HOSPITALITY MARKETING AND CONSUMER BEHAVIOR

Creating Memorable Experiences

Advances in Hospitality and Tourism

HOSPITALITY MARKETING AND CONSUMER BEHAVIOR

Creating Memorable Experiences

Edited by

Vinnie Jauhari, PhD

Apple Academic Press Inc.
3333 Mistwell Crescent
Oakville, ON L6L 0A2 Canada

Apple Academic Press Inc.
9 Spinnaker Way
Waretown, NJ 08758 USA

Printed in the United States of America on acid-free paper
International Standard Book Number-13: 978-1-77188-378-8 (Hardcover)
International Standard Book Number-13: 978-1-315-36622-7 (CRC Press/Taylor & Francis eBook)

Library and Archives Canada Cataloguing in Publication

Hospitality marketing and consumer behavior : creating memorable experiences / edited by Vinnie Jauhari, PhD.
(Advances in hospitality and tourism book series)
Includes bibliographical references and index.
Issued in print and electronic formats.
ISBN 978-1-77188-378-8 (hardcover).--ISBN 978-1-315-36622-7 (PDF)
1. Hospitality industry--Marketing. 2. Consumer behavior. I. Jauhari, Vinnie, author, editor II. Series: Advances in hospitality and tourism book series
TX911.3.M3H67 2017 647.94068'8 C2016-908266-0 C2016-908267-9

Library of Congress Cataloging-in-Publication Data

Names: Jauhari, Vinnie, editor.
Title: Hospitality marketing and consumer behavior : creating memorable experiences / editor, Vinnie Jauhari, PhD.
Description: Toronto ; Waretown, NJ, USA : Apple Academic Press, 2017. |
Includes bibliographical references and index.
Identifiers: LCCN 2016057229 (print) | LCCN 2016058093 (ebook) | ISBN 9781771883788 (hardcover : alk. paper) | ISBN 9781315366227 (CRC Press/Taylor & Francis eBook)
Subjects: LCSH: Hospitality industry--Marketing. | Consumer behavior.
Classification: LCC TX911.3.M3 H674 2017 (print) | LCC TX911.3.M3 (ebook) | DDC 647.94068/8--dc23
LC record available at https://lccn.loc.gov/2016057229

Apple Academic Press also publishes its books in a variety of electronic formats. Some content that appears in print may not be available in electronic format. For information about Apple Academic Press products, visit our website at **www.appleacademicpress.com** and the CRC Press website at **www.crcpress.com**

ABOUT THE EDITOR

Vinnie Jauhari, PhD (IITD)

Vinnie Jauhari, PhD, is Director of Education Advocacy at Microsoft Corporation India Ltd., where she is responsible for evangelizing education initiatives at Microsoft. She leads and manages strategic engagements in higher education and K-12 and also works on policy issues related with education. She works on programs leading to capacity development for teachers through initiatives in pedagogical innovation. These are both in public and private sector domain. She has initiated programs that involve confluence of content, technology, and pedagogy. Some of these workshops are in the domain of vision and leadership and creative curriculum development.

Previously Dr. Jauhari was Director and Professor of Strategy at IIMT (now Vedatya Institute), Gurgaon, India. She has developed strategic linkages for the institute with some leading international universities as well as partnered with industry to create employability for students and was responsible for academic leadership and research strategy. In her role at IIMT, she initiated and managed several international conferences and fostered strong linkages with schools and other higher education institutions.

Vinnie was earlier Region Lead for HP Labs Open Innovation Office for India. She has received numerous awards for her work at HP Labs as well as her academic achievements. She won the Director's Award for Innovation in the worldwide team in 2008–2009. She is also a recipient of the HP Empower grant for women during her tenure at HP Labs. She has over 19 years of experience across industry and academic assignments.

Dr. Jauhari has authored twelve books on services, innovation, and technology management. Having authored over 100 papers in international and national journals of repute, she is the Founding Editor of *Journal of Services Research* and the *Journal of Technology Management for Growing Economies*. She has been a guest editor of numerous international journals, and some of her papers have won awards and global recognition. Her areas of interest span across strategy, technology, entrepreneurship, and sustainability across service sectors.

Vinnie received her PhD in the domain of corporate entrepreneurship from IIT Delhi. She received a Postdoctoral Fellowship at United Nations University, Tokyo, in the area of sustainable technologies.

CONTENTS

LIST OF CONTRIBUTORS

Watson Baldwin
Lecturer and Chef, Club at Gateway Center, University of North Texas – Hospitality & Tourism Management, Denton, Texas, USA

Sonia Bharwani
Manchester Business School, UK

Vinay Chauhan
Associate Professor, The Business School, University of Jammu, Jammu, India

Kartik Dave
School of Business, Public Policy and Social Entrepreneurship, Ambedkar University Delhi, India

Kirti Dutta
G.L. Bajaj Institute of Management & Research, Plot 2, Knowledge Park III, Greater Noida 201306, India

Charles Foster
Lecturer and General Manager, Club at Gateway Center, University of North Texas – Hospitality & Tourism Management, Denton, Texas, USA

Sanjaya S. Gaur
Professor and Head of the Department of Marketing, Sunway University Business School, Sunway University, No. 5 Jalan Universiti, Bandar Sunway, 47500 Selangor Darul Ehsan, Malaysia. E-mail: sanjayag@sunway.edu.my

Shaphali Gupta
Assistant Professor, Marketing Area, Management Development Institute, Gurgaon, India. E-mail: shaphali.gupta@mdi.ac.in

Halimin Herjanto
Assistant Professor, Marketing School of Business, McKendree University, USA. E-mail: herjanth@gmail.com

Vinnie Jauhari
Director, Education Advocacy, Microsoft Corporation India Pvt. Ltd. E-mail: Vinnie.jauhari@yahoo.com

Bharath M. Josiam
Professor, Hospitality & Tourism Management, College of Merchandising, Hospitality & Tourism, University of North Texas, 1155 Union Circle #311100, Denton, Texas, 76203-5017, USA. E-mail: Josiamb@unt.edu

Navdeep Kaur Kular
Visiting Faculty, Vedatya Institute (formerly IIMT), Gurgaon, India. E-mail: novikular@rediffmail.com; novikular@gmail.com

Rosa Malave
Lecturer, Club at Gateway Center, University of North Texas – Hospitality & Tourism Management, Denton, Texas, USA

Kamal Manaktola
School of Hospitality, Auro University, Surat, India

Deepak Manhas
Assistant Handicrafts Training Officer, Handicrafts Department, J&K Government, India. E-mail: manhasdeepak2009@gmail.com

Parul G. Munjal
Sushant School of Art and Architecture, Ansal University, Gurgaon, India. E-mail: Parul.g.munjal@gmail.com

Sandeep Munjal
Vedatya Institute, Gurgaon, India. E-mail: Sandeep.munjal1973@gmail.com

David Njite
University of New Orleans, Lester E. Kabacoff School of Hotel, Restaurant and Tourism Administration, 2000 Lakeshore Drive, New Orleans, LA 70148, USA

H.G. Parsa
Daniels College of Business, University of Denver, 344 Joy Burns Center, 2044 East Evans Avenue, Denver, Colorado 80208, USA. E-mail: hparsa@du.edu

Dinesh Sharma
Assistant Professor, SJMSOM, IIT Bombay, Mumbai, Maharashtra, India

Anjana Singh
Institute for International Management and Technology, Gurgaon, India

Gaurav Tripathi
BIMTECH, Greater Noida, India

Parul Wasan
Associate Professor, Manav Rachna International University, Faridabad, Haryana, India

LIST OF ABBREVIATIONS

ANOVA	analysis of variance
BYOC	bring your own computer
BYOD	bring your own device
CA	Cronbach's alpha
CETs	customer engagement technologies
CMS	content management system
CQ	cultural intelligence
CRM	customer relationship management
CRS	central reservations systems
CRSP	consumer retail search process
CS	customer satisfaction
EFA	exploratory factor analysis
EQ	emotional intelligence
EV	eigen values
FL	factor loadings
FMCG	fast-moving consumer goods
FOH	front of the house
FSR	full service restaurant
GDP	gross domestic product
GDS	global distribution systems
GOI	Government of India
HI	hospitality intelligence
HM	hospitality management
HR	human resource
IHHA	Indian Heritage Hotels Association
IQ	intelligence quotient
IT	information technology
ITP	intention to patronize
KMO	Kaiser-Meyer-Olkin
MF	mean of factor
MMCF	Maharana of Mewar Charitable Foundation
MTES	memorable tourism experience scale
NFC	near field communication

OCE	overall customer experience
PMS	property management systems
POS	point of sales
PQ	people quotient
QSR	quick service restaurant
R&D	research and development
RM	revenue management
SD	standard deviation
SOA	service-oriented architecture
SPSS	statistical package for social sciences
SRR	student-run restaurant
VE	variance explained
VM	variable mean
VOC	voice of the customer
WTP	willingness to pay
WTR	willingness to return

ADVANCES IN HOSPITALITY AND TOURISM BOOK SERIES BY APPLE ACADEMIC PRESS, INC.

Editor-in-Chief:
Mahmood A. Khan, PhD
Professor, Department of Hospitality and Tourism Management, Pamplin College of Business, Virginia Polytechnic Institute and State University, Falls Church, Virginia, USA
Email: mahmood@vt.edu

Books in the Series:

Food Safety: Researching the Hazard in Hazardous Foods
Editors: Barbara Almanza, PhD, RD, and Richard Ghiselli, PhD

Strategic Winery Tourism and Management: Building Competitive Winery Tourism and Winery Management Strategy
Editor: Kyuho Lee, PhD

Sustainability, Social Responsibility and Innovations in the Hospitality Industry
Editor: H. G. Parsa, PhD
Consulting Editor: Vivaja "Vi" Narapareddy, PhD
Associate Editors: SooCheong (Shawn) Jang, PhD,
Marival Segarra-Oña, PhD, and Rachel J. C. Chen, PhD, CHE

Managing Sustainability in the Hospitality and Tourism Industry: Paradigms and Directions for the Future
Editor: Vinnie Jauhari, PhD

Management Science in Hospitality and Tourism: Theory, Practice, and Applications
Editors: Muzaffer Uysal, PhD, Zvi Schwartz, PhD, and
Ercan Sirakaya-Turk, PhD

Tourism in Central Asia: Issues and Challenges
Editors: Kemal Kantarci, PhD, Muzaffer Uysal, PhD, and Vincent Magnini, PhD

Poverty Alleviation through Tourism Development: A Comprehensive and Integrated Approach
Robertico Croes, PhD, and Manuel Rivera, PhD

Chinese Outbound Tourism 2.0
Editor: Xiang (Robert) Li, PhD

Hospitality Marketing and Consumer Behavior: Creating Memorable Experiences
Editor: Vinnie Jauhari, PhD

Women and Travel: Historical and Contemporary Perspectives
Editors: Catheryn Khoo-Lattimore, PhD, and Erica Wilson, PhD

Wilderness of Wildlife Tourism
Editor: Johra Kayeser Fatima, PhD

Medical Tourism and Wellness: Hospitality Bridging Healthcare (H2H)©
Editor: Frederick J. DeMicco, PhD, RD

Sustainable Viticulture: The Vines and Wines of Burgundy
Claude Chapuis

The Indian Hospitality Industry: Dynamics and Future Trends
Editors: Sandeep Munjal and Sudhanshu Bhushan

ABOUT THE SERIES EDITOR

Mahmood A. Khan, PhD, is a Professor in the Department of Hospitality and Tourism Management, Pamplin College of Business at Virginia Tech's National Capital Region campus. He has served in teaching, research, and administrative positions for the past 35 years, working at major U.S. universities. Dr. Khan is the author of seven books and has traveled extensively for teaching and consulting on management issues and franchising. He has been invited by national and international corporations to serve as a speaker, keynote speaker, and seminar presenter on different topics related to franchising and services management. He is the author of *Restaurant Franchising: Concepts, Regulations, and Practices, Third Edition, Revised and Updated*, published by Apple Academic Press, Inc.

Dr. Khan has received the Steven Fletcher Award for his outstanding contribution to hospitality education and research. He is also a recipient of the John Wiley & Sons Award for lifetime contribution to outstanding research and scholarship; the Donald K. Tressler Award for scholarship; and the Cesar Ritz Award for scholarly contribution. He also received the Outstanding Doctoral Faculty Award from Pamplin College of Business.

He has served on the Board of Governors of the Educational Foundation of the International Franchise Association, on the Board of Directors of the Virginia Hospitality and Tourism Association, as a Trustee of the International College of Hospitality Management, and as a Trustee on the Foundation of the Hospitality Sales and Marketing Association's International Association. He is also a member of several professional associations.

PREFACE

Creating memories and joyous experiences for consumers is a key dimension that can impact the profitability and growth of a hospitality firm. Creating these positive experiences is an outcome of an interplay of number of factors. These factors range from impact of vision, structuring of systems and policies aligned to consumer expectations and market needs, policies, resources, ethical orientation of an organization, leadership, physical and work environment, and employee orientation, among many other factors. As the world becomes more complex, technology can help create many value-added services that can drive consumer experience.

This book covers a wide theme of marketing areas that focus on and contribute to memorable consumer experiences, drawing from global experiences. The book covers marketing research, different elements of the marketing mix, consumer feedback and recovery, technology, people aspects, and how they impact consumer experience. The book offers insights from emerging economies as well as some distinct insights from global practices.

The world is changing like never before, and technology is driving a lot of change as well. Wearable technologies, mobility, cloud, and easy-to-use access devices have changed the way consumers make their decisions. The way marketers and consumers relate is also evolving very quickly. The social media has put an enormous power in the hand of consumers. There is also a new kind of entrepreneurship and hospitality products is are emanating. Young dynamic entrepreneurs who have deployed technologies that drive value to guests such as Zomato are a case in point. How do these new firms drive value to the consumers?

The concept of consumer experience is also witnessing a huge change. Do consumers really feel welcomed by the hotels and restaurants and retail outlets? What are the aspects that drive consumer engagement? What kind of people, practice, and system insights enable consumer engagement? Today, consumers have a wide array of options to express their opinions as well. The presence of social media that also acts as a forum for expression of pleasure and displeasure can impact the business of the firm. While opting for reservations, consumers look at reviews posted by other consumers. Information about organizations and their performance is easily available. So in that context, how transparent systems can be created which capture consumer satisfaction and also have a greater understanding of the consumers is also important.

The book also captures consumer aspirations for various marketing mix elements. Their expectations from hotels and restaurants would reflect the changing aspirations of the markets and consumers. Consumer loyalty as a concept in changing times is also explored. Sustainability as a concept would be a necessity in the new framework. How would the concept of sustainability be marketed to the consumer and what are the challenges around the same?

This book will appeal to potential consumers and also would be unique as it brings global perspectives. The Gen Y has very different expectations, and they also are heavy users of technology. The conventional approach toward consumer satisfaction is also evolving. In the changing scenario, it is important that the new framework of marketing is understood and new strategies are debated and documented.

This book provides an insight into marketing and consumer behavior in the context of hospitality and tourism. The dynamics of emerging economies have been captured, and some lessons drawn from best practices across the globe.

I am grateful to the authors who have made an immense contribution by sharing their work. I am also indebted to the journals which have facilitated the copyright for the work of the authors. I would like to acknowledge the support that I have received from Professor Mahmood Khan for all these years and this great opportunity to share my work. I would also like to acknowledge the support from Apple Academic Press—Ashish and his team, in getting this work published.

Heartfelt thanks to my family—Sunil, Shaurya, my parents, and my in-laws—for their support in all my endeavors.

—Vinnie Jauhari, PhD

CHAPTER 1

CONSUMER EXPERIENCES: AN INTRODUCTION

VINNIE JAUHARI*

[1]*Director Education Advocacy, Microsoft Corporation India Pvt. Ltd.*†

**E-mail: Vinnie.jauhari@yahoo.com*

CONTENTS

†The views presented are by the author and nowhere reflect the organization's point of view.

ABSTRACT

This chapter gives an introduction to the concept of consumer experience and how it could contribute to business growth and driving value to the customer. There is a context to consumer experience and the parameters contributing to satisfaction may vary. There are variables which are linked with culture and socio-economic aspects which could also impact consumers. Outstanding experiences can only be created through a combination of investments in people, organization structure, deployment of technology, resources among many other aspects. The chapter also gives an overview of themes covered in this book and provides insight into each of the paper. The sector span across hospitality, retail, aviation, and restaurants. The papers are a combination of empirical and conceptual framework and the contributions from the globe.

It is an age where experiences are becoming extremely important part of any consumer interface, be it face to face or digital. Memories are important and association with organizations must drive value. Technology is altering the way experiences are being created for consumers.

There are also experiences around everyday life which start from commuting to workplace, telecommunication, banking, dining, entertainment, sports, travel, education, and citizenship services. It is the quality of experiences which results in consumer satisfaction and engagement. It is around concern for people's time, convenience, and meaningful engagements which also generate opportunities for revenue generation as well. Technology drives a lot of new ways of engaging with consumers and also providing access. Also, experiences are transcending the barriers of time and geography. Firms such as Flipkart and Amazon and their success in India demonstrate how conventional barriers for entrepreneurship can be broken and how a novelty of experience and convenience can lead to success in the marketplace.

When one thinks of experiences, there are a number of contexts to draw from. On one hand, it could be a Disneyland which powerfully recreates experiences from fables and stories taking one to the land of imagination and dreams. The whole experience is a powerful blend of creativity, engagement, and a mapping of service offering at a standardized level. It is a powerful engagement story, though one could argue the monotony of repetitiveness. There are also experiences in the arena of sports which draw an unparalleled euphoria and involvement. Gaming is also another such example. There is passion for teams and players and love for the sport that contributes to loyalty. The football clubs across the globe especially Europe, the love for cricket in India, and the League matches that attract big investments demonstrate a very distinct consumer experience for sports lovers. Also, there may be very ordinary engagements around consumption of food through home delivery or online channels which demonstrate a very different kind of consumer experience where value of money, timeliness, and convenience elements may be more important considerations in consumer interface. Hence, there is a spectrum of values on which consumer experience can be assessed and the value drivers may be very distinct for different segments.

Experience has many facets which vary with the context in which they are being created. There is no standard form, but some of the outlying principles may be common such as consumer orientation, understanding of value drivers, keeping up the delivery promise, innovation, and excellence, among other aspects. To calibrate an experience, the context in which it is based needs to be understood. Multiple scenarios can be looked at for understanding the consumer experience. Some of these are enumerated below.

1. Typology

Consumer experiences and their understanding may be widely different when the following come into play:

a. Culture background
b. Socioeconomic factors
c. Geography

The demand–supply dynamics play an important role. When the demand outstrips the supply, maintaining a consumer experience in that context is a very different ballgame. Whether it is accommodation, food, travel experience, entertainment. However, charging premium or different prices comes in through differentiated consumer experience. In India, despite the lags in standards in Railway experiences, yet it is so hard to get tickets during peak seasons. Here, convenience far outweighs the experience element. However, consumers would happily pay for a differentiated experience if the supplier charges higher amount of money.

Chowdhury (2009) in his study of consumer experience in the context of banking industry discussed about the differences in dimensions of consumer experience. First, there are two dimensions of discrimination between the levels of customer satisfaction. The first dimension is typified by work culture and fulfillment of expectations, which may be indicative of relational qualities. The second dimension is characterized by quality service and customers' loyalty. The consumers of first generation are a delighted lot. The consumers of Grameen Banks are high on loyalty, and their perceptions on quality also vary.

Consumer aspirations may also vary with the segment to which they belong. However, consistency in promise/offering is something which every consumer expects.

The cultural background impacts perceptions of experience. Warmth, going beyond the call of duty are some of the expectations in India and when guests visit international destinations, the expectations are also at the same level. However, cultural experiences vary, and despite paying a premium, the experience may still not have the warmth.

The experience also vastly differs with the ability to pay, and the expectations also vary with what one is willing to pay.

2. **Engagement aspects**

   These also vary depending on the context of a service being consumed. The value drivers may be different for different kinds of services.

   - Value for money: Consumers staying in the budget hotels have limited expectations, but if a brand is able to offer hygiene with good food and convenience elements, the experience would have to be created which brings out value for money proposition.
   - Premium experience: Here, the expectations are very high and consumers must feel delighted for the investments that they are making. Fun, surprise, premium, and uniqueness, coupled with staff that helps delivers the experience, would be important elements.
   - Fulfilling a unique need: This could be a scenario such as a religious/pilgrimage visit or a visit for wellness purpose. The key here is the availability of a competent resource and everything else is weaved around it. If the therapist is incompetent, all other luxuries would have no meaning around the same.

3. New products/services

There are many new products and services which have been launched. The technology enables development of many new services and products. Whether it is WhatsApp or Skype, all exemplify simplicity of experience and convenience. The ability to share free data and images has led to WhatsApp being deployed and used in multiple scenarios. The newness of experience is also very helpful. For instance, a wide spectrum of educators across the globe use tools such as Skype to create collaborative scenarios for their students. Mystery Skype is used by many primary schools to develop knowledge about countries across geographies. The deployment of geographic information system (GIS)-based navigation services for even tourism can have immense applications. One of the largest growing segments in India is food delivery through online channels.

4. Simplicity of experiences

The ease of going through an experience is very important. A visit to a monument or a tourist place which is facilitated by easy booking and access and also paying a premium for a faster access could be important to some consumers. Anything which is complex and requires a lot of effort to consume a service will never be able to build the marketplace. The success of many services such as MakeMyTrip or Yatra, Expedia, Hotels.com is the ability to create comparisons and offer value services to consumers. These online companies and portals have redefined the dynamics of the business and have been disruptive in their approach. Their success lies in redefining consumer value and simplifying their lives while making choices which suit their requirements.

5. Innovation

The space tourism is a novel concept where consumers have not undertaken an experience before, but it would entail training and also insurance as it would be a new ballgame altogether. There are consumers who are willing to adapt to this novel situation. Also, whether it is about cultural extravaganza or going through culinary tours in a country, a newness of experience is always welcome. Wellness trips also come in this category where an experience is taken beyond the realms of accommodation and culinary journeys.

The price paid by the consumer also has a bearing on their expectations. Higher investment raises expectations on an experience being truly exceptional. At lower investments, expectations are also reasonable. For flexibility and entertainment context, the experience expectations may be very different.

6. **Emotional bonding**

   Sometimes there are emotional values attached with a visit. This may be a trip back to a native place or a heritage or spiritual journey. The elements of nostalgia and values attached to the visit may far outweigh the logical dimensions in such a case.

7. **Technological aspect**

   Transformations in technology have led to enhanced contributions and many new products and services. Technology has enabled emergence of many new forms of entrepreneurship and also simplified the access to the services.

   The online availability of product offerings and also convenience aspect have a huge influence on consumer buying patterns.

1.1 ASPECTS THAT MATTER/CONTRIBUTE TO EXPERIENCE

There is a lot of evidence on aspects that influence customer experience. These factors are related to the following:

- Employee skills
- Processes and systems
- Concept and offerings
- Hygiene elements
- Desirable demand characteristics

Mather (1993) talks about the market conditions. He discusses the role of competition, customer buying habits, seasonality influences, and so forth. Also, the dynamism caused by the marketer or the competition initiated actions.

1.2 ABOUT THE BOOK

This book is an attempt to provide insights on various dimensions that contribute to consumer experience. This book provides insights into aspects that could contribute to better engagement with consumers. It brings in multiple insights from various segments such as restaurants, food firms, and retailing. It also brings in perspectives on experience elements and how frontline staff in context of hospitality industry can drive more engaged experiences. It brings in dimensions such as consumer behavior, pricing strategies, and sustainability to reach out to consumers. Aspects around technology and social media are also covered in the book.

Bharwani and Jauhari (2015) in their work "Creating Memorable Customer Experiences – Insights From Hospitality Sector" have delved upon the role of competencies in contributing to consumer experience, especially in the context of frontline staff.

The purpose of this paper is to identify and map competencies required by frontline employees to enhance guest experience in the hospitality industry, in the context of an emerging experience economy. This work is based on secondary research through extensive review of relevant literature in the area of experience economy and hospitality management. This study proposes a new construct of "hospitality intelligence" (HI) encompassing mainly emotional intelligence (comprising interpersonal intelligence and intrapersonal intelligence), cultural intelligence, and hospitality experiential intelligence dimensions. Practitioners and human resource (HR) professionals in the field of hospitality would find the HI construct useful in recruiting and training frontline employees, while educationists could use the findings of this study in designing curricula and pedagogical interventions for developing the right skill set for the hospitality industry. This study proposes a competencies framework and develops a construct of HI required by frontline employees in the hospitality industry to elevate guest experience from a simple interaction to a memorable experience.

Kular (2015) in her work "Creating Memorable Consumer Experiences: Insights from Hospitality and Tourism Industry" brings in insights from quality perspective on consumer experience.

This paper explores the concept of consumer experiences which appeals to the emotions, dreams, and desires as opposed to the functionality or utility of hospitality services. The advancement of technology has generated awareness and information for the consumer and has provided access to unlimited possibilities. The expectations of consumers have risen and service quality and reliability are taken for granted. The role of the consumer has changed from passive audience to an active participant in the service delivery process. The management of services through theatrical performance with the consumer as the star leading to the cocreation of the memorable experience is the differentiator in the competitive hospitality industry. The physical surroundings and the ambience of the place stimulates the five senses of taste, touch, sight, sound, and smell and are an integral part of the experience. The values, attitudes, and beliefs of the consumer are personal and they make the experience unique for each customer. The literature has been reviewed to arrive at managerial implications. The insights from emerging economies have been incorporated to illustrate the creation of memorable consumer experiences.

Herjanto and Gaur (2015) in their work "Creating Memorable Experiences: Lessons from World's Top 10 Hotels" bring in global perspectives on consumer experience.

The aim of this study is to investigate and identify the key themes that help create positive memorable experiences for hotel customers. This study is qualitative in nature and employs the thematic analyses technique. First, an extensive review of current literature is carried out to understand the factors that contribute to the creation of positive memorable experiences for hotel customers. An initial thematic map is developed based on this. A sample of the world's top 10 hotels is chosen based on TripAdvisor's "2014 Travellers Choice – Top 25 Hotels in the World" report. A total of 248 reviews and feedback (indicating positive memorable experiences) posted over a period of 12 months by real customers of sampled hotels were identified. These are then content analyzed using thematic analysis to confirm the themes that create memorable experience for the guests of the world's top 10 hotels. A final thematic map is then prepared based on these confirmed themes.

Six themes emerged in the study. Perceived hospitality and professionalism of the hotel staff, perception of travel experience, and hotel space management were found to be the most important factors that create a memorable experience for the hotel guests.

The findings of this research are based on the analysis of real customer reviews and feedback. Therefore, this study offers important insights for hotel management staff, as they now have the means to identify the source of customers' memorable hotel experience. This study amalgamates customers' real experience and feedback to assist hoteliers in increasing customers' memorable hotel experience.

Chauhan and Manhas (2015) in their work "Dimensional Analysis of Customer Experience in Civil Aviation Sector" have provided insights into various dimensions of consumer experience.

Creating a superior customer experience has been gaining increased attention in the service sector. The diverse market offerings that stimulate enduring experience, which customers cherish, have competitive edge over most competing products or services. Customer experience acts as an emerging opportunity in this fast-paced highly competitive world, especially in the new horizon of experience economy. Due to an increasing growth rate and diversity of airline passengers, customer experience is emerging as a critical element in civil aviation sector. It is crucial for airlines to offer great experiences to passengers in order to gain a competitive advantage. This paper thus examines the nature and extent of customer experience in civil aviation sector. More specifically, the study explores dimensions of customer experience in civil aviation sector. The study is based on data of sample size of 1005 respondents from selected airlines namely Air India, Jet Airways, and Kingfisher.

Gupta and Sharma (2015) in their work "Dimensions of Retail Service Convenience in Emerging Market Settings—A Qualitative Investigation" have explored measures of consumer convenience which is an important contributor to the experience element.

The existing measures of service convenience, developed and validated in context of developed service economies, do not adequately capture customers' perception of service convenience for retail stores (i.e., stores which offers both goods and services), especially in the emerging markets. Current study examines perceptions of and identifies a comprehensive inventory of service convenience for retail stores in emerging market setting, India. Based on convenience literature and three separate qualitative studies, authors proposed retail store service convenience as a multidimensional construct consisting of six dimensions. Both retailers and shoppers were included in the study. Selection and assurance were found as novel dimensions for retail service convenience. Perceived risk of service fairness, resulting in exertion of cognitive energy, is seen as major concern among respondents. Study elucidates the critical role of store staff in building affirmative convenience perception. The present study enhances the understanding of retail service convenience in an emerging market (India) context. Thus, this study expands the domain of service convenience construct by further exploring the dimensions and measures set out by earlier researchers. This study explores new dimensions of convenience and proposes items for developing a measure for retail store service convenience. The implications of proposed dimensions are discussed, both for retailers and future research.

Josiam, Malaye, Foster, and Baldwin (2015) in their work "Assessing Quality of Food, Service and Customer Experience at a Restaurant: The Case of a Student Run Restaurant in the USA" have focused on perspectives on quality aspect of consumer experience from the context of a standalone restaurant.

In the restaurant business, satisfied customers will return and provide positive word of mouth to peers. Studies have shown that restaurants that generate repeat patronage have six significant attributes in common, namely food quality, service quality, consistency of food and service, menu variety, cost/price–value relationship, atmosphere/ambience, and hygiene/cleanliness. University-level hospitality management programs regard the student-run restaurant (SRR) as an essential part of the curriculum. Despite many such restaurants housed in universities in the USA and across the world, little information is available about how these restaurants assess quality and promote usage and loyalty. This study addresses this subject by identifying the perceptions of the patrons of a SRR, segmenting the customer base, and ascertaining the quality of drivers of repeat and referral patronage. A total of 503 guests were surveyed at a university SRR in the southwestern region of the USA. Overall, patrons were satisfied with the food quality, service quality, value for money, and convenience of location. However, satisfaction levels were lower for convenience of payment methods and portion size. Significant differences were found between males and females, as well as between younger and mature patrons. Significant differences also existed between the perceptions of heavy users and light users. These findings suggest the SRR serves distinct segments, which emphasizes a need to focus on customized strategies for customer retention. More information about patrons and the quality of restaurant attributes that drive their choices will assist hospitality faculty in SRRs and restaurateurs to competitively position their restaurants for success in the marketplace.

Tripathi and Dave in their work "Exploration of Service Quality Factors in Restaurant Industry: A Study of Selected Restaurants in

New Delhi Region" have focused on quality factors in the restaurant industry.

The purpose of this paper is to explore the underlying key dimensions of service quality in restaurants. Service quality items pertaining to the restaurants are extracted from extensive review of literature including the consideration of unique factors from Indian cultural orientation. The study was conducted in New Delhi and its adjoining cities wherein the restaurant customers were surveyed using a structured questionnaire. Factor analysis was used to bring out the underlying dimensions of service quality. The dimensions extracted are cultural orientation, aesthetics, ambient settings, empathy, privacy and entertainment, first impression, reliability, and responsiveness. The Indian market is contextually different in contrast to various other countries where such research studies have been widely carried out. Hence, this study provides departure from previous studies and presents greater insight into the service quality factors as perceived by the consumers in India. This will help the restaurant managers to ponder on the factors, which are more pertinent for the Indian markets. Importantly, this study attempts to test the variables pertaining to cultural orientation from the Indian context as dimensions of the restaurant service quality and hence attempts to create a more suitable scale for the Indian market.

Parsa, Gregory, Self, and Dutta in their study "Consumer Behaviour in Restaurants: Assessing the Importance of Restaurant Attributes in Consumer Patronage and Willingness to Pay" have discussed about experience in the context of consumer behavior.

The purpose of the paper is to explore the relationship between restaurant attributes and consumers' willingness to patronize. Current research shows that the most common factors affecting restaurant guests while making this decision are: food quality, service quality, and overall restaurant environment. The present paper explores these three factors and their effect on consumers' willingness to pay and their willingness to patronize when these factors are modified from low to high and vice versa. A dynamic comparison method using scenario-based experimental primary research has been used for the current study. It is a $2 \times 2 \times 3$ experiment with two types of restaurants (full service and quick service), two levels of performance (high and low), and three major attributes (food quality, service, and ambience). Contrary to the commonly held notion in economic literature that the relationship between consumers' willingness to pay and the elasticity (intention to patronize) for restaurants' attributes is linear, the current results indicated that this relationship is not linear thus demanding further investigation. Additionally, questioning the earlier conclusions that all restaurant attributes are equally important in consumer decision-making, the current results indicated that consumers place differential importance on each attribute. And the level of importance placed on each attribute varies with the type of restaurant, upscale or quick service. This is one of the major contributions of the paper questioning the long-held belief and early empirical studies about restaurant attributes. The obtained results also indicated that food quality is more important than service and ambience for consumers in upscale restaurants, while speed of service is more important than food quality and ambience in quick service restaurants. Customers in both upscale and quick service restaurants are willing to spend more if the restaurants' resources are focused on attributes that are appropriate for that segment. These findings are significantly important to the restaurant industry as they identify the critical attributes for each segment of the restaurant industry.

Singh and Manaktola (2015) have expressed their thoughts in their work "Driving Value through Pricing: Strategies Adopted by Managers in Price Sensitive and Fierce Competitive Markets."

Hotel managers have always faced the challenge of use of pricing strategies to achieve both revenue and customer satisfaction. The objective of this paper is to identify existing practices of price setting in hotels of National Capital Region and strategies adopted by managers in price-sensitive and fierce-competitive market. This information will enable us to analyze the thoughts and price pressures hotel managers go through in driving value for customers through pricing strategies and to make recommendations accordingly.

The chapter uses qualitative primary research through structured open-ended interview to discuss in detail pricing strategies. The interviews will be conducted with senior management responsible for pricing decisions like revenue managers or general managers from a spectrum of hotels in National Capital Region of India. It is imperative for the hotels to understand the perceived customer value of the product or service in a global context and respond appropriately to change in the market conditions. This research will provide the understanding of the intentions of the hotels toward pricing strategies and the overall aim to be achieved through pricing. This makes this research quite valuable for academic researchers and practitioners to understand the factors that could be important for sustainable pricing strategy.

Wasan (2015) in her work "Managing Technologies for Consumer Engagement" discusses technology-led consumer experience.

The passive consumer of analog media has rapidly evolved into an active creator of content moving across multiple digital media channels (Baker, 2010).

The emerging technologies epitomize the consumer lifestyles. Additionally, it also point toward increased Internet activity and social media usage through integrated media apps through mobile devices.

The consumer is usually at the epicenter of the convergence trend, and more often than not, consumer leads the technology adoption curve, while a hotel enterprise is forced to play catch up in order to pursue customers in the domain of consumer engagement.

Adoption of technology has altered both the operational and the philosophical aspect of how any hotel enterprise looks at customer engagement.

Emerging insights are now pointing toward trends that fuel merger of consumer technologies, mobile and convergence technology, and the social media for creating opportunities and expectations for enhancing guest services and guest expectations in hospitality industry. Then there are brands that are scaling up the social competencies of their websites in order to bond with their customer. Additionally, they synchronize their strategies to achieve deeper customer engagements.

The industry has started to use new technologies (also known as "funware") and the power of social networking. An example of a new strategy is the new buzz word "gamification." It offers a powerful marketing strategy to hospitality companies for little or no cost. Gamification techniques challenge and motivate customers through competition, recognition, and rewards. Further, because the dynamics of gamification are highly transferable, they can be applied to achieve many different goals: to create viral PR and buzz, increase loyalty or compliance, crowdsource new products or solutions, gain feedback, recruit talent, and so forth.

Kumar (2015) in her work "Social Media and Engaging with Consumers in Hospitality Sector" discusses about role of social media and possibilities for engagement with consumers.

Social media is a valuable tool to engage with the customers. The emerging media landscape has provided new opportunities for the consumer connect. It has altered the manner in which consumers search for information and make their decision choices. The academic literature along with the technology literature available from vendors in public domain has been synthesized to present the opportunities and challenges for hospitality sector. This chapter ponders over the importance of social media and how businesses can interact, engage, and participate with the online users. It suggests the ways and means to enhance customer acquisition, customer development, and retention. Customer opinions and evaluation of services can be used for collaboration and cocreation of products and services. It also highlights the challenges in quantifying social media's influence on the customers. The case studies illustrate the social media measures adopted by various hospitality organizations for consumer engagement. These can provide insights to others to emulate the best practices and develop a sustainable social media strategy.

Munjal and Munjal (2015) in their work "Heritage hotels in India – offering unique experiences to customers with sustainable practices as a differentiator" have provided insights on consumer experience from sustainability perspective.

Adaptive reuse of heritage structures in the form of hotels has shown impressive growth in India in recent years. While this conversion poses challenges, it also presents opportunities as end users are showing interest in staying at heritage hotels to experience our rich cultural heritage.

The objective of the research is to explore the success of heritage hotels in India in offering a value-added product to the customers, and also probe the sociocultural and economic impact of heritage hotels from a perspective of sustainability. The study focuses especially on heritage hotels, because these have emerged as a high-growth segment, typically located in areas with historical contexts. They offer an inimitable experience due to the physical features and heritage value on one hand are also receiving patronage due to the sustainable practices they are adopting.

The sustainability indicators prescribed by the Ministry of Tourism in India have been used to assess the impact of selected heritage hotels taken up for study.

The research effort highlights the success or challenges that the case study hotels have achieved in offering a unique experience to its expanding customer base, with the practice of principles of sustainability as a distinguishing feature. These findings can be helpful directives for more reutilization of heritage structures as potential heritage hotels.

Heritage hotels represent opportunities for putting heritage assets to commercial use and simultaneously ensuring their conservation. The inferences can help establish heritage hotels as drivers of social development, especially in regions that are suffering from poverty, unemployment, and lack of education. If appropriate processes are followed, a mutually interdependent and beneficial relationship can be forged and promoted that can sustain the cultural component at the local, regional and as a result, national level.

KEYWORDS

- **products**
- **services**
- **consumer experiences**
- **technology**
- **innovation**

REFERENCES

Chowdhury, U. K. Delighting Customers: An Exploration into the Discriminating Factors. *Total Qual. Manag.* **2009,** *20(2)*, 253–266.

Mather, H. F. Do More than Just Satisfy Your Customer – Profitably Delight Them. *Ind. Manag.* **1993,** *35*, 10–15.

PART I

Perspectives on Customer Experience

CHAPTER 2

CREATING MEMORABLE CONSUMER EXPERIENCES: INSIGHTS FROM THE HOSPITALITY AND TOURISM INDUSTRY

NAVDEEP KAUR KULAR

Visiting Faculty at Vedatya Institute (formerly IIMT), Gurgaon, India

E-mail: novikular@rediffmail.com; novikular@gmail.com

CONTENTS

ABSTRACT

This paper explores the concept of consumer experiences which appeals to the emotions, dreams, and desires as opposed to the functionality or utility of hospitality services. The advancement of technology has generated awareness and information for the consumer and has provided access to unlimited possibilities. The expectations of consumers have risen and service quality and reliability are taken for granted. The role of the consumer has changed from passive audience to an active participant in the service delivery process. The management of services through theatrical performance with the consumer as the star leading to the cocreation of the memorable experience is the differentiator in the competitive hospitality industry. The physical surroundings and the ambience of the place stimulates the five senses of taste, touch, sight, sound, and smell and are an integral part of the experience. The values, attitudes, and beliefs of the consumer are personal and they make the experience unique for each customer. The literature has been reviewed to arrive at managerial implications. The insights from emerging economies have been incorporated to illustrate the creation of memorable consumer experiences.

2.1 INTRODUCTION

Consumers are looking for new and unusual places to explore and different activities to undertake (Scott et al., 2009). In the experience economy of today, the search is on for experiences that provide fantasy, feelings, and fun (Holbrook and Hirchman, 1982). Consumers see beyond the functional and economical usage of the services and also consider the emotional, social, ethical, and environmental aspects (Nordin and Kowalkowaski, 2010). The emotional, aspirational, and participative over the rational or functional aspects of the products and services are increasingly being given importance to by the consumers. The hedonic and pleasure seeking values are shadowing the utilitarian and intrumental values. Guests today are looking for well-being and emotional satisfaction. The tourism, hospitality, and leisure services being people oriented have unique characteristics and evaluation criteria with high-risk purchase element and concern for customer satisfaction (Reisinger, 2001). The hospitality and tourism industry has the emotional, aspirational, hedonic, and aesthetic appeal which distinguishes it from other services like banking and insurance. The hospitality industry is based on the host–guest relationship with social and cultural connotation attached to it as compared to other services which predominantly have a commercial manager–customer relationship (Hemmington, 2007). The level of customer participation in the hospitality and tourism services is much more as compared to other services which lead to a unique experience for each customer. The hospitality and tourism experience is dynamic and complex which is cocreated when the consumer interacts with the staff in the ambience provided by the organization while production and consumption go on at the same time.

The consumer profile of travelers is undergoing a change. The customers today are sophisticated, well traveled, and more demanding as compared to those in the mid-20th century. The customers expect to be entertained and have an experience which leads to a return trip and/or positive interactions with the organization (Jayawardena et al., 2013). The expectations of consumers have risen and the service quality and reliability are taken for granted. The standard service is no longer a differentiator and the organizations need to market experiences in order to remain competitive in the marketplace. The prosperity in the emerging economies has produced enough high net-worth individuals aware of the offerings around the world and expecting the same level in the home countries. The rising middle class is letting go off its pent up desire to travel and is exploring destinations in far off places. The sophisticated visitor's expectations are high. There is increase in diversity in the international travelers with increasing number of visitors from emerging economies especially from China and India traveling to various destinations around the world.

The rapid advancement in technology has made consumers aware of destinations around the world and the experiences they offer. Technology has also provided access to the compare and shop for products and services online. At the same time, the reduced cost of technology has made it possible for organizations to store and sift through large amounts of data and process it further to provide personalized service. The customer's demographics, psychographics, and behavior patterns can be studied using data mining and customized products can be prepared to make the experience personal and memorable.

In the competitive environment prevalent today, it is of utmost importance to engage the customer through experiences to create value rather than just providing service. In hospitality industry there is high degree of involvement of the consumer is in the experience. The values, attitudes, and beliefs of the consumers are personal and they make the experience unique for each customer.

The increased competitive intensity, changing tastes, and preferences of customers and advances in technology have opened doors for creating more innovative experiences. The service delivery through theatrical metaphors and cocreation of a personal experience appealing to the emotions and aspirations of consumer can be achieved. The search is on for creating novelty, moments of surprise, and amazement which makes the experience unique and memorable for consumers.

2.2 TYPES OF EXPERIENCES

An experience is the series of events that one lives through which is evaluated in totality. The experiences are intangible and connect with the customers better than the products or services as they provide value to them and become memorable (Binkhorst and Dekker, 2009). The experience encompasses the encountering and living through situations throughout the travel continuum. Experiences can be unique to a particular location or those that can be had anywhere. The experiences give the consumer "sensory, emotional, cognitive, behavioral and relational values that replace the functional values" (Schmitt, 1999). The wealth is no longer concentrated in the hands of the elite and more and more people are aspiring for personal and customized services. The pursuit of good life filled with contentment, happiness, and pleasure can be seen all around us (Van Boven and Gilovich, 2003). There are emotional aspects in making decisions rather than rational cognition in consumption choices (Scott et al., 2009). The experiences act as a bridge between the customer's lifestyle and choices and the brand and have meaning in the broader social context. Bruwer and Alant (2009) showed that it is the sensual and pleasure seeking experiences within a social context that drive the tourists to the wine destinations. Whenever the experience is not defined it is assumed to be a pleasant one.

Tourism experience provides a break from ordinary spatial and temporal structures of everyday life and improves the quality of life. It gives an opportunity to absorb and immerse in the new places, things, and ideas and enriches the visitors. If successfully executed, the experience gives the guests memories to cherish for a lifetime. The vast variety of experiences calls for a systematic classification to make an in-depth study. The pleasurable experiences have been classified into the following four types by Dube and Le Bel (2003):

1. Sensory or physical pleasure derived from the pleasant sensations experienced
2. Social pleasure which comes from interaction with other human beings (or otherwise, as in solitary pursuit of some activity)
3. Emotional pleasure derived from the feelings, ideas, and mental images
4. Intellectual pleasure derived from deciphering the subtleties and complexities of stimuli around us.

Classification of Experiences

Sensory Pleasure

Sight: The exquisite locales please the sight and the picture is etched in our memory. The pristine beaches, snow clad mountains, or rustic locales of a jungle safari present a unique setting appealing to the human eye.

Smell: The inviting fragrance of the flowers set at the dining table of the garden restaurant, the ambience in the front office of a hotel, or the freshness of the laundry all add to the delight of the customers.

Sound: The soothing background music playing in the restaurants sets the ambience for a pleasant evening. The innovations in materials to minimize echo and disturbing sounds in atriums, banquet halls, and conference halls increase the guest's satisfaction level. In music festivals, the melodies of the songs attract visitors.

Taste: The gastronomical element is of utmost importance in restaurants. It increases the amount a consumer spends at a given time and forms the basis of narrative to others.

Touch: The velvet couches and the comfortable beds are an important aspect in providing the guests with relaxing stay in hotels.

Social Pleasure

Hotels and restaurants provide the ambience for social outings with family, friends, and colleagues. This satisfies the social needs of human beings. Whether it is a birthday celebration party at Pizza Hut or time spent in the coffee shop with friends, the social aspect of the experience makes it memorable. The opportunity is there to learn more about each other and spend some quality time away from the routine. The group can explore new places and things and can build a bond for a lifetime. They can learn from each other. The adventure sports arenas provide a space to compete against each other and hold team building exercises for the business guests. The collective well-being creates a deeper and shared meaning of the experience which can be revisited and cherished for a long time to come.

Emotional Pleasure

The visit to an upscale restaurant or a destination appeals to the emotions in human beings. Great stories and mental images of a place let you soar high in your dreams. They create a magic spell on the guests and leave them craving for more.

Intellectual Pleasure

The visit to the historical or heritage site imparts the guest new insights into the life and time of the inhabitants. The study tours by experts to study the flora and fauna species increases the knowledge of the streams by uncovering the new complexities of the ecosystem and gives them the intellectual pleasure. A visit to a Japanese or Italian restaurant is a learning experience for a foreign national as he can in the future distinguish between the food and ambience of these two distinct cultures. The wine tasting workshops or the reading festivals bring together people from a specialized field and give them the opportunity to share their experience and build their knowledge further from these interactions. The debates and discussions are intellectually stimulating and prod the participants to think further and explore new realms.

Pine and Gilmore (1999) have classified experiences into four sets namely education, entertainment, escapist, and aesthetic. There is a wide variety of experiences which the hospitality sector offers to the guests. These experiences are created because of the exquisite locales the destinations are set in, ethnic cuisines they offer, art and culture of the place that they showcase ,and various other reasons. These unique experiences are not only relevant to adventure sports but also for nature walks, cuisine and wine tasting, or appreciating a new culture, historical or heritage site, religious place, or in a wild life safari context. Whether it is the tasting of wine or specialty/signature dish, skiing, surfing, rock climbing, water sports, ice hockey, skating, diving, shopping, pottery, artifact making/ purchasing, participating in the music festival, or a sports event, an experience can become memorable when it touches the chord of the heart.

2.3 STAGING EXPERIENCE TO GAIN COMPETITIVE ADVANTAGE/DIMENSIONS IN CONSUMER EXPERIENCE

The production and the consumption of the experience take place simultaneously and it is only after the experience that a consumer can evaluate whether it matched or exceeded or fell short of the expectations. When customers are better off after the service then value for the customer is created (Gronroos, 2008). Value creation implies the well-being of the customer, that the customer is better off in some respect after the experience. In some cases there may be erosion of value for the customer when the experience does not turn out to be up to the expectations. The experience can turn out to be either an enjoyable one or can be deficient in some respects and the consumer continuously makes efforts to improve it. The service quality expectation and perception is influenced by the synergy between people, process, and physical evidence (Titz, 2001). At tourist destination, experience is influenced by multiple factors and their interaction such as accommodation, intangibles, airlines, and local inhabitants. Chan and Baum (2007) in their study found the experience of ecotourists to be multidimensional based upon the activities available, service site staff, socialization on site, and quality of information provided on wildlife and culture.

Staging the experiences is a complex process which involves the consumers and employees in the context of the physical surroundings according to the processes and systems of the organization within the vision of the entrepreneur. Each experience is influenced by the personal beliefs, values, and attitudes of the customers and the response to these by the staff. Prahalad and Ramaswamy (2004) propose that the experiential marketing needs to go beyond the Disney type of experience where the guests are the human props in the staged experiences. Morgan et al. (2008) in their article 'Drama in the dining room' have used the metaphor of theatrical performance where the customer is not a mere spectator but is the star cast with the staff acting in the supporting roles to cocreate the experience. The processes are the scripts, and the physical surroundings provide the props and sets for the experience.

2.3.1 PHYSICAL ENVIRONMENT

The importance of physical surroundings in experience comprising multisensory cues, space and functions, signs and symbols, art and artifacts has been highlighted by many researchers (Zemke and Pullman, 2008; Walls et al., 2011). The physical surroundings provide multisensory cues regarding the quality of experience. The ambience of the place stimulates the five senses of taste, touch, sight, sound, and smell and is an integral part of the experience. The ambient conditions such as lighting, music, aroma, artifacts, and colors convey the quality message and set the mood for the experience (Walls et al., 2011). The atmosphere of the place influences the tourist experience ((Prebensen and Foss, 2011). The physical environment, design and setting, ambience of the service impacts the service quality and the experience that is provided to the customer. The aesthetics give a dramatic effect and can mesmerize a guest.

The Vineyards of Nashik

Set in the picturesque locales, surrounded by the Western Ghats, the vineyards of Nashik is the destination for wine tourists. It is India's own Napa valley which has fertile land with lush green vines adding to the scenic beauty of the place. The gentle slopes of the landscape and the wineries attract visitors from both home and abroad. The panorama of the place enthralls the visitors. The wine drinking is a lifestyle activity which provides hedonic pleasure and is an experience in itself whether it is for the occasional drinker or a connoisseur. The wine guru unravels the mysteries of the wine making process and enhances the wine tasting experience by explaining its intricacies. The friendly and hospitable people make the experience more enjoyable. The tourists lose track of time and immerse in the pleasure of an extraordinary experience.

The décor of the restaurant, lighting, music, flower arrangements at the table, the plate settings, the folding of napkins, and the attire of the service personnel are a prelude to the staged performance later. The physical environment provides the tangible basis to the customers to form a viewpoint regarding the anticipated service (Walls and Berry, 2007; Walter and Evardsson, 2012). The design and layout of the restaurant or the bar can increase or decrease the chances of interaction between guests and impacts the overall experience. The open kitchens of restaurants reassure the guests about the hygiene and provide opportunity to the chefs to display their skills (Alonso and O'Neill, 2010). This enhances the experience of the guests and adds entertainment value.

The hotel's atmosphere and the facilities provide help in relaxing and escaping the routine. Value for the customers is created through employees, servicescape, service equity, processes, service convenience, and price fairness. Servicescape is the strongest driver of service value followed by service equity (Martin-Ruiz et al., 2012). It is important for the guest to feel welcomed in the environment. It has to be comfortable and relaxing. For those traveling for relaxation, the cognitive image of the destination influences the intent to recommend it to others, whereas for those traveling to experience fun and excitement the destination personality is an important predictor (Sahin and Baloglu (2014).

2.3.2 *GUEST–EMPLOYEE INTERFACE*

The human interactions are those with the employees and other guests. The intangible nature of the hospitality products places responsibility on the employees to provide the experience. The role of the front office staff and other members of the organization is determined by the policies of the organization. The service interactions and encounters with the front office staff and tour guides are extremely important in tourism experiences (Prebensen and Foss, 2011). Baum (2006) highlighted that the emotional intelligence of employees and their engagement in their roles can enhance the experience for the consumer. Employees who are in direct contact with the customers are a key factor in making the experience extraordinary. The customers want the employees to provide quick and efficient service. They should be available to provide the requisite help whenever required but should respect the privacy of the guests and should not come in the way of normal course of the experience. Their appearance should be neat and professional and the behavior courteous. They should be knowledgeable and skilled to perform the task to the expectation level of the guests. Attentive, sensitive, efficient, knowledgeable, and skilled employees in appropriate attire are the ones who make the guests feel welcomed at the property and provide proactive service. The employees should be adept at improvising. They pave the way for valuable cocreation of experiences. Happy and empowered staff members create memorable experiences for the customers turning them into brand ambassadors for the hotel.

Bharwani and Jauhari (2013) have developed a hospitality intelligence construct based upon emotional intelligence, cultural intelligence, and hospitality experiential intelligence to map the competencies of hospitality employees. It is important to recruit the new employees with the right skill set and to train the present one to acquire the requisite skills.

Rejuvenating the mind, body, and spirit

The Ananda Spa set in the tranquil foothills of the Himalayas, amidst the Sal forest and overlooking the Ganga provides a perfect retreat for relaxation and rejuvenation. Away from the hustle and bustle of the cities and crowds, the panoramic landscapes soothe the eyes and bring in peace and tranquility to the mind. The knowledge of Ayurveda, Yoga, and Vedanta is integrated with the international therapies to provide the consumer with an enchanting experience.

The routine is decided according to the needs and desires of the guest. The personalized attention and care to the requirements make the guest feel special. The centuries of wisdom is packed in the ayurvedic oils and creams and is used to relax and tone up the body. The therapeutic ingredients work wonders on the body and enthrall the guests. The magic hands massage the wear and tear suffered from the daily routine of busy life and brings the tissues back to life. The pores are cleansed and the skin starts shining. The experience is relaxing. The guest gets the feeling of being taken care of in a special way. The holistic experience rejuvenates the mind, body, and the spirit.

2.3.3 GUEST-TO-GUEST INTERFACE

Consumers crave for the social and entertainment value in addition to the transactional relationship they have with hospitality organizations. Consumers derive value from creating, enjoying, and remembering the experience with the cooperation of other consumers (Wikstrom, 2008). The fellow customer's demeanor, appearance, behavior, and interactions have an influence on the stay experience of a customer in a property (Walls et al., 2011). Finsterwalder and Kuppelwieser (2011) studied the multiple consumer cocreation efforts in the service interactions and found that the consumer engagement in the group task had positive influence on the perceived consumer-to-consumer social interaction.

In restaurants, customer experience is influenced by the basic food offering, culinary finesse, ambience, and company at the table and other guests in the restaurant (Andersson and Carlback, 2009). The company at the table and other guests are beyond the control of the management of the restaurants but rest of the factors can be designed and managed to provide optimum experience to the consumer.

2.3.4 PERSONAL CHARACTERISTICS OF THE CONSUMER

The company can provide the ambience and the actors for the experience but it is the state of mind and the mood of the customer which determines the quality of the experience (Pine and Gilmore, 1999; Morgan et al., 2009). The consumers can play a disruptive or creative role in the staging of the experience. The reactions to the events and exchanges are personal to each consumer. The outcome of the experience depends upon the reaction of the consumer to the staged encounter based on his frame of mind, cultural background, thoughts, and feelings. The emotions and individual and collective well-being contribute to experiences (Prebensen and Foss, 2011).

The service spaces alone cannot orchestrate experiences, for that engagement of the guests is necessary. The experience may involve the consumer physically, emotionally, intellectually, and spiritually (Mossberg, 2007). The active interest and participation of the consumer are prerequisites for a successful experience. The level of participation varies from consumer to consumer. The knowledge and skills the consumer possesses influence action in the servicescapes (Pareigis et al., 2012). The consumer's ability to observe, listen, interact, and empathize may determine the quality of the social experience. Lugosi (2008) has used the term capability to refer to the individual's knowledge, skills, and competences to create meaningful experiences. Consumers need to tap their capabilities developed outside and inside the service environment to enjoy the experience. The consumer's need for self-development is fulfilled by undertaking creative tasks (Richards and Wilson, 2006). With each experience, the customer acquires knowledge and skills to outperform the previous standard achieved. It enhances the self-confidence and self-image of the consumer (Morgan, 2006). Some transformational change is there. The drive is there to repeat the experience to further advance the knowledge. Foodservice is an art created by talented professionals and requires skilled consumers to appreciate it (Morgan et al., 2008).

Roles in Consumer Experience

The type and setting of the hospitality organization determine the roles played by consumer in experiences. Many restaurants and bars have live band or orchestra playing to provide an enhanced experience to the consumers. Others have singers or performers engaged in entertaining the guests while they enjoy their meal or drink. At some hotels, novel activities are organized to keep the guests involved and happy. The physical layout within which such events take place determines the amount of interaction customers have with individuals outside their group. The song request by one customer in a particular group can increase the attention and interest in the live singer of customer seated in another group if it has an emotional connect with the second customer. The customer can talk about the context and encourage others in his group to enjoy the song of his choice. If the singer asks the customer to sing along and then the pleasure of the experience can be taken to the next level. Others can join in the singing or can watch, clap, and enjoy the moment. Similarly, talented customers can play a musical instrument or dance along in the performance if given an opportunity. The opportunity for interaction between different groups of consumers increases in bars and restaurants which telecast sports events live and attract the sports enthusiasts. The customers may go in groups to cheer their favorite sportsperson or teams together and may also join others with similar interests to increase the level of fun and excitement. When such events bring customers from different groups together in the experience, the social dimension of the experience is enhanced. The service providers and their customers may play different roles during the consumption experience. For a memorable social experience within the service space, the staff and the consumers may play the roles of initiator, enhancer, director, and/or facilitator (Lugosi, 2008). The initiator focuses on the activity that brings the group together; the enhancer acts as a catalyst for interactions and reinforces the significance of the activity; the director steers the performance toward objective and the facilitator who actively or passively brings the group together.

2.3.5 CONTEXTUAL FEATURES IN EXPERIENCE

The events that form an experience have a contextual connotation and are set in a particular time period. These events unfold over the continuum of the travel. Tourism experience is impacted by network of stakeholders whether they are persons or things – real, virtual, or even dreams. The factors such as reasons for the travel, the ease/difficulty of making reservations, the nature and service of the airlines, the on-time departure and arrival of aircrafts, and the rental car services all contribute toward an experience. The reasons for undertaking the trip are foremost in forming an opinion about the experience. The business and leisure trips may excite the consumer in different ways. The relations with the colleagues accompanying the consumer for business purposes determine whether the consumer is looking forward to the experience or not. In leisure travel, the family members or friends accompanying the consumer have influence over the experience. The company of the family and friends on special occasions presents an opportunity for extraordinary hospitality experiences. The celebrations can be made memorable through the ample fun and entertainment opportunities provided by the hospitality organizations. Also, the destination for a particular trip may vary the consumer's enthusiasm level for the upcoming trip. These are the factors over which hospitality organizations have little control. The businesses can provide as much information about the destination as possible so that the consumers make wise choices are not disappointed at arrival. The alliances with travel agents, airlines, and rental car companies should be in place to provide a seamless experience.

A series of events determined by the consumer which gives him the freedom of self-expression and spontaneity in an ambience set by the hospitality organizations sets the stage for memorable experiences. The living through these experiences can lead to the consumer learning new skills, testing his limits, and enhancing his knowledge leading to personal transformation. The meaning derived from the experience is very personal and depends upon the influence it has had on the consumer and the value it had generated for him. Communicating experiences in terms of meanings and narratives, symbols and episodes enhances their value and allows the bearer to relive them. The narrative value of the experience by the consumer adds deeper meaning to the experience and when it is shared with others, it can induce desire in them to emulate the same. The company and its network, the consumer and the consumer community all play a vital role in the cocreation of experiences in the ambient environment provided by the businesses through continuous interaction.

White Water Rafting in the Ganges

The banks of Ganges uphill of the religious town of Rishikesh in the northern province of Uttarakhand in India are dotted with permanent and seasonal hotels which provide the adventurous experience of white-water rafting. The intrinsic beauty of the place is an attraction for local and foreign nationals alike. Thousands throng to this place to have fun and adventure in the summer months. The living in the tents on the banks of this mighty river is a novel experience in itself. The gushing waters of the river provide the melodious ambient sound enhancing the experience. For the city folk, the amenities provided are bare minimum with the electricity being generated in the house using diesel and lights are switched off at a set time. The guests are then handed out one lantern per group to enjoy the evening. The three levels of rapids in the river provide the opportunity to visitors to customize their adventure outing. The guests are given a short training discourse to enjoy the adventure to the fullest while taking all safety precautions. The safety of the guests is ensured through the use of life jackets and trained lifeguards on each raft. The excitement and joy one experiences while approaching a rapid in a raft and crossing it is a memorable experience for the guests. The ambience of festivity in the air has to be seen to be believed. The brave and sporty ones can master the technique and build reputation in the group. They can guide others to avoid falling in the river and enjoy the rapids. The guest can also experience other activities such as trekking, playing beach volleyball, cliff jumping, slithering, rappelling, rock climbing, nature walks, doing yoga by the riverside, diving, and swimming. The guests look forward to the gourmet food offered in the makeshift dining hall after the strenuous physical activity throughout the day. The variety in food provided at such remote destination is remarkable. The care and the attention to the detail of the caretakers at the lodge make the experience special. It is an experience worth having for the city bred to enjoy the natural environs and at the same time experience an adventurous activity.

The memorable customer experiences are not only enjoyable and entertaining but also leave the customers with a feeling of fantasy and nostalgia encouraging them to relive the experience (Price, 2011). This brings in repeat revenues for the organizations and opportunities for cocreating again and again. Consistent positive experiences reinforce the consumer connect with the brand. They are part of the customer's memory for a lifetime and make the customers brand advocates inducing potential customers to experience the magical feeling.

Brilliant Cast and Gripping Story Make the Experience Memorable

Dramatizing the service encounter adds an element of mystery to the experience. The well-trained staff of the organization is the cast that keeps the guest interested and involved in the happenings by brilliant portrayal. Intrigue and the drama keep the guests on the edge of their seats anticipating more entertainment. All elements of the performance are steered together in tandem to create synergy between the disparate units. The aesthetics and creativity of the place add a dramatic effect to the whole experience. The guests are mesmerized by the soul-stirring performance. Spellbounding experience brings the smile on the lips of the guests. Enthralled, the guests leave the premises totally delighted and craving for more. The lovely moments can be shared and relived with family and friends.

2.4 EXPERIENCE DESIGN

The experience quality needs to be consistent with the image projected. Jayawardena et al. (2013) emphasize the fact that hospitality organizations need to study in depth the factors that influence, differentiate, and delight a customer at each of the stages of the travel experience. Long-term relationship with valued customers requires a comprehensive approach more than service quality and customer satisfaction (Martin-Ruiz et al., 2012). As the income of the consumer increases, experience becomes an important value determinant (Yu and Fang, 2009). Torres and Kline (2013) provide a useful framework for providing customer delight in hospitality experiences by conceptualizing the behaviors and actions that achieve this objective.

It is possible to design experiences to increase the customer satisfaction. The potential guests to the area and the opportunities available in the host environment present the canvas for creation of experiences. The elements of variety and novelty need to be inculcated in experiences to create and maintain the visitor interest. A different space and form needs to be created to make the experience unique (Lin, 2010). The food experience needs to be contrast, more intense, and an extension of the everyday life of the consumer (Quan and Wang, 2004). There should be congruence between the theme of the restaurant, décor and food served (Lin and Mattila, 2010). Businesses need to identify, enhance, and deliver their experiential offers to the customers (Williams, 2006). The customer has to be provided with ample options to choose from and derive the pleasure associated with this. The choice provided to the guests on the menu gives the consumer the opportunity to make decision. Similarly, the availability of abundant activities at a resort conveys generosity.

The experiences need to be novel and unique in order to be memorable. The design of the experiences requires creativity. Enough flexibility needs to be embedded in the design for it to be improvised while the consumer experience is under way. Wide range of activities available at or around the destination increases the choices available to the consumer. Variety is the name of the game. Consumers when choose from a variety of options provided to them on the property, experience a sense of control over the experience. They get the pleasure of plenty and the satisfaction of choice. The service can be tailored according to the individual's need giving a personalized touch (King, 2002).

The ambience needs to appeal to all the five senses of the visitors to provide sensational pleasure. The environment should be entertaining, stimulating and educational (Knutson et al. 2006). The right environment and setting need to be created for the experiences to emerge (Schmitt, 1999). A threshold-level requirement is to maintain clean spaces, proper air quality and lighting, soothing temperature, humidity, noise levels, and have appropriate background music. A clear signage dispels ambiguity regarding the service spaces in unfamiliar new environment of hotels in faraway places and makes the guests feel safe and comfortable. To please the guest, appealing architecture, landscaping, art works, paintings, chandeliers, color schemes, fabrics, fixtures, and furnishings need to be put in place to make the experience memorable. The servicescapes should be such that they invite and attract the visitors and once inside the ambience and the comfort make them forget time and enjoy the visit. The approach response should be stimulated in the guests rather than the avoidance response to the physical environment. Evardsson et al. (2010) have proposed a dynamic approach to physical environment comprising the static (physical artefacts, intangibles, customer placement, and technology) and the interactive dimensions (customer's involvement and interaction with employees).The servicescape design should be such that the social dimensions of the experience are also taken care of (Johnstone, 2012). The customers interact with the physical environment's functional and social dimension and derive their own meanings of the experience which are expressed as feelings, thoughts, imagination, and behavior (Walter and Evardsson, 2012). The design should be intuitive, meaningful, and easy to use to support the customer processes (Pareigis et al., 2012). The experience design should incorporate features that avoid crowding and at the same time, makes the place lively and entertaining. The organizations need to create experience spaces which facilitate the staging of the experience.

Canvas for fun and entertainment

The magic shows and puppet shows on birthday parties of the kids enthrall the audience with the mystery element.

The bowling alleys, ice-skating arenas, rappelling, and other adventure sports provide the thrill to the teenagers and adults alike. This leads to an increase in the consumer spend at the hospitality destination in addition to providing an experience for the lifetime.

The cafes provide the setting for the friends or colleagues to unwind and share their experiences.

The pubs and restaurants provide the ambient setting for live bands and singers and can enchant the audience with sing along competitions.

The nature walks, hiking and trekking and mountaineering at destinations provide a unique experience.

The jungle safaris have an inherent element of adventure. The spotting of the tiger during the safari is an experience to remember for a lifetime. The wolf and bear trails encompass a novel experience.

The pottery making, art and handicraft workshops educate the consumers in addition to entertaining them.

The historical and heritage sites bring insights regarding the life and times of the inhabitants.

The crowds cheering at the sports events telecast live while enjoying meals at restaurants add a special meaning to the experience.

Walking trails to the old city areas imparts knowledge along with being entertaining.

Open-air concert arenas bring together strangers and create a unique experience.

The businesses need to bear in mind that the customer is the focal point instead of the service. The guests should feel genuinely valued and welcomed. Range of possibilities can be explored to cater to different behavioral segments of consumers and appeal to their desires and dreams. The service needs to be customized according to the needs of the customer. The interactive mode should be deployed to give the consumer access to the information required to tailor the experience according to individual needs and level of involvement sort. Juttner et al. (2013) propose that applying the sequential incident laddering technique based on customer feedback can provide the guidelines for service experience design. The sequential incident laddering technique is customer centric as it starts with the customer-defined scope, process and memorable incidents that form the experience. It provides a mechanism for measuring emotions and integrating emotion-driven actions in the managerial processes.

The first generation of experiences has concentrated on providing the fun and entertainment for consumers, whereas the second generation of experiences focus on cocreation. The novel experience can be cocreated by the involvement of the consumer and the desire of the businesses to delight the guests. The cocreation of the experience is developed with central point being the consumer and matched with the personal, social, and cultural values that the consumer holds. Being sensitive to wishes, desires, and needs of guests and a positive interpersonal interaction initiate the cocreation of an experience (Binkhorst and Dekker, 2009). The customers feel a sense of empowerment when they play a greater role in the exchange process (Hoyer et al., 2011). Not all guests are inclined toward participating in the cocreation activities. The company should approach and interact according to the guest's comfort level with the involvement in various activities. There should be clarity of task, the customer should be competent enough and be motivated to contribute toward coproduction of the experiences. Roggeveen et al. (2012) have demonstrated how the cocreation not only enhances the consumer experience but is also a cost-efficient strategy for service recovery as compared to compensation when the customers must deal with severe delays.

The Internet with access to immense possibilities has brought about a change in which the consumers are made aware of the services and the manner in which these are provided. People are well informed and can search for alternatives. Technological developments facilitate meaningful dialogue and provide a platform for the cocreation of experiences which are unique and authentic. Most of the cocreation of experiences is consumer generated and businesses are playing a reactive role of providing solution to their queries. Hospitality organizations need to be more proactive in design of tourism cocreation experiences and need to integrate these in their business processes. The empowered, well-informed, and influential customers of today are playing an active role of coproducers and co-designers of the experiences. The knowledge of the skilled, informed, and active customers can be leveraged to embark on a mutually beneficial journey of cocreation by the firms (Saarijarvi, 2012).The experiences should be designed and managed in such a way that they lead to sustained competitive advantage for the firm.

Unique Characteristics of Destinations

The Fort and Palace Hotels in India

The architectural grandeur of the fort and palace hotels of India which cannot be replicated anywhere else in the world attracts visitors from near and far-off places. It combines with a culture that equates the guests to God and believes in taking care of their well-being provides a fertile ground for creating remarkable consumer experiences. The rich cultural heritage and excellent customer service provide a memorable experience for the guests.

The Himalayas

The snowclad peaks and the mountain passes of the world's highest mountain range, the Himalayas is host to many tourist destinations from Leh in the northern state of Jammu and Kashmir to Sikkim in the northeast. The natural beauty and the vast expanse of Nubra Valley beyond the Khardungla pass has to be experienced to be appreciated. The white sand along the river bed, the double-humped camels, the sulfur springs, and the wild flowers all adorn this unique destination.

The Kaziranga Wildlife Sanctuary

The Kaziranga Wildlife Sanctuary sprawled over 430 acres is home to the Indian one-horned rhino and is a world heritage site. It is also habitant of large population of elephants, Indian bison, sloth bears, and leopards. Several species of birds can be sighted in the sanctuary. The highlight of the place is its elephant safaris. The mahouts are apt at handling these elephants and guide the visitors through the safari. The coffee and rubber plantation along the Karbi Anglog are the other sightseeing activities available. The guests can also visit the tea gardens of Assam.

Cruise to Lakshadweep

Lakshadweep Islands are to the west of coast of Kerala in the Arabian Sea. Spread over 32 km^2 and 36 islands out of which only 10 are inhabited. It is known as the tropical paradise of India. The cruise starts from the coastal city of Cochin .Visitors can enjoy scuba diving, snorkeling kayaking, glass-bottomed boat rides and tourist attractions like the marine museum. The corals are visible through the shallow blue waters of the sea. Fishing, coir making, and coconut cultivation are the main occupations of the native population. The islands are a great place for exploring wildlife and ecotourism.

The Pristine Beaches of the Maldives

The pristine beaches of the Maldives with their white sand and picturesque panorama provide an excellent opportunity for hospitality organizations to provide memorable experiences to the guests. The fun and excitement provided by the sun and sand experiences is enhanced by the service par excellence by the staff. The swimming, surfing, snorkeling, and diving are some of the activities that the guest can enjoy. The beach rooms look out on to the exquisite shoreline. The tranquil setting and the natural beauty of the place is at par with the best in the world.

2.5 MANAGEMENT OF EXPERIENCES

Customer engagement leads to the integration of the customer resources into the core offering of the product. The purpose of experience management is to capture customer feedback and integrate it in experience design, to ascertain business practices that require improvement and to reduce undesirable consumer experiences (Fatma, 2014). The value is created through guest's accumulated experiences with resources and processes in the physical, social, mental, temporal, and spatial contexts (Gronroos and Voima, 2013). Customer's engagement in the service delivery process leads to memorable experiences for the customers and better financial performance, customer retention, and loyalty for the organizations (Tigu et al., 2013). Care and sensitivity is required to manage experiences. The customer database with relevant and updated information can support the frontline employees, providing a personalized attention stimuli to enhance the experience (Juttner et al. 2013).The hotel owners need to formalize their guest encounters so that meaningful information could be derived out of it for usage by the staff.

Employees are the interface between the organization and the guests. Happy and satisfied employees provide quick resolution to customer queries and complaints. They are the ones who make the guest feel valued and respected. Their timely interaction, assistance, and guidance lead to superior customer service (James, 2013). Their behavior and service help the guest make an emotional connection with the company and leave the premises happy. "Highly motivated and engaged employees can create memorable experiences" (Varma, 2012). Customer experience management is the offerings provided to fill in the gaps between expectations and experience (Meyer and Schwager, 2007), whereas customer relationship management may drive cross selling by bundling products in demand with those that are not. Employees must be adequately trained and compensated as they are an important cast member in the staging of experiences.

One of the challenges in providing memorable experiences is the guest–employee interface where the employee is untrained and is in the job for less time (Jayawardena et al., 2013). Focus at operational level is on commoditization and cost reduction. Operational freedom is not there. The budget is not there for training, coaching, or for promoting the destination. Low-cost employees, frequent turnover, attrition some of the challenges that the hospitality organizations are facing. This leads to the inability to improvise and adapt the service (Morgan, 2009). Clash between hospitality notion and profitability objectives is there when offering experiences (Hemmington, 2007; Morgan et al. 2008,). The economic relationship with the customer should be dealt with only once preferably before the experience so that the staff can be generous and hospitable.

The social dimensions of the hospitality experiences should be managed. Consumers with matching profiles should be encouraged to sit at adjacent tables in restaurants and vice versa. Any aggrieved guest should be taken aside and prompt resolution of problem should be offered so that it does not dilute the experience of other guests.

The experience should be provided in close coordination with other stakeholders whether they are online travel agents or tour operators or rental car services. As the experiences are evaluated in totality, attempt should be made to make it as smooth and hassle free as possible. Healthy partnerships with all stakeholders should be built and maintained to enhance the experience.

The customer experience factors should be incorporated in planning and customer experience delivery should be monitored (Popa and Barna, 2013). The company should drive growth using the customer experience as a differentiator. The consumer experiences should be managed to turn them into personally valued experiences so as to generate brand loyalty.

2.6 EXPERIENCE EVALUATION

The initial service evaluation is based upon the service attributes as the consumption starts. Once the consumer accumulates experiences, the evaluation is done on them. The consumers evaluate the actual experiences in relation to their expectations from experiences rather than in absolute terms. The mental state and emotions of the consumer play a vital role in defining experiences. The subjective personal responses and feelings make the experience unique for each guest. The psychographics, the social environment, and the emotional state of the consumer influence their evaluation (Scott et al., 2009). Some researchers have named these factors as the trip-related factors and personal characteristics of the consumer. Personal values reflecting consumer's self-concept and aspirations determine the intent to form long-term associations (Martin-Ruiz et al., 2012). Kauppinen-Raisanen and Gummerus (2013) found that consumers remember positive food-related experiences in terms of food, context, self, place and time. The quality of experiences are evaluated based both the functional elements provided by the service suppliers and the emotional elements brought in by the consumers (Chan and Baum, 2007). Knutson et al. (2006) have identified seven attributes on which experiences can be evaluated. These are Environment, Convenience, Accessibility, Benefit, Utility, Incentive, and Trust. Yang (2011) has developed a "customer-delight barometer" and "competitiveness index" to measure the quality attributes.

Chang and Horng (2010) have prepared an experience quality construct based upon ambience, service providers, other consumers, consumer's companions, and the consumers themselves. Atmosphere, concentration, imagination, and surprise elements have been considered while preparing the physical surroundings dimension. Atmosphere refers to the décor and design; concentration to the time the customer spends enjoying the experience; imagination to the stories and dreams; and surprise to the novelty and amazement experienced. The impact of companions on the quality of experience has been emphasized by many researchers. Each experience provides the customer with the cognitive learning opportunity.

The factors making the experience memorable have time and again been studied in the past. Kim et al. (2012) have prepared a 24-item list for development of a scale to assess the memorable tourism experiences. The scale comprises seven parameters of refreshment, local culture, hedonism, knowledge, meaningfulness, involvement, and novelty. Kim and Ritchie (2014) studied psychometric properties of the memorable tourism experience scale (MTES) on a Taiwanese sample and confirmed that the seven dimensions of the scale are valid in cross-cultural context.

Harris et al. (2011) have proposed a discursive approach for evaluation of experiences in order to debate and critique further and to evaluate the experience as a whole rather than on various dimensions. This approach also brings out the aesthetic details of the experience not within the purview of current instruments used for evaluation. The role of the customers before, during, and after the experience as coresearchers and cocreators is highlighted.

The functional as well as the emotional value of the experience should be considered while doing the evaluation of experiences (Chan and Baum, 2007). The production cost of the experience needs to be studied in detail along with the value of the experience for the customer. The experience accounting systems need to be put in place so as to attain a fine balance between various factors that create value for the customer. Andersson and Carlback (2009) showed through experience evaluations in monetary terms that restaurants need to reallocate resources from food expenses and service toward the ambience of the place in order to meet the customer expectations.

2.7 CONCLUSION

The consumers are in pursuit of hedonic or pleasure-seeking values in addition to the rational or functional values provided by the hospitality experiences. The experiential offerings of the organizations should be matched to the needs and wants of the consumers The organizations need to provide abundant choice to the consumers in order to excite and engage them in the process. The active participation of the consumers is essential to make the experiences extraordinary. The element of surprise should be there which the consumer can discover during the consumption phase. The pleasant ambient environment plays an important role in making the experience enjoyable. The meaningful social interactions with the staff and other consumers play a vital role in the experience being memorable. The opportunity should be there for knowledgeable consumers to cocreate the experience and enhance it. The experience should meet or exceed the expected level. High engagement/involvement with the product is there when the consumer is enjoying the service and is unlikely to switch even when there are minor flaws (Laws, 2004). Committed customer relationships bring in greater payoffs in the form of referrals, positive word-of-mouth, customer satisfaction, loyalty, and diminished price sensitivity (Martin-Ruiz et al. 2012).The product is important to the consumer's belief system and the consumer identifies with it which leads to pro-company consequences of brand loyalty and brand advocacy (Stokburger-Sauer et al., 2012). The customer experience management leads to customer satisfaction, customer loyalty, and customer equity (Fatma, 2014). Consumer takes back memories of a lifetime and is compelled to make a return visit. Consumer shares the experiences with family and friends and acts as the brand ambassador of the organization. It is a win-win situation for both the consumers and the hospitality organization. The management of the experience with theatrical performance with the consumer leading as the star to cocreate the experience is going to be the differentiator in today's competitive hospitality sector.

KEYWORDS

- **memorable experiences**
- **customer experiences**
- **cocreation**
- **hospitality and tourism industry**
- **emerging economies**
- **theatrical metaphor**

REFERENCES

Alonso, A. D.; O'Neill, M.A. To What Extent Does Restaurant Design Influence Consumer Eating Out Experience? An Exploratory Study. *J. Retail Leisure Prop.* **2010,** *9*(3), 231–246.

Andersson, T. A. Carlback. Experience Accounting: An Accounting System that Is Relevant for Production of Restaurant Experiences. *Serv. Ind. J.* **2009,** *29*(10), 1377–1395.

Baum, T. G. Reflections on the Nature of Skills in the Experience Economy: Challenging Traditional Skills Models in Hospitality. *J. Hosp. Tour. Manag.* **2006,** *13*(2), 124–135.

Binkhorst, E.; Dekker, T. D. Agenda for Co-creation Tourism Experience Research. *J. Hosp. Mark. Manag.* **2009,** *18*(3), 311–327.

Bharwani, S.; Jauhari, V. An Exploratory Study of Competencies Required to Co-Create Memorable Customer Experiences in the Hospitality Industry. *Int. J. Contemp. Hosp. Manag.* **2013,** *25*(6), 823–843.

Bruwer, J.; Alant, K. The Hedonic Nature of Wine Tourism Consumption: An Experiential View. *Int. J. Wine Bus. Res.* **2009,** *21*(3), 235–257.

Chan, J.K.L.; Baum, T. Ecotourists' Perception of Ecotourism Experience in Lower Kinabatangan, Sabah, Malaysia. *J. Sustain. Tour.* **2007,** *15*(5), 574–590.

Chang, T.; Horng, S. Conceptualizing and Measuring Experience Quality: The Customer's Perspective. *Serv. Ind. J.* **2010,** *30*(14), 2401–2419.

Dube, L.; Le Bel, J. The Content and Structure of Laypeople's Concept of Pleasure. *Cognit. Emot.* **2003,** *17*(2), 263–295.

Evardsson, B.; Enquist, B.; Johnston, R. Design Dimensions of Experience Rooms for Service Test Drives: Case Studies in Several Service Contexts. *Manag. Serv. Qual.* **2010,** *20*, 312–327.

Fatma, S. Antecedents and Consequences of Customer Experience Management – A Literature Review and Research Agenda. *Int. J. Bus. Commer.* **2014,** *3*(6), 32–49.

Finsterwalder, J.; Kuppelwieser, V. G. Co-Creation by Engaging Beyond Oneself: The Influence of Task Contribution on Perceived Customer-to-Customer Social Interaction During a Group Service Encounter. *J. Strategic Mark.* **2011,** *19*(7), 607–618.

Gronroos, C. Service Logic Revisited: Who Creates Value? And Who Co-Creates? *Eur. Bus. Rev.* **2008,** *20*(4), 298–314.

Gronroos, C.; Voima, P. Critical Service Logic: Making Sense of Value Creation And Co-Creation. *J. Acad. Mark. Sci.* **2013,** *41*, 133–150.

Harris, K.; Harris, R. Elliot; D.; Baron, S. A Theatrical Perspective on Service Performance Evaluation: The Customer-Critic Approach. *J. Mark. Manag.* **2011,** *27*(5–6), 477–502.

Hemmington, N. From Service to Experience: Understanding and Defining Hospitality Business. *Serv. Ind. J.* **2007,** *27*(6), 747–755.

Holbrook, M. B.; Hirschman, E. C. The Experiential Aspects of Consumption: Consumer Fantasies, Feelings and Fun. *J. Consum. Res.* **1982,** *9*, 132–140.

Hoyer, W.D.; Chandy, R.; Dorotic, M.; Krafft, M.; Singh, S.S. Consumer Cocreation in New Product Development. *J. Serv. Res.* **2011,** *13*, 283–296.

James, J. The Heart that Makes the Mouse: Disney's Approach to Brand Loyalty. *J. Brand Loyal.* **2013,** *2*(1), 16–20.

Jayawardena, C.; McMillan, D.; Pantin, D.; Taller, M.; Willie, P. Trends in the International Hotel Industry. *Worldw. Hosp. Tour. Themes*. **2013,** *5*(2), 151–163.

Johnstone, M. The Servicescape: The Social Dimensions of Place. *J. Mark. Manag.* **2012,** *28*(11–12), 1399–1418.

Juttner, U.; Schaffner, D.; Windler, K.; Maklan, S. Customer Services Experiences: Developing and Applying Sequential Incident Laddering Technique. *Eur. J. Mark.* **2013,** *47*(5/6), 738–768.

Kauppinen-Raisanen, H.; Gummerus, J. Remembered Eating Experiences Defined by Self, Place, Food, Context and Time. *Br. Food J.* **2013,** *115*(5) ,666–685.

King, J. Destination Marketing Organizations-Connecting the Experience Rather Than Promoting the Place. *J. Vacat. Mark.* **2002,** *8*(2), 105–108.

Kim, J.; Ritchie, J.R.B. Cross-Cultural Validation of a Memorable Tourism Experience Scale (MTES). *J. Travel Res.* **2014,** *53*(3), 323–335.

Kim, J.; Ritchie, J. R. B.; McCormick, Bryan Development of a Scale to Measure Memorable Tourism Experiences. *J. Travel Res.* **2012,** *51*(1), 12–25.

Knutson, B.J.; Beck, J.A.; Kim, S. H.; Cha, J. Identifying the Dimensions of the Experience Construct. *J. Hosp. Leisure Mark.* **2006,** *15*(3), 31–47.

Laws, E. *Improving Tourism and Hospitality Services*; CABI Publishing: Wallingford, 2004. 100–129.

Lin, I.Y. The Combined Effect of Color and Music on Customer Satisfaction in Hotel Bars. *J. Hosp. Mark. Manag.* **2010,** *19*, 22–37.

Lin, I.Y.; Mattila, A.S. Restaurant Servicescapes, Service Encounter and Perceived Congruency on Customers' Emotions and Satisfaction. *J. Hosp. Mark. Manag.* **2010,** *19*, 819–841.

Lugosi, P. Hospitality Spaces, Hospitable Moments: Consumer Encounters and Affective Experiences in Commercial Settings. *J. Foodserv.* **2008,** *19*, 139–149.

Martin-Ruiz, D.; Barosso-Castro, C.; Rosa-Diaz, I. M. Creating Customer Value Through Service Experiences: An Empirical study in the Hotel Industry. *Tour. Hosp. Manag.* **2012,** *18*(1), 37–53.

Morgan, M. Making Spaces for Experiences. *J. Retail and Leisure Property*. **2006,** *5*(4), 305–313.

Morgan, M.; Watson, P.; Hemmington, N. Drama in the Dining Room: Theatrical Perspectives on Foodservice Encounters. *J. Foodserv.* 2008, *19*, 111–118.

Morgan, M.; Elbe, J.; Esteban, C. J. Has the Experience Economy Arrived? The Views of Destinations Managers in Three Visitor-Dependent Areas. *Int. J. Tour. Res.* **2009,** *11*, 201–216.

Mossberg, L. A Marketing Approach to the Tourist Experience. *Scand. J. Hosp. Tour.* **2007,** *7*(1), 59–74.

Nordin, F.; Kowalkowski, C. Solutions Offerings: A Critical Review and Reconceptualisation. *J. Serv. Manag.* **2010,** *24*(4), 441–459.

Pareigis, J.; Echeverri, P.; Edvardsson, B. Exploring Internal Mechanisms Forming Customer Servicescape Experiences. *J. Serv. Manag.* **2012,** *23*(5), 677–696.

Pine, B. J.; Gilmore, J. H. *The Experience Economy: Work Is Theatre and Every Business a Stage*; Harvard Business School Press: Boston, 1999; 30–50.

Popa, V.; Barna, M. Customer and Shopper Experience Management. *Valahian J. Econ. Stud.* **2013,** *4*(2), 81–88.

Prahalad, C. K.; Ramaswamy, V. *The Future of Competition: Co-creating Unique Value with Customers*; Harvard Business School Press: Boston, 2004; 265–285.

Prebensen, N. K.; Foss, L. Coping and Co-Creating in Tourist Experiences. *Int. J. Tour. Res.* **2011,** *13*, 54–67.

Price, F.W. Creating Memorable Moments: When Customer Service Isn't Enough, *Tourist Attractions & Parks*. **2011**. http://tapmag.com/2011/06/01/creating-memorable-moments-when-customer-service-isn%E2%80%99t-enough/. accessed 10 July 2014.

Quan, S.; Wang, N. Towards a Structural Model of the Tourist Experience: An Illustration from Food Experiences in Tourism. *Tour. Manag.* **2004,** 25, 297–305.

Reisinger, Y. Unique Characteristics of Tourism, Hospitality and Leisure Services. In *Service Quality Management in Hospitality, Tourism and Leisure;* Kandampully, J., Mok, C., Sparks, B., Eds.;Haworth Hospitality Press: Binghamton, NY; 2001; 67–84.

Roggeveen, A.; Tsiros, M.; Grewal, D. Understanding the Co-Creation Effect: When does Collaborating with Customers Provide a Lift to Service Recovery. *J. Acad. Mark. Sci.* **2012,** *40*(6), 771–790.

Richards, G.; Wilson, J. Developing Creativity in Tourism Experiences: A Solution to the Serial Reproduction of Culture? *Tour. Manag.* **2006,** *27*, 1209–1223.

Saarijarvi, H. The Mechanisms of Value Co-Creation. *J. Strategic Mark.* **2012,** *20*(5), 381–391.

Sahin, S.; Baloglu, S. City Branding: Investigating a Brand Advocacy Model for Distinct Segments. *J. Hosp. Mark. Manag.* **2014,** *23*(3), 239–265.

Schmitt, B. Experiential Marketing. *J. Mark. Manag.* **1999,** *15*, 53–67.

Scott, N.; Laws, E.; Boksberger, P. The Marketing of Hospitality and Leisure Experiences. *J. Hosp. Mark. Manag.* **2009,** *18*, 99–110.

Stokburger-Sauer, N.; Ratneshwar, S.; Sen, S. Drivers of Consumer Brand-Identification. *Int. J. Res. Mark.* **2012,** *29*(4), 406–418.

Tigu, G.; Iorgulescu, M.; Ravar, A.S. The Impact Creativity and Innovation in the Hospitality Industry on Customers. *J. Tour. Chall. Trends.* **2013,** *6*(1), 9–34.

Titz, C. The Impact of People, Process and Physical Evidence on the Tourism, Hospitality and Leisure Service Quality. In *Service Quality Management in Hospitality, Tourism and Leisure*; Kandampully, J., Mok, C., Sparks, B., Eds.; Haworth Hospitality Press: Binghamton, NY; 2001; 15–49.

Van Boven, L.; Gilovich, T. To do or to have? That is the question. *J. Pers Soc. Psychol.* **2003,** *85*, 1193–1202.

Varma, R.T.R. Enhancing and Empowering Customer Experience, *SCMS J. Indian Manag.* **2012,** July–Sep, 71–78.

Walls, E.A.; Berry, L.L. The Combined Effect of Physical Environment and Employee Behavior on Customer Perception of Restaurant Service Quality. *Cornell Hotel Restaurant Adm. Q.* **2007,** 48, 58–69.

Walls, A.; Okumus, F.; Wang, Y.; Kwun, D.J. Understanding the Consumer Experience; an Exploratory Study of Luxury Hotels. *J. Hosp. Mark. Manag.* **2011**, *20*, 166–197.

Walter, U.; Evardsson, B. The Physical Environment as a Driver of Customers' Service Experiences at Restaurants. *Int. J. Qual. Serv. Sci.* **2012,** *4*(2), 104–119.

Wikstrom, S. R. A Consumer Perspective on Experience Creation. *J. Cust. Behav.* **2008,** *7*(1), 31–50.

Williams, A. Tourism and Hospitality Marketing: Fantasy, Feeling and Fun. *Int. J. Contemp. Hosp. Manag.* **2006,** *18*, 482–495.

Yang, C. Identification of Customer Delight for Quality Attributes and its Application. *Total Qual. Manag.* **2011,** *12*(1), 83–98.

Yu, H.; Fang, W. Relative Impacts from Product Quality, Service Quality and Experience Quality on Customer Perceived Value and Intention to Shop for the Coffee Shop Market. *Total Qual. Manag.* **2009,** *20*(11), 1273–1285.

Zemke, D. M. V.; Pullman, M. E. Assessing the Value of Good Design in Hotels. *Build. Res. Inform.* **2008,** *36*(6), 543–556.

CHAPTER 3

CREATING MEMORABLE EXPERIENCES: LESSONS FROM THE WORLD'S TOP 10 HOTELS

HALIMIN HERJANTO[1] and SANJAYA S. GAUR[2*]

[1]*Assistant Professor, Marketing School of Business, McKendree University, USA*

E-mail: hherjanto@mckendree.edu

[2]*Professor and Head of the Department of Marketing, Sunway University Business School, Sunway University, No. 5 Jalan Universiti, Bandar Sunway, 47500 Selangor Darul Ehsan, Malaysia*

[*]*Corresponding author. E-mail: sanjayag@sunway.edu.my*

CONTENTS

ABSTRACT

Purpose: The aim of this study is to investigate and identify the key themes that help create positive memorable experiences for hotel customers.

Design/Methodology/Approach: This study is qualitative in nature and employs the thematic analyses technique. First, an extensive review of current literature is carried out to understand the factors that contribute to the creation of positive memorable experiences for hotel customers. An initial thematic map is developed based on this. A sample of the world's top 10 hotels is chosen based on TripAdvisor's "2014 Travellers' Choice – top 25 hotels in the world" report. A total of 248 reviews and feedback (indicating positive memorable experiences) posted over a period of 12 months by real customers of sampled hotels were identified. These are then content analyzed using thematic analysis to confirm the themes that create memorable experience for the guests of the world's top 10 hotels. A final thematic map is then prepared based on these confirmed themes.

Findings: Six themes emerged in the study. Perceived hospitality and professionalism of the hotel staff, perception of travel experience and hotel space management were found to be the most important factors that create a memorable experience for the hotel guests.

Practical Implications: The findings of this research are based on the analysis of real customer reviews and feedback. Therefore, this study offers important insights for hotel management staff, as they now have the means to identify the source of customers' memorable hotel experience. The study also has implications for academia. It provides a range of themes for future researchers to empirically validate and test their contribution to the creation of memorable experiences in terms of the hospitality sector in general and hotels in particular.

Originality/Value: This study amalgamates customers' real experience and feedback to assist hoteliers in increasing customers' memorable hotel experience. The research approach used in this study makes it valuable not only for the practitioners in hospitality by giving them much required guidance but it also contributes to the hospitality literature by opening up an avenue for useful further research.

3.1 INTRODUCTION

Despite the political unrest in Ukraine, violent public protests in Thailand, transportation disasters such as the disappearance of Malaysian Airlines MH-370 and the sinking of a commuter boat in South Korea, and despite general world calamities, the prestigious Howart Hotel, Tourism and Leisure (2014) report suggests that the sentiments toward the global hotel market remain strong and positive. This report states that significant local and global economic growth and improvement in local tourism trends are the strongest factors affecting the global hotel market. In reaction to the lucrative and increasing demand for hotel rooms, worldwide hotel operators are increasing their hotel's room capacity. For example, in the next 3 years, Saudi Arabian hotel operators are expected to add about 50,000 more hotel rooms (anonymous, 2013). In addition, the largest global hotel group – Intercontinental Hotel Group (IHG), the operator of well-known Intercontinental Hotels and Resorts, Crowne Plaza Hotels and Resorts, Holiday Inn, and HI Express has increased their room capacity to more than 600,000 rooms in more than 100 countries around the world (Hospitality Net, 2013) and 250,000 more rooms addition is expected in the near future (Miles, 2014). These capacity expansions are expected to accommodate 40 million members (LRA, 2013).

The IHG group is renowned as one of the best hotel providers in the world and has repeatedly won several respected hotel achievement awards such as Best Business Hotel Chain Worldwide by Business Traveler Awards, Australasia World Travel Awards, Asia's Leading Honeymoon Resort and Luxury Resort and Best Urban Hotel (IHG, 2014). However, de Klumbis (2009) suggests that such achievements need to be supported by the ability of IHG to create a memorable hotel experience. To him, these achievements are meaningless as they are no longer enough to draw hotel customers to stay in such hotels because such customers are now looking for more than luxury and a clean as well as comfortable stay; rather, they are looking for something special that they can remember.

By definition, a memorable experience refers to the positive or negative circumstances that one is directly or indirectly involved in – an experience that makes one feel something, gives them a good or bad "gut feeling" (Gonzales and Svensson, 2011) and can be recalled after the event has occurred (Kim et al., 2012). This definition of a memorable experience, clearly supports Lo's (2012) view that experience is the most important and influential factor in determining customers' emotions. Scholars argue that when hotel customers have positive emotional experiences, they will remember them with reference to the effect on their sense of satisfaction (Lo, 2013), their future purchasing decisions (Hung et al., 2014) and their positive word of mouth (Kim, et al., 2010).

Although the importance of a memorable hotel experience has been long identified, understood, and attracted a large number of scholars, findings on this issue are still mixed and inconclusive (Hudson and Ritchie, 2009). For example, some scholars (Ariffin and Maghzi, 2012; Lo, 2012; Kim, 2014) believe that psychological elements are the most influential in producing memorable hotel experiences. Chandalal and Valenzuela (2013) suggest that cognitive factors are more important in creating memorable experiences, while Walls et al. (2014) believe that physical factors are the most important element in generating memorable hotel experiences. Ariffin and Maghzi (2012) suggest that in order to reduce this confusion and to get a better understanding of this phenomenon, scholars need to replicate existing studies in order to identify the most important elements of a memorable hotel experience. Thus, our study aims to bridge this gap by broadening the understanding of the most important factors leading to customers' memorable hotel experience. Specifically, our study attempts to answer the following research question:

RQ: What are the most important factors that create a memorable hotel experience for its customers?

3.2 LITERATURE REVIEW

The tourism industry is known as one of the most lucrative (Lewis-Cameron, 2010) and competitive business (Hajiyeva and Jafarli, 2013). According to Wong (2008), this competitiveness is due to the race by tourism operators to please their customers by offering different ranges of accommodation, tourist activities, cultural experiences, and world class cuisines. To be successful, these offerings must exceed customer expectations (Wong, 2008) and generate a memorable guest experience (Verma, 2003).

Generally, a memorable experience refers to a specific circumstance that impresses customers and creates positive feelings (Gonzales and Svensson, 2011). For example, Lo's (2012) study on heritage tourism found that a combination of a high level of information on historical sites and tourist operators' communication skills make a visit to such sites worthwhile, and increase tourist appreciation and satisfaction. In contrast, Kim (2014) suggests that a negative memorable experience happens when customers face a negative circumstance that generates a negative feeling. The author argues that a negative memorable experience may be the result of internal and external factors. For example, internal factors, such as a sickness and external factors, such as unprofessional and inconsistent service from tourist operators, create an unpleasant experience which in turn leads to adverse feelings, such as sadness or anger.

In this study, a memorable tourist experience refers to a positive hotel experience that stays in a hotel guest's memory. Such an experience is believed to improve a hotel guest's emotional, cognitive, and behavioral values (de Klumbis, 2009), and to create a closer bond between a host and hotel guests (Horvarth, 2013). Consequently, a positive memorable experience promotes a high level of satisfaction (Lo, 2012), positive word of mouth (Kim et al., 2010) and ultimately enhances revisit intention (Hung et al., 2013). Numerous scholars believe that a memorable experience is a complex phenomenon (Ayeni, 2013; Kim et al., 2010). That is, a memorable experience is formed by a large number of different factors. For example, Gonzales and Svensson (2011) found that a high level of learning experience and hotel guests' willingness to engage with activities determine a memorable experience, while Curtin (2010) suggests that the charisma of the destination and its environmental factors are responsible for creating a highly memorable experience. In addition, Ariffin and Maghzi (2012) reveal that personalization and the host's genuine relationships with hotel guests are the most important elements in building a memorable experience. In sum, Ayeni (2013) argues that both individually and together, these elements potentially promote a memorable hotel guest experience. An intensive review of the literature on a memorable experience shows that all the factors causing such an experience can be classified into physical, cognitive and affective factors.

The first factor is concerned with physical components, such as ambience, multisensory, space management, and signs, symbols, and artifacts (Walls et al., 2011; Ajala, 2008). Each of these is detailed in the following section:

3.2.1 AMBIENCE

Ambience refers to an individual's perception and appraisal of the inter-sensorial space and situation around him or her (Thibaud, 2011). In this study, ambience more directly refers to the favorable atmosphere that is experienced by hotel customers during their stay. It is produced by cleanliness, comfort, elegance, landscaping, quality of the surrounding environment, safety/security, and the softness of lighting. Berry et al. (2002) believe that a positive perception and experience of ambience generate positive emotions, strong beliefs, and bodily sensations that lead to positive behavior toward the positive ambience providers.

3.2.2 MULTISENSORY

Historically, the term multisensory refers to individuals' sensory experience and response to two or more categories of stimulus at one time (Booth et al., 2011). Such multisensory capabilities serve as a feedback tool to maintain the balance of activities within the human body when dealing with incoming stimuli (Lewan, 1999). According to Nordenfalk (1985), the term multisensory refers to the five different senses: sight, hearing, smell, touch, and taste and each of these senses help individuals to evaluate incoming stimuli (color, odor, temperature, and humidity, noise, music, and view) and produce a perception (Shimomura and Oyabu, 2010) and memory (La Poidevin, 2004). In other words, the integration of overall positive multisensory experience stimulates hotel guests' positive emotions (Martuzzi et al., 2007) which lead to a memorable experience (La Poidevin, 2004).

3.2.3 SPACE OR THE PHYSICAL HOTEL ENVIRONMENT

Knutson et al. (2009) argue that space or the physical hotel environment can be seen as one of the most important element in creating a memorable experience. These physical features of the hotel can include the architectural layout and arrangement (i.e., size of the room, bathroom, bed etc.), space maintenance, furnishing, and the hotel's equipment (i.e., elevators, pool etc.). Scholars believe that any interactions with the hotel's physical appearance or space will stimulate affective and cognitive perception

(Pijls et al., 2011), which in turn affects an individual's memory (Johnston and Clark, 2001).

3.2.4 SIGNS, SYMBOLS, AND ARTIFACTS

In this study, signs, symbols, and artifacts refer to the clarity and uniqueness of the hotel signage and directions. Factors such as the availability and appearance of direction notices within the hotel premises, the availability of local maps and the appearance and tidiness of the staff are examples of this category. Scholars believe that the clarity of signage and the tidiness of the staff uniform are tangible clues of professionalism (Newman, 2007). Such professionalism is then believed to increase the positive mood which shapes hotel customers' memories (Schauder, 2012). Walls et al. (2011) argue that physical components are fundamental to hotel guests' experience, because they offer a tangible value and a first impression leading to positive emotions.

The second factor is concerned with cognitive components (Chandralal and Valenzuela, 2013). These are based on hotel guests' evaluation of their subjective tourism experience, also termed as a guest's perception of experience. Howe (1996) refers to the perception of experience as individuals' unique ability to translate, conceptualize, and apprehend their involvement and engagement in an activity. In other words, the perception of an experience is a product of individuals' unique and exclusive interpretation (Winkler, 2006) of selected stimuli (Budzinski, 2003) that appear (Winkler, 2006) and matter (McDonald, 2011) to individuals' emotions at that time (Homann, 2010). Scholars believe that strength and consistency (Tsoukas, 1991) as well as the relevance (Archibald, 2012) of an experience to the individual, at that point in time, generate a memorable experience. The perceptions of meaningfulness, opportunity to learn, significance, novelty, social interaction, and emotional arousal are believed to shape individuals' perception of experience.

3.2.5 PERCEPTIONS OF MEANINGFULNESS

According to Chandralal and Valenzuela (2013), perceived meaningful refers to a guest's memorable experience formed by a significant experience which occurs when the hotel guest finds their experience enriching their intellectual development (i.e., gaining new knowledge about their visited place) and improving their relationship with significant others (i.e., family togetherness).

3.2.6 PERCEPTIONS OF OPPORTUNITY TO LEARN

A perceived opportunity to learn refers to the hotel guest's ability to experience an actual life experience (Chandralal and Valenzuela, 2013). This perception occurs when guests receive an actual life experience by exploring and having hands-on experience related to remote lifestyles and indigenous local culture, for example, a cooking experience with indigenous people.

3.2.7 PERCEPTIONS OF SIGNIFICANCE

The significance of an experience is perceived as a result of specific elements of the guest experience (Chandralal and Valenzuela, 2013). These elements include a high level of extremeness and exclusiveness or personalization. Chandralal and Valenzuela (2013) believe the higher the extremeness, the more memorable the experience. For example, a hotel guest will easily remember their stay in an expensive and world famous hotel.

3.2.8 PERCEPTIONS OF NOVELTY

Gonzales and Svensson (2011) describe perceived novelty as an extraordinary experience that is different from previous experiences. Such a novel experience provides a first-time contact with a strange and unfamiliar situation. As a result, a hotel guest perceives the novelty of experience as a game changer. For example, exposure to a new culture or a new type of food promotes an enthusiasm which inspires the guest to involve themselves in this new experience.

3.2.9 PERCEPTIONS OF SOCIAL INTERACTION

A positively perceived social interaction is regarded as one of the most important element in the perception of experience (Walls et al., 2011). According to Ap and Wong (2001), positive perceptions of social interaction could include a guest's interaction with a tour operator as well as other guests, allowing the guest to share their opinions within a common understanding and without worrying about being judged. Such a high level of understanding not only provides the guest with a sense of well-being, but more importantly offers an opportunity to solve potential problems that may arise during their stay or trip (Ap and Wong, 2001).

3.2.10 PERCEPTIONS OF SPONTANEITY AND SURPRISE

Perceptions of spontaneity and surprise refers to a hotel guest's view of a positive unexpected experience (Chandralal and Valenzuela, 2013). To Curtin (2001), a perception of spontaneity occurs when a hotel guest has no expectation and therefore when something pleasant occurs, the hotel guest feels pleasantly surprised and excited, leading to a memorable experience.

3.2.11 PERCEPTIONS OF HOSPITALITY

Perceived hospitality directly relates to the relationship between the host and the hotel guest (Walls et al., 2011). The dimension of this relationship includes the host's attitude, professional behavior, proactive service, and level of personalization. Ariffin and Maghzi (2012) believe that the effect of perceived hospitality promotes a very special relationship between the host and hotel guest. They believe that perceived hospitality offers a sense of well-being that "touches the heart" of a hotel guest.

The third factor is affective factor. This factor relates to the emotional aspect of a memorable experience. According to Kim (2014), the affective factor can be classified into positive and negative.

3.2.12 POSITIVE AND NEGATIVE FACTORS

A positive memorable experience happens when a hotel guest faces a positive circumstance that generates positive feelings such as happiness and pleasure, while a negative memorable experience occurs when a hotel guest deals with a negative circumstance and experiences negative feelings such as anger, frustration, and sadness. Kensinger and Schacter (2006) argue that both positive and negative emotions generate positive and negative memorable experiences, respectively.

3.3 METHODOLOGY

This study is qualitative in nature and employs a thematic analysis to identify the factors (themes) creating memorable hotel experience.

3.3.1 THE SAMPLE

A sample of the world's top 10 hotels was chosen based on TripAdvisor's 2014 Travellers' Choice – top 25 hotels in the world report. Hotels, thus selected represent the leading accommodation providers for upmarket tourists worldwide and are listed in Table 3.1. Each of these hotels has been reviewed by its customers on the TripAdvisor website (www.tripadvisor.com). Customers have rated their overall experience with the hotel using a five-point scale: Excellent, Very Good, Average, Poor and Terrible and have written comments detailing their good or bad experiences in their reviews. Because our objective is to understand the positive nature of a memorable hotel experience, we include only those reviews in our study which were rated as Excellent and Very Good, and published over a period of 12 months (during March 1, 2013 and March 1, 2014). In this way, a total of 7265 positive reviews and feedback posted by real guests of sampled hotels were gathered. Each of these 7265 reviews were carefully read to identify those reviews which indicated a memorable experience and not just a high level of satisfaction. Based on this, 7017 of these were excluded from the further analyses because these were positive reviews but not reflecting a memorable experience. Finally, 248 relevant reviews were found to be useful for further analyses in this research.

TABLE 3.1 The Top 10 Hotels in the World.

No	Hotel	Country	Overall customer rating		Memorable reviews
			Excellent	Very good	
1	Grand Hotel Kronenhof	Switzerland	413	17	6
2	The Upper House	Hong Kong	673	56	28
3	Gili Lankansfushi	Maldives	602	27	38
4	Naraya Hotel, Spa & Gardens	Costa Rica	1638	159	42
5	The Oberoi Udaivillas	India	739	63	42
6	Casa Gangotena	Ecuador	199	9	6
7	Lindos Blu	Greece	471	58	11
8	The St. Regis Punta Mita Resort	Mexico	880	62	40
9	The Oberoi Mumbai	India	713	119	25
10	Trump International Hotel & Tower Toronto	Canada	330	37	10
			6658	607	248

3.3.2 ANALYTICAL PROCEDURE

Thematic analysis is a powerful analytical tool that helps researchers in identifying themes or patterns within the existing qualitative data (Olds and Hawkins, 2013) by arranging and unfolding data in detail (Braun and Clarke, 2006) to highlight the strength of the evidence (Olds and Hawkins, 2013). As per Braun and Clarke's (2006) suggestion, our thematic analysis followed a five-step process: identification of memorable experience related themes, initial coding determination, identification of possible themes, feedback analysis, and validated themes. The first three steps of this process involved preliminary theme identification, and the last two steps of this process were used for the finalization of the research themes. Data used for the first three steps is the literature discussed under the section on literature review. Based on this initial thematic map is created which is presented in Figure 3.1. For the clarity reason, Figure 3.1 is then divided into three subfigures: Figure 3.1a–c. Figure 3.1a shows the initial themes identified from the literature for the physical factors, Figure 3.1b for the cognitive factors and Figure 3.1c for the affective factors.

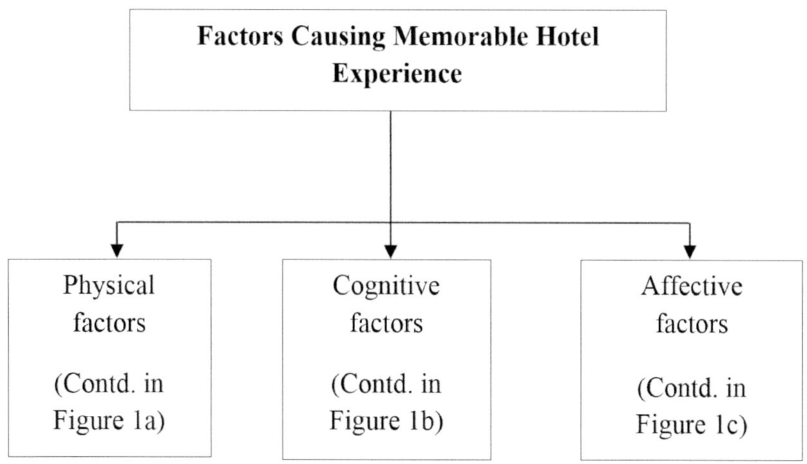

FIGURE 3.1 Initial thematic map of memorable hotel experience.

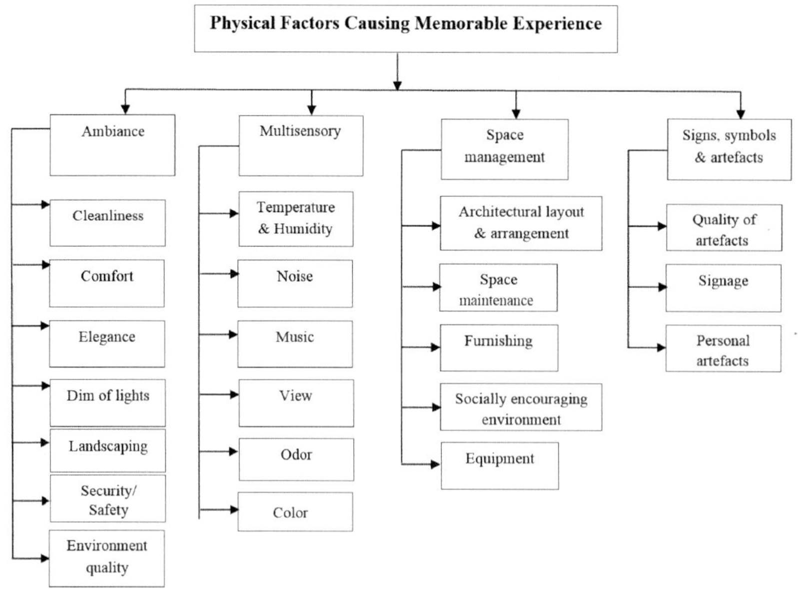

FIGURE 3.1A Initial thematic map of memorable hotel experience (Physical factors).

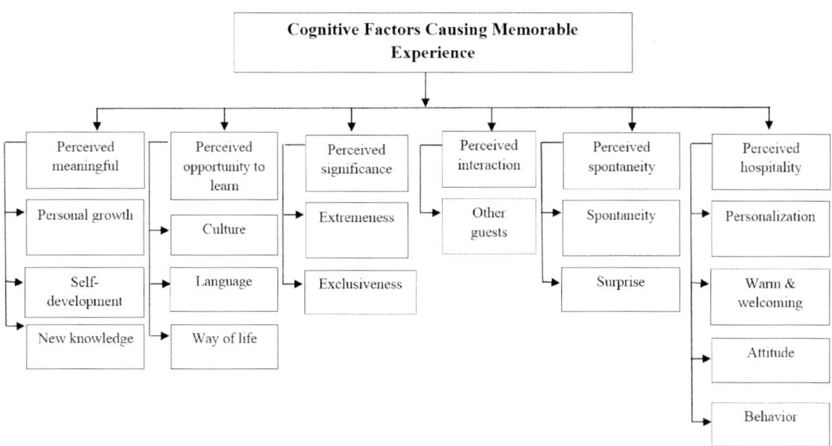

FIGURE 3.1B Initial thematic map of memorable hotel experience (Cognitive factors).

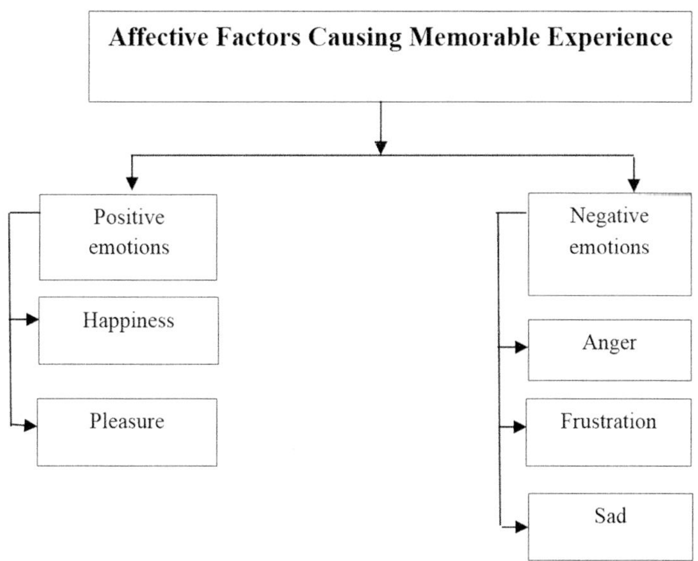

FIGURE 3.1C Initial thematic map of memorable hotel experience (Affective factors).

Next 248 reviews from real customers of the best 10 hotels in the world were coded to identify and confirm the themes presented in initial thematic maps. The final thematic map was then constructed to show the factors causing a memorable hotel experience. These are shown in Figure 3.2.

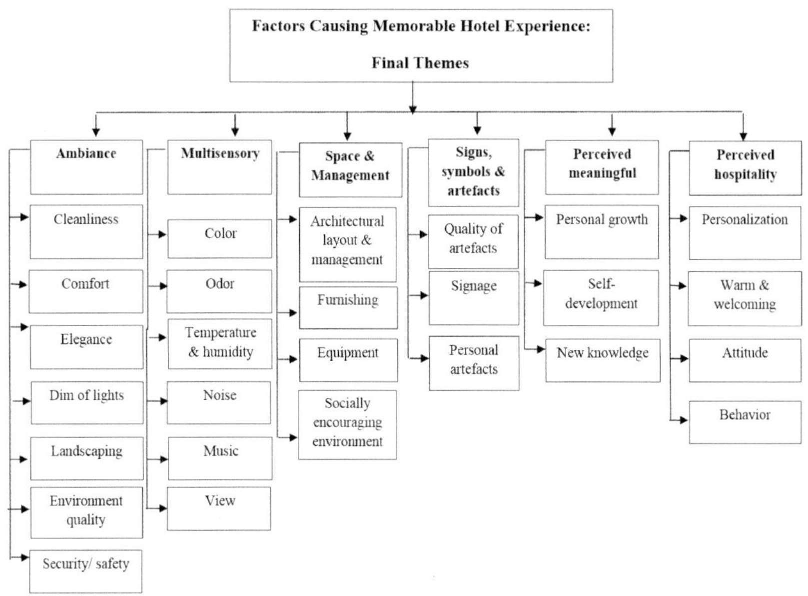

FIGURE 3.2 Final thematic map of memorable hotel experience.

3.4 FINDINGS AND DISCUSSION

As a result of in-depth analysis of customers' reviews and feedback on their hotel experience, six themes emerged as the most important factors in creating a memorable hotel experience: ambience, multisensory, space, signs, symbols, and artifacts, perception of experience and finally perceived hospitality. This study found that in addition to hotel customers' comments on each theme, they also gave their comments based on the combination of two or more of the themes above. Perceived hospitality, perception of experience, and space management were the most commented on by hotel customers. These themes received 178 (44%), 109 (27%), and 57 (14%) comments, respectively. In addition, 68% or 17% of these comments were based on the combination of themes above.

According to Lobo and Antunes (2013), ambience is an important ingredient in creating relaxation by reducing stress and anxiety. Consequently, ambience enhances individuals' positive feelings (Slatten et al., 2009) which thereby improves and reinforces an enjoyable experience and sense of satisfaction (Wansink and van Ittersum, 2012), memory (Matsumoto and Stanny, 2006), and individuals' willingness to revisit and replicate their hotel experience (Marinkovic et al., 2014). The following comments support this argument:

"We saw the sun rise in the mornings off our back deck and we watched the sun set out our front door. The large reef out toward the ocean from our villa produced just the right amount of ambient waves-crashing sounds that kept us remembering where we were. We could sleep with our door and windows open at night or close them for an air conditioned bedroom. All in all, the very most special and exquisite vacation we've yet to take! We'd love to come back someday and stay in villa 28 again."

In addition to the natural environment, other comments show that prime location and resort landscape also produce positive ambience.

"This is the place to truly feel complete and content without doing much at all. The staff, the resort grounds, and the location itself will provide you with every comfort and ambience, in our case for a perfect and unforgettable getaway."

The above comments by happy hotel customers show that on both occasions, ambience was responsible for creating a memorable hotel experience. These findings support Sloan, Kelleher, and MacNamee (2011) who suggest that different types and strengths of ambience can create different awareness or memorable experiences.

As discussed earlier, Nordenfalk (1985) argues that the term multisensory includes sight, hearing, smell, touch, and taste. Each of these senses help individuals to evaluate incoming stimuli and produce a perception (Shimomura and Oyabu, 2010) and memory (La Poidevin, 2004). The following comments support this premise:

"The room was amazing with great views over the harbour and watching the 8pm ICC light show from the luxury of the deep baths is something that I will remember for a long, long time."

"A design feature I really loved was the music in every room. Oh, and the bathroom. What an outstanding space. Truly the relaxing retreat we were hoping to find.... It really was one of the most memorable holidays we've had and we can't wait to return."

As can be identified in both comments above, customers' memorable hotel experience was generated by the multisensory nature of the situation.

Both sight and hearing senses are responsible for creating good perceptions and memories.

According to Pijls, et al. (2011), the physical environment of a hotel serves as an important gateway to the hotel customers' memorable experience. Customers start experiencing and building their initial perception of their stay by evaluating the physical appearance of the hotel from the time they arrive on the hotel premises. In addition, Orsingher and Marzochhi (2003) confirm that process of a memorable experience is also regulated by customers' positive emotions (i.e., ease and relaxation) that are initially generated by the comfort of the hotel facilities, such as the room, lobby, and hall. The comments below support this argument:

"I have stayed in some of the best hotels that the world has to offer but nothing really compares to this piece of heaven on earth. Sashi and Kristina were fabulous as the Guest Experience Managers – and the iPod technology that controlled everything from check in to room service made the whole stay wonderfully easy (and very 21st century). These really are rooms with a view – and particularly from the bathroom. Floor to ceiling windows and baths that you can sleep in. Ren accessories and spacious room plans made for a truly unforgettable stay (and I was only here on business)."

The following comment also confirms the statement above:

"The room was amazing with great views over the harbor and watching the 8pm ICC light show from the luxury of the deep baths is something that I will remember for a long, long time."

Newman (2007) argues that signs, symbols, and artifacts can be classified as some of the most important ingredients in creating a memorable hotel experience. To him, for example, clear and visible signage around hotel premises is essential as it provides guests with directions and reflects the professionalism of the hotel. Such professionalism, according to Schauder (2012), allows a guest peace of mind and increases their positive mood which further improves the memorable experience. This argument is supported and illustrated by the following comments:

"As we went to the shores of the lake near the palace, we were taken in by another set of hotel staff. As we entered the reception through the royal pathways (signage) and extraordinary structures brimming with richness, red rose petals showered on our head from top and it was nothing short of feeling like heaven!... It was really an out of the world experience and many thanks to all the staff of XXX! You really care for your guests and worth the visit!"

"The pools, the Jacuzzis and walking around the hotel paths (signage) will be forever remembered, and we will definitely come back here. Really, this place makes every other five-star review I've published on Trip Advisor worthless."

Both the comments above show that clear and visible signage around the hotel premises creates a high level of ease and confidence for hotel customers when they are using or experiencing hotel facilities (i.e., the hotel footpath).

The next theme that we identified in this study was the *perception of experience.* Howe (1996) refers to the perception of experience as individuals' unique ability to translate, conceptualize, and apprehend their involvement and engagement in an activity. In other words, the perception of an experience is a product of individuals' unique and exclusive interpretation (Winkler, 2006) of selected stimuli (Budzinski, 2003) that appear (Winkler, 2006) and matter (McDonald, 2011) to individuals' emotions at that time (Homann, 2010). Scholars believe that strength and consistency (Tsoukas, 1991) as well as the relevance (Archibald, 2012) of an experience to the individual, at that point in time, generate a memorable experience. The perceptions of meaningfulness, significance, novelty, and social interaction are believed to shape individuals' perception of experience. These arguments are supported by the following comments:

3.4.1 PERCEPTION OF SIGNIFICANCE (PRICE)

"[I] rang ahead to book us a space for cocktails and a view of the "light symphony" which illuminates HK's buildings and can only be seen from the mainland.... Marcel and his team could not be faulted for their smiles and genuine willingness to help. Yes of course it's expensive but it's an experience you won't forget. I promise."

3.4.2 PERCEPTION OF MEANINGFULNESS (HONEYMOON)

"We recently honeymooned at the XXX and it far exceeded our expectations. Not only is the property beautiful and pristine, but the service and staff are amazing. The General Manager called our room to check on us, bought us drinks by the pool and always remembered our faces when he saw us. He is the most hands on General Manager that I have ever encountered. We are so sad to leave, but will definitely be back. Thank you for the most wonderful Honeymoon that we could have ever dreamed of!"

3.4.3 PERCEPTION OF NOVELTY (NEW FOOD)

"This is our second trip to the XXX (see previous review). It was everything we remembered and more. It was nice to see that some of the menus had changed and that there were some new food options including a pizza oven. We can't wait to go back!"

3.4.4 PERCEPTION OF SOCIAL INTERACTION (NEW FRIEND)

"Perhaps the best testament to how good a job the hotel does is how easily you will make friends with fellow guests while staying here. It's great to meet people on vacation, when everyone is relaxed and having fun.... Kudos to the XXX for helping their guests, many new friends, and for helping families makes such good memories. We will definitely be back."

The perceived hospitality theme is categorized to capture the professionalism and the hospitable attitude of the staff. This theme refers to a special value that is offered by the staff (Vollebergh and Huiberts, 1997) through their professionalism, attitude (i.e., warm, welcoming, and friendly), and behavior (i.e., helpful, proactive, committed, and dedicated to their jobs and customers). Hallmann et al. (2013) point out that positively perceived hospitality improves the hotel image and hotel customers' intention to revisit. More importantly, perceived hospitality fulfills individuals' information seeking experience, which further remains in their memory (Chalkiti, 2012). Several supporting comments are listed below:

"The employees at this resort make your stay memorable.... Liz (greeting you every morning with a smile) and Danny (serving up the best green juice) at breakfast; Gustave, Antonio, & Jose (with his great snacks and sunglass cleaning skills) at the pool; Bladamir at Dinner; and who could forget the incredible butler service from Efran & Louis."

In the same vein, the following comment also shows that staff attitude creates memorable experiences for hotel customers:

"All-in-all K, Frankie and the XXX staff did an amazing job, we'd like to thank Frankie, Michelle, Vinchi, Kim and Raymond for making our stay so memorable. We'll definitely be returning to the XXX and we'll be recommending others to stay at XXX hotels in the future."

Finally, we found that memorable hotel experiences are also generated by two or more of the themes above. The following two comments illustrate:

"This is one of the very best properties I have ever stayed at! Outstanding! Impeccable and warm service from the moment you arrive until the second you leave. Beautifully designed rooms, public areas, restaurant and bar. I had the chance to stay in a One-Bedroom Suite *with* dramatic views over Hong Kong. The bathroom is very spacious including a very large shower and bathtub with amazing view. Go to the Bar (Cafe Gray) on the top floor, order Champagne with some oysters and experience the magic moment when the sun goes down and the lights of the city start to blink. It is an unforgettable experience, I'm telling you."

"A delicious breakfast in XXX, relaxing at the Sea Breeze pool, a snack in the afternoon with a small cake for my dad, the Champagne ritual in the Altamira Lobby and finally dinner at Sea Breeze, where I got my Mita Mary =). The room was so lovely and especially my mum was overwhelmed from the bathroom with the outdoor shower. It was just an amazing time and each family member enjoyed every second. Thank you very much for this beautiful memory we will never forget!!!"

3.5 CONCLUSION, LIMITATIONS, AND RECOMMENDATIONS

This study has reiterated the importance of creating a memorable hotel experience and has offered important information to hoteliers who now have the knowledge to determine the sources of customers' memorable hotel experiences. Through thematic analysis, six themes (ambience, multisensory, space, signs, symbols, and artifacts, perception of experience, and perceived hospitality) concerning a memorable hotel experience have emerged. We found that perceived hospitality, perception of experience, and space management are the most commented themes and responsible for 85% of hotel customers' memorable experience. In addition, this study has also identified that memorable hotel experiences are generated by a combination of themes.

This study was carried out by utilizing data from the tripadvisor.com website published between March 1, 2013 and March 1, 2014. The reason for limiting the study to this time period was that the selected hotels were part of TripAdvisor's 2014 Travellers Choice – top 25 hotels in the world report. Without this limitation, a greater number of comments and feedback would have been gathered and analyzed. The small sample therefore places constraints on generalizing the findings. Although this study provides important insights, an extended time period of hotel reviews and feedback may offer a different perspective of a memorable hotel experience.

Further, the present study has exclusively reviewed themes apparent in hotel customers' reviews and feedback relating to the world's five-star hotels and may not be applicable to all hotels (i.e., resort hotels, business hotels, family hotels etc.). Thus, an investigation of customers' memorable experience in different types of hotels and different cultures or countries would provide an important addition to this study.

3.6 IMPLICATIONS FOR HOTELIERS

Findings of this study offer important implications for the hoteliers.

This study suggests that it is important for hotel management to carry on, maintain and ensure the positive attitude of their staff towards hotel customers. The research has identified that most hotel customers regard the attitude of the staff as the most appreciated and important element in creating their memorable experience. In fact, one out of every two hotel customers commented that their experience was a lot more memorable when they received good treatment from the hotel staff. Such positive treatment helps hotel customers to feel welcomed and important. Therefore, we suggest that it is very important for hotel management to select the right persons for their staffing. It is also recommended that hoteliers maintain staff's positive attitude by offering more training, fair remunerations and treating them as partners rather than the employees. As Beatson et al. (2008) explain, creating a happy working environment and a happy staff are the essential ingredients to an excellent performance that produces happy customers.

In addition to the staffing issue, hoteliers are also recommended to continuously maintain and refresh their hotel property. The appropriateness of the furniture selections, faultless equipment, and property maintenance are also responsible for ensuring customers comfort and good experience. The findings show that even if hoteliers have a limited budget for expenditure, hotel property maintenance needs to be prioritized. As Johnston and

Clark (2001) suggest, the physical appearance of a hotel serve as the most important first impression for customers. Thus, we recommend that hoteliers allocate enough budget for maintenance and have a robust, frequent and consistent property refreshing plan.

KEYWORDS

- **memorable experience**
- **world's top 10 hotels**
- **thematic analysis**
- **hotels**
- **TripAdvisor**

REFERENCES

Ajala, O. A. Employment and Income Potentiality of Tourism Development in Amhara Region Ethiopia. *Ethiop. J. Environ. Stud. Manag.* **2008,** *1*(2), 74–82.

Anonymous. Hotel Room Capacity Rises 54%. [Online] 2013.http://www.arabnews.com/news/463080 (accessed May 2 2014).

Ap, J.; Wong, K. K. F. Case Study on Tour Guiding: Professionalism, Issues and Problems. *Tour. Manag.* **2001,** 22, 551–563.

Archibald, M. M. The Holism of Aesthetic Knowing in Nursing. *Nurs. Philos.* **2012,** *13*(3), 179–188.

Ariffin, A. A. M.; Maghzi, A. A Preliminary Study on Customer Expectations of Hotel Hospitality: Influences of Personal and Hotel Factors. *Int. J. Hosp. Manag.* **2012,** *31*, 191–198.

Ayeni, D. A. Promoting Sustainable Tourism through Tourism Infrastructure Development in Nigeria. *Scott. J. Arts Soc. Sci. Scien. Stud.* **2013,** *9*(1),3–14.

Beatson, A.; Lings, I.; Gudergan, S. P. Service Staff Attitudes, Organisational Practices and performance Drivers. *J. Manag. Organ.* **2008,** *14*, 168–179.

Berry, L. L.; Sneider, K.; Grewal, D. Understanding Service Convenience. *J. Mark.* **2002,** *66*(3), 1–17.

Booth, D. A.; Sharpe, O.; Freeman, R. P. J.; Conner, M. T. Insight into Sight, Touch, Taste and Smell by Multiple Discriminations from Norm. *Seeing Perceiving* **2011,** *24*, 485–511.

Braun, V.; Clarke, V. Using Thematic Analysis in Psychology. *Qual. Res. Psychol.* **2006,** *3*, 77–101.

Budzinski, O. Cognitive Rules, Institutions, and Competition. *Const. Polit. Econ.* **2003,** *14*, 213–233.

Chalkiti, M. Knowledge Sharing in Dynamic Labour Environment: Insights from Australia. *Int. J. Contemp. Hosp. Manag.* **2012,** *24*(4), 522–541.

Chandralal, L.; Valenzuela, R. F. Exploring Memorable Tourism Experiences: Antecedents and Behavioural Outcomes. *J. Econ., Bus. Manag.* **2013,** *1*(2), 177–182.

Curtin, S. What Makes for Memorable Wildlife Encounters? Revelations from 'serious' wildlife tourists. *J. Ecotur.* **2010,** *9*(2), 149–168.

de Klumbis, D. F. Seeking the Ultimate Hotel Experience. *Working paper, ESADE Escuela Universitaria de Turismo San Ignasi, ramon Llull University, Spain.* pp. 1–13.[Online] 2009 www.esade.edu/cedit2003/pdfs/danielafreund.pdf (accessed April 23 2014).

Geng, J.; Wasinwasukul, M. Innovative value propositions in the experience economy. The case of Chiva-som hotel and iceHotel. *Unpublished master thesis,* Kalstad Business School, Sweden. [Online] 2012. http://www.diva-portal.org/smash/get/diva2:567067/FULLTEXT01.pdf.

Gonzales, D., Svensson, O. Stadium Experience: A Qualitative Study about the Experience Economy in the Swedish Allvenskan. *Unpublished Master Thesis,* Linnaeus University, Sweden. [Online] 2011.www.diva-portal.org/smash/get/diva2:422760/FULLTEXT01.pdf (accessed April 23 2014).

Hallmann, K.; Zehrer, A.; Muller, S. Perceived Destination Image: An Image Model for a Winter Sports Destination and Its Effect on Revisit. *J. Travel Res.* **2013,** *XX*(X), 1–13.

Homann, K. B. Embodied Concepts of Neurobiology in Dance/Movement Therapy Practice. *Am. J. Ther.* **2010,** *32*, 80–99.

Horvarth, Z. Cultural value perception in the memorable tourism experience. *Cultural Tourism Handbook*; Richard, G., Smith, M, Eds; Routledge: London.

Horwart HTL Global Leader in Hospitality Consulting – Global Hotel Market Sentiment Survey. [Online] 2012. http://horwathhtl.com/files/2012/06/Global-GHMSS-H1-2014.pdf (accessed 25 April 25 2014).

Hospitalitynet. World ranking 2013 of Hotel Groups and Brands. [Online] 2013 www.m.hopitalitynet.org/news/4060119.html (accessed April 25 2014).

Howe, D. Client Experiences of Counselling and Treatment Interventions: A Qualitative Study of Family Views of Family Therapy. *Br. J. Guid. Couns.* **1996,** *24*(3), 367–375.

Hudson, S.; Ritchie, J. R. B. Branding a Memorable Destination Experience. The Case of Brand Canada. *Int. J. Tour. Res.* **2009,** *11*, 217–228.

Hung, W. L.; Lee, Y. J; Huang, P. H. Creative Experiences, Memorability and Revisit Intention in Creative Tourism. *Curr. Issues Tour.* **2014,** 1–8.

IHG IHG InterContinental Hotels Group – Award Wins. [Online] 2014. www.ihgplc.com/index.asp?pageid=948 (accessed May 1 2014).

Johnston, R.; Clark. G. *Service Operations Management,* Prentice-Hall, London, 2001, 214.

Kensinger, E. A.; Schacter, D. A. When the Red Sox Shocked the Yankees: Comparing Negative and Positive memories. *Psychon. Bull. Rev.* **2006,** *13*(5), 757–763.

Kim, J. H. The Antecedents of Memorable Tourism Experience: The Development of a Scale to Measure the Destination Attributes Associated with Memorable Experiences. *Tour. Manag.* **2014,** *44*, 34–45.

Kim, J. H.; Ritchie, J. R. B; McCormick, B. Development of a Scale to Measure Memorable Tourism Experiences. *J. Travel Res.* **2012,** *5*(1), 12–25.

Kim, J. H.; Rithcie, J. R. B; Tung, V. W. S. The Effect of Memorable Experience on Behavioural Intention in Tourism: A Structural Equation Modelling Approach. *Tour. Analysis* **2010,** *15*, 637–648.

Knutson, B. J.; Beck, J. A.; Kim, S., Cha, J. Identifying the Dimensions of the Guest's Hotel Experience. *Cornell Hosp. Q.* **2009,** *50*(1), 44–55.

Lewan, L. Why Human Societies Need Sustainability Analyses Based on Biophysical Assessment. *Ecol. Econ.* **1999,** *29*, 57–60.

Lewis-Cameron, A. Port of Spain: The Meeting and Conventions Capital of the Southern Caribbean. In. Marketing Island Destinations: Concepts and Cases; A. Lewis-Cameron, S. Roberts, Eds., Elsevier: Burlington, MA,2010; 135–146.

Lo, K. P. Y. *Service Design Strategies for Customisation. Implication of Conflicting Emotions and Concerns*, Paper is presented at Proceeding of 8th International Design and Emotion Conference, London, Sept 11–14, 2012.

Lobo, L., Antunes, D. Chest CT in Infants and Children", *Eur. J. Radiol.* **2013,** *82*, 1108–1117.

LRA IHG (interContinental Hotels Group) Expands EMEA Quality Assurance Program. 2009. www.lraworldwide.com/press_2009-01-27_IHG_EMEA.html (accessed May 1 2014).

Marinkovic, V.; Senic, V.; Ivkov, D.; Dimitrovski, D.; Bjelic, M. The Antecedents of Satisfaction and Revisit Intentions for Full-Service Restaurants. *Mark. Intelligence Plan.* **2014,** *32*(3), 331–327.

Martuzzi, R.; Murray, M. M.; Michel; C. M., Thiran; J. P.; Maeder, P. P.; Clarke, S., Meuli, R. A. Multisensory Interactions within Human Primary Cortices Revealed by BOLD Dynamics. *Neuroscience.* **2007,** *17*(7), pp. 1672–1679.

Matsumoto, A., Stanny, C. J. Language Dependent Access to Autobiographical Memory in Japanese-English Bilinguals and US Monolinguals. *Memory* **2006,** *14*(3), 378–390.

McDonald, S. M. Perception: A Concept Analysis. *Int. J. Nurs. Termin. Classif.* **2011,** 1–8.

Miles, A. Check Out the Largest Hotel Chain in the World.[Online] 2014.www.mudlusciouspress.com/check-out-the-largest-hotel-chain-the-world/ (accessed May 1 2014).

Newman, A. J. Uncovering Dimensionality in the Servicescape: Towards Legibility. *Serv. Industries J.* **2007,** *27*(1), 15–28.

Nordenfalk, C. The Five Senses in Late Medieval and Renaissance Art. *J. Warburg Courtauld Inst.* **1985,** *48*, 1–22.

Olds, K.; Hawkins, R. *Conceptualising the Generic Competencies Required Providing Clinincal Supervision to Australian Psychologists: A Thematic Analysis*, Advances in Clinical Supervision Conference, Sydney, Australia, Jun 4–6, 2013. www.nswiop.nsw.edu.au/conference/resources/monograph.pdf#page=28 (accessed May 1 2014).

Orsingher, C.; Marzocchi, G. L. Hierarchical Representation of Satisfactory Consumer Service Experience. *Int. J. Serv. Industry Manag.* **2003,** *14*(2), 200–216.

Pijls, R.; Schreiber, G. H.; van Marle, R. S. F. *Capturing the Guest Experience in Hotels*, Proceeding of the 29th EuroCHRIE annual conference Dubrovnik, Croatia, Oct 19–22, 2011.

Poidevin, L. The Experience and Perception of Time. in *The Stanford Encyclopaedia of Philosophy*; Edward. N. Zalta (Ed) [Online] 2004.www.plato.stanford.edu/archieves/win2004/entries/time-experience (accessed March 28 2014).

Schauder, A. Exit Through the Gift Shop. *Australian Leisure Management, 36,*July-August, 2012, 38–40.

Shimomura, Y.; Oyabu, T. *Analysis for Human Five Sense Images on Onsen*, Proceeding of the 11th Asia Pacific Industrial Engineering and Management Systems Conference and the 14th Asia Pacific Regional meeting of International Foundation for Production Research, Malaka, Dec 7–10, 2010.

Slatten, T.; Krogh, C.; Connolley, S. Make It Memorable: Customer Experiences in Winter Amusement Parks. *Int. J. Cult., Tour. Hosp. Res.* **2011,** *5*(1), 80–91.

Sloan, C.; Kelleher, J. D.; MacNamee, B. *Feeling the Ambience: Using Smart Ambience to Increase Contextual Awareness in Game Agents*, Proceeding of *the 8th* International Conference on Advances in Computer Entertainment, 2011.

Thibaud, J. P. The Sensory Fabric of Urban Ambiences. *Senses Soc.* **2011,** *6*(2), 203–215.

Tripadvisor Travellers' Choice 2014 – Top 25 Hotels in the World. [Online] 2014. www.tripadvisor.com/TravelersChoice-Hotles-cTop-g1 (accessed April 25, 2014).

Tsoukas, H. The Missing Link: A Transformational View of Metaphors in Organizational Science. *Acad. Manag. Rev.* **1991,** *16*(3), 566–585.

Verma, H. V. Customer Outrage and Delight. *J. Serv. Res.* **2003,** *3*(1), 119–133.

Vollebergh, W. A. M., Huiberts, A.M. Stress and Ethnic Identity in Ethnic Minority Youth in the Netherlands. *Soc. Behav. Personality* **1997,** *25*(3), 249–258.

Walls, A.; Okumus, F.; Wang, Y.; Kwun, D. J. W. Understanding the Consumer Experience: An Exploratory Study of Luxury Hotels. *J. Hosp. Mark. Manag.* **2011,** 20(2), 166–197.

Wansink, B.; van Ittersum, K. Fast Food Restaurant Lightning and Music can Reduce Calorie Intake and Increase Satisfaction. *Psychological Rep. Hum. Resour. Mark.* **2012,** *111*(1), 228–232.

Winkler, R. Husserl and Bergson on Time and Consciousness. *Analecta Husserliana* **2006,** *90*, 93–115.

Wong, L. My Home Away from Home. *Spasifikmag.com.* [Online] 2008.http://www.spasifikmag.com/travelpage_31march08lenawong/(accessed May 2, 2014).

PART II
Sector Insights

CHAPTER 4

DIMENSIONAL ANALYSIS OF CUSTOMER EXPERIENCE IN THE CIVIL AVIATION SECTOR

VINAY CHAUHAN[1] and DEEPAK MANHAS[2*]

[1]*Associate Professor, The Business School, University of Jammu, Jammu, India*
[2]*Assistant Handicrafts Training Officer, Handicrafts Department, J&K Government, India*
**Corresponding author. E-mail: manhasdeepak2009@gmail.com*

CONTENTS

Originally published as Chauhan, V. and Manhas, D. (2014) "Dimensional Analysis of Customer Experience in Civil Aviation Sector," in Journal of Services Research, 14:1, pp. 75-98. Published by the Institute for International Management and Technology. Reprinted with permission.

ABSTRACT

Creating a superior customer experience has been gaining increased attention in the service sector. The diverse market offerings that stimulate enduring experience, which customers cherish, have competitive edge over most competing products or services. Customer experience acts as an emerging opportunity in this fast-paced, highly competitive world, especially in the new horizon of experience economy. Due to an increasing growth rate and diversity of airline passengers, customer experience is emerging as a critical element in civil aviation sector. It is crucial for airlines to offer great experiences to passengers in order to gain a competitive advantage. This paper thus examines the nature and extent of customer experience in civil aviation sector. More specifically, the study explores dimensions of customer experience in civil aviation sector using exploratory factor analysis (EFA). The study is based on data of sample size of 1005 respondents from selected airlines, namely Air India, Jet Airways, and Kingfisher. The results of EFA, hierarchical regression model, and ANOVA depict that customer experience is a multidimensional construct. It further suggests that there is a significant impact of experiential dimensions on overall customer experience and there exists a significant difference on the basis of airlines regarding customer experience. The results also reveal that Jet Airways has higher level of customer experience followed by Kingfisher and Air India.

4.1 INTRODUCTION

Customer experience acts as an emerging opportunity in this fast-paced, highly competitive world, especially in the new horizon of experience economy. The notion of customer experience, and its impact on business, is now receiving great attention (Prahalad and Ramaswamy, 2004; Klaus, 2011). Managing customer experience has become a crucial strategic ingredient for service organizations (Klaus, 2011). Airlines and other stakeholders are beginning to pay attention to customer experience (Graham, 2001), thereby improving customers' air travel experiences. Customer experience originates from a set of interactions between a customer and an organization, which provoke a reaction. This experience implies that the customer's involvement at different levels is rational, emotional, sensorial, physical, and spiritual (Gentile et al., 2007). Customer experience is the difference between what the customer think they should be getting and the experience that they receive (Millard, 2006). Customer experience is intended at enhancing relationships with customers and building customer loyalty. Creating superior customer experiences is now seen as a key objective for service organizations (Verhoef et al., 2009) in their efforts to build customer loyalty. The feelings and reactions of customers while consuming a service have recently been recognized as an important part of customer evaluation and satisfaction with service (Otto and Richie, 1995). The concept "customer experience" was formulated in 1982 by Holbrook and Hirschman as a new experiential approach to consumer behavior. From a managerial point of view, the landmark work by Pine and Gilmore (1998) ignited extensive interest into a new management paradigm which emphasizes the switch from service delivery to experience creation.

The current trend in business world is to create lasting experiences for the customers (Carbone, 1998; Pine and Gilmore, 1998; Rowley, 1999; Berry et al., 2002; Gilmore and Pine, 2002). Differentiating solely on the traditional physical elements such as price, delivery and lead times is no longer an effective business strategy because the new differentiator today is customer experience (Shaw and Ivens, 2002). In the past, companies have primarily focused on the physical aspects of the product, while totally neglecting the emotional and value aspects and hence, losing many customers in the long run (Nunes and Cespedes, 2003). Additionally, Berry et al. (2002) argued that the emotion clues are just as important to the customer experience and work synergistically with functional clues. It is the composite of all the clues that make up the customer's total experience. To compete successfully in this customer experience territory, a growing number of organizations are systematically applying the principles and tools of total customer experience to generate, strengthen, and sustain lasting customer loyalty.

According to Pine and Gilmore, the experiences provided are directly related to the business's ability to generate revenue. Consumers develop the recognition of a company, brand, product, or service from the provider after they get experiences from attending activities and being stimulated by them (Schmitt, 1999). Experiences that are stored in consumers' memory are valuable information sources which act as internal information for future decision-making (Hoch and Deighton, 1989). Pine and Gilmore (1999) opined that the world's economy has changed drastically from service based to experience based in the past few years and will continue to change as our needs and societies change. In past years, both research and management practices have focused on quality and productivity, as they are critical in marketing a business' services. However, their concerns are limited in addressing imperative issues like consumer experience. An experience occurs when a company intentionally provides superior services to engage individual customers in a way that creates a memorable event (Pine and Gilmore, 1998). These experiences engage the customers to create memories within them (Gilmore and Pine, 2002). Hence, the diverse market offerings that generate enduring experience that customer cherishes have competitive edge over most competing products or services. This understanding of customer experience necessitates examining and factoring dimensions affecting customer experience in civil aviation sector

4.2 REVIEW OF LITERATURE

The subsequent section summarizes the existing literature on service experience research. Researchers like Schembri (2006) believe that the customers' service experience should be the focus of research as it is the key determinant of consumers' service delivery. The "Customer Experience" concept has aroused interest amongst researchers around the world. Providing superior products and excellent service are critical factors in today's business world. Customers are becoming more and more experience oriented and airline companies have to be aware of the factors that have an influence on customer experience. Frow and Payne (2007), in a research study examined the concept of customer experience and suggested strategies for achieving outstanding customer experience at an affordable cost, leading to customer loyalty. Verhoef et al. (2009) examined the customer experience by proposing a conceptual model to discuss the various determinants of customer experience. The results revealed that prior customer experience will influence future customer experiences. Kim, Ritchie, and McCormick (2012) developed a valid and reliable measurement scale comprising of seven domains viz., hedonism, refreshment, local culture, meaningfulness, knowledge, involvement, and novelty. Further, Otto and Ritchie (1996) enhanced the understanding of the service experience in tourism by developing and testing a scale across three different tourism industries viz., hotels, airlines, and tours and attractions. Pareigis et al. (2011) identified and described that various dimensions like customer involvement, safety, and physical artifacts that are important for the customer experience in the context of public transport travelers. The results showed the importance of interactions with other customers and the physical environment in enhancing the customer's experience. This view point is also supported by Tsiros and Parasuraman (2006) who found that interactions among customers can have profound effects on the service experience. Pentina et al. (2011) identified different categories of online shopping experiences and concluded that online shopping experiences increased browser satisfaction and increased sales and traffic to online stores. Klaus and Maklan (2012) empirically validated multiple-item scale for measuring customers' service experience and found that the service experience has a significant impact on customer satisfaction, loyalty, and word-of-mouth intentions. Lemke et al (2010) in their study proposed a conceptual model for customer experience quality and found that customer experience positively influenced customer relationship outcomes. Bel (2005) conducted the research study to integrate key concepts into a comprehensive managerial framework for experience marketing in the airline industry. The framework accounts for the sequential unfolding of the air travel experience and provide a customer-centric perspective of the air travel experience. In another study, Grace and Cass (2004) found that the service experience was found to significantly affect feelings, satisfaction, and brand attitudes. Moufakkir (2010) empirically examined policy of pay for in-flight food and drinks on travelers' experience. Most travelers did not support this policy and related issues, such as intention to pay, pay arrangement, and desired mode of payment.

Xu and Chan (2010) explored service experience in the context of package tours and decomposed it into four dimensions, namely "recognition and escapism," "peace of mind and relaxation," "hedonics," and "involvement," which have direct influence on overall tourist satisfaction and behavioral intention. Jensen (2012), in a research paper, investigates how consumers' travel experience and shopping orientation toward travel shopping influences their tendency to shop for travel products on the Internet. Using data from 256 respondents, the results revealed that shopping orientation and travel experience both influence travelers' intentions to shop travel products online. Pine and Gilmore (1999) argued that creating a distinctive customer experience can provide enormous economic value for firms. Ruiping and Yujuan (2006) found that the service delivery system based on customers' experience helps the customers obtain the good experiences and improve the profitability of customers. Therefore, what comes out as a synthesis based on the above findings of review of literature is that the customer experience directly influences service quality, customer relationship, customer satisfaction, sales, feelings, satisfaction and brand attitudes, behavioral intention, enormous economic value for firms, and profitability of customers. Marketers today believe that enhancing customer experience and lasting customer loyalty are important for maintaining customer focus and creating customer preference.

4.2.1 RESEARCH GAP

A large number of research studies have been conducted dealing with impact of customer experience in context of service organizations. However, most of them have restricted themselves to customer experience outcomes and its impact on the tourist satisfaction (Xu and Chan, 2010; Pentina et al., 2011), customer loyalty (Klaus and Maklan, 2011), and behavioral intentions (Jensen (2012). Whereas less consideration is given to measure and conduct research on the dimensions of customer experience in Indian civil aviation sector, which necessitates the need and relevance of present study. The study is descriptive, exploratory, and comprehensive in nature as it validates the various dimensions of customer experience scale. Therefore, in order to bridge the gap in extant literature, present study is undertaken to investigate the customer experience in Indian civil aviation sector in terms of objectives and hypotheses as discussed below.

4.3 OBJECTIVES

The objectives of the study are outlined as:

- To examine the nature and extent of relevance of customer experience in civil aviation sector,
- To explore dimensions underlying the customer experience,
- To investigate the impact of experiential dimensions on overall customer experience,
- To identify the significant differences in various airlines regarding customer experience.

4.4 HYPOTHESES FORMULATION

- Customer experience is a multidimensional construct.
- There is significant impact of experiential dimensions on overall customer experience.
- There exists significant difference on the basis of airline regarding customer experience.

4.5 RESEARCH METHODOLOGY

The primary data have been collected with the help of a questionnaire developed after extensive review of literature (Kim et al., 2012; Palmer, 2010; Otto and Ritchie, 1996; Xu and Chan, 2010; Gentileet al., 2007; Oliver et al., 1997; Pine and Gilmore, 1998; Kim et al., 2010) and discussions with the experts. The primary data was obtained from the respondents travelled in airlines under study through stratified sampling technique (Liu and Liu, 2008; Hsu, 2009). The questionnaire was finalized after conducting a pilot survey to ensure its reliability and validity. There are different qualitative and quantitative techniques to measure customer experience. Due to convenience of survey research, its versatility, efficiency, and generalizability, survey method (Otto and Ritchie, 1999; Novak et al., 2000) was employed to collect data from respondents in order to measure customer experience. However, discussions with some of the representative sample have also been used as an input, while drawing conclusions and making suggestions. The questionnaire comprised of two sections. Section A consisted of 6 items relating to respondents' profiling, whereas section B had 46 items relating to customer experience measurement. One additional item in the form of 47th statement, "Overall Customer Experience is Memorable" was been incorporated in the questionnaire as an independent measure of overall customer experience. All the statements in the section B were based on a 5-points Likert scale ranging from 5 = strongly agree and 1 = strongly disagree. Cronbach alpha and split half as a test of reliability (Malhotra, 2008) have been worked on the total number of respondents (N = 1005). The data have proved quite reliable in terms of split half reliability as mean obtained from both halves of respondents are satisfactory (Group I = 3.72 and Group II = 3.67). Moreover, Cronbach's alpha value of .869 also proved reliability as it is greater than the threshold value of .70 (Table 4.1). The content and construct validity was duly assessed through review of literature and discussions with the experts representing both academia and practicing managers of representative airlines. Moreover, higher Kaiser–Meyer–Olkin measures of sampling adequacy values (.846) and Bartlett's test of sphericity (2948.051) and variance explained (71.641%) also represent the construct validity. Convergent validity has also been satisfied as communalities of all items were above .50 (Field, 2003).

TABLE 4.1 Split Half Reliability and Cronbach Alpha.

Group	Mean and alpha
Group I	3.72
Group II	3.67
Cronbach's alpha	.869

For making the study exhaustive and representative, the respondents have been surveyed from the five airports of North India viz., Jammu airport, Chandigarh airport, Srinagar airport, Amritsar airport, and New Delhi airport; traveling in three major airlines of civil aviation sector. In order to draw proportionate sample for each strata, a sample size of 1005 customers was contacted in five select airports, that is, 201 from each airport viz., Jammu (201), Srinagar (201), Chandigarh (201), Amritsar (201), and New Delhi (201). The data after purification through factor analysis were subjected through various statistical tools like ANOVA and regression analysis.

4.6 FINDINGS AND DISCUSSIONS

The findings and discussion of the study have been summarized as below:

The demographic factors of the customers in select airports of India have been discussed in detail on the basis of their respective percentage values, which are as follows:

Out of the total respondents of 1005, the number of male respondents figured higher (684, 68%) than their female counterparts (321, 32%). More than half of the total respondents were married (603, 60%). The number of respondents (444, 44%) in the age group of 21–40 years is the highest followed by respondents (419, 42%) in the age group of 41–60 years.

Majority of the respondents are postgraduates (465, 46%) followed by graduates (333, 33%). Majority of the respondents are employed in public sector (34%) followed by private sector (31%). Out of the total respondents, 327 (33%) respondents were from Air India, 327 (32%) respondents were from Kingfisher, and 351 (35%) respondents were from Jet Airways. This detail is summarized in the Table 4.2.

TABLE 4.2 Customer Profiling (Demographics).

Variables	N	%	Variables	N	%
Gender			***Occupation***		
Male	684	68	Self employed	195	19
Female	321	32	Employed (private sector)	315	31
Marital status			Employed (public sector)	340	34
Single	402	40	Others	155	15
Married	603	60	***Airline***		
Age			Air India	327	33
Less than 21	55	5	Jet Airways	351	35
21–40	444	44	Kingfisher	327	32
41–60	419	42			
Above 60	87	9			
Qualification					
Up to graduation	333	33			
Post-graduation	465	46			
Professional	207	21			

4.7 COMPARATIVE ANALYSIS OF CUSTOMER EXPERIENCE AMONG THE SELECT ORGANIZATIONS

Customer experience in the civil aviation sector is reflected in Table 4.3 which shows that the respondents of Jet Airways have rated "airline has efficient baggage handling mechanism" the highest value (4.68) and "flight schedules are convenient" the lowest value (2.24), whereas respondents of Kingfisher Airline have rated "employees show sincere interest in solving problems (flight cancellation, baggage loss, etc.)" the highest value (4.25) and "flight schedules are convenient" the lowest value (2.45). Similarly, respondents of Air India have rated, "I was doing something thrilling" the highest value (4.34) and "planes are safe from all sorts of threat" the lowest value (2.16). Additionally, respondents of Jet Airways have rated, "I could communicate freely with employees" the highest value (4.47) followed by respondents of Kingfisher airline (3.64) and Air India (3.53), whereas respondents of Kingfisher airline have rated "I felt a sense of cooperation between employee and me" the highest value (3.96) followed by respondents of Air India (3.64) and Jet Airways (3.53).

Additionally, respondents of Kingfisher airline have rated "Airline provides excellent quality in-flight services" the highest value (3.68) followed by respondents of Air India (3.58) and Jet Airways (2.76), whereas respondents of Jet Airways have rated "I felt a sense of cooperation between employee and me" the highest value (3.76) followed by respondents of Air India (3.33) and Kingfisher airline (3.23). The respondents of Jet Airways have rated "Airport is safe place against threat of all sorts" the highest value (4.40) followed by respondents of Air India (3.78) and Kingfisher airline (3.67), whereas respondents of Jet Airways have rated "Airline has efficient baggage handling mechanism" the highest value (4.68) followed by respondents of Air India (2.83) and Kingfisher airline (2.78). However, on the whole, the respondents have accorded the highest mean score to the items, "Employees show sincere interest in solving problems (flight cancellation, baggage loss, etc.)" (4.34), followed by "I was doing something thrilling" (4.18), followed by "The air travel felt like a change from routine" (4.15), followed by "The air travel truly felt like an escape" (4.14), followed by "Airline staff are interested in customers" well-being (4.14), followed by "I felt like I was on an adventure" (4.11), followed by "My boredom was alleviated while air travelling" (4.04). However, the respondents assigned lowest mean scores to the items, namely "Flight Schedules are Convenient" (2.34), followed by "Planes are safe from all sorts of threat" (2.54), followed by "I was in a different world" (2.64), followed by "I had a good time because I was able to act on the "spur of the moment"" (2.94), followed by "I felt really lucky during this travel" (3.15), followed by "Airline provides modern aircraft for passengers" (3.15).

Therefore, it can interpreted from the above that respective airlines must keep up the good work for all the items with mean values more than 3 on 5 point scale simultaneously improvising on all variables with mean values less than the mid value of 3 on 5 point scale.

TABLE 4.3 Comparative Analysis of Customer Experience among the Select Organizations.

Serial No.	Variables	Mean			GM
		JA	KA	AI	
1	Airline makes one feel that one can trust them and have confidence in them	**4.26**	3.96	4.11	4.11
2	Airline provides modern aircraft for passengers	**3.76**	3.03	2.66	3.15
3	Planes are safe from all sorts of threat	**2.78**	2.68	2.16	2.54
4	Employees show sincere interest in solving problems (flight cancellation, baggage loss, etc.)	**4.60**	4.25	4.17	4.34
5	I could communicate freely with employees	**4.47**	3.64	3.53	3.88
6	I enjoyed being immersed in exciting new products	**3.69**	3.43	3.47	3.53
7	I felt a sense of personal security	2.79	3.42	**3.48**	3.23
8	It was a very nice time out	2.59	**3.43**	3.31	3.11
9	I felt a sense of cooperation between employee and me	3.76	3.96	4.13	3.95
10	The air travel truly felt like an escape	**4.19**	4.19	4.04	4.14
11	I was doing something thrilling	3.95	4.24	**4.34**	4.18
12	I was having a once in a lifetime experience	3.09	**3.98**	3.88	3.65
13	I felt quite relaxed during air travel	**3.93**	3.11	2.89	3.31
14	I felt like an element of surprise	3.58	**3.83**	3.75	3.72
15	Airline provides excellent quality in-flight services	2.76	**3.68**	3.58	3.34
16	I feel my belongings are safe during air travel	**3.76**	3.23	3.33	3.44
17	I was doing something new and different	2.84	**3.76**	3.66	3.42
18	Airline has comfortable seats	**3.38**	3.13	3.18	3.23
19	Airport is safe place against all sorts of threat	**4.40**	3.67	3.78	3.95
21	I had some choice in the way things were done	2.95	**3.65**	3.54	3.38
22	The time spent in air travel was truly enjoyable	3.40	3.55	**3.67**	3.54
23	I continued to travel, not because I had to, but because I wanted to	3.26	3.50	**3.56**	3.44
24	I had a good time because I was able to act on the "spur of the moment"	**3.75**	2.50	2.57	2.94
25	The air travel felt like a change from routine	**4.63**	3.96	3.86	4.15
26	I feel extremely safe during air travel	**3.82**	3.55	3.58	3.65

TABLE 4.3 *(Continued)*

Serial No.	Variables	Mean			GM
		JA	KA	AI	
27	I was in a different world	2.59	2.65	**2.68**	2.64
28	I was doing something I really like to do	**3.49**	3.36	3.41	3.42
29	I was being stimulated or challenged in some way	3.18	**3.78**	3.72	3.56
30	I had a chance to meet interesting people	**4.10**	3.45	3.52	3.69
31	I felt really lucky during this travel	2.97	3.22	**3.26**	3.15
32	Airline staff are interested in customers' well-being	**4.58**	3.89	3.95	4.14
33	I felt like I was on an adventure	**4.30**	3.97	4.06	4.11
34	My boredom was alleviated while air traveling	3.92	**4.11**	4.09	4.04
35	I feel safe when buying online tickets	**3.88**	3.56	3.45	3.63
36	Customer can check-in through Internet by themselves	3.43	**3.48**	3.44	3.45
37	Flight schedules are convenient	2.24	**2.45**	2.33	2.34
38	The airline has comfortable waiting lounges	**3.95**	3.79	3.75	3.83
39	Customer can book tickets online easily	**3.74**	3.61	3.63	3.66
41	Airline provide hassle free check-in	4.07	3.31	3.33	3.57
42	The airline has other travel related partners (e.g., car rentals, hotels)	3.50	**3.55**	3.51	3.52
44	Employees of airline are willing to help passenger	**4.35**	3.44	3.49	3.76
45	I played a role in or contributed to the service process	**3.77**	3.11	3.05	3.31
46	During air travel, I felt the excitement of the hunt	**3.98**	3.78	3.82	3.86
47	My overall service experience is memorable	**4.67**	3.88	3.78	4.11

JA= Jet Airways, KA= Kingfisher Airline, AI= Air India, GM= Grand Mean.

4.7.1 TESTING OF HYPOTHESES

H1: Customer experience is a multidimensional construct.

The multidimensional nature of customer experience has received considerable academic attention in the past few years. But, the way the customer experience constructs have been operationalized and the relative contribution of each dimension on overall customer experience is still shrouded in uncertainty. The present study adopts customer experience as a multidimensional construct. Also, previous dimensions and research studies were adequately considered before explaining factorial dimensions of customer experience. The technique of EFA has been used through Statistical Package for Social Sciences (SPSS, 17 Version) with principal component analysis along with varimax rotation for summarization of the total data into minimum meaningful factors. The items having factor loading less than 0.5 and Eigen values less than 1 were ignored for the subsequent analysis (Hair et al., 2009). With the application of factor analysis, the customer experience measurement scale comprising of total 46 statements was reduced to 35 statements that converged to five factors with 71.641% of variance explained (Table 4.3).

TABLE 4.4 EFA: Customer Experience and Factors Influencing Customer Experience in Airlines Dimensions.

	Variables	VM	SD	FL	C	MF	EV	VE	CA
Hedonism	The air travel truly felt like an escape	4.14	0.93	.976	.960	**3.64**	**8.133**	**20.572**	**.973**
	During air travel, I felt the excitement of the hunt	3.86	0.85	.953	.955				
	While travelling, I was able to forget my problems	3.23	0.74	.921	.951				
	The time spent in air travel was truly enjoyable	3.54	0.77	.916	.941				
	It was a very nice time out	3.63	0.56	.877	.923				
	I enjoyed being immersed in exciting new products/service	3.53	0.73	.853	.916				
	I felt really lucky during this air travel	3.15	0.67	.800	.648				
	I felt like I was on an adventure	4.11	0.47	.797	.643				
Novelty	I was doing something thrilling	4.18	0.90	.970	.951	**3.78**	**5.962**	**19.042**	**.967**
	I was doing something new and different	3.54	0.78	.944	.943				

TABLE 4.4 *(Continued)*

	Variables	VM	SD	FL	C	MF	EV	VE	CA
	I felt like an element of surprise	3.72	0.86	.911	.934				
	The air travel felt like a change from routine	4.15	0.69	.879	.910				
	I was having a once in a lifetime experience	3.65	0.80	.848	.906				
	I felt quite relaxed during air travel	3.31	0.78	.839	.888				
	My boredom was alleviated while air travel	4.04	0.63	.637	.456				
	I had a chance to meet interesting people	3.69	0.84	.636	.474				
Safety	Airport is safe place against all sorts of threat	3.95	0.69	.834	.860	**3.39**	**4.294**	**12.070**	**.905**
	Planes are safe from all sorts of threat	2.54	0.72	.811	.854				
	I feel my belongings are safe during air travel	3.44	0.98	.779	.839				
	I feel safe when buying online tickets	3.63	0.74	.745	.657				
	Airline provides modern aircraft.	3.15	0.83	.723	.655				
	I feel extremely safe during air travel	3.65	0.57	.692	.517				
Recognition	Employees show sincere interest in solving problems (flight cancellation, baggage loss, etc.)	4.34	0.73	.861	.781	**3.96**	**2.591**	**10.780**	**.875**
	Airline makes you feel that you can trust them and have confidence in them	4.11	0.87	.860	.782				
	I could communicate freely with employees	3.88	0.63	.858	.780				
	I had some choice in the way things were done	3.38	0.83	.730	.605				

TABLE 4.4 *(Continued)*

	Variables	VM	SD	FL	C	MF	EV	VE	CA
	I felt a sense of cooperation between employee and me	3.95	0.53	.728	.602				
	Airline staff are interested in customers' well-being,	4.14	0.96	.658	.500				
Comfort	Airline provide hassle free check-in	3.57	0.46	.756	.582	**3.51**	**1.095**	**8.997**	**.784**
	The airline has comfortable waiting lounges	3.83	0.89	.732	.542				
	Customer can book tickets online easily	3.66	0.95	.677	.524				
	The airline has comfortable seats	3.23	0.68	.612	.495				
	Airline provides excellent quality in-flight services	3.34	0.77	.608	.485				
	The airline has other travel related partners (e.g., car rentals, hotels, travel insurance)	3.52	1.03	.603	.503				
	Airline has efficient baggage handling mechanism	3.43	0.64	.597	.493				
Grand		3.65 (Mean)						71.641 (VE)	

VM=Variable mean, SD=Standard deviation, FL=Factor loadings, C=Commonalities, MF= Mean of factor, EV=Eigen values, VE= Variance explained and CA=Cronbach alpha.

4.7.2 CUSTOMER EXPERIENCE

The overall mean score of this dimension was 3.65 indicating high level of customer experience being felt by those passengers who travel on airlines under study. The total variance explained for customer experience was 71.641. This dimension came up with five factors viz., Hedonism,

Novelty, Safety, Recognition, and Comfort. These factors are discussed in detail as follows:

Hedonism (F1): The first factor having mean = 3.64 with Eigen value 8.133 comprised of eight items (Table 4.4). The item "the air travel truly felt like an escape" has the highest factor loading (.976) indicating high association with this factor. The item "felt like an adventure" having the least factor loading (.797) and therefore stands least associated with this factor.

Novelty (F2): The second factor having mean = 3.78 with Eigen value 5.962 comprised of eight statements. The item "doing something thrilling" has the highest factor loading (.970) and therefore this item stands highly associated with this factor. About 87% of the total respondents felt their boredom was alleviated while traveling by air (4.04) and had a chance to meet interesting people (3.69). The mean values of the items under this factor range from 3.69 to 4.18.

Safety (F3): The third factor having mean = 3.39 with Eigen value 4.294 comprised of six statements. The item "Airport is safe place against threat of all sorts" has the highest factor loading (.834) and therefore this item stands highly associated with this factor. The item "feel extremely safe during air travel" has the lowest factor loading (.692) and therefore stands least associated with this factor.

Recognition (F4): The fourth factor having mean = 3.96 with Eigen value 2.591 comprised of six statements. About 84% of the total respondents felt "a sense of cooperation between employee and me" (3.95) and had some choice in the way things were done (3.38). The mean values of the items under this factor range from 4.14 to 4.34.

Comfort (F5): The fifth factor having mean = 3.51 with Eigen value 1.095 comprised of seven statements. The item "Airline provide hassle free check-in" has the highest factor loading (.756) and therefore this item stands highly associated with this factor. About 52% of the total respondents observed airline provide hassle free check-in (3.57) and about 51% of the total respondents found customer can book tickets online easily (3.66).

Therefore, the results support the hypothesis "Customer experience is a multidimensional construct."

H2: There is significant impact of experiential dimensions on overall customer experience.

TABLE 4.5 Regression Analysis: Impact Analysis of Customer Experience Dimensions on Overall Customer Experience.

Model	R	R^2	Adjusted R^2	Standard error of estimate	F-value ANOVA	Significance level	β	Durbin–Watson
a	.413	.170	.170	.29999	206.065	.000	.394	2.077
b	.566	.320	.319	.27165	236.228	.000	.415	
c	.689	.474	.473	.23903	301.123	.000	.397	
d	.770	.593	.592	.21038	364.580	.000	.349	
e	.829	.687	.685	.18462	438.633	.000	.308	

a. Predictors: (Constant), Safety.
b. Predictors: (Constant), Safety, Hedonism.
c. Predictors: (Constant), Safety, Hedonism, Novelty.
d. Predictors: (Constant), Safety, Hedonism, Novelty, Recognition.
e. Predictors: (Constant), Safety, Hedonism, Novelty, Recognition. Comfort.
f. Dependent Variable: Overall Customer Experience is Memorable.

The regression model equation is as follows:

$$OCE = \alpha + \beta 1F1 + \beta 2F2 + \beta 3F3 + \beta 4F4 + \beta 5F5$$

$$OCE = .242 + .394H + .415N + .397S + .349R + .308C$$

where α = constant, β1 β2 β3 β4 β5 represents coefficient of regression for the different independent factors, OCE = Overall Customer Experience, H = Hedonism, N = Novelty, S = Safety, R = Recognition, and C = Comfort. When H is increased by one unit, OCE increases by .394. Similarly, when N, S, R, C increases by one unit, OCE increases by .415, .397, .349, .308, respectively. The result of step-wise regression analysis enticed five independent factors as significant in predicting the dependent variable. These were: "Safety", "Hedonism", "Novelty" and "Recognition", and "Comfort". The correlation between predictor and outcome is positive with values of R as .413, .566, .689, .770, and .829, which signifies high correlation between predictor and the outcome.

In model "a," R is .413 which indicates 41% association between dependent and independent variable. R-square for this model is .170 which means that 17% of variation in overall customer experience can be explained from the independent variable. Adjusted R-square (.170) indicates that if anytime another independent variable is added to the model, the R-square will increase. Further beta values reveal significant relationship of independent variables with dependent variable. Similarly, in model "e," R is .829 which indicates 82.9% association between dependent and independent variables. R-square for this model is .687 which means that 68.7% of variation in overall customer experience can be explained from the independent variables, namely Safety, Hedonism, Novelty, Recognition, and Comfort. Adjusted R-square (.685) indicates that if anytime another independent variable is added to model, the R-square will increase, but in the present context, since the value is quite close to 0.7, therefore it rejects the need for inclusion of more variables. *Safety* has emerged as the strongest predictor whereas *Comfort* is found to be the weakest as represented by relative *t*-values. Change in R-square is also found to be significant with *F*-values significant at 5% confidence level. Therefore, the aforesaid findings support the hypothesis "There is significant impact of experiential dimensions on overall customer experience."

H3: There exists significant difference among various airlines regarding customer experience.

To test third hypothesis, the respondents have been classified into three categories on the basis of airline, viz., Air India (33%), Kingfisher (35%), and Jet Airways (32%). To find out the mean difference among different airline groups regarding customer experience measurement, univariate analysis of variance (ANOVA) was applied.

TABLE 4.6 ANOVA: Differences in Overall Customer Experience among Select Airlines.

Dimension	Source of variations	Sum of squares	df	Mean square	F	Significant
Overall customer experience	Between groups	2.384	2	1.192	14.342	.000
	Within groups	83.292	1002	.083		
	Total	85.676	1004			

On the whole, ANOVA reveals significant mean difference of customer experience among the respondents belonging to different airline groups (F = 14.342, Sig. = .000, Table 4.6). Further, individual factor wise analysis also disclosed significant mean difference in three factors out of five factors, viz., F2 (F2: Sig. = .001), F3 (F3: Sig. = .0016), F4 (F4: Sig. = .002). Only two factors F5 (F5; Sig. = .365) and F1 (F1: Sig. = .695 had insignificant difference regarding customer experience measurement among respondents belonging to different airline. Further, post hoc test was applied to examine the significant mean differences of customer experience among respondents belonging to different airline groups. Results revealed significant mean difference between Air India and Jet Airways (Sig. = 0.000), and Kingfisher and Jet Airways (Sig. = 0.001) but insignificant mean difference between Air India and Kingfisher (Sig. = 0.058, Table 4.8). Therefore, the results support the hypothesis "There exists significant difference among various airlines regarding customer experience."

TABLE 4.7 ANOVA: Differences in Dimension-wise Customer Experience among Airlines.

Dimensions	Source of variations	Sum of squares	df	Mean square	F	Significant
Hedonism (F1)	Between groups	.341	2	.171	.364	.695
	Within groups	469.640	1002	.469		
	Total	469.981	1004			
Novelty (F2)	Between groups	7.016	2	3.508	7.159	.001
	Within groups	491.046	1002	.490		
	Total	498.063	1004			
Safety (F3)	Between groups	3.841	2	1.920	4.173	.016
	Within groups	461.078	1002	.460		
	Total	464.919	1004			
Recognition (F4)	Between groups	4.744	2	2.372	6.370	.002
	Within groups	373.133	1002	.372		
	Total	377.877	1004			
Comfort (F5)	Between groups	.713	2	.357	1.009	.365
	Within groups	353.979	1002	.353		
	Total	354.692	1004			
	Total	85.676	1004			

TABLE 4.8 Post Hoc Tests.

Multiple comparisons

Least significant difference

Dependent variable	(I) Airline	(J) Airline	Mean difference (I–J)	Standard error	Significant	95% Confidence interval	
						Lower bound	Upper bound
Hedonism (F1)	Air India	Kingfisher	.01133	.05322	.831	−.0931	.1158
		Jet Airways	−.03198	.05275	.545	−.1355	.0715
	Kingfisher	Air India	−.01133	.05322	.831	−.1158	.0931
		Jet Airways	−.04331	.05275	.412	−.1468	.0602
	Jet Airways	Air India	.03198	.05275	.545	−.0715	.1355
		Kingfisher	.04331	.05275	.412	−.0602	.1468
Novelty (F2)	Air India	Kingfisher	−.12538*	.05442	.021	−.2322	−.0186
		Jet Airways	−.20247*	.05394	.000	−.3083	−.0966
	Kingfisher	Air India	.12538*	.05442	.021	.0186	.2322
		Jet Airways	−.07710	.05394	.153	−.1829	.0287
	Jet Airways	Air India	.20247*	.05394	.000	.0966	.3083
		Kingfisher	.07710	.05394	.153	−.0287	.1829
Safety (F3)	Air India	Kingfisher	.01893	.05273	.720	−.0845	.1224
		Jet Airways	−.11990*	.05227	.022	−.2225	−.0173
	Kingfisher	Air India	−.01893	.05273	.720	−.1224	.0845
		Jet Airways	−.13884*	.05227	.008	−.2414	−.0363
	Jet Airways	Air India	.11990*	.05227	.022	.0173	.2225
		Kingfisher	.13884*	.05227	.008	.0363	.2414

TABLE 4.8 *(Continued)*

Dependent variable	(I) Airline	(J) Airline	Mean difference (I–J)	Standard error	Significant	95% Confidence interval	
						Lower bound	Upper bound
Recognition (F4)	Air India	Kingfisher	−.08560	.04744	.071	−.1787	.0075
		Jet Airways	−.16782*	.04702	.000	−.2601	−.0756
	Kingfisher	Air India	.08560	.04744	.071	−.0075	.1787
		Jet Airways	−.08222	.04702	.081	−.1745	.0100
	Jet Airways	Air India	.16782*	.04702	.000	.0756	.2601
		Kingfisher	.08222	.04702	.081	−.0100	.1745
Comfort (F5)	Air India	Kingfisher	−.03280	.04620	.478	−.1235	.0579
		Jet Airways	−.06506	.04580	.156	−.1549	.0248
	Kingfisher	Air India	.03280	.04620	.478	−.0579	.1235
		Jet Airways	−.03226	.04580	.481	−.1221	.0576
	Jet Airways	Air India	.06506	.04580	.156	−.0248	.1549
		Kingfisher	.03226	.04580	.481	−.0576	.1221
Overall customer experience	Air India	Kingfisher	−.04248	.02241	.058	−.0865	.0015
		Jet Airways	−.11732*	.02221	.000	−.1609	−.0737
	Kingfisher	Air India	.04248	.02241	.058	−.0015	.0865
		Jet Airways	−.07484*	.02221	.001	−.1184	−.0312
	Jet Airways	Air India	.11732*	.02221	.000	.0737	.1609
		Kingfisher	.07484*	.02221	.001	.0312	.1184

*The mean difference is significant at the 0.05 level.

4.8 RESEARCH CONTRIBUTION

This research study can provide airline marketers with an understanding on how to convert their customer experience into a strategic input for making management strategies more effective. The results are likely to help academicians and marketers to collect information and plan appropriate customer experience enhancement strategies. This is one of the few studies that have addressed the significance of customer experience in civil aviation sector in the highly competitive service industry. The present research provides theoretical contribution by filling gaps in the extant literature. The outcome of the study will provide useful insight for further research in the area. Creating a superior customer experience has been gaining increasing attention from retailers. However, there has been a dearth of a commensurate level of scholarly research on this topic. The present paper is an attempt to provide a holistic portrayal of the customer experience construct and subsequently, discusses specific determinants of customer experience, highlighting those that are especially in need of further research. This paper offers practical insights for developing and implementing effective experience-based strategies.

4.9 MANAGERIAL IMPLICATIONS

Although there are several aspects that require further research and vindication, the findings of this study provide useful implications for marketing managers. From a managerial perspective, it is important to know that the customer experience must be to be taken into account by any airline given its positive effects on the customer loyalty. It reveals that delivering memorable customer experience provides an opportunity for managers to create additional value and benefits for consumers. Moreover, it also affirms that by focusing on experiences, organizations can gain a competitive edge (Pine and Gilmore, 1998). This research highlights that experiences that engage the consumer by giving him/her recognition and establish an emotional connection with him/her can create customer loyalty. This paper focuses on possibilities to increase comfort and the potential marginal benefits that the airlines may gain by providing more comfort to passengers, thereby attracting more passengers. This paper also discusses that airline must focus on safety of the travelers as it is an imperative dimension of customer experience. In addition to the delivering superior customer experience, managers should give substantial emphasis on developing the skills of its employees since they interact with customers directly or indirectly, their enthusiasm, passion, and commitment have a bearing on the extent of customer engagement and the experience as a whole. The findings of this study also imply that it is vital for organizations to continuously innovate and improve the offering to overcome boredom and increase novelty (Pine and Gilmore, 2000). Companies should identify and analyze favorable and unfavorable service experiences and thus create a knowledge base for designing services that deliver favorable service experiences as only those companies that deliver the favorable and right experience to customers will succeed in the global marketplace (Seddon and Sant, 2007). The research findings provide some advices for the industry players in drafting various managerial strategies to increase the customer experience, by emphasizing on the different perspectives of customer experience such as hedonism, novelty, safety, recognition, and comfort.

4.10 SUGGESTIONS AND LIMITATIONS

Airlines are advised to capture rich information across all customer interactions with the service provider to enhance customer experience. It is suggested that airlines should obtain a direct measure of customer experience by conducting periodic surveys by sending questionnaires or make telephone calls to a random sample of their recent customers to find out how they feel about various aspects of the airline's performance. Airlines are advised to be customer-centric and to maximize the ease with which customers can inquire, make suggestions, or complain. There should be no tendency on the part of the airlines to discount the complaints under the assumption that they come from a small percentage of the customers because this minimal number of complaints can become spectacularly more significant because of the word of mouth communication.

Though all efforts have been made to maintain the study exhaustive, objective, reliable, and valid, yet it has certain limitations which must be taken care of whenever its findings are considered for implementation. Every effort has been made to keep the objectivity in research but the element of subjectivity cannot be ruled out as response obtained may be actuated by personal likes and dislikes. The element of subjectivity cannot be ruled out as respondents might hide some information though all the efforts have been made for maintaining the objectivity of the research. In addition, Kingfisher's operations are stopped now, hence research study suggests very limited value, however can be useful for its future operations.

4.11 CONCLUDING REMARKS AND SCOPE FOR FUTURE RESEARCH

Customer experience is the necessary prerequisite for building strong customer loyalty and the key driver of customer retention in a service-dominated economy. Consumers indisputably desire superior experiences and more and more businesses are responding by designing and promoting them. Leading-edge airlines will find that the next competitive battleground lies in delivering lasting experiences (Pine and Gilmore, 1998). To realize the full benefit of delivering such lasting customer experiences, businesses must deliberately design appealing experiences in what they produce and offer by combining functional and emotional benefits in their offerings. Emotional bonds between companies and customers are difficult for competitors to imitate. The results of factor analysis, hierarchical regression model, and ANOVA revealed that customer experience is a multidimensional construct. *There is significant impact of experiential dimensions on overall customer experience* and there exists significant difference among various airlines regarding customer experience. The results depict that Jet Airways has higher level of customer experience followed by Kingfisher and Air India. The study provides fresh insights into multiple dimensions of customer experience construct. The domain of customer experience offers a rich agenda for future research.

The present study is based on the perceptions of passengers of three airlines, namely Air India, Jet Airways, and Kingfisher. Further research thus needs to take in the perceptions of other airlines in the civil aviation sector. This research should encourage researchers to explore the customer experience in different service sectors such as banking, hospital industry, and hotel industry. Comparative study can be done by studying perceptions of the three groups of participants in the air travel market, namely airlines, travel agents, and passengers regarding customer experience.

KEYWORDS

- **Air India**
- **customer experience**
- **Jet Airways**
- **Kingfisher**
- **civil aviation sector**

REFERENCES

Anderson, J. C.; Narus, J. A.; van Rossum, W. Customer Value Propositions in Business Markets. *Harv. Bus. Rev.* **2006,** *84*(3), 90–99.

Berry, L. L.; Carbone, L. P.; Haeckel, S. H. Managing the Total Customer Experience. *Sloan Manag. Rev.* **2002,** *43*(3), 85–90.

Bettencourt, L. A.; Gwinner, K. Customization of the Service Experience: The Role of the Frontline Employee. *Int. J. Serv. Ind. Manag.* **1996,** *7*(2), 3–20.

Bonnie J. K.; Jeffrey A. B.; Seunghyun K.; Jaemin C. Identifying the Dimensions of the Guest's Hotel Experience. *Cornell Hosp. Q.* **2009,** *50*, 44–55.

Carbone, L. P. Total Customer Experience Drives Value. *Manag. Rev.* **1998,** *87*(7), 62.

Frow, P.; Adrian P. S. Toward the Perfect Customer Experience. *J. Brand Manag.* **2007,** *15*(2), 89–101.

Gentile, C.; Spiller N.; Noci, G. How to Sustain the Customer Experience: An Overview of Experience Components that Co-Create Value with the Customer. *European Manag. J.* **2007,** *25*(5), 395–410.

Gilmore, J. H.; Pine, J. B. Customer Experience Places: the New Offering Frontier. *Strategy Leadersh.* **2002,** *30*(4), 4–11.

Grace, D.; Cass, A. Examining Service Experiences and Post-Consumption Evaluations. *J. Serv. Mark.* **2004,** *18*(6), 450–461.

Graham, A. (2001) *Managing Airports: An International Perspective;* Butterworth-Heinemann publications: Burlington, MA, **2001**.

Gupta, S.; Vajic, M. The Contextual and Dialectical Nature of Experiences.*In New Service Development: Creating Memorable Experiences;* Fitzsimmons, J. A., Fitzsimmons. M. J. Eds.; SAGE Publications, Inc.: Thousand Oaks, CA, **2000**; pp 33–51.

Hair, J. F.; Black, W. C.; Babin, B. J.; Anderson, R. E. *Multivariate Data Analysis* (6th edn); Pearson Prentice Publishers: New Delhi, **2009**.

Harris, R.; Harris, K.; Baron, S. Theatrical Service Experiences: Dramatic Script Development with Employees. *Int. J. Serv. Ind. Manag.* **2003,** *14*(2), 184–99.

Hoch, S.; Deighton, J. Managing What Consumers Learn from Experience. *J. of Mark.* **1989,** *53*, 1–20.

Hsu, H. Y. Study of Factors Influencing Online Auction Customer Loyalty, Repurchase Intention, and Postitive Word of Mouth: A Case Study of Students from Universities in Taipei, Taiwan. In *Advances in Information Technology;* Springer: Berlin, Heidelberg, **2009**; pp 202–210.

Ismail, A. R. Experience Marketing: A Review and Reassessment. *J. Mark. Manag.* **2009,** *25*(6), 167–201.

Jensen J. M. Shopping Orientation and Online Travel Shopping: the Role of Travel Experience. *Int. J. Tour. Res.* **2012,** *14*(1), 56–70.

Jones, T. O.; Sasser, E. W. Why Satisfied Customers Defect. *Harv. Bus. Rev.* **1995,** *73*(6), 88–99.

Jordan L.; Le Bel, J. L. Beyond the Friendly Skies: An Integrative Framework for Managing the Air Travel Experience. *Manag. Serv. Qual.* **2005,** *15*(5), 437–451.

Kim, J. H.; Ritchie, J. R. B.; McCormick, B. Development of a Scale to Measure Memorable Tourism Experiences. *J. Travel Res.* **2010,** *51*(1), 12–25.

Klaus, Ph. Quo vadis, customer experience? In *Beyond CRM: Customer Experience in the Digital Era. Strategies, Best Practices and Future Scenarios in Luxury and Fashion;* Rusconi, C. Eds.; Franco Angeli: Milano, **2011**.

Klaus, Ph.; Maklan, S., Bridging the Gap for Destination Extreme Sports: A Model of Sports Tourism Customer Experience. *J. Mark. Manag.* **2011,** *27*(13–14), 1341–1365.

Klaus, P.; Maklan, S. EXQ: A Multiple-Item Scale for Assessing Service Experience. *J. Serv. Manag.* **2012,** *23*(1), 5–33.

Lemke, F.; Clark, M.; Wilson, H. Customer Experience Quality: An Exploration in Business and Consumer Contexts Using Repertory Grid Technique. *J. Acad. Mark. Sci. Mark. Theory* **2010,** *6*(3), 381–392.

Liu, J.; Liu, J. An Empirical Study on the Relationship between Service Encounter, Customer Experience and Repeat Patronage Intention in Hotel Industry. In *Wireless Communications, Networking and Mobile Computing, 2008*; WiCOM'08, 4th International Conference on IEEE, **2008**; pp 1–7.

Malhotra, N. *Marketing Research: An applied Orientation* (5th edn); Prentice Hall of India: New Delhi, **2008**.

Millard, N. Learning from the Wow Factor: How to Engage Customers through the Design of Effective Affective Customer Experiences. *BT Technol. J.* **2006,** *24*(1), 11–16

Moufakkir, O. The Pay for In-Flight Food and Drinks Policy and Its Impact on Travelers' Experience. *Tour. Anal.* **2010,** *15*(1), 99–110.

Novak, T. P.; Hoffman, D. L.; Yung, Y. F. Measuring the Customer Experience in Online Environments: A Structural Modeling Approach. *Mark. Sci.* **2000,** *19*(1), 22–42.

Nunes, P. F.; Cespedes, F. V. The Customer Has Escaped. *Harv. Bus. Rev.* **2003,** *81*(1), 96–105.

Oliver, R. L.; Rust, R. T.; Varki, S. Customer Delight: Foundations, Findings, and Managerial Insight. *J. Retail.* **1997,** *73*(3), 311–336.

Otto, J. E.; Ritchie, J. R. The Service Experience in Tourism. *Tourism Manag.* **1996,** *17*(3), 165–174

Palmer, A. Customer Experience Management: A Critical Review of an Emerging Idea. *J. Serv. Mark.* **2010,** *4*(3), 196–208.

Pareigis, J.; Edvardsson, B.; Enquist, B. Exploring the Role of the Service Environment in Forming Customer's Service Experience. *Int. J. Qual. Serv. Sci.* **2011,** *3*(1), 110–124.

Pentina, I.; Amialchuk, A.; Taylor, D. G. Exploring Effects of Online Shopping Experiences on Browser Satisfaction and E-Tail Performance. *Int. J. Retail Distrib. Manag.* **2011,** *39*(10), 742–758.

Pine, B. J.; Gilmore, J. H. *The Experience Economy: Work is Theatre and Every Business a Stage;* Harvard Business School Press: Boston, **1999**.

Pine, J. B.; Gilmore, J. H. Welcome to the Experience Economy. *Harv. Bus. Rev.* **1998,** *76*(4), 97–106.

Popovic, V.; Kraal, B. J.; Kirk, P. J. *Passenger Experience in an Airport: An Activity-Centred Approach,* IASDR 2009 Proceedings, **2009**; pp 1–10.

Prahalad, C.; Ramaswamy, V., Co-Creation Experiences: The Next Practice in Value Creation. *J. Interact. Mark.* **2004,** *18*(3), 5–14.

Richards, L. G.; On the Psychology of Passenger Comfort, In *Human Factors in Transport Research;* Oborne; D. J.; Levis, J. A. Eds.; Academic Press, **1980**; vol. 2, pp 15–23.

Rojas, C; Camarero, C. Visitors' Experience, Mood and Satisfaction in a Heritage Context: Evidence from an Interpretation Center. *Tour. Manag.* **2008,** *29*, 525–537.

Rowley, J. Measuring Total Customer Experience in Museums. *Int. J. Contemp. Hosp. Manag.* **1999,** *11*(6), 303–310.

Ruiping, X.; Yujuan, Z. The Construction of Service-Marketing System Based on Customers' Experience. *Can. Soc. Sci.* **2006,** *2*(6), 87–92.

Schembri, S. Rationalizing Service Logic, or Understanding Services as Experience. *Mark. Theory* **2006,** *6*(3), 381–392

Schmitt, B. *Experiential Marketing: How to Get Customers to Sense, Feel, Think, Act and Relate to Your Company and Brands*; Free Press: New York, **1999**.

Seddon, J.; Sant, R. Increasing Business Value through Improved Customer Experiences. *E-Perspectives* [online], **2007**. Available from URL:http://www.millwardbrown.com (cited 22 October 2012)

Severt, D.; Tesone, D.; Murrmann, S. Prior Experience Satisfaction and Subsequent Fairness Perceptions within the Service Experience. *J. Hosp. Leis. Mark.* **2006,** *13*(3–4), 121–137.

Shaw, C.; Ivens, J. *Building Great Customer Experiences;* Palgrave Macmillan: Basingstoke, **2002**.

Klaus, Ph.; Maklan, S. Bridging the Gap for Destination Extreme Sports: A Model Sports Tourism Customer Experience. *J. Mark. Manag.* **2011,** *27*(13–14), 1341–1365.

Tsiros, M.; Parasuraman, A. The Anatomy of Service Encounter Evaluations: A Conceptual Framework and Research Propositions. *Asian J. Mark.* **2006,** *12*(1), 4–22.

Verhoef, P.; Lemon, K.; Parasuraman, A.; Roggeveen, A.; Schlesinger, L.; Tsiros, M. Customer Experience: Determinants, Dynamics and Management Strategies. *J. Retail.* **2009,** *85*(1), 31–41.

Xu, J. B.; Chan, A., Service Experience and Package Tours. *Asia Pacific J. Tour. Res.* **2010,** *15*(2), 177–194.

CHAPTER 5

DIMENSIONS OF RETAIL SERVICE CONVENIENCE IN EMERGING MARKET SETTINGS: A QUALITATIVE INVESTIGATION

SHAPHALI GUPTA[1*] and DINESH SHARMA[2]

[1]*Assistant Professor, Marketing Area, Management Development Institute, Gurgaon, India*
[2]*Assistant Professor, SJMSOM, IIT Bombay, Mumbai, Maharashtra*
[*]*Corresponding author. E-mail: shaphali.gupta@mdi.ac.in*

CONTENTS

Originally published as Gupta, S. and Sharma, D. (2014) "Dimensions of Retail Service Convenience in Emerging Market Settings: A Qualitative Investigation," in Journal of Services Research, 14:1, pp. 99-122. Published by the Institute for International Management and Technology. Reprinted with permission.

ABSTRACT

The existing measures of service convenience, developed and validated in context of developed service economies, do not adequately capture customers' perception of service convenience for retail stores (i.e., stores which offer both goods and services), especially in emerging markets. The current study examines perceptions and identifies a comprehensive inventory of service convenience for retail stores in emerging market setting in India. Based on convenience literature and three separate qualitative studies, authors proposed retail store service convenience as a multidimensional construct consisting of six dimensions. Both retailers and shoppers were included in the study. Selection and assurance were found as novel dimensions for retail service convenience. Perceived risk of service fairness, resulting in exertion of cognitive energy, is seen as a major concern among respondents. Study elucidates the critical role of store staff in building affirmative convenience perception. The present study enhances the understanding of retail service convenience in an emerging market (India) context. Thus, this study expands the domain of service convenience construct by further exploring the dimensions and measures set out by earlier researchers. This study explores new dimensions of convenience and proposes items for developing a measure for retail store service convenience. The implications of proposed dimensions are discussed, both for retailers and future research.

5.1 INTRODUCTION

With the several societal trends, such as tremendous socioeconomic changes, rapid technological progress, increasing number of women in workforce, more competitive business environment and increased interest toward leisure and self-development activities, there has been seen a significant effect on the consumer's perception about their time and energy usage (Brown, 1990; Berry et al., 2002). With higher disposable incomes, credit cards, familiarity of the Western shopping way of life and deep desire of improved living standards, emerging market consumers are ready to spend in an unprecedented manner with huge expectations in terms of value and experience (Indian Retail report, 2011).[1] Indeed, from

[1]India Retail Report, 2011, research by Images Retail Intelligence Services (IRIS).

a retailing perspective, Treadgold (1999) noted that "*the most compelling [Asian retail] opportunities are at the value end of the market given that consumers in Asia today are much more value conscious than they were in the mid-1990s*." It is suggested that a firm can increase value of their offering either by providing better quality products or services, or by lowering price of the products or services, or by decreasing nonmonetary cost incurred by consumers during buying process (Zeithaml and Bitner, 2008). In the domain of consumer behavior and marketing management, decrease in the expenditure of time and effort expended by consumers in the process of buying, acquiring, and consuming products or services, both in or offline environment, is termed as "convenience."

Although the term "convenience," coined by Copeland (1923), has been identified as a significant variable in plethora of studies focused on consumer satisfaction, loyalty, and store patronage, few efforts have been taken to understand it as an absolute construct (Farquhar and Rowley, 2009); it is only recently that it has received its long overdue recognition as a multidimensional construct in its own right (Berry et al., 2002; Brown, 1990; Seiders et al., 2000). It otherwise was neglected and was poorly defined as a unidimensional construct. "Convenience," in an era of service economy, was conceptualized as service convenience which is defined as "consumers' time and effort perceptions related to use or buy of a service." This comprised five types of service convenience, each one affecting an overall convenience evaluation of a service (Berry et al., 2002). To much of our current knowledge about service convenience construct is based on the studies conducted in developed countries. There is a possibility that existing convenience construct and measures do not adequately capture consumers' perception of service convenience in emerging markets, for example, the in-store phase of the consumer decision journey tends to be longer and more important in emerging markets than in developed ones. Emerging market consumers have a penchant for visiting multiple stores multiple times and for collecting information methodically, especially when they purchase big-ticket items. These consumers like to test products and interact with sales representatives in order to collect product information and negotiate with retailers to get the best deal (Atsmon et al., 2012). Also, the shopping context in Asian and other emerging markets often differs from that of developed markets. Emerging market consumers do not necessarily shop in hypermarkets like Walmart and Carrefour. In India, as in small town and rural China, traditional trade still dominates.

This results in a unique dynamics between shopper and seller which can strongly influence consumer choices.

The objective of present study is to examine the perceptions and to explore the dimensions of retail service convenience among Indian consumers. Examining retail service convenience in Indian context is both appropriate and significant in the present economic scenario. First, the Indian growth story over last few years in spite of economic down turn has been encouraging. India has been ranked second fastest growing economy after China, fourth in global purchasing power parity and would be third largest economy in term of gross domestic product (GDP) in next five years. It has also been considered as one of the lucrative emerging economies by both domestic and international retailers. The retail sector in India is expected to grow by 18.8% and to generate revenues of US$866 billion by 2010 (Indian Retail Report, 2013)[2]. Second, retail literature has frequently cited convenience as an important variable (Huddleston et al., 2004; Schrader and Schrader, 2004; Pan and Zinkhan, 2006; Arnold and Luthra, 2000; Aggarwal, 2000; Sinha and Banerjee, 2004; Grewal et al., 2004; Mohanty and Sikaria, 2011) and recently acknowledged it as a multidimensional construct (Berry et al., 2002; Seiders et al., 2007) in its own right. Though the extant literature is helpful to understand convenience as a construct, the lack of validation (or partial validation) of service convenience dimensions and scale instigates further investigation. Convenience, being a perceptual phenomenon, is idiosyncratic in nature; thus much work needs to be done for the further understanding of service convenience, in different context (Farquhar and Rowley, 2009), especially in emerging societies.

This chapter opens with the review of convenience-related literature, elucidating the odyssey of convenience construct from an attribute to a multidimensional construct. Further chapter describes the qualitative studies conducted by authors of present study to understand the perception for retail service convenience among Indian consumers. The chapter concludes with proposed dimensions and perception items for retail service convenience.

---

[2]India Retail Report, 2013, research by Images Retail Intelligence Services (IRIS).

5.1.1 REVIEW OF LITERATURE

There have been two streams of literature which are salient to our study. The first stream focuses on consumer convenience orientation, explaining the factors why some consumers are more likely than others to buy convenient goods and services. The second stream focuses on the studies. It has played a significant role in conceptualizing convenience as a multidimensional construct.

5.1.2 CONVENIENCE ORIENTATION

Consumer's convenience orientation is defined as the value and preference consumers place on convenient goods and services with inherent time- and effort-saving characteristics (Brown, 1990; Berry et al., 2002) and convenience oriented consumer is characterized as "one who wish to accomplish a task in the shortest time with the least expenditure of human energy"(Morganosky, 1986). At the outset, Anderson (1969, 1971a, b, 1972) examined convenience and proposed the term convenience oriented consumption. He defined it as: (1) satisfies some immediate want or need and (2) releases time or energy or both for alternative uses. The former part of the definition was influenced by Copeland's (1923) perspective on convenience goods, where convenience deals with ease of acquisition, convenient to purchase and accessible. Second part of the definition recognized the multidimensionality of convenience construct where consumer wants to save their time and effort so that they can invest that time and energy in some other high valued tasks. The latter part of definition opened up the discussion for further scope in convenience literature. Anderson argued about time and energy aspect of convenience which consumer has to forego while using any goods and services, and discussed convenience as an inherent attribute in product and services used by consumers which can reduce their time and energy cost. Literature demonstrates that convenience orientation was mostly dealing with two dimensions: time saving and effort/energy saving, and suggested that understanding expenditure of consumer's time and effort during consumption is an important step in creating buyer's value. Stages in family life cycle, socioeconomic status, annual household income, occupation, wife's employment, education and age have been found as significant determinants of convenience orientation (Anderson, 1969, 1971a, b, 1972).

5.1.3 CONVENIENCE—AN ATTRIBUTE TO A MULTIDIMENSIONAL CONSTRUCT

In conjunction with the above mentioned studies focused on convenience-oriented consumption and which viewed convenience as a product attribute, few researchers consistently worked on building convenience, as a rich multidimensional construct, to understand its complex role in consumer buying process. In an effort Yale and Venkatesh (1986) suggested convenience as a crucial concept for marketer and mentioned that the rise of service economy requires the systematic examination of convenience as "primary salient product attribute." They argued for the multidimensionality of the construct and mentioned that operationalizing convenience with only time-saving attribute is wrong understanding of the construct, as many empirical studies viz. Douglas (1976); Reilly (1982); Strober and Weinberg (1977, 1980), have found few significant differences between working women and nonworking women, using convenience products. They put forward convenience as a complex and a crucial concept for marketer and suggested that studying convenience issue can help them to recognize and to understand the consumer's convenience orientation and to find out the demand for the convenience attribute in products. They proposed number of variables and factors which affect the perception or need of convenience among consumers (see Table 5.1). Though exclusivity of all the factors or classes was questionable, as few of the classes were quite subjective and therefore difficult to measure; also there could be some overlap between the classes mentioned. Nevertheless, contribution of this study was worthy in terms of supporting time and effort aspects of convenience and identifying four convenience classes. This study also emphasized on consumer perspective of convenience, especially as a service rather than the product attribute view.

Although it was acknowledged that convenience consists of several dimensions (Anderson and Shugan, 1991; Sediers et al., 2000; Reimers and Clulow, 2000; see Table 5.1), there was no agreement on what were these dimensions. For example, Brown (1989, 1990) argued for the attribute classes given by Yale and Venkatesh (1985) and claimed that conceptualization was very ambiguous, was not supported by any theory and it was difficult to measure. Brown (1989, 1990) proposed five dimensions based on utility theory of economics which says that consumer desires for time, place, possession, and form utility.

TABLE 5.1 Convenience as a Multidimensional Construct.

Author (year)	Contribution to convenience literature
Yale and Venkatesh (1986)	Convenience influencing variables: economical/temporal, spatial, psychological, sociological, philosophical, and situational. Proposed six conveniences classes: time utility, accessibility, handiness, appropriateness, portability, and avoidance of unpleasantness.
Lew G. Brown (1990)	Proposed five dimensions of convenience: Time: product availability at convenient time Place: products are available at the place which is convenient to the customers Acquisition: customers can acquire products or services with less effort Execution: hiring or getting someone else to do the task for the customer Use: customer can use the product and services easily
Anderson and Shugan (1991)	Convenience from customization perspective. Value- added convenience
Seiders et al. (2000)	Retail store convenience Access: reach Search: locating the right product Possession: acquire the product Transaction: completion and amendment of transaction
Vaughan Reimers; Dr. Val Clulow (2000)	Shopping convenience for retail stores(temporal, spatial, and effort costs): composition, compatibility, concentration, access, parking, trading hours, design, enclosure, and shopping services and amenities
Berry, Seiders and Grewal (2002)	A conceptual model of service convenience and introduction to five types of service convenience (with time and effort dimensions), including waiting time perception Decision convenience: during make purchase or use decisions Access convenience: to initiate service delivery Transaction convenience: to effect a transaction Benefit convenience: to experience the service's core benefits Post benefit convenience: during reinitiating contact with a firm

5.1.4 SERVICE CONVENIENCE CONSTRUCT

Rapidly embedding its critical importance in the field of consumer behavior research and business practices, "convenience," in an era of service economy, was conceptualized as service convenience and had its first conceptual model by Berry et al. (2002). The proposed model was based on the five stages consumer go through during buying process (Engel and Blackwell 1982) and suggested five convenience types, that is, decision, access, benefit , transaction, post benefit. They mentioned that past works have not adequately explored the complex interrelationships between time and effort in regards to the dynamic processes by which convenience is initiated and sustained, for example, nature and type of services influence customer's sensitivity to time and effort.

Researchers took enough efforts to understand this construct conceptually, but literature mostly falls short of empirical support. Post Berry et al. (2002), few researchers attempted to develop and validate measurement scales for service convenience in different setting (Chou, 2002; Seiders et al., 2007; Colwell, 2008). The first empirical study was done by Chou (2002) on scale development of service convenience and testing of the construct. He developed 19-item scale, measuring different kinds of service convenience demands. However, Chou's (2002) work evidence is available in form of unpublished master dissertation report and it has not received much recognition. So far, the most recognized scale is the *Servcon*, a 17-item comprehensive instrument for measuring service convenience, developed and validated by Seiders et al. (2007) in context of specialty retail store. Researchers strengthen *Servcon* scale by providing nomological validity, and substantiate it with antecedents and consequences of convenience. The contribution of this study is significant as it exhibits, for the first time, rigorous empirical inquiry into convenience. However, study displayed some flaws in item generation and statistical process, as was demonstrated by Farquhar and Rowley (2009). First, the word convenience was used in all three items measuring access convenience dimension, which created a circularity problem in scale development process; and second, study lacked data for final stage of post benefit convenience and provided a statistically derived substitute. Later, another empirical study was done by Colwell et al. (2008), who developed 17 items to psychometrically valid scales for measuring the service convenience in cell phone and internet services. These two studies produced much required empirical investigation into convenience, but lacked generalizability, as very little work is done to validate the scales. Therefore, there is a possibility that generated convenience items may not be suitable for other service contexts, for example, *Servcon* tested in an Indian setting in context of food and grocery store was found to be only partially validated. This study suggested further investigation on other dimensions to reveal underlined nuances of Indian consumers' perception on expenditure of nonmonetary resources, that is, time, energy, and effort (Aagja et al., 2011). Moreover, it was concluded that though measures of service convenience for pure service environment and for retail environment are likely to share some common dimensions, measures of retail service convenience must capture additional dimensions, especially in emerging societies, where consumers are yet not fully exposed to and acquainted to the kind of retail services developed countries demonstrate.

5.2 QUALITATIVE INVESTIGATION—TRIANGULATION APPROACH

For the purpose of understanding underlined nuances of retail service convenience among Indian consumers, we employed three distinct qualitative techniques—phenomenological interviews, exploratory in-depth interviews and customer tracking through store (adopted from Dabholkar et al., 1996) which are discussed below.

5.2.1 PHENOMENOLOGICAL INTERVIEWING

Phenomenology, "as both a philosophy and a methodology has been used in organizational and consumer research in order to develop an understanding of complex issues that may not be immediately implicit in surface responses" (Smith et al., 2009). Phenomenology is a qualitative research approach committed to the examination of how people make sense of their major life experience; it is concerned with exploring experience in its own terms (Dabholkar et al., 1996; Smith et al., 2009). In the context of this study, six phenomenological interviews (including both organized and unorganized retailers and shoppers) were conducted, to understand "convenience" as a phenomenon and to assign meaning to the shopping experience as the participant sees it, and not as what the researcher perceives it.

The interview commenced with an introduction by the researcher about themselves and the research study. Respondents were then asked about their background and shopping interest. Gradually, the conversations were focused on availability of various retail store categories and on respondents' patronage stores. Respondents were requested to mention their expectations from a retail store and also about what they like in the store which they prefer above other stores. In an attempt to explore their perceptions about convenience in shopping, participants were inquired about their inconveniences during shopping, as to understand broader picture of their expectations in terms of services. Later, they were probed about the factors which provide them a feel of comfort and convenience during a shopping trip. They were also requested to narrate incidences of good or bad service experience which had a strong impression on them and which affected their decision of store choice every time they go shopping. In an attempt to explore their perceptions about convenience during shopping, respondents were allowed to mention their aggregate shopping experience regardless of retail type (modern or traditional retail store) and category type (fast-moving consumer goods (FMCG), durables and apparels). Each interview lasted for 45–60 minutes and key points of the interview were taken verbatim during the course of discussion and with 24-hour rule by Eisenhardt and Bourgeois (1988), discourse was transcribed immediately after interviews.

This study revealed that shoppers are most concerned with behavior of store staff. Respondents said although new formats have everything on display, they needed the store staff to make their shopping easy and mentally comfortable. Availability of well-informed and knowledgeable staff makes their shopping process smooth and comfortable. During interviews few respondents mentioned that they are still loyal to few traditional retail stores for the sole reason that the store owner treats them well and thoroughly understands their requirements and taste. To quote one respondent:

"I would like to go to the store where store staff would suggest me about patterns, colours and style which goes well with my personality ... that's why I prefer to go to boutiques where I get personalized service and advice of expertise ... less efforts at my end ...." (Female, 32 years, employed)

Respondents submitted their concern for untrained staff in modern retail stores, where they take long time to answer customer queries and most of the times give unsatisfactory response. As one respondent said:

"When I approached the salesman to get more information about the fabric of the merchandise I was buying (as I always wear 100% cotton and information was not mentioned on tag) that person had no clue about the fabric and the brand ...." (Male, 33 years, employed)

Another important attribute mentioned both by retailer and consumers was the assortment and good display of merchandise, consumers expect to find everything they need quickly in the store and therefore, assortment of products in the store is very relevant. More variety provides convenience to shoppers as they get a large set of merchandise to select from, which further save their efforts and time.

"Store should have large variety of merchandise and accessories, with all sizes available, so that I am able to find quickly what I like and what fits me well" (Female, 32, housewife).

Layout of the store too received a significant mention during the interviews, as an important attribute to store convenience. One participant who travels quite frequently mentioned:

"Planned store layout makes shopping comfortable, it provides easy navigation and I can cover whole store in less time ... do not miss anything without getting exerted ... also if chain of stores have standardized layout policy, then it becomes so easy to locate things ... irrespective of the location of the store ... in or with in cities." (Male, 36, self-employed)

Other salient convenience attributes cited by respondents were better proximity of store from home or office, parking area, less travel time to reach, less crowded, one stop shopping and less waiting in queues at billing counters. Both by consumers and retailers, home delivery and proximity of store have been seen as most convenient features offered by traditional store.

5.2.2 EXPLORATORY IN-DEPTH INTERVIEW

The second technique employed was in-depth telephonic and personal interviews, to discover relevant determinants of retail service convenience not yet identified. Respondents were requested to recall their whole shopping trip, leaving from home to end of purchase and were told to mention their expectations with regards to apparel, food and grocery, and durables' shopping, regardless of retail type (modern or traditional retail store) and to comment on factors producing convenience during the shopping process. The definition of convenience was not given to the respondents, in an attempt to explore their perceptions about word convenience in shopping. It was assumed that the more a particular factor related to convenience was cited, the more salient it was in the minds of respondents, and thus the retail service convenience component became more prominent to them. The group of 60 shoppers was interviewed and the method used was nonrandom convenience sampling. Size of sample population was decided based on "Concept of Saturation" of Glaser and Strauss (1967), when collection of new data and information does not put any further light on the subject under research. The demographic profile of the shoppers is presented in Table 5.2.

TABLE 5.2 Demographic Profile of Respondents.

Total sample	**60**
Age	**Number of respondents**
18–25	14
25–40	25
40–65	19
65 and above	2
Gender	
Female	42
Male	18
Annual income	
<5 lac	24
5–10 lac	1-6
10–15 lac	9
15–20 lac	7
>20 lac	4
Total sample	60
Occupation	
Employed	32
Self-employed	3
Students	12
Retired	3
Housewife	10

Some of the findings of this study were similar to the phenomenological study, for example, consumers were concerned about sales-people's behavior, proximity of store, product assortment, hassle-free exchange procedure, space in store, store layout, parking facility. In addition to this, other significant factors emerged from exploratory in-depth interviews were shoppers' concern for trust and value perceived during the process. Perception of value and trust are a subjective phenomenon and was weighted differentially by different consumers. Some consumers obtain value from all relevant "get" and "give" components Zeithaml (1998), whereas others view value as getting product at the lowest price. In the present study, value ratio is proposed as "give" factors both in terms of monetary and nonmonetary cost incurred by consumers and "get" factors in terms of assurance of quality, trust, dependability and keeping promises given by retail store.

"Once I went to buy some stuff at nearby store, what I saw was so disgusting ... Shopkeeper opened one body lotion bottle and apply it over his dry hands ... and again kept that on the shelf space to sell ... that was so unethical" (Female 26, housewife).

Further, respondents displayed their apprehensions about getting fair deals from retailers; they had a fear of being cheated by the retailer's hard sell marketing strategies. Such kind of selling practices force any shopper to be more judgmental and to spend more of his cognitive and emotional efforts in trying to get a fair deal. Other convenience attributes mentioned by respondents included, less time in locating things in store, extended store hours during weekdays, proper signage and membership cards, and discounts. Although discounts and offers were frequently cited by respondents especially in white goods and food and grocery category buying. Although we recognize discounts and offers as an important component having an impact on store choice, for the purpose of this study we view it as distinct from the convenience construct.

5.2.3 TRACKING THE CUSTOMER

Finally, "tracking" was taken as a third technique for qualitative investigation, to observe the thought process and service expectations of consumers during their shopping trip. In tracking method "researcher unobtrusively monitors the customer experiences in the store, information regarding identified components of the shopping experience, and the consumers."

Interactions with these elements was collected without significantly altering the natural flow of the experience (Dabholkar et al., 1996). Researcher took the permission from the consumers and followed them through the store for the purpose of the current study. Researcher observed and noted down their experiences as mentioned by them their interactions with store employees, store services and merchandise; their pleasure and discontentment attached with that particular excursion. Participants gave their comments especially on sales-people's behavior, space in the store, layout of the store, waiting queue at billing counter, and crowd in store and cleanliness. Participants were also vocal about incorrect labelling of price and offers on merchandise shelves.

5.3 RETAIL SERVICE CONVENIENCE—PROPOSED DEFINITION AND DIMENSION STRUCTURE

Adopted from Berry et al. (2002), present study defined retail service convenience as "consumers' perception of their time and effort (physical, cognitive, and emotional) required during the course of achieving underlined shopping goal, initiating from problem recognition stage to post purchase stage."

For the purpose of extracting dimension structure of retail service convenience, emerged attributes from qualitative study were subjected for thematic content analysis, done by one PhD student, one retail marketing specialist and one professor, who independently examined and extracted themes for the emerged items and arranged the data into meaningful categories. After doing the thematic content analysis all emerged attributes category-wise were put in the preset and emergent retail service convenience dimensions. Researcher started with five preset service dimensions proposed by Berry et al. (2002) and added few new dimensions as they become apparent through the data. Researcher adjusted the definition of the given dimensions (if required and gave a new name to that dimension) and identified new dimensions to accommodate data that did not fit the existing labels. Analysis represents human interpretation of the themes which emerged from the data; no software package has been used for analysis. Integrating our qualitative study findings with review of convenience literature, we put forward that retail service convenience has a multidimensional structure consisting of six dimensions, that is, information search convenience, access convenience, selection convenience, assurance convenience, transaction convenience and post purchase convenience.

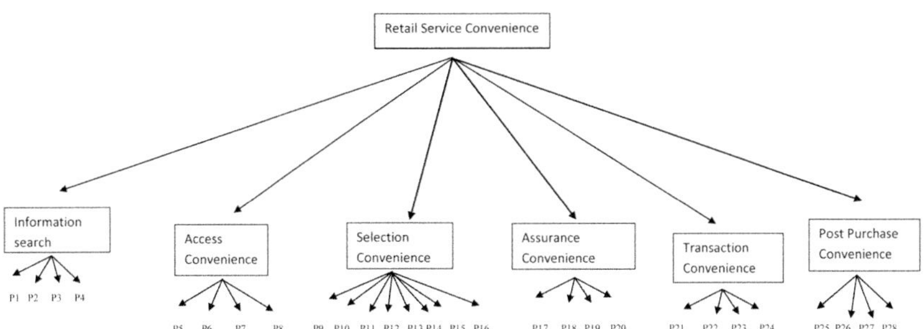

FIGURE 5.1 Proposed dimensional structure for retail service convenience.

The first dimension we propose is "***information search convenience***," which is similar to the Berry et al.'s (2002) decision convenience dimension, except few variations, in terms of information availability of product's offers and surety of getting what consumers are looking for in a particular store. Our depth interview revealed that information about the merchandise that a store possesses removes the anxiety regarding the nonavailability of products in store in the consumers' mind ("*I don't like hopping from one store to another to get what I want ... it is very irritating*"). Respondents mentioned that advertisement via various channels is an important source for them to get informed. Another variation in this dimension is the availability of the information regarding ongoing offers and schemes a particular store initiates, as phenomenological interview revealed consumers' sensitivity toward money-saving deals and offers. These interviews also concluded that lack of such information enhances consumers' cognitive and emotional inconvenience. Thus, it is suggested that retailers should be more careful and alert while forming their communication strategies so that right message and right information is delivered to potential consumers (Berry et al., 2002). We view this dimension of convenience as salient as it takes place prior to the actual service exchange.

Second dimension of convenience is "***access convenience***," which is similar to the Berry et al.'s (2002) access convenience dimension. It can be described as the proximity of the store from home or office, sufficient and safe parking area, less travel time and convenient operating hours. Access convenience is another convenience dimension, which too takes place before initiating actual buying process. Our in-depth interviews revealed that an easy and comfortable access to store stimulates more frequent purchases and occasions to buy from the given store (*"If two stores are providing me same facilities then I will prefer a store which is near to my place"*). Access convenience is more salient in case of inseparable services as compared with separable services, for example, people shop when store is open (Berry et al., 2002). Therefore, easy access to the store, parking facilities and comfortable store hours would enhance the perception of convenience among consumers (Seiders et al., 2000). Access convenience diminishes the physical efforts and serves as time convenience to the shoppers. It plays a more complex role for inseparable services as nothing can happen until consumers' gain access to the service (Berry et al., 2002). The speed and ease with which consumers can access the service may powerfully influence the choices they make.

The third dimension we propose is "***selection convenience***," which refers to consumers' perceived time and effort expenditure in searching and selecting products in the store. Although this dimension would also involve the consumers' perceived time and effort expenditure to experience the core benefits as explained by benefit convenience dimension of Berry et al. (2002), it is specifically related to all those activities which support shoppers to locate things in the store and facilitate them in selecting products of their choice with less time and effort expenditure. The retail shopping experience provides consumers with an opportunity to interact with a variety of personal (employees, consumers) and nonpersonal (products and decor) elements in the environment (Bitner, 1992), which otherwise is missing in a pure service environment. A significant number of respondents reported that wide range of assortment, well organized display, store layout, knowledgeable store staff, availability of stock and appropriate signage reduced their shopping efforts and saved their time during the selection process.

The rationale of this dimension comes from consumer retail search process (CRSP), a process by which consumers physically search through retail shopping environments (Titus and Everett, 1995). Past research suggests that consumers interact with retail shopping environments for a variety of reasons (Tabuer, 1972). Such interactions generally comprise either goal-oriented prepurchase search activity or an ongoing search activity such as browsing behavior (Bloch et al., 1986).In any of such case, consumers must find their way through the retail environment. During indepth interviews behavior of store staff has emerged as one critical parameter while selecting the products (*"I don't like sales people chasing me in store while looking at things but at the same time I want them to be available as and when their help is required, it helps me in finding right stuff in less time"*). Uninformed sales staff increase time and energy expenditure of shoppers. Sales staff also give a personal touch during shopping trip, especially in modern retail stores where shoppers do not know and interact with store owners personally. The inability to locate desired products and information may develop negative feelings of anger and irritation among shoppers. These feelings if severe enough may lead to abandoning of the search effort, or a permanent withdrawal of their patronage (Titus and Everett, 1995).

Fourth novel dimension we propose is "***assurance convenience***"; it involves customer expenditure of time and effort for perceiving trust and fairness during the course of buying, from the given retailer. This dimension of retail service convenience deals with the anxiety and fear shoppers have in their mind because of unfair business practices and availability of inferior products in the market. Also, new age retail stores lack personal relationship-based trust between retailer and shopper, therefore stores need to assure them and require to instill faith in them through their genuine practices throughout the process.

Trust being a key element of social capital, has been considered as an essential component in exchange relations (Mayer et al.,1995) and is closely related to fundamental outcomes of a firm, i.e. performance, competitive advantage, satisfaction and other economic outcomes like transaction cost (Balasubramanian et al., 2003; Cummings and Bromiley, 1996; Handy, 1995) and search cost reductions (Gulati, 1995). Gwinner et al. (1998) found that consumers' confidence in service provider's services (reduced anxiety and faith in the trustworthiness of the service provider) is the utmost benefit to consumers for maintaining long-term relationship with a service firm. Plank et al. (1999) recognized three elements, viz sales person, product and company as critical referents to consumer trust and accordingly defined trust as a buyer's belief that sales personnel, product and company will fulfil their obligations as understood by them. Thus assurance is seen as an important dimension amongst respondents as it reduces their anxiousness, enhances their trust in store and lessens their physical, mental and emotional exertion while buying. Comments included (*"I feel confident about the store where I shop," "the behavior of people enhances my trust every time I visit the store"* and *"I need to be alert and ... while shopping and transacting with the store"*).

The fifth dimension, "***transaction convenience***" comprises consumers' expenditure of time and effort to carry out a transaction to obtain the right of ownership of the given product (merchandise). Transaction convenience in retail store is specifically related with the perception of time and energy spent at waiting in queue at a billing counter, nonfunctional scanner machine, price code not entered in the system, nonacceptance of credit cards and untrained staff on billing machine. Long-waiting queue at billing counter is the most concerning factor during the transaction process ("*I expect a fast check out as soon as I am over with my selection of merchandise*"). The waiting time literature explains the negative after effects for companies that make the consumers wait too long to pay (Larson, 1987; Tom and Lucey, 1997). Waiting to pay can be the least rewarding act required of the consumers. Transaction inconvenience is an opportunity cost as consumers whose presence is required in a queue, cannot make a concurrent use of that time. Moreover, consumers tend to perceive waiting time to be longer than they actually are (Hornik, 1984). Transaction inconvenience also can take an emotional toll on consumers who get trapped in the slower line or who question the fairness of the service system (Larson, 1987). The consequences of transaction inconvenience are critical as this is the stage where consumers pay for both nonmonetary cost (time and effort) and monetary cost for services before they experience them.

Our sixth dimension, "***post purchase convenience***" is similar to post benefit convenience proposed by Berry et al. (2002), it is related with the expenditure of consumers' time and effort at the time when they want to reconnect with the retailer for any exchanges and to acquire after sale services. Post purchase activities typically include exchange of any defective product, customer's change of mind, any billing error or functional problem within warranty time, etc. Interview data reveals that shoppers' after sale service experience with retail store subsequently affects their repurchase intentions for next shopping trip. Respondents have submitted that most of the Indian stores lack in quick exchange policies and procedures ("*product return is the most difficult stuff to perform as I have to explain so many things to concern store staff*"). Past researches validate the importance of the post purchase experience to the overall consumer satisfaction (Bitner et al., 1990; Berry and Parasuraman, 1991). With the support of justice theory framework, it was found that perceived convenience of handling complaints increases consumers' satisfaction with the process (Tax et al., 1998). As Berry et al. (2002) mentioned that consumers spend their time and effort resources to receive benefits and they need more incentive in the form of additional benefits, if they are to spend more of their resources.

5.3.1 PROPOSED MEASURES FOR RETAIL SERVICE CONVENIENCE

Based on the qualitative study data, literature review and existing *Servcon* scale, items were constructed to tap each of the six dimensions of retail store service convenience. The initial item generation process generated pool of 105 items, with an iterative process, which involves systematic reviews; we revised and refined the set of items to articulate items that would be suitable to retail store services. Panel of marketing faculty members and retail store managers then evaluated the items for content and face validity. The members were given the conceptual definitions of retail service convenience along with illustrative quotes from the data, and instructions were given to retain items based on their representation of convenience domain, clarity of words and subject to modification. Candidate for deletion were items that were not clear and were open to misinterpretation. On the basis of panel's categorization and several follow-up conversations, a substantial number of redundant items were eliminated and several items were modified. This process resulted in 28 convenience measurement items for measuring six dimension of retail store service convenience, including 12 revised items from *Servcon*. Table 5.3 displays the proposed perceptual items for the retail service convenience construct.

TABLE 5.3 Proposed Item Descriptions for Retail Service Convenience Dimensions.

SERVCON dimension	Retail service convenience dimension	Perception item
Decision	**Information search**	P1. Prior to shopping, I can easily determine whether store will offer what I need
(NI)	**Information search**	P2. I can quickly get information about product availability in store (via Internet, newspaper, television or radio advertisement)
(NI)	**Information search**	P3. Store updates me regularly about special schemes offered by the store.

TABLE 5.3 *(Continued)*

SERVCON dimension	Retail service convenience dimension	Perception item
Decision	**Information search**	P4. Deciding to shop at this store is quick and easy
Access	**Access**	P5. I am able to get to store quickly
Access	**Access**	P6. I am able to reach store easily
(NI)	**Access**	P7. Store offers suitable store hours
(NI)	**Access**	P8. Store provides easy parking
Benefit	**Selection**	P9. Store has well organized layout
Benefit	**Selection**	P10. Store is spacious enough for comfortable movement in between aisles
(NI)	**Selection**	P11. Store has appropriate sign boards
(NI)	**Selection**	P12. Store offers wide variety of offering.
Benefit	**Selection**	P13. It is easy to get information related with product specifications, quality and price
(NI)	**Selection**	P14. It is easy to locate things; I am looking for in store.
(NI)	**Selection**	P15. It is easy to locate staff for assistance
(NI)	**Selection**	P16. It is easy to get store staff advice while selecting the product
(NI)	**Assurance**	P17. I feel safe while doing transactions with store
(NI)	**Assurance**	P18. I don't feel cheated in the store
(NI)	**Assurance**	P19. I find it safe and secure shopping in the store
(NI)	**Assurance**	P20. I have a faith in the management of the store
Transaction	**Transaction**	P21. I do not have to wait for long at billing counter to pay.
Transaction	**Transaction**	P22. I am able to complete my purchase transaction quickly.
Transaction	**Transaction**	P23. It takes little time to pay for my purchase
(NI)	**Transaction**	P24.Store accepts all major cards and coupons and they are processed easily
Post Benefit	**Post purchase**	P25 It is easy to process returns and exchanges at retail store.

TABLE 5.3 *(Continued)*

SERVCON dimension	Retail service convenience dimension	Perception item
Post Benefit	**Post purchase**	P26. Store takes care of product exchanges and returns promptly.
Post Benefit	**Post purchase**	P27. Any after-purchase problems I experience are quickly resolved.
(NI)	**Post purchase**	P28. Store provides home delivery of purchased product , if required

Note: The items are labeled P to denote perceptions. (NI) = Item is not included in SERVCON.

5.4 DISCUSSIONS

5.4.1 THEORETICAL CONTRIBUTION

Our main objective of this research was to investigate service convenience construct in a retail environment, in the context of emerging market, India. This study was an effort also to address the literature call of conducting an exploratory qualitative study to understand the nuances of service convenience in the Indian context, so that a service convenience construct and a scale grounded in an Indian context can be developed (Aagja et al., 2011). We proposed retail service convenience as a multidimensional construct consisting of six dimensions, that is, information search, access, selection, assurance, transaction and post purchase convenience. We found that in emerging retail market situation assurance has emerged as an important dimension for retail store service convenience, due to the perceived risk of fairness and "ages long" trust between traditional retailer and consumers. Our research also suggests that interaction with store staff is a crucial element for consumers during buying process, especially in the markets where organized retailing is still in its nascent stage and dominated by traditional retailing model where personal relationship between customer and retailer plays an important role. Qualitative research displayed a critical importance of store staff in up surging trust and assurance among consumers for the given store.

5.5 MANAGERIAL IMPLICATIONS

As the discussion in the preceding section illustrates, the theoretical contribution of this study is in terms of exploring convenience perception among Indian consumers; the findings from this study contains a number of implications for retailers as well. First, an understanding of role of convenience construct in consumer decision-making process is useful for retailers in constructing better services and implementing specific convenience oriented actions to enhance consumer value and loyalty. Retailers could use the proposed convenience dimensions to investigate the direction and strength of convenience needed among their current consumers. Further, the retailers would be well positioned to assess convenience strength of different shopper groups and could foster tailored convenience strategies to serve them better. For example, a shopper with hedonic motive is likely to perceive higher service convenience as compared with a utilitarian shopper, who would perceive convenience differently. The retailer could focus on one or all of the convenience dimensions in investigations of mean levels of convenience across consumers groups based on age, race/ethnicity, gender and even profitability. Such findings would help retailers focus on those critical issues in the store which would enhance shoppers' convenience perception and to eliminate the trivial ones.

5.6 DIRECTIONS FOR FUTURE RESEARCH

This chapter provides a conceptual framework designed to stimulate further research in the domain of retail service convenience. This study offers avenues for further research for conducting an empirical research to assess and to validate the six dimensions of retail service convenience in various contexts. This research represents the first step of expanding domain of service convenience in an emerging market context, because as Berry et al. (2002) suggest, service convenience is an uncharted territory and requires further investigation in order to increase understanding of this phenomenon.

KEYWORDS

- **retail service convenience**
- **emerging markets**
- **satisfaction**

REFERENCES

Aagja, J. P.; Mammen, T.; Saraswat, A. Validating Service Convenience Scale and Profiling Customers: A Study in the Indian Retail Context. *VIKALPA*. **2011,** *36*(4), 25.

Aggarwal, A. Current Issues in Indian Retailing. *Eur. Retail. Dig*. **2000,** *25*, 70–71.

Anderson, W. T. *The Convenience Oriented Consumer*; Bureau of Business Research, Graduate School of Business, University of Texas: Austin, TX, 1971a.

Anderson, W. T. An Analysis of the Correlates of Convenience-Oriented Consumer Behavior: With Special Emphasis on Selected Convenience Foods and Durable Goods. Unpublished Doctoral Dissertation, Michigan State University, East Lansing, Mich, 1969.

Anderson, W. T. Jr. Identifying the Convenience-Oriented Consumer. *J. Mark. Res*. **1971,** *8*(5)179–183.

Anderson, W. T. Jr. Convenience-Oriented and Consumption Behaviour. *J. Retail*. **1972,** *48*(3), 49–71.

Arnold, S. J.; Luthra, M. N. Market Entry Effects of Large Format Retailers: a Stakeholder Analysis. *Int. J. Retail. Distrib. Manag*. **2000,** *28*(4/5), 139–154.

Atsmon, Y., Kuentz, J. F. Seong, J. Building Brands in Emerging Markets. *McKinsey Quarterly* [online] **2012**. http://www.mckinsey.com/insights/winning_in_emerging_markets/building_brands_in_emerging_markets (accessed September, 2012).

Balasubramanian, S.; Konana, P.; Menon, N. M. Customer Satisfaction in Virtual Environments: a Study of Online Investing. *Manag. Sci*. **2003,** *49*(7), 871–889.

Berry, L. L.; Seiders, K.; Grewal, D. Understanding Service Convenience. *J. Mark*. **2002,** *66*(7), 1–17.

Berry, L. L.; Parasuraman, A. *Marketing Services: Competing Through Quality*; The Free Press: New York, 1991.

Bitner, M. J. Servicescapes: The Impact of Physical Surroundings on Customers and Employees. *J. Mark*. **1992,** *56*(April), 57–71.

Bitner, M. J.; Booms, B. H.; Tetrault, M. S. The Service Encounter: Diagnosing Favorable and Unfavorable Incidents. *J. Mark*. **1990,** *54*(1), 71–84.

Bloch, P. H.; Sherrell, D. L.; Ridgway, N. M. Consumer Search: An Extended Framework. *J. Cons. Res*. **1986**, *13*(1), 119–126.

Brown, L. G. The Strategic and Tactical Implications of Convenience in Consumer Product Marketing. *J. Consum. Mark*. **1989,** *6*(3), 13–19.

Brown, L. G. Convenience in Services Marketing. *J. Serv. Mark*. **1990,** *4*(1), 53–59.

Carmon, Z. J.; Shanthikumar, G.; Carmon, T. F. A Psychological Perspective on Service Segmentation Models: The Significance of Accounting for Consumers' Perceptions of Waiting and Service. *Manag. Sci.* **1995,** *42*(11), 1806–1815.

Chou, T-T. Advancing the Service Convenience Construct: A Scale Development Study on Customer Perceptions of Convenience in the Airline Service Encounter, Master's dissertation, National Kaohsiung First University of Science and Technology, Taiwan, 2003.

Colwell, S. R.; Aung, M.; Kanetkar,V.; Holden, A. L. Toward a Measure of Service Convenience: Multiple-Item Scale Development and Empirical Test. *J. Serv. Mark.* **2008,** *22*(2), 160–169.

Copeland, M.T. Relation of Consumers Buying Habits to Marketing Methods. *Harv. Bus. Rev.* **1923,** *1*(4), 282–289.

Cummings, L. L.; Bromiley, P. The Organizational Trust Inventory (OTI): development and validation. R. M. Karamer, T. R. Tyler (eds.), *Trust in Organizations: Frontiers of Theory and Research*; Sage: Thousand Oaks, CA, 1996; pp 302–320.

Dabholkar, P. A.; Thorpe, A. I.; Rentz, J. O. A Measure of Service Quality for Retail Stores: Scale Development and Validation. *J. Acad. Mark. Sci.* **1996,** *24*(1), 3–16.

Douglas, S. P. (1976). Cross-national Comparisons and Consumer Stereotypes: A Case Study of Working and Non-working Wives in the US and France. *J. Cons. Res.* **1976,** *3*(1), 12–20.

Eisenhardt, K.; Bourgeois, L. Politics of Strategic Decision Making in High Velocity Environments: Towards Mid Range Theories. *Acad. Manag.* **1988,** *31*(4), 737–770.

Engel, J. F.; Blackwell, R. D. *Consumer Behavior*, 4th ed., The Dryden Press: New York, 1982.

Farquhar, J. D.; Rowley, J. Convenience: A Services Perspective. *Mark. Theory.* **2009,** *9*, 425.

Glaser, B.; Strauss, A. *The Discovery of Grounded Theory: Strategies of Qualitative research*; Wiedenfeld and Nicholson: London, 1967.

Grewal, D.; Levy, M.; Lehmann, D. R. Retail Branding and Customer Loyalty: an Overview. *J. Retail.* **2004,** *80*(4), ix–xii.

Gulati, R. Does Familiarity Breed Trust? The Implications of Repeated Ties for Contractual Choice in Alliances. *Acad. Manag. J.* **1995,** *38*(1), 85–112.

Gwinner, K. P.; Gremler, D. D.; Bitner, M. J. Relational Benefits in Services Industries: The Customer's Perspective. *J. Acad. Mark. Sci.* **1998,** *26*(2), 101–114.

Handy, C. Trust and the Virtual Organization. *Harv. Bus. Rev.* **1995,** *73*(3), 40–50.

Hornik, J. Subjective vs. Objective Time Measures: A Note on the Perception of Time in Consumer Behavior. *J. Consum. Res.* **1984,** *11*(6), 615–18.

Huddleston, P.; Whipple, J.; Van Auken, A. Food store loyalty: Application of a Consumer Loyalty Framework. *J. Target. Meas. Anal. Mark.* **2004,** *12*(3/2), 213–230.

Larson, R. C. Perspectives on Queues: Social Justice the Psychology of Queuing. *Oper. Res.* **1987,** *35*(11/12), 895–904.

Mayer, R. C.; Davis, J. H.; Schoorman, F. D. An Integrative Model of Organizational Trust. *Acad. Manag. Rev.* **1995,** *20*(3), 709–734.

Mohanty, S.; Sikaria, C. Creating a Difference – The Store Ambience in Modern Day Retailing. *Glob. J. Manag. Bus. Res.* **2011,** *11*(3), 1–9.

Morganosky, M. Cost- Versus Convenience-Oriented Consumers: Demographic, Lifestyle, and Value Perspectives, *Psychology and Marketing*, 1986; Vol. 3, Spring, pp. 35–46.

Pan, Y.; Zinkhan, G. M.; Determinants of Retail Patronage: A Meta-Analytical Perspective. *J. Retail.* **2006,** *82*(3), 229–243.

Plank, R. E.; Reid, D. A.; Pullins, E. B. Perceived Trust in Business-to-Business Sales: A New Measure. *J. Pers. Sell. Sales Manag.* **1999,** *19*(3), 61–71.

Reilly, M. D. Working Wives and Convenience Consumption. *J.Cons. Res.* **1982,** *8*(4), 407–418.

Reimers, V.; Clulow, V. *Shopping and Convenience: A Model for Retail Centers*. Monash University, Faculty of Business and Economics, Department of Management. 2000.

Schrader, T. J.; Schrader, W. R. Consumer Patronage of Four Types of Food Outlets: The Impact of Retail Image Attributes. *J. Food. Prod. Mark.* **2004,** *10*(1), 25–46.

Seiders, K.; Larry G. Attention Retailers: How Convenient Is your Convenience Strategy. *Sloan Manag. Rev.* **2000,** *49*(3), 79–90.

Seiders, K.; Voss, G. B.; Godfrey, A. L.; Grewal, D. SERVCON: Development and Validation of a Multidimensional Service Convenience Scale. *Acad. Mark. Sci. J.* **2007,** *35*(1), 144.

Sinha, P. K.; Banerjee. A. Store Choice Behaviour in an Evolving Market. *Int. J. Retail. Distrib. Manag.* **2004,** *32*(10), 482–494.

Smith, J. A.; Flowers, P.; Larkin, M. *Interpretative Phenomenological Analysis-Theory, Method and Research*; Sage: London 2009.

Strober, M. H.; Weinberg, C. B. Strategies Used by Working and Nonworking Wives to Reduce Time Pressures. *J. Cons. Res.* **1980,** *6*(4), 338–348.

Strober, M. H.; Weinberg, C. B. Working Wives and Major Family Expenditures. *J. Cons. Res.* **1997,** *4*(3), 141–147.

Tauber, E. M. Why Do People Shop? *J. Mark.* **1972,** 46–49.

Tax, S. S.; Chandrashekaran, M. Customer Evaluations of Service Complaint Experiences: Implications for Relationship Marketing. *J. Mark.* **1998,** *62*(4), 60–76.

Tom, G.; Lucey, S. A Field Study Investigating the Effect of Waiting Time on Customer Satisfaction. *J. Psychol.* **1997,** *131*(6), 655–660.

Titus, P. A.; Everett, P. B. The Consumer Retail Search Process: A Conceptual Model and Research Agenda. *J. Acad. Mark. Sci.* **1995,** *23*(2), 106–119.

Treadgold, A. The Outlook for Asian Retailing. *Discount Merch.* **1999,** *39*(5), 45–46.

Yale, L.; Venkatesh, A. Toward the Construct of Convenience in Consumer Research. *Adv. Consum. Res.* **1986,** *13*, 403–408.

Zeithaml, V. A. Consumer Perceptions of Price, Quality and Value: A Means-End Model and Synthesis of Evidence. *J. Mark.* **1998,** *53*(7), 2–22.

Zeithaml, V. A.; Bitner, M. J. *Services Marketing: Integrating Customer Focus Across the Firm,* (4th edn); Tata McGraw-Hill: New Delhi, India, 2008.

CHAPTER 6

ASSESSING QUALITY OF FOOD, SERVICE AND CUSTOMER EXPERIENCE AT A RESTAURANT: THE CASE OF A STUDENT-RUN RESTAURANT IN THE USA

BHARATH M. JOSIAM[1*], ROSA MALAVE[2], CHARLES FOSTER[3], and WATSON BALDWIN[4]

[1]*Professor – Hospitality & Tourism Management, College of Merchandising, Hospitality & Tourism, University of North Texas, 1155 Union Circle #311100, Denton, Texas, 76203-5017, USA*

[2]*Lecturer – Club at Gateway Center, University of North Texas – Hospitality & Tourism Management, Denton, Texas, USA*

[3]*Lecturer and General Manager – Club at Gateway Center, University of North Texas – Hospitality & Tourism Management, Denton, Texas, USA*

[4]*Lecturer and Chef – Club at Gateway Center, University of North Texas – Hospitality & Tourism Management, Denton, Texas, USA*

[*]*Corresponding author. E-mail: Josiamb@unt.edu*

CONTENTS

Originally published as Josiam, B.M., Malave, R., Foster, C. and Baldwin, W. (2012) "Assessing Quality of Food, Service and Customer Experience at a Restaurant: The Case of a Student Run Restaurant in the USA," in Journal of Services Research, 14:1, pp. 49-73.
Published by the Institute for International Management and Technology. Reprinted with permission.

ABSTRACT

In the restaurant business, satisfied customers will return and provide positive word of mouth to peers. Studies have shown that restaurants that generate repeat patronage have six significant attributes in common, namely food quality, service quality, consistency of food and service, menu variety, cost/price–value relationship, atmosphere/ambience, and hygiene/cleanliness. University-level hospitality management programs regard the student-run restaurant (SRR) as an essential part of the curriculum. Despite many such restaurants housed in universities in the USA and across the world, little information is available about how these restaurants assess quality and promote usage and loyalty. This study addresses this subject by identifying the perceptions of the patrons of a SRR, segmenting the customer base, and ascertaining the quality of drivers of repeat and referral patronage. A total of 503 guests were surveyed at a university SRR in the southwestern region of the USA. Overall, patrons were satisfied with the food quality, service quality, value for money, and convenience of location. However, satisfaction levels were lower for convenience of payment methods and portion size. Significant differences were found between males and females, as well as between younger and mature patrons. Significant differences also existed between the perceptions of heavy users and light users. These findings suggest that the SRR serves distinct segments, which emphasizes a need to focus on customized strategies for customer retention. More information about patrons and the quality of restaurant attributes that drive their choices will assist hospitality faculty in SRRs and restaurateurs to competitively position their restaurants for success in the marketplace.

6.1 INTRODUCTION

On-campus restaurants where students both prepare and serve meals are rich learning environments unique to hospitality management programs. These restaurants provide opportunities for active involvement in operations, thereby linking theoretical principles to real-world business situations. Students readily transfer knowledge gained through these experiences to the workplace, resulting in enhanced career success. The term *student-run restaurant* (SRR) has been adopted for this paper to describe these on-campus restaurants. Research has shown that hospitality management programs in the USA with a SRR generate more graduates who enter the foodservice industry than those without such an experience (Nies, 1993).

6.2 NEED FOR THE STUDY

The most recent research conducted specifically on SRRs was in 1993 by Nies, in which 38 out of the 77 4-year US hospitality programs reported the use of an SRR. Despite the fact that SRRs are an integral part of the curriculum of all reputed hospitality programs, there is very limited literature on this topic. A thorough literature search for this study could identify only two papers directly pertaining to this study namely, Nies (1993), and West and Farley (1991). Therefore, the purpose of this study is to fill the gap in the literature by identifying the perceptions of patrons of a SRR on a US campus regarding the following attributes related to *repeat and referral patronage:* food quality, service quality, price-value issues, convenience, motivation for dining, and ambience.

Little information is available, however, concerning the criteria used in these programs to assess quality of food, service, and customer experiences and the steps taken to maintain their customer base and encourage patronage. West and Farley (1991) focused on cost reduction through sharing facilities with a foodservice contractor and improved educational outcomes due to greater student involvement in a simulated business environment. Nies (1993) reported on the prevalence of SRRs and their role in educating students. Almost half of all the American hospitality programs operate a SRR (Nies, 1993). The cost of operating SRR is substantial; investment in kitchen equipment alone is much greater than the cost of facilities for a lecture-based classroom. Less than half of all SRRs in the USA earn a profit (Nies, 1993). Therefore, in addition to controlling operating expenses, there is a need to generate more income. This is certainly true for all restaurants, not just for SRRs. To improve revenues, drivers of customer satisfaction and their quality needs to be assessed.

One strategy for measuring food and service quality is the comment card. A number of SRRs utilize this approach to evaluate service success (Nies, 1993). Unfortunately, the construct validity of customer comment cards is often too poor for management to confidently use them in making strategic decisions (Lewis and Pizam, 1981; Schall, 2003). There is a need, then, for research on customer perception of SRRs using an in-depth survey, with a broader, more representative sample. The results of such research would provide information beyond that of the limited, self-selected comment card data that typically suffers an inadequate sample size and shallowness of scope

6.3 LITERATURE REVIEW

The increasing complexity of the hospitality industry is a result of its numerous and diverse service components (Harris and Cannon, 1995). It is often hailed as "one of the largest (industries) in the world" handicapped by ineffectively trained employees (Harris and Bonn, 2000, p. 321). Hospitality management programs have recognized the values of experiential learning as an effective tool toward career preparation (Daly, 2001; Feinstein, 2001; Hawkins and Weiss, 2004). Hawkins and Weiss (2004) state its value as assisting students with information retention, problem solving, and providing an invaluable experience, as they become overall more effective self-learners. The presence of SRRs within hospitality management curriculums is based upon this focus on experiential learning. Students receive instruction and gain experience in the requirements for quantity food production and the principles of dining room services (Nies, 1993). In the following literature review, SRR management and marketing issues will be extensively discussed. Parallels will be drawn to the methods by which commercial restaurants succeed in competitive markets.

6.3.1 THE SRR BUSINESS

The description of SRRs in the USA is primarily based upon the research completed by Nies in 1993. Most SRRs in the USA are located on campus and have a typical capacity of 30–100 seats. Unlike their commercial counterparts, these restaurants operate only on weekdays and are often closed during shorter summer sessions. The majority concentrate on lunch service due to the lack of dinner demand, though a few do serve both. Lunch checks have an average range from US$2 to $8, while dinner checks range from US$4 to $30. Cafeteria service is found in only 25% of on-campus restaurants and buffet service in 6%. The majority of SRRs feature a full-service dining experience with student wait staff on hand.

The cornerstone of any foodservice operation is the menu (Frei, 1995). According to Frei, the menu "determines the image, price range, and profit potential of a restaurant" (1995). SRRs in the USA structure their menus to maximize the student experience while operating within the constraints of a modest budget. Most menus afford a limited selection of *entrees* to choose from, in order to manage service expediency and food quality. Only a minority restrict their offering to a selection among soups, salads, or desserts. Alcoholic beverages are available at less than half of the SRRs. Theme menus are also popular, in which case both the meal and the overall dining experience reflect a unifying theme such as Thanksgiving or Valentine's Day. Theme menus represent a changing slate of offerings for the customer, with a new dining experience on each visit (Nies, 1993; Jennings, 2005).

Student operations are as vulnerable to failure as their commercial counterparts. Although SRRs are housed in educational institutions and typically have nonprofit status, maintaining a break-even operation is still necessary. As is true in the business world, SRRs require a substantial capital investment of facilities, equipment, as well as monies for daily operation (Nies, 1993; Walker and Lundberg, 2000). Unfortunately, a considerable amount of time is also necessary to obtain profit over this initial investment, which is the cause of failure for many restaurant ventures. Previous research indicates a failure rate of 27% for restaurants in the first year of business that rises to 50% by the end of the third year (Walker and Lundberg, 2000). As a nonprofit entity, the management of SRRs is further challenged by the complexity of balancing its educational responsibility alongside profitability goals (Rojas, 2000). Similarly, many SRRs struggle to breakeven or fail altogether in their attempt to avoid substantial loss (Nies, 1993).

6.3.2 IMPORTANCE OF CUSTOMER RETENTION

Dining out is an important part of the lifestyle of many Americans. Research conducted by Kant and Graubard on this activity revealed "in 1999–2000, three or more weekly commercially prepared meals were reported by 48% of males and 35% of females" in the USA (2004). Repeat customers are the bedrock of solvency for a successful business venture, as they generate more profit than new guests (Zeithaml, 2000). Blattbert et al. (2001) found that "30 percent of the company's (loyalty card) customers represented over 75% of its profits" (2001). A key indicator of return patronage is customer satisfaction (Dube et al. 1994; Kivela et al. 1999; Schall, 2003).

Although there is no guarantee that a satisfied customer will return, statistics indicate that over 90% of dissatisfied customers will *not* return to a restaurant associated with a negative dining experience (Stevens et al. 1995). Researchers have delineated certain attributes that are associated with repeat business. The top six restaurant attributes that generate repeat customers are (1) food quality, (2) consistency, (3) menu variety, (4) an attractive price–value relationship, (5) ambience, and (6) cleanliness. Restaurant operators that focus on these attributes stand to strengthen customer loyalty and retention (Dube et al., 1994; Soriano, 2002; Koo et al. 1999; Josiam and Monteiro, 2003; Josiam et al. 2007). In addition, regularly conducting customer satisfaction research will guide management in their efforts to better satisfy their customers, as the findings can help restaurateurs better understand how their operations are performing with regards to the drivers of customer satisfaction (Brierley et al. 2003).

6.3.3 MEETING EXPECTATIONS OF CONSUMERS

Customers are becoming more sophisticated and expectations have risen concomitantly. Service providers are routinely expected to go beyond the commonplace and provide an exemplary dining experience (Bojanic and Rosen, 1994; Grindy, 1999). For many customers food quality is almost indistinguishable from service quality, and most agree that both must be present for a restaurant to qualify for a repeat visit (Koo et al., 1999; Soriano, 2002). The value considerations of these lifestyle customers, in regards to their dining experiences, surpass the issue of price. They respond more emphatically to ambience, hygiene, and cleanliness (Soriano, 2002; Yuksel and Yuksel, 2002; Yuksel, 2003). As a consequence, unique restaurant concepts grow in importance. Conversely, an outdated look or static design disenchants lifestyle customers and adversely affects profitability (Soriano, 2002).

6.3.4 FOOD QUALITY

Food is often seen as the single most important overall aspect of the dining experience (Kivela et al., 1999; Raajpoot, 2002; Sulek and Hensley, 2004). Maintaining a high level of food quality is absolutely necessary to satisfy the needs and expectations of the restaurant customers (Peri, 2006). It is important to recognize how food quality is viewed in a restaurant; the literature has identified the following attributes most commonly used in evaluating food quality in restaurants: presentation, taste, freshness, and temperature. These attributes are used as the tangible cues of food quality in restaurants. Presentation is seen as how attractively food is presented as a tangible cue for customer perception of quality and it has been seen as a key food attribute in modeling dining satisfaction (Kivela et al., 1999). Food presentation is also seen as on the product/service factors in the tangible quality scale (Raajpoot, 2002). Taste is also a key aspect in food that influences restaurant customer satisfaction and future behavior intentions (Kivela et al., 1999). Freshness refers to the state of food associated with its crispness, juiciness, and aroma (Péneau et al., 2006). Temperature is another element of evaluating food quality (Johns et al., 1996; Kivela et al., 1999). Temperature interacts with the three of the major sensory properties: taste, smell, and sight which have a strong connection with the flavor of food and its associated evaluation (Delwiche, 2004).

6.3.5 SERVICE QUALITY

One of the most researched aspects of service marketing is service quality (Fisk et al., 1993). The scale used to measure service quality is SERVQUAL, which was introduced by Parasuraman et al. (1988) and is the single most used scale for the conceptualization and measurement of service quality constructs (Brady et al., 2002). SERVQUAL is a useful starting point for assessing and improving service quality, but it is not a final solution (Parasuraman et al., 1991). SERVQUAL utilizes five quality dimensions for its scale of measurement: reliability, assurance, tangibles, empathy, and responsiveness. These five dimensions can be viewed as the perceived service quality evaluations (Wakefield and Blodgett, 1999). In Parasuraman et al.'s (1988) original model, each of the five dimensions held their own definitions. *Reliability* refers to the ability to perform the promised services dependably and accurately. *Assurance* is defined as the knowledge and courtesy of employees, as well as their ability to convey trust and confidence. *Empathy* refers to the provision of caring and individualized attention to customers. *Responsiveness* means willingness to help customers and provide prompt service. Finally, *tangibles* is defined as the physical facilities, equipment, and appearance of personnel. These elements of service quality need to be addressed and periodically measured in both commercial restaurants and in SRRs to evaluate customer's perception of the services being delivered.

Additionally, customers expect a full representation of modern technology and frown upon antiquated methods of payment (Mehta, 1999). In 2003, electronic forms of payment, such as debit and credit cards, exceeded cash and check payments for the first time in the USA (ATM Marketplace, 2003). Increasing preference for electronic forms of payment imply that credit/debit card usage at restaurants is rising (National Restaurant Association, 2002).

6.3.6 MARKET SEGMENTATION

An effective strategy for optimizing the match between expectations and service is to identify those factors that result in homogeneous purchasing behaviors of discrete market segments. Market segmentation capitalizes on the predictive power of customer satisfaction resulting in increased sales and profits (Yuksel and Yuksel, 2002; Yuksel, 2003). A variety of factors, such as demographics, lifestyle, service usage, and ethnic origin have been used as a basis for segmentation. In response to an increasingly diverse society, restaurateurs have learned to consider age, gender, income, and ethnicity as differentiating factors that have significant financial implications (Shank and Nahhas, 1994; National Restaurant Association, 1999; Silver, 2000; Soriano, 2002; Josiam and Monteiro, 2003; Josiam et al., 2007). While Soriano (2002) found no gender-based difference in the importance of food quality, service, cost/value, and place/ambience, an earlier study of service quality by Silver (2000) found that women consider service more important than men. SRRs would benefit from emulating their commercial counterparts and determine the distinctive profiles of their current market segments, and tailor their offerings to better serve them.

An important and growing segment in the USA is the mature market. The 2000 US Census revealed that people 55 years of age or older made up 20% of the population (Moschis et al., 2003). Estimates are that these mature adults will comprise 25% the population by 2015 and 33% the population by 2050 (Shank and Nahhas, 1994). Mature consumers control three-fourth of all US financial assets and half of all discretionary spending. In fact, they enjoy a higher level of discretionary spending than other age segments and are willing to purchase experiences in addition to products (Moschis et al., 2003). In terms of dining experiences, the mature market favors breakfast and lunch over dinner, making them an important segment for a SRR (Fu and Parks, 2001). SRRs generally offer a relatively full-service dining experience with a pricing structure that competes at a higher average than the standard convenience food options provided by campus cafeterias. The mature market is an ideal market segment for SRRS due to their market characteristics. They are more loyal and less price conscious than younger customers, as well as less concerned with speed of service, because they place greater value on discounts, nutrition, convenience, friendly service, and individualized attention (Knutson and Patton, 1993; Shank and Nahhas, 1994; Fu and Parks, 2001; Moschis et al., 2003).

6.4 PURPOSE AND OBJECTIVES OF THE STUDY

Despite the large number of SRRs in hospitality management programs across the world, there have been no studies to date of customer concerns in SRRs. To address this gap in the literature, the current study looks at customer satisfaction and retention in SRRs. The findings can assist hospitality management programs worldwide to sustain their SRR as a financially and educationally viable part of the hospitality curriculum. The purpose of the current study is to fill the gap in the literature by identifying the perceptions of patrons of a SRR in the USA. The study will be guided by the main elements of quality management (Breyfogle et al., 2001; George, 2003). These include a process that defines, measures, and analyses current process to improve and control them. This process, as applied to service quality needs to incorporate the Voice of the Customer (VOC). The findings of this study will expand knowledge of SRR performance and assist universities in increasing customer retention and enhancing financial stability. A better understanding of the relationship between operations and customer satisfaction would benefit hospitality management programs that operate a SRR. Furthermore, it would benefit restaurant operators by helping them to better understand how to assess the quality of their food, service, and customer experiences.

This study explores factors that influenced the decision of patrons to dine at a SRR operated by a Hospitality Management program at a university campus in the southwestern region of the USA. The objectives of the study were as follows:

Identify the most important SRR attributes as viewed by customers.

Identify differences between SRR patrons, and segment them based on gender, age, level of usage, and membership in campus community.

Identify the attributes of the SRR that drive referral and revisit patronage.

6.5 METHODOLOGY

6.5.1 *QUESTIONNAIRE*

This study collected data on factors that contributed to return patronage at a SRR operated by a leading Hospitality Management program in the south-western region of the USA. Students enrolled in a Dining Room Service and Management course operated the dining room, while those enrolled in a Quantity Food Production and Management course prepared the meals. A three course *Table-de-hoté* meal priced at US $6.50 was served 3 days per week during a long semester. A book of nine tickets was available for purchase discounting the cost of each meal by 10%. The SRR served 75–250 meals daily during the period of investigation. The typical patrons at the SRR were university students, university staff, members of the local community, and visitors to campus.

A self-administered questionnaire was developed for the purpose of collecting data. The questionnaire included questions on both demographic and other variables expected to influence the decision to dine at the SRR. A five-point Likert scale was utilized and respondents were asked to rank their degree of agreement with a list of statements that were categorized under the headings of service, food, reason to dine, barriers to dining more often, overall evaluation, and referral and repeat visit intention. The points on the scale were: 1 = strongly disagree, 2 = somewhat disagree, 3 = neutral, 4 = somewhat agree, and 5 = strongly agree. Demographic and usage questions were given as multiple-choice options.

Several terms were adopted for descriptive purposes of this study. *Mature consumers* were defined as those who were 55 years of age or older. *Heavy users* were defined as patrons who had purchased a book of nine meal tickets, whereas *light users* were those who did not purchase ticket books.

6.5.2 SAMPLE SELECTION, DATA COLLECTION, AND DATA ANALYSIS

A convenience sampling method was employed, given the constraints on time and resources. The researchers surveyed patrons during lunch service at the SRR over a 6-week period. A researcher would approach the patrons during their meal and ask if they would be willing to complete the anonymous and confidential survey. Completed surveys were retrieved by the researchers from willing participants. No compensation was provided to respondents.

Data was analyzed using SPSS. Descriptive statistics, including frequencies and means, were calculated. Analysis of variance (ANOVA) analysis was conducted to identify significant differences between demographic groups and other usage segments. Correlation analysis was conducted to examine the relationship between age and importance of SRR attributes. Multiple-regression analysis was conducted to examine the relationships between restaurant attributes and intention to revisit or recommend the SRR.

6.6 FINDINGS AND DISCUSSION

A sample size of 500 was targeted, and a total of 503 usable responses were collected. Over half of the respondents were university employees and students. Approximately, 68% of respondents were female. Just over a third (33%) were mature customers (age 55 or older). This gender composition was confirmed as representative of the sample base, by comparing the researchers' observations and those of the SRR General Manager.

Approximately, 40% of the respondents were first-time/light-user patrons, while the other 60% were repeat/heavy users. Similarly, 60% of the respondents bought the book of meal tickets for the SRR (Table 6.1). Approximately, 40% of the patrons of the SRR reported an annual household income in the US$49,999 or less category, while over 40% reported an annual household income of over US$75,000. The median US household has an income of US$42,228 (US Census Bureau, 2001). It appears that many SRR patrons come from more affluent households and are more educated than the general US population, with only 7.1% indicating their highest academic credentials to be a high-school diploma.

TABLE 6.1 Demographic Characteristics of SRR Patrons.

Demographics	N	%
Gender		
Male	137	32.5
Female	284	67.5
Occupation		
University students	153	32.5
University employees	123	26.1
Others	195	41.4
Annual household income		
Less than $24,999	105	26.3
$25,000–$49,999	60	15.0
$50,000–$74,999	60	15.0
$75,000–$99,999	52	13.0
$100,000–$124,999	54	13.5
$125,000–$149,999	27	6.8
$150,000 and over	42	10.5
Age		
Less than 55 years	322	64.0
55 and older	166	34.0
Psychographics/usage	N	%
First time or repeat patron of SRR		
First time guest	197	41.0
Repeat patron	283	59.0
Purchased book of tickets		
Yes	172	40.8
No	250	59.2

Note: Totals differ due to missing data.

6.6.1 *OBJECTIVE 1: IDENTIFY THE PERCEPTIONS OF SRR ATTRIBUTES*

Respondents answered questions related to attributes associated with dining at the SRR, on a five-point Likert scale ranked from Strongly

Disagree (1) to Strongly Agree (5). Using a study by Yuksel and Yuksel (2002) as a guideline, the attributes were grouped into various categories (Table 6.2). Mean scores for individual variables were consistently above 4.00 for all categories. On the whole, it appears that patrons perceived that food, service, and the overall experience were of good quality, and that the SRR provided good value for money. Multiple questions related to these issues generated mean scores ranging from 4.3 to 4.87 (Agree to Strongly Agree). With respect to barriers to increased patronage, the highest scores were for "Convenience," "Parking," and "Credit Cards/ Payment Methods." This suggests that patrons are currently satisfied with food, service, and price/value issues, but that they seek conveniences such as multiple payment methods, and better parking. The high overall scores bode well for repeat and referral patronage of the SRR. Both referral and revisit intentions received high scores, with means of 4.70 and 4.77, respectively.

TABLE 6.2 Mean Scores of Attributes by Category.

Categories and attributes	N	Mean	SD
Food			
The amount of food is right	500	4.46	0.828
Plate presentation is attractive	500	4.59	0.723
Food is flavorful	497	4.56	0.765
Food is fresh	493	4.62	0.702
Temperature of food is right	498	4.40	0.832
Food is consistent across cuisines	450	4.30	0.864
Service quality dimensions			
Staff is clean and well dressed	498	4.87	.441
Staff is knowledgeable	501	4.67	.668
Staff is approachable	500	4.79	.520
Staff anticipates my needs	499	4.57	.697
Staff gives prompt service	499	4.63	.723
Staff is well trained	497	4.69	.607
Staff serves food as ordered	474	4.69	.670
Staff makes effort to handle my special requests	457	4.64	.737
Staff provides consistent service	492	4.72	.598

TABLE 6.2 *(Continued)*

Categories and attributes	N	Mean	SD
Motivations to patronize SRR			
SRR is convenient	489	3.66	1.067
I dine at SRR to entertain guests	481	3.78	.998
SRR gives me value for money	489	4.22	.942
SRR offers a different menu each day	483	3.99	.965
Motivations – support and showcase school/ university			
Support school of merchandising and hospitality management	490	4.38	0.860
Support hospitality management (HM) students	497	4.45	0.802
SRR provides learning for HM students	496	4.70	0.661
Showcase the university	480	3.73	1.042
Barriers to patronage (I would dine more often if :)			
If menu was "set"	483	2.73	1.101
If wine/beer were served	488	2.74	1.418
If portion sizes were larger	482	2.82	1.274
If I could get in-out in 30 minutes	486	2.96	1.182
If parking was more convenient	487	3.69	1.235
If credit/debit cards were accepted	488	3.37	1.254
If ambience was more attractive	480	2.75	1.179
Overall evaluation			
Overall – food quality is good	499	4.60	.667
Overall – service is good	497	4.82	.480
Overall – experience is good	499	4.69	.595
Referral and return intentions			
I would recommend this SRR	498	4.70	0.621
I would dine again at this SRR	497	4.77	0.610

Note: 1 = strongly disagree, 2 = somewhat disagree, 3 = neutral, 4 = somewhat agree, 5 = strongly agree.

6.6.2 OBJECTIVE 2: IDENTIFY DIFFERENCES BETWEEN RESTAURANT PATRONS, AND SEGMENT THEM BASED ON GENDER, AGE, LEVEL OF USAGE, AND MEMBERSHIP IN CAMPUS COMMUNITY

6.6.2.1 GENDER

ANOVA revealed that significant differences existed between the perceptions of male and female patrons (Table 6.3). Males perceived more menu choices within a set menu, acceptance of credit/debit cards, larger portion size, the availability of wine and beer, and ambience as the biggest barriers of the SRR. Females perceived that the SRR delivered better value for money. These differences point to segmentation issues.

TABLE 6.3 Analysis of Variance of Restaurant Attributes by Gender.

Categories and attributes	Male		Female		F
	N	Mean	N	Mean	
Food/menu issues					
The SRR offers a different menu each day	131	3.85	277	4.06	4.626*
Patronize SRR more if "set" menu	134	2.96	270	2.64	7.675**
Patronize SRR more if wine/beer served	135	3.14	273	2.58	14.947***
Payment/value issues					
The SRR gives me value for money	134	4.06	277	4.30	6.188*
Patronize SRR more if credit cards accepted	134	3.58	276	3.27	5.598*
Portion size issues					
The amount of food is right	136	3.13	283	4.57	17.568***
Patronize SRR more if portions were larger	132	2.78	272	2.64	22.288***
Ambience					
Patronize SRR more if ambience more attractive	132	2.92	269	2.67	4.193*

Note: 1 = strongly disagree, 2 = somewhat disagree, 3 = neutral, 4 = somewhat agree, 5 = strongly agree. $^{*}p < 0.05$; $^{**}p < 0.01$; $^{***}p < 0.001$.

6.6.2.2 AGE

Significant differences were found between the perceptions of younger patrons and mature patrons. Younger patrons place greater value on menu choices, credit card payment options, price, and larger portion sizes. Mature patrons were significantly more likely to agree that the SRR provided good food, good service, and good experience. Additionally, mature patrons would like alcohol to be served, and expressed less concerned with other barriers such as parking or payment with credit cards (Table 6.4). It appears that the SRR is meeting the needs of the mature patrons very well. While that bodes well for attracting the mature segment, it also points to the importance of better understanding and serving the younger patron segment.

TABLE 6.4 Analysis of Variance of Restaurant Attributes by Age Categories.

Categories and attributes	Younger (less than 55)		Mature (55 and older)		F
	N	Mean	N	Mean	
Food issues					
Food is flavorful	317	4.51	165	4.67	4.760*
Food is fresh	315	4.54	163	4.75	9.806**
Plate presentation of food is attractive	320	4.53	165	4.72	7.376**
Overall – food quality is good	319	4.56	165	4.68	3.936*
Menu issues					
The SRR offers a different menu each day	313	3.93	157	4.12	4.265*
Patronize SRR more if "set" menu	314	2.85	155	2.52	9.758**
Patronize SRR more if wine/beer served	316	3.04	158	2.19	41.375***
Payment/value issues					
The SRR gives me value for money	316	4.10	160	4.43	12.750***
Patronize SRR more if credit cards accepted	315	3.70	159	2.73	74.171***
Portion size issues					
The amount of food is right	320	4.39	165	4.58	5.890*
Patronize SRR more if portions were larger	311	3.14	157	2.24	59.712***
Ambience					
Patronize SRR more if ambience better	310	2.97	156	2.31	35.597***
Service quality issues					
SRR staff is knowledgeable	321	4.63	164	4.76	4.034*
SRR staff is approachable	321	4.73	165	4.88	9.200**
Motivation/barriers for dining at SRR					
I dine at SRR to entertain guests	313	3.62	155	4.06	20.886***
Dine more at SRR if get in–out in 30 min	135	3.16	157	2.57	27.795***
Referral and return intentions					
I would recommend SRR to others	319	4.66	165	4.78	3.932*

6.6.2.3 HEAVY VERSUS LIGHT USERS/TICKET BOOK PURCHASE

Significant differences were found on several attributes between patrons who purchased a book of tickets and those who did not (Table 6.5). Purchasers reported significantly higher scores on "to support the students and the school." Purchasers also indicated that they dined at the SRR, because it was convenient. Ticket book purchasers gave relatively high scores to the SRR on food and service attributes. However, it is troubling to note that their scores were significantly lower than those of casual visitors. Perhaps, ticket book holders have higher expectations than casual patrons. Management needs to better understand and meet the needs of this important long-term, heavy-user segment. The findings also suggest that the restaurant serves two distinct usage segments and strategies for customer retention need to be crafted accordingly.

TABLE 6.5 Analysis of Variance of Restaurant Attributes by Purchase of Ticket Books.

Categories and Attributes	Purchased		Not Purchased		F
	N	Mean	N	Mean	
Food issues					
Plate presentation of food is attractive	172	4.53	248	4.67	4.212^{*}
Menu issues					
The SRR offers a different menu each day	168	4.14	239	3.89	6.843^{**}
Payment/value issues					
Patronize SRR more if credit cards accepted	169	3.15	240	3.51	8.429^{**}
Portion size issues					
The amount of food is right	172	4.38	248	4.58	6.094^{*}
Service quality issues					
SRR staff is clean and well dressed	169	4.82	248	4.92	6.146^{*}
SRR staff is knowledgeable	171	4.58	249	4.77	9.459^{**}
SRR staff is approachable	171	4.76	248	4.86	5.264^{*}
Staff anticipates my needs	171	4.47	248	4.68	10.443^{**}
Staff gives prompt service	171	4.56	249	4.73	5.760^{*}
Staff is well trained	171	4.61	246	4.76	6.040^{*}
Motivation/barriers for dining at SRR					
I dine at SRR, because it is convenient	168	3.88	242	3.50	12.706^{***}
I dine at SRR to support HM students	172	4.62	246	4.35	11.305^{**}
I dine at SRR to support SMHM	168	4.51	244	4.31	5.103^{*}

Note: 1 = strongly disagree, 2 = somewhat disagree, 3 – neutral, 4 – somewhat agree, 5 = strongly agree. $^{*}p < 0.05$; $^{**}p < 0.01$; $^{***}p < 0.001$.

6.6.2.4 UNIVERSITY COMMUNITY AND OUTSIDERS

Significant differences were also found between the perceptions of the off-campus patrons and the university community (Table 6.6). Off-campus customers placed greater importance on different menus, availability of wine and beer, value for money, service and dining experiences, and wishing to eat every day. University employees and students had significantly higher scores than off-campus patrons for more menu choices, loyalty programs, payment method options, parking, larger portion size, and formal atmosphere Respondents from the campus community indicated that they dined at the SRR, because it was convenient. Consistent with this, they found parking, and the service time to be barriers to patronage. They also gave significantly lower scores to the size of food portions. Respondents from the campus community gave relatively high scores to the SRR on food and service attributes. However, it is troubling to note that their scores were significantly lower than those of off-campus and presumably casual visitors (Table 6.6). Perhaps, the campus community has higher expectations than casual patrons. This again suggests that the restaurant serves two distinct segments and strategies for customer retention need to be crafted accordingly. Management needs to be sure that the campus community is not taken for granted and that their needs are being met.

TABLE 6.6 Analysis of Variance of Restaurant Attributes by On/Off University Identity.

Categories and attributes	University community		Non-university community		F
	N	Mean	N	Mean	
Menu issues					
Patronize SRR more if wine/beer served	273	3.00	184	2.45	16.864***
Payment/value issues					
Patronize SRR more if credit cards accepted	272	3.71	185	2.94	43.938***
Portion size issues					
The amount of food is right	274	4.38	194	4.53	3.918*
Patronize SRR more if portions were larger	271	3.11	181	2.50	26.390***
Ambience					
Patronize SRR more if ambience better	268	2.94	182	2.51	15.135***

TABLE 6.6 *(Continued)*

Categories and attributes	University community		Non-university community		F
	N	Mean	N	Mean	
Service quality issues					
SRR staff is knowledgeable	275	4.59	194	4.75	6.387*
SRR staff is approachable	275	4.71	193	4.87	10.110**
SRR staff anticipates my needs	275	4.48	193	4.66	7.655**
SRR staff gives prompt service	274	4.53	193	4.74	9.147**
Overall – Service at SRR is good	273	4.77	192	4.87	4.388*
Motivation/barriers for dining at SRR					
I dine at SRR, because it is convenient	274	3.78	184	3.41	13.447***
Dine more at SRR if get in-out in 30 min	274	3.16	182	2.70	17.394***

Note: 1 = strongly disagree, 2 = somewhat disagree, 3 = neutral, 4 = somewhat agree, 5 = strongly agree. *$p < 0.05$; **$p < 0.01$; ***$p < 0.001$.

6.6.3 OBJECTIVE 3: IDENTIFY THE ATTRIBUTES OF THE SRR THAT PREDICT REFERRAL AND REVISIT PATRONAGE

To identify the attributes of the SRR that predicts referral and revisit patronage, two multiple regression analyses were employed with SRR attributes as the independent variables and referral and revisit intention as the dependent variables. All food, service, motivations, barriers, and demographic variables were initially entered into the regression equation. An iterative process was utilized to identify the most powerful predictors, taking into consideration issues of multicollinearity (Table 6.7).

Both regression equations were found to be significant with relatively high predictive power. The variables in the equation were able to predict 74.1% of the variance in the case of referral intention and 63.5% in the case of revisit intention, respectively. The most powerful and significant predictors of both referral and revisit intention were the perceived overall experience, followed by overall food quality. As expected, select service attributes were also found to be significant predictors, as was the desire to support students. Among barriers to patronage, time taken for lunch service was found to be important for potential repeat guests (Table 6.7).

Previous research identified food quality, service quality, overall experience, and convenience to be key drivers of customer satisfaction in restaurants (Dube et al., 1994; Soriano, 2002; Koo et al., 1999; Josiam, and Monteiro, 2003; Josiam et al., 2007). The findings of this study are consistent with the literature on customer satisfaction in restaurants. Not surprisingly, this study found those that perceived that the SRR provided high quality food and experience were the most likely to refer or revisit, while time-related convenience was found to be a barrier to revisit. In line with this, number of prior visits was a significant predictor of revisit, suggesting that satisfied customers were likely to return.

TABLE 6.7 Regression Analyses: Predictors of Referral and Return Visit Intentions.

Predictor variables	Referral intention beta values	Revisit intention beta values
Overall – experience at SRR is good	0.670***	0.540***
Overall – food quality at SRR is good	0.197***	0.163***
Overall – service at SRR is good	NS	0.094**
SRR staff provides consistent service	−0.087**	NS
SRR staff makes the effort to handle my special requests	0.058*	NS
SRR lets me support Hospitality Mgmt. students	−0.094**	−0.070*
SRR lets me support school	0.147***	NS
SRR provides learning for Hospitality Mgmt. students	NS	0.198***
SRR gives me value for money	0.090**	NS
Would dine more at SRR, if I could get in-out in 30 min	NS	0.063*
Number of visits to the SRR	NS	0.072*
Model statistics		
Degrees of freedom	426	446
F value	175.063***	111.882***
Adjusted R square	0.741	0.635

Note: $^{*}p < 0.05$; $^{**}p < 0.01$; $^{***}p < 0.001$, NS = not significant.

6.7 DISCUSSION

By analyzing the preferences of each market segment, managers of SRRs can gain insights leading to more effective strategies addressing the needs of different target markets. Although a number of differences were found between segments, it is noteworthy that food quality, service quality, consistency, price/value, and payment methods were important issues for all segments. While the management of the SRR can take comfort in the high scores on the core issues of food and service, they now have new opportunities to improve customer satisfaction. Acting upon study results, the SRR can make improvements in menu variety, portion sizes, and service time. Payment options can be widened by accepting debit and credit cards. Management can examine the costs and benefits of serving wine and beer. These changes have a high potential to enhance the probability of repeat and referral patronage.

6.7.1 GENDER

The results are consistent with Soriano's study (2002), which found no differences between males and females regarding value and service. In other areas, however, gender does pose differences. The heightened importance of a larger portion size to males may be correlated to a higher awareness of caloric intake among women due to their increased tendency to diet (Wardle et al., 2004; Pew Research, 2006). Furthermore, women may view the restaurant as a place to socialize, while men may view it as an avenue for business entertainment. Hence, the greater importance attributed by men to ambience, time, service of alcohol, and acceptance of credit cards, as these attributes would facilitate a business lunch.

6.7.2 AGE

Study findings concerning the relationship between age and perceptions agree with Shank and Nahhas (1994), who found positive correlations between age and convenient location, loyalty, and the need for individualized attention, and negative correlations between age and frequency of dining out with friends and co-workers, shopping for low prices, having discounts available, and quality of food. It is not surprising that older patrons were more comfortable in the somewhat formal atmosphere of the SRR and gave higher scores to food, service, and ambience and were less concerned with barriers to patronage.

6.7.3 MATURE MARKET POTENTIAL

The percentage of mature patrons within the sample was higher than the national average of 20% of the population (Moschis et al., 2003). The researchers found that residents of nearby retirement communities and nursing homes patronize the SRR for lunch on a regular basis, which is consistent with the previous literature on the preference of mature patrons on lunchtime dining (Fu and Parks, 2001). The mature demographic group is thus a valuable market segment for SRRs due to their stability as a consumer base. Management should pursue further advertising and sales opportunities to sustain and nurture the growth of this market in nearby retirement communities and nursing homes.

6.7.4 HEAVY- AND LIGHT-USER PERCEPTION

Significant differences were found between the perceptions of heavy-use patrons and light-use patrons with respect to different menu, price and value, support and showcase school/university, service quality attributes, dining experiences, and convenience. The findings support the contention of Silver (2000), that infrequent restaurant-goers value service more than frequent restaurant-goers. However, menu, price and value, overall dining experiences, convenience, and support and showcase school/university are important attributes associated with heavy users. They are similar to previous findings that consistency of service, menu variety, cost/price–value relationship, and atmosphere/ambience are important restaurant attributes across different segments (Dube et al., 1994; Soriano, 2002; Koo et al., 1999; Josiam and Monteiro, 2003; Josiam et al., 2007).

6.7.5 SHOWCASE THE SCHOOL

One attribute common to SRRs is "to support and showcase school/ university." The mean score ranging from 3.73 to 4.45 puts respondents in the categories "agree" and "strongly agree." The relatively high score on this category is not surprising. Students involved in the operation of a restaurant tend to invite family and friends to dine at the restaurant, and sell books to them and the faculty. Nies (1993) indicated that operating a SRR was not only an educational tool but also an opportunity to showcase the hospitality program. Indeed, the researchers saw many university administrators and faculty entertaining outside guests in the restaurant. The SRR serves as a university showcase for potential students and other stakeholders, demonstrating how university students can develop professional competencies via practical experiences.

6.7.6 TICKET BOOKS

Generally, patrons who purchased the ticket book showed high, but significantly lower levels of satisfaction with the restaurant. Perhaps, ticket book buyers are satisfied customers of the restaurant from previous semesters, hence their willingness to commit in advance. At the same time, their expectations could be higher. It should be noted that although patrons who did not purchase books of tickets were less price and value sensitive compared to ticket buyers, they still consider these attributes as important factors for dining out. The university has a campus community of over 30,000, but despite this large local population, the number of ticket books sold, at around 200 a semester, is relatively low. Furthermore, with over 25,000 students, the proportion of student patrons is very low. Aggressive marketing communication directed at students and staff of the university will help tap into this locally available customer base.

6.7.7 ALTERNATIVE PAYMENT

The desire for multiple payment methods such as credit and debit cards tends to support the contention that consumers regard not only food, but also various other aspects of service as key criteria for choosing restaurants (Koo et al., 1999; Soriano, 2002). The preference for electronic forms of payment is consistent with national trends in this regard (National Restaurant Association, 2002; ATM Marketplace, 2003). A university SRR should seriously consider adding electronic payment options to attract and retain customers.

6.7.8 *PORTION SIZES*

Large portion size can enhance the price/value perception of customers (Grindy, 1999). Large portion size and loyalty programs could increase their perceived value for money (Grindy, 1999). Consistent with this, more menu choices would allow younger patrons to choose more affordable menu items. An alternative explanation is that mature patrons may be more driven by the overall dining experience, while younger customers are more focused on food, convenience, and value large portion sizes.

It should be noted that the researchers make no claims as to the generalizability of this study to other SRRs in the USA or in other parts of the world. The publication of this study is first and foremost a demonstration of how a study can be conducted at a restaurant to assess various dimensions of quality and yield actionable findings to enhance customer loyalty and increase revenues. It is to be expected that management of other SRRs would have findings unique to their operations and customer base. Restaurants worldwide are encouraged to conduct similar in-depth studies to gain a deeper understanding of their customers. Furthermore, such a survey can become a tracking survey, if conducted periodically, to measure the changing perceptions of customers over time, as the food, service, and consumer expectations change.

6.8 CONCLUSIONS

Greater understanding of university-affiliated SRRs is of value to all hospitality management programs. The student learning that takes place in these restaurants is unique. More information about the patrons and the attributes that influence their choices will assist faculty as they position their restaurants for optimal support. The maintenance of a healthy customer base is an excellent way to ensure a successful future of these invaluable learning environments. Furthermore, understanding gained by customer feedback, obtained from a data-driven survey, to assess different dimensions of quality in the SRR operations, can be of immense help to the restaurateurs.

6.9 LIMITATIONS

This study has limitations in terms of both methodology and application. The study used a non-random convenience sample due to time, access, and budgetary constraints. In addition no attempt was made to sample non-customers and identify barriers to their patronage. Non-customers may be different from the convenience sample both behaviorally and demographically. In addition, the investigation was conducted at one university during one semester. Customers' perceptions may be different at other places and at other times.

KEYWORDS

- **customer experience**
- **hospitality management program**
- **student-run restaurant**
- **service**
- **quality**

REFERENCES

Arora, R.; Singer, J. Customer Satisfaction and Value as Drivers of Business Success of Fine Dining Restaurants. *Serv. Mark. Q.* **2006,** *28*(1), 89–102.

ATM Marketplace. 2003. Electronic Payments Surpass Cash, Checks. http://www.atmmarketplace.com/news. (accessed 30 March 2004).

Blattbert, R. C.; Getz, G.; Thomas, J. S. *Customer Equity*. Harvard Business School Press: Cambridge, 2001.

Bojanic, D. C.; Rosen, L. D. Measuring Service Quality in Restaurants: An Application of the SERVQUAL Instrument. *Hosp. Res. J.* **1994,** *18*(1), 3–14.

Brady, M. K.; Cronin, J. J.; Brand, R. R. Performance-only Measurement of Service Quality: A Replication and Extension. *J. Bus. Res.* **2002,** *55*(1), 17–31.

Brierley, J.; MacDougall, R.; Hill, N. *How to Measure Customer Satisfaction.* 2nd edn. Gower Publishing, Ltd: Burlington, 2003.

Breyfogle, F. W. III; Cupello, J. M.; Meadows, B. *Managing Six Sigma: A Practical Guide to Understanding, Assessing and Implementing the Strategy that Yield Bottom-line Success*. John Wiley & Sons, Inc: Chicester, 2001.

Daly, S. P. Student-operated Internet Businesses: True Experiential Learning in Entrepreneurship and Retail Management. *J. Mark. Edu.* **2001,** *23*(3), 204–215.

Delwiche, J. The Impact of Perceptual Interactions on Perceived Flavor. *Food Qual. Pref.* **2004,** *15*(2), 137–146.

Dube, L.; Renaghan, L. M.; Miller, J. M. Measuring Customer Satisfaction for Strategic Management. *Cornel. Hotel Restaur Adm. Q.* **1994,** *35*(1), 39–47.

Feinstein, A. H. An assessment of the Effectiveness of Simulation as an Instructional System in Foodservice. *J. Hosp. Tour. Res.* **2001,** *25*(4), 421–443.

Fisk, R. P.; Brown, S. W.; Bitner, M. J. Tracking the Evolution of the Services Marketing Literature. *J. Retail.* **1993,** *69*(1), 61–103.

Frei, B. T. The Menu as Money Maker. *Rest. Institut.* **1995,** *105*(6), 144–145.

Fu, Y. Y.; Parks, S. C. The Relationship between Restaurant Service Quality and consumer Loyalty among the Elderly. *J. Hosp. Tour. Res.* **2001,** *25*(3), 320–336.

George, M. L. *Lean Six Sigma for Service.* McGraw-Hill: New York, 2003.

Grindy, B. 1999 Value Judgments' *in* Restaurants USA. http://www.restaurant.org/. (accessed 23 January 2004)

Harris, K. J., Bonn, M. A. Training Techniques and Tools: Evidence From the Foodservice Industry. *J. Hosp. Tour. Res.* **2000,** *24*(3), 320–335.

Harris, K. J.; Cannon, D. F. Opinions of Training Methods used in the Hospitality Industry: A Call for Review. *Int J. Hosp. Manag.* **1995,** *14*(1), 76–96.

Hawkins, D. E.; Weiss, B. L. Experiential Education in Graduate Tourism Studies: An International Consulting Practicum. *J. Teach. Travel Tour.* **2004,** *4*(3), 1–29.

Jennings, L. Fine-dining Operators' Theme Nights Break Routines, Boost Covers. *Nation Restaur. News* **2005,** 39(31), 1–5.

Johns, N.; Tyas, P.; Ingold, T.; Hopkinson, S. Investigation of the Perceived Components of the Meal Experience, Using Perceptual Gap Methodology. *Int. J. Tour. Res.* **1996,** *2*(1), 15–26.

Josiam, B. M.; Monteiro, P. A. Tandoori Tastes: Perceptions of Indian Restaurants in America', *Proceedings of the 5th Biennial Conference on Tourism in Asia: Development, Marketing, & Sustainability. May 2002, Hong Kong SAR, PRC. International Journal of Contemporary Hospitality Management, 16*(1), 18–26.

Josiam, B. M.; Sohail, S. M.; Monteiro, P. A. Curry Cuisine: Perceptions of Indian Restaurants in Malaysia. *Tour. Int Multidiscip. J Tour.* **2007,** *2*(2), 25–37.

Kant, A. K.; Graubard, B. I. Eating out in America, 1987–2000: Trends and Nutritional Correlates. *Prevent. Med.* **2004,** *38,* 243–249.

Kivela, J.; Inbakaran, R.; Reece, J. Consumer Research in the Restaurant Environment, Part 1: A Conceptual Model of Dining Satisfaction and Return Patronage. *Int. J. Contemp. Hosp. Manag.* **1999,** *11*(5), 205–24.

Knutson, B. J.; Patton, M. E. Restaurants can find Gold Among Silver Hair: Opportunities in the 55+ Market. *J. Hosp. Leis. Mark.* **1993,** *1*(3), 79–90.

Koo, L. C.; Tao, F. K. C.; Yeung, J. H. C. Preferential Segmentation of Restaurant Attributes through Conjoint Analysis. *Int. J. Contemp. Hosp. Manag.* **1999,** *11*(5), 242–250.

Lewis, R. C.; Pizam, A. Guest Surveys: A Missed Opportunity. *Cornel. Hotel Restaur. Adm. Q.* **1981,** *22,* 37–44.

Parasuraman, A.; Berry, L.; Zeithaml, V. Refinement and Reassessment of the SERVQUAL Scale. *J. Retail.* **1991,** *67*(4), 420–450.

Parasuraman, A.; Zeithaml, V.; Berry, L. SERVQUAL: Multiple-item Scale for Measuring Consumer Perception of Service Quality. *J. Retail.* **1988,** *63,* 12–40.

Mehta, S. Strategic Implications of an Emerging Cashless Society in the US. *Electron. Mark.* **1999,** *9*(1/2), 93–103.

Moschis, G.; Folkman, C.; Bellenger, D. Restaurant Selection Preferences of Mature Consumers. *Cornel. Hotel Restaur. Admin. Q.* **2003,** *44*(4), 51–59.

National Restaurant Association. Diverse Diners. 1999, http://www.restaurant.org/rusa/magArticle.cfm?ArticleID=26. (accessed 20 January 2004).

National Restaurant Association. Credit-card ownership increasing. 2002. http://www.restaurant.org/research/magarticle.cfm?ArticleID=796. (accessed 22 January, 2004).

Nies, J. I. The Role of Student-operated Restaurants in the Hospitality Curriculum. *Hosp. Tour. Educ.* **1993,** *5* (3), 21–24.

Pew Research Center, Social Trends Report. Eating More; Enjoying Less. 2006 http://pewresearch.org/assets/social/pdf/Eating.pdf. (accessed 1 August 2006).

Rojas, R. R. A Review of Models for Measuring Organizational Effectiveness Among for-Profit and Nonprofit Organizations. *Nonprofit Manag. Leadersh.* **2000,** *11*(1), 97–104.

Raajpoot, N. A. TANGSERV: A Multiple Item Scale for Measuring Tangible Quality in Foodservice Industry. *J. Foodserv. Bus. Res.* **2002,** *5*(2), 109–127.

Schall, M. Best Practices in the Assessment of Hotel-guest Attitudes. *Cornel. Hotel Restaur. Adm. Q.* **2003,** *44*(2), 51–65.

Shank, M. D.; Nahhas, F. Understanding the Service Requirements of the Mature Market. *J. Restaur. Foodserv. Mark.* **1994,** *1*(2), 23–43.

Silver, D. Active Service Restaurants and Institutions. 2000. http://www.rimag.com/004/sr.htm. (accessed 20 January 2004)

Soriano, D. R. Customers' Expectations Factors in Restaurants: The Situation in Spain. *Int. J. Qual. Reliab.* **2002,** *19*(8/9), 1055–1068.

Stevens, P.; Knutson, B.; Patton, M. DINESERV: A Tool for Measuring Service Quality in Restaurants. *Cornel. Hotel Restaur. Adm. Q.* **1995,** *36*(2), 56–61.

Sulek, J. M.; Hensley, R. L. The Relative Importance of Food, Atmosphere, and Fairness of Wait: The Case of a Full-service Restaurant. *Cornel. Hotel Restaur. Adm. Q.* **2004,** *45*(3), 235–247.

U.S. Census Bureau. Money income in the United States: 2001. 2001 http://www.census.gov/prod/2002pubs/p60-218.pdf. (accessed 22 January 2004)

Wakefield, K. L.; Blodgett, J. G. Customer Response to Intangible and Tangible Service Factors. *Psychol. Market.* **1999,** *16*(1), 51–68.

Walker, J. R.; Lundberg, D. E. *The Restaurant from Concept to Operation* (3rd edn). John Wily & Sons, Inc: New York, 2000.

Wardle, J.; Haase, A. M.; Steptoe, A.; Nillapun, M.; Jonwutiwes, K.; Bellisle, F. Gender Differences in Food Choice: The Contribution of Health Beliefs and Dieting. *Soc. Behav. Med.* **2004,** *27*(2), 107–116.

West B. M.; Farley, G. A. A Cost-effective Quantity Food Lab Through the use of Shared Resources. *Hosp. Tour. Educat.* **1991,** *4*(1), 15–20.

Yuksel, A.; Yuksel, F. Measurement of Tourist Satisfaction with Restaurant Services: A Segment-based Approach. *J. Vacat. Market.* **2002,** *9*(1), 52–68.

Yuksel, A. Market Segmentation Based on Customers' Post-purchase Performance Evaluation: A Case of Tourist Diners. *J. Travel Tour. Market.* **2003,** *15*(1), 1–18.

Zeithaml, V. A. Service Quality, Profitability, and the Economic Worth of Customers: What We Know and What We Need to Learn. *J. Acad. Market. Sci.* **2000,** *28*(1), 67–85.

PART III

Value Drivers: HR Competencies

CHAPTER 7

AN EXPLORATORY STUDY OF COMPETENCIES REQUIRED TO COCREATE MEMORABLE CUSTOMER EXPERIENCES IN THE HOSPITALITY INDUSTRY

SONIA BHARWANI[1] and VINNIE JAUHARI[2*]

[1]*Manchester Business School, U.K.*

[2]*Director Education Advocacy, Microsoft Corporation India Pvt. Ltd.*

[*]*Corresponding author. E-mail: Vinnie.jauhari@yahoo.com*

CONTENTS

This paper was originally published as Sonia Bharwani, Vinnie Jauhari (2013) "An exploratory study of competencies required to co-create memorable customer experiences in the hospitality industry", International Journal of Contemporary Hospitality Management, Vol. 25 Iss: 6, pp.823–843. Reprinted with due permission from Emerald Group Publishing Limited.

ABSTRACT

Purpose: The purpose of this paper is to identify and map competencies required by frontline employees to enhance guest experience in the hospitality industry, in the context of an emerging experience economy.

Design/methodology/approach: Secondary research through extensive review of relevant literature in the area of experience economy and hospitality management.

Findings: This study proposes a new construct of "Hospitality Intelligence" (HI) encompassing mainly emotional intelligence (EQ) (comprising interpersonal intelligence and intrapersonal intelligence), cultural intelligence (CQ), and hospitality experiential intelligence dimensions.

Practical implications: Practitioners and HR professionals in the field of hospitality would find the HI construct useful in recruiting and training frontline employees, while educationists could use the findings of this study in designing curricula and pedagogical interventions for developing the right skill set for the hospitality industry.

Originality/value: This study proposes a competencies framework and develops a construct of HI required by frontline employees in the hospitality industry to elevate guest experience from a simple interaction to a memorable experience.

7.1 HOSPITALITY IN THE EXPERIENCE ECONOMY

With the liberalization, privatization, and globalization of economies the world over, the hospitality industry has undergone transformation through which it has emerged as an industry with a global orientation (Erdly and Kesterson-Townes, 2003). Over the past quarter of a century, there has been an evolution in the hospitality and tourism consumption behavior in terms of increasing levels of importance being attributed to leisure time pursuits (Williams, 2006). Hospitality consumers have evolved to become qualitatively more discerning, more demanding, and more diverse. Research suggests that the contemporary world traveler is becoming increasingly hedonistic and self-indulgent (Hirschman and Holbrook, 1982; Van Boven and Gilovich, 2003), seeking a superlative-quality, integrated, multicultural yet consistent hospitality experience (Scott et al., 2009; Salovey and Mayer, 1990; Miao, 2011). The hospitality industry, the world over, is transforming from a product-focused, physical-asset intensive business to a customer-focused, experience-centric one (Knutson et al., 2006).

There has been a paradigm shift in the way economic value is perceived across the globe. According to Pine and Gilmore (1998, p. 97), "as services, like goods before them, increasingly become commoditized, experiences have emerged as the next step in what we call the progression of economic value .... Economists have typically lumped experiences in with services, but experiences are a distinct economic offering, as different from services as services are from goods."

In the emerging experience economy, hospitality and leisure businesses are focusing on providing individually customized hospitality and travel experiences to their guests (Erdly and Kesterson-Townes, 2003) to cater to their unique personal tastes and requirements by developing distinct value-added components to their product and service offerings which are already of a consistent and high functional quality (Oh et al., 2007). According to Hemmington (2007, p. 749), "customers do not buy service delivery, they buy experiences; they do not buy service quality, they buy memories." Thus, for effective delivery of hospitality products and services, it is critical for hospitality organizations to keep the customers' perspectives central while designing customer experiences.

In the hospitality and tourism context, consumer experiences are "multi-dimensional takeaway impressions or outcomes" (Walls et al., 2011a, p. 18) which result from engaging encounters that involve consumers on a sensory level, emotionally, cognitively, behaviorally, and relationally rather than merely on a functional level, thereby creating memorable experiences (Schmitt, 1999; Oh et al., 2007; Lashley, 2008). "While commodities are fungible, goods tangible and services intangible, experiences are memorable." (Pine and Gilmore, 1999, p. 11). Thus, the traditional hospitality service offerings of lodging and boarding are being purposefully encased in engaging experiences to create memorable events. Hotels are channelizing their efforts to provide holistic experiential service offerings which connect with each individual guest on a personal and emotional level to create memorable experiences.

Hemmington (2007) quotes Lashley (2008), who state that "hospitality is essentially a relationship based on hosts and guests" and emphasize that it is the host-guest relationship which is the main distinctive characteristic of hospitality from which several other dimensions emerge. In order to gain competitive advantage, frontline employees can be used as operant resources to cocreate customer experiences (Lusch et al., 2007). This highlights the need for understanding the competencies required by frontline hospitality employees for effective guest engagement.

7.2 OBJECTIVE OF THE STUDY

Thus, in the context of the evolution of the hospitality industry in the emerging experience economy, there is a need to explore the competencies required by frontline employees to transition from simply being "service providers" to taking on the mantle of "experience providers."

This raises important questions such as:

- What kind of competencies should the frontline staff have over and above the basic technical competencies, to cocreate positive customer experiences?
- What kind of training interventions should be initiated by hospitality firms to develop these competencies in their frontline staff?
- What could be done at academic level to develop the competencies for frontline positions?

This study proposes a new construct of "Hospitality Intelligence" (HI) and also a conceptual framework for the same. It also clarifies various dimensions of HI and the sub-constructs which constitute these dimensions. HI mainly encompasses (EQ) (comprising interpersonal intelligence and intrapersonal intelligence), cultural intelligence (CQ), and hospitality experiential intelligence dimensions. HI can play a crucial role in enabling frontline employees to elevate guest experience from an ordinary encounter to a memorable one.

In the context of the hospitality industry, earlier studies have endeavored to examine the importance of EQ in human interaction and service performance but these pertain to EQ in context of managerial performance or leadership roles (Langhorne, 2004; Scott-Halsell et al., 2008). Similarly, research related to CQ is more generic in terms of importance of CQ in international and globalized work environments and for expatriate managers. There is very limited research specifically related to EQ, CQ, and hospitality experiential intelligence in context of frontline employees in the hospitality industry.

This paper builds on these concepts to put forward the conceptual framework for HI which include competencies required by frontline employees to transform themselves from being merely "executors of service delivery mechanisms" into "facilitators of experience architecture" (Carbone and Haeckel, 1994).

7.3 APPROACH TO THE STUDY

This paper is based on an exhaustive review of literature conducted on guest experience and competencies of frontline staff in the context of the hospitality industry. The literature review initially focuses on the dimensions which influence consumer experience, highlighting the important role that human interactions play in creating memorable guest experience in context of the hospitality industry.

Thereafter, literature and research on EQ and CQ is examined to determine the various dimensions and sub-constructs which are relevant for engendering a memorable hospitality experience. The broad dimensions drawn from EQ and CQ are used to develop and propose the HI construct and a preliminary conceptual framework keeping in mind guest experience. The various sub-constructs which make up each of the HI dimensions have been drawn from existing competencies-related literature in the hospitality industry. Thus, the HI construct encompasses the competencies that are required by frontline staff in the hospitality industry (in addition to the basic technical competence) to create memorable experiences for their guests.

7.4 DIMENSIONS INFLUENCING CONSUMER EXPERIENCE

Merely offering superior quality products and services is not sufficient for engendering sustainable competitive advantage in today's economic setting. Research has shown that with regard to the hospitality and tourism industry, the experience value of the products and services offered is increasingly playing a dominant role in influencing the consumers' motivation to purchase the service (Otto and Ritchie, 1996; Brunner-Sperdin and Peters, 2009; Yoo et al., 2011). By de-commoditizing their business offerings and systematically managing customer experiences, hospitality organizations can endeavor to develop an emotional and personal connect with their customers to engender higher levels of customer engagement and commitment to the brand (Berry and Carbone, 2007; Lashley, 2008). "Connecting emotionally with customers requires an organization to create a cohesive, authentic and sensory-stimulating total customer experience that resonates, pleases, communicates effectively and differentiates the organization from the competition" (Berry and Carbone, 2007, p. 26). Designing and developing customer experiences keeping in mind the different experience design dimensions which engage customers on an emotional level can go a long way in enhancing customer satisfaction and eliciting customer commitment and loyalty (Pullman and Gross, 2004).

A review of literature shows that several researchers have sought to put forward a range of elements that influence consumer experiences. The material product, employee behavior and attitude, environment, interpersonal relationships, and technical quality (Reuland et al., 1985; Bitner, 1992; Carbone and Haeckel, 1994; Berry et al., 2002) are some of the important elements of experiential design that have a direct impact on consumers' experiences and consequently on their levels of satisfaction.

While most of the studies mentioned above relate to consumer experience in general in service industries, there is some research specifically in the context of the hospitality industry. Brunner-Sperdin and Peters (2009) have explored dimensions of customers' service experience which impact guest emotions in context of high-quality hotels in Europe and used the terms "hardware," "software," and "humanware" to describe the operational, organizational, and personal dimensions, respectively. Hemmington (2007) in his seminal paper has taken hospitality beyond services management and gone on to define hospitality as a commercial experience. He identified the host-guest relationship, generosity, theatre and performance, "lots of little surprises," and safety and security of the guests as the five key dimensions of hospitality experience. A more recent study by Walls et al. (2011b) has succinctly brought together the various dimensions of consumer experience discussed above in context of luxury hotel guests. These dimensions include the physical environment, human interaction (of guests with employees as well as fellow guests), the personal characteristics of guests, and other trip-related factors such as purpose of the trip, nature of the hotel, and the experience continuum.

Table 7.1 summarizes the focus of different studies conducted on various facets which influence consumer experience.

TABLE 7.1 Dimensions Influencing Customer Experience.

Authors	Material product	Employee behavior and attitude	Environment	Interpersonal relations	Technical quality
Reuland et al. (1985)	✓	✓	✓		
Bitner (1992)		✓	✓		
Carbone and Haeckel (1994)	✓	✓	✓	✓	
Berry et al. (2002)	✓	✓	✓	✓	✓
Pullman and Gross (2004)	✓			✓	
Brunner-Sperdin and Peters (2009)	✓	✓		✓	✓
Hemmington (2007)		✓	✓	✓	
Walls et al. (2011b)	✓	✓	✓	✓	

As the table highlights, several of the studies have focused on the behavior and attitude dimension and also on environment. Attitudes are influenced by number of factors. Behavior is an outcome of certain competencies and is influenced by attitudes, knowledge, and skills. However, gaps exist in the current literature in terms of elaborating in greater detail about the behavior and attitude of the frontline staff–what are the specific competencies that are required to make frontline staff more effective in their job roles which involve guest interface? Walls et al. (2011b) have discussed consumer experience in luxury hotels and the role of physical environment and human interaction dimensions contributing to the same. However, competencies dimension of frontline staff, which could impact the effectiveness of the interaction between the consumer and the employee, have not been elaborated upon. Most of the literature is silent on what aspects of behavior and attitude could contribute to competencies which would help in engendering a superior customer experience. Thus, it can be seen that the competency dimension impacting the customer experience in the context of the hospitality industry is a relatively unexplored field.

The focus of this study is the competencies of the frontline hospitality employees who are involved in the guest/customer interface. The study, however, presupposes that the frontline employees already possess the requisite technical competencies required to perform their job in the specific areas of operations they are involved in. Thus, the current study on HI tries to clarify what helps shape the behavior and attitude of employees involved in guest interface, which impacts the overall guest experience.

7.5 HUMAN INTERACTION

Given various nomenclatures by different researchers–ranging from "humanics" (Carbone and Haeckel, 1994) to "humanware" (Brunner-Sperdin and Peters, 2009), to "relational cues" (Pullman and Gross, 2004)–human interaction has emerged as an important dimension which influences customer experiences in the hospitality industry. Employees are considered to be "key determinants of service quality, customer satisfaction and loyalty, competitive advantage and organizational performance" (Kusluvan et al., 2010, p. 172). Morgan et al. (2009) stress the importance of emotional, aspirational, and participative aspects of customer experience over the functional and rational dimensions. They highlight the need for service delivery strategies which encompass the theatrical metaphors of staging, casting, and performance (Pine and Gilmore, 1999) in the process of cocreating unique and memorable experiences for hospitality guests and go on to argue that to be successful in the experience economy. It is important to train and develop hospitality professionals who understand the nuances of social behavior and are capable of better anticipating and catering to the requirements and wants of their guests (Morgan, 2004, 2006).

In the context of the experience economy, the increasing competition levels and growing complexity in the global hospitality sector has changed the strategic and operational landscape in the industry (Kandampully and Suhartanto, 2000) and the skills set needed by hospitality employees–especially the frontline employees–to work competently reflect these changes (Chung, 2000). In order to promote customer experience centricity, hospitality organizations need to inculcate a deep understanding of consumers while designing their service experience offerings (Prahalad and Ramaswamy, 2004; Binkhorst and Den Dekker, 2009). The customer interaction has to be managed in such a manner so as "to cocreate value with customers while addressing customer-specific idiosyncratic needs" (Chathoth et al., 2013, p. 13). Further, hospitality organizations should use their customer-contact employees as "operant resources" (Shaw et al., 2011) and develop in them competencies which will enable them to achieve "a level of engagement with role and guests that goes significantly beyond that encapsulated within traditional skills model of the sector" (Baum, 2006, p. 126).

While the literature reviewed does address the constructs of the human interaction dimensions of consumer experience, the discussion is largely limited to enumerating some broad traits and characteristics of employees (Morgan, 2004; Brunner-Sperdin and Peters, 2009; Walls et al., 2011b). And though existing literature covers EQ and cultural exposure as contributors to improving interpersonal interaction, these aspects have not been explicitly covered in the context of a memorable customer experience. EQ and CQ could be important contributors in building the requisite competencies which would impact the behavior of frontline staff and improve their interactions with customers. This paper seeks to further develop the human interaction constructs by exploring the competencies required by frontline employees to transition from simply being "service providers" to taking on the mantle of "experience providers." Thus, a new construct of "Hospitality Intelligence" encompassing EQ (comprising interpersonal intelligence and intrapersonal intelligence), CQ, and hospitality experience-related dimensions has been proposed, keeping in mind the evolving customer experience centricity of the hospitality offerings.

7.6 INTELLIGENCE AND COMPETENCE

In its most common connotation, intelligence refers to an individual's ability to learn and reason (Kihlstrom and Cantor, 2000). Conventionally, the study of intelligence focused mainly on cognitive aspects such as memory and problem solving and the traditional view was that intelligence was something you were born with, had only a certain amount of and that you could not do much to augment the levels of your intelligence (Gardner, 1997). However, the conventional definition of intelligence, mainly in the context of cognitive and academic abilities may be a rather narrow construct (Sternberg, 1996).

Several psychologists and researchers such as Thorndike (1920) and Wechsler (1958) early on recognized the importance of non-cognitive aspects of intelligence. Thorndike (1920) in his classic formulation "Intelligence and its uses" came up with the concept of understanding intelligence as an amalgam of three different facets:

1. *Mechanical Intelligence:* Ability to understand and manage concrete objects.
2. *Abstract Intelligence:* Ability to understand and manage ideas.
3. *Social Intelligence:* Ability to understand and manage people.

Thus, social intelligence, which related to the ability of an individual "to act wisely in human relations" (Thorndike, 1920) and to engage in adaptive social interactions, was considered to be an important dimension of intelligence beyond the traditional cognitive elements.

Building on Thorndike's concept of social intelligence, Gardner (1983) included interpersonal and intrapersonal intelligences as part of seven intelligence domains in his theory of multiple intelligences. Gardner observed that interpersonal and intrapersonal intelligences are as important as the type of intelligence typically measured by IQ and related tests (Gardner, 1983; Cherniss, 2000). Other researchers like Sternberg (1996) have used labels such as "practical intelligence" and "successful intelligence" to denote constructs which blend cognitive abilities with other underlying competencies to result in effective or superior job performance.

On a parallel front, in his paper "Testing for Competence rather than Intelligence," David McClell (1973) questioned the validity of traditional measures of intelligence such as IQ tests and scholastic aptitude tests as predictors of job performance. According to McCllelland (1973), "It is better to observe what good performers actually do to be successful than make assumptions about intelligence and other underlying traits" and he pioneered the concept of competencies in management literature.

Boyatzis (1982) defined competency in a generic form as any underlying characteristic an individual possesses and utilizes, which leads to successful performance in a job role. Competencies refer to behavioral dimensions that an individual brings to a position to enable him to perform the job competently. Thus, the term competency presupposes the willingness and the capability to behave in a competent manner and incorporates knowledge, skills, behavior, and attitude into a single core unit.

A review of literature shows that competencies and intelligence (in its broad connotation which includes non-cognitive aspects) have been used interchangeably or have been closely related in meaning (Morand, 2001; Boyatzis et al., 2002; Langhorn, 2004). The relationship between the two constructs has been brought out most lucidly by Goleman (1998) who defines competence as a learned capability based on intelligence which results in superior work performance.

The authors have kept this relationship between intelligence and competencies in mind while formulating the construct of HI. Thus, HI includes knowledge, skill, attitude, and behavioral competencies which are critical for customer-interfacing employees in the hospitality industry to perform their job competently and deliver on a superior customer experience. This new construct–HI–mainly draws from EQ and CQ which are discussed below. It also includes hospitality experience-related competencies which are essential for designing and developing service offerings in the newly emerging experience economy in the hospitality in industry.

7.7 EMOTIONAL INTELLIGENCE

According to Kunnanatt (2004), "Emotional intelligence is the ability of a person to use emotions as guiding tools for interpersonal effectiveness in his or her social environment." emotionally intelligent people produce win–win outcomes for themselves by creating a magnetic field of emotional attraction around them. According to Goleman (1995), EQ competencies can be classified as personal competencies and social competencies. Personal competencies are about dealing with one's own self and social competencies are about dealing with others and managing one's relationships. Goleman (1995) observes that "the contribution of emotional intelligence to effective performance at work is as much as 66% for all jobs and 85% for leadership job." This has huge implications especially for the hospitality industry which is predominantly a customer-oriented and experience-based segment.

Aydin et al. (2005) in their study suggest that HRM specialists have to test both IQ and EQ in the hiring process to create a high performing work force in the organization. They suggest that in a high performance context, the achievement involves not only technical analytical intelligence or educational background and expertise but the capacity of managing oneself and interpersonal relationships. Aydin et al. (2005) used 17 factors in their study to explain the relationship between preeminent achievement in organizations and two different dimensions of intelligence–IQ and EQ. They have suggested that with IQ as a base, EQ with its interpersonal and intrapersonal dimensions creates preeminent achievement in the workplace. The key competencies for interpersonal intelligence are:

- Motivating others;
- Influence and persuasion;
- Team capabilities;
- Communication; and
- Collaboration and co-operation.

The competencies for intrapersonal intelligence are:

- Optimism and positive thinking;
- Honesty and persuasion;
- Perseverance;
- Commitment;
- Tolerance;
- Self-confidence; and
- Self-consciousness and self-control.

Gardner (1983), in his path-breaking book "Frames of Mind: The Theory of Multiple Intelligences" postulated the concept of interpersonal intelligence as one of the seven different facets of multiple intelligences that individuals possess. Interpersonal intelligence refers to the ability of individuals to interact with and work well with other people and the different aspects of people-smart skills possessed by an individual can be labeled as People Quotient (PQ) (Silberman, 2001). While researchers like Salovey and Mayer (1990) who coined the term "emotional intelligence" and Goleman (1995, 1998) who popularized it, included interpersonal intelligence as a facet of EQ, the various sub-dimensions of interpersonal intelligence were not explored in detail. However, Silberman (2001) in concept, proposed different dimensions which enhance the understanding of the underlying facets of the interpersonal intelligence construct such as empathy and understanding, effective communication, emotional resilience, seeking and assimilating feedback, influencing skills, conflict resolution skills, flexibility, and team playing.

7.8 CULTURAL INTELLIGENCE

Cultural dimensions play a big role in fostering relationships. In a hospitality context, when guests and hosts are from different nationalities, sensitivity to cultures could play an important role in building memorable interactions. Cultural underpinnings may impact values, behavior, and quality of communication. Fitzgerald (1998) discusses differences in cultures could create situations which would need to be addressed in context of service delivery. She also offers comments on how service preferences may vary across cultures. She remarks, "In Japan ... they expect at all times, polite, smiling attention from all service personnel ....They think it impolite if staff speak to someone else ... while attending to their needs." while "Germans usually expect fast, efficient, 'no nonsense service'" (Fitzgerald, 1998, p. 48).

According to Fitch (1998, p. 2), culture refers to "a pervasive, generally invisible system of symbolic resources and shared beliefs arising from shared experiences of a group of people that stands outside but still shapes their understanding of how the world works." As such, culture then impacts the relational practices, perceptions, emotional cues, and behavior of individuals. However, the ability to understand emotions in the home culture does not mechanically transfer to unfamiliar cultures (Earley et al., 2006).

Taking cognizance of the challenges of cultural diversity thrown up as a result of globalization. Earley and Ang (2003) conceptualized a multidimensional framework of CQ based on Sternberg's (1986) theories of intelligence. CQ refers to the malleable capabilities of individuals to function and interact effectively in diverse intercultural settings involving different races, ethnicities, and nationalities. It explains the difference in abilities of individuals to navigate culturally disparate environments. CQ, thus, refers to the capabilities of an individual to intelligently deal with situations marked by cultural diversity.

According to Earley et al. (2006), CQ comprises four dimensions:

1. Metacognitive CQ;
2. Cognitive CQ;
3. Motivational CQ; and
4. Behavioral CQ.

Metacognition refers to the cognition of cognitive processes used by individuals themselves and by others–it is the process of thinking about thinking (Flavell, 1979). In context of CQ, metacognitive CQ refers to higher-order mental processes that individuals use to acquire knowledge of and control over individual thought processes relating to culture (Ang et al., 2007). Those with well-developed metacognitive CQ are knowingly mindful of cultural preferences and norms before and during interactions (Ng et al., 2009).

Cognitive CQ deals with general knowledge about the cultural practices and norms of different cultures which is acquired through experience or education. It includes understanding of the frameworks of cultural values and the social systems of different cultures and subcultures. People with high cognitive CQ have the ability to recognize and predict commonalities and differences across various cultures (Ang et al., 2007).

Besides mental understanding of diverse cultures, CQ also encompasses the motivational capability required to cope with ambiguous and culturally unfamiliar settings. Motivational CQ relates to the mental capacity to direct attention and sustain energy toward gathering knowledge about and functioning in situations marked by cultural differences (Earley and Ang, 2003). According to Kanfer and Heggestad (1997, p. 39), motivational CQ "provides agentic control of affect, cognition and behavior that facilitate goal accomplishment."

Behavioral intelligence refers to outward manifestations or overt expressions in terms of what people do rather than what they think (Sternberg, 1986). Thus, the last facet of CQ acknowledges that cultural understanding (cognition) and interest (motivation) must be accompanied by situation-appropriate behavior culled from a broad repertoire of culture-specific verbal and nonverbal actions, while interacting with people from diverse cultures.

EQ focuses on the prowess of an individual to perceive and manage emotions in a culture-neutral context. CQ provides individuals with insights and capabilities to deal with multicultural situations and engage in cross-cultural encounters. However, an important aspect of commonality between both these concepts is that in both cases individuals tend to have "a propensity to suspend judgment – to think before acting" (Earley and Mosakowski, 2004, p. 140). Thus, CQ is essentially EQ across a cultural context.

It was found that research related to emotional and CQ was rather generic–in the context of leadership roles or managerial performance in international and globalized work environments. There is very limited research related to specifically emotional and CQ in the frontline staff in the hospitality industry. However, few researchers have highlighted the importance of EQ (Baum, 2006, Lashley, 2008) for frontline employees in creating a memorable hospitality experiences. Baum (2006) also touches upon the skills that are needed of customer contact employees while engaging in cross-cultural encounters in the hospitality industry. This paper builds on these concepts to put forward the conceptual framework for HI.

7.9 CONCEPTUAL FRAMEWORK FOR HOSPITALITY INTELLIGENCE (HI)

For any customer interface in the context of the hospitality industry, the frontline staff play a key role. There are numerous touch points which are created wherein a customer and an employee interface happens. These touch points or interaction points could be in various operations areas such as food and beverage, front office, concierge, travel desk, housekeeping, spa, and so on. The context may be a luxury, upscale, mid-segment or a budget segment hotel. In each of these, employee interface is a key determinant of customer satisfaction. If the service encounter is positive, it would have a positive impact of the customer experience.

Scripting the role of employees in guest interactions has received criticism from several authors on the grounds that it spawns "mindless" and "habitual" behaviors in the frontline staff (Harris et al., 2003) and leads to contrived and inauthentic hospitality experiences (Lynch, 2005). Using the metaphor of theatre, stage, and performance (Pine and Gilmore, 1999), Morgan et al. (2008) suggest that rather than playing their part by rote and surface acting, service performers need to get under the skin of the character by "intelligently" putting something of themselves into the part.

To this end, the authors propose a conceptual framework for competencies required for successful employee–guest interactions for creating a memorable experience. Though a memorable experience is influenced by many other aspects (Walls et al., 2011b), the competencies of the frontline staff play a key role in human interactions between the employees and the guests. These competencies can be clubbed under the domain of HI. Thus, HI comprises a set of competencies required by hospitality staff, over and above the technical competencies they possess, to create authentic, convincing, and memorable hospitality experiences. It is composed of three dimensions: EQ, CQ, and hospitality experiential intelligence dimensions. EQ comprises of elements of both interpersonal intelligence and intrapersonal intelligence.

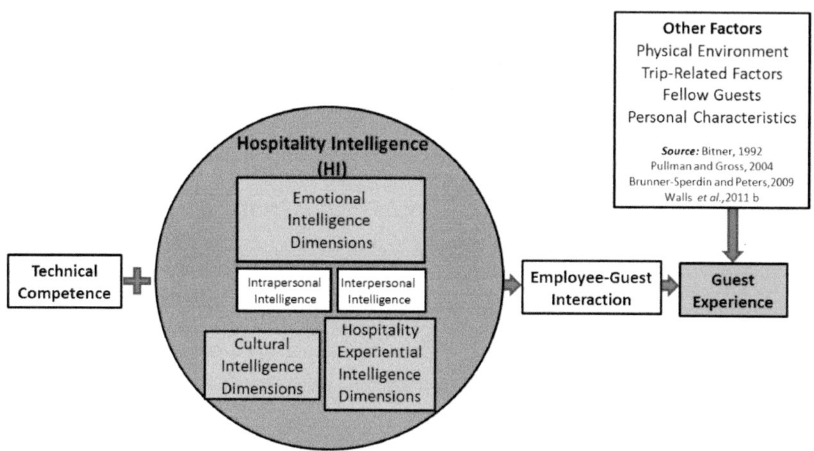

FIGURE 7.1 Conceptual framework of hospitality intelligence (HI).

The three proposed dimensions of the HI–EQ (including both interpersonal and intrapersonal intelligence), CQ and hospitality experiential intelligence dimensions are elaborated in Table 7.2. The various constructs which make up each of the HI dimensions have been drawn from existing competencies-related literature in the hospitality industry. Several authors have mentioned these competencies in their studies. Tas (1988) in his study on competencies for management trainees in the hotel industry discussed that the following competencies are important: understanding guest problems; sensitivity to guest issues; maintaining professional and ethical standards; effective communications; developing positive customer relations; and striving to achieve a positive working relationship. Chung-Herrera et al. (2003) have put forward "Self management" composed of flexibility, adaptability, and self-development as an important competency. But, there is a need to elaborate on these competencies and relate them to the critical factors for success for the hospitality industry (Jauhari, 2006). Thus, these competencies are detailed in Table 7.2 to bring out their meaning in context of the role they play in enabling frontline staff in engendering memorable guest experiences through successful guest interactions.

TABLE 7.2 Constructs and Dimensions of Hospitality Intelligence (HI).

Construct	Meaning	Author(s)
Emotional Intelligence Dimension		
Interpersonal intelligence		
Empathy	Ability to actively listen, understand and relate to feelings of the guest, interpret the unspoken, and appreciate and acknowledge diverse viewpoints.	Parsuraman et al., 1988; Tas, 1988; Brunner-Sperdin and Peters, 2009; Walls et al., 2011b
Effective communication	Clarity in expressing oneself in order to get the message across succinctly and effectively and keeping dyadic channels open to facilitate two-way flow of information.	Tas, 1988; Kay and Russette, 2000; Walls et al, 2011b
Influencing skills	Assertively persuading guests by connecting with them, unearthing their needs, and reducing their resistance to new ideas through well reasoned lines of argument.	Lenehan, 2000
Seeking and assimilating guest feedback	Ability to gather information about guest reactions and utilize this for improved future interactions and performance.	Lenehan, 2000
Anticipating guest needs	Ability to predict and respond to guest requirements and wants before they are overtly vocalized.	Carbone and Haeckel, 1994; Erdly and Kesterson-Townes, 2003; Walls et al, 2011b
Responsiveness–"Yes, we can" attitude	Attentiveness, willingness, and promptness in dealing with guest requests, complaints, and problems.	Parsuraman et al, 1988; Brunner-Sperdin and Peters, 2009; Walls et al, 2011b
Flexibility	Ability to accommodate, adapt to or respond to uncertainties arising due to the variability in guest needs and service situations.	Kay and Russette, 2000
Conflict resolution skills	Ability to negotiate differences in a calm, non-defensive manner and resolve matters by devising creative resolutions to problems.	Kay and Russette, 2000; Raybould and Wilkins, 2006; Stanton-Reynolds et al, 2009

TABLE 7.2 *(Continued)*

Construct	Meaning	Author(s)
Team playing	Ability to co-ordinate the efforts of team members and work effectively to advance the collective goal of the team through collaboration and co-operation for superior guest experience.	Tas, 1988; Chung-Herrera et al., 2003; Jauhari, 2006
Intrapersonal intelligence		
Emotional resilience	Ability to remain calm and confident in face of provocation and adversity.	Baum, 2006; Lashley, 2008
Optimism	Positive outlook and the ability to engender a feeling of bonhomie.	Lashley, 2008; Langhorn, 2004
Commitment	Passion for work which is driven by motivations other than money or status such as genuine hospitality toward guests.	Hemmington, 2007; Lashley, 2008
Self-awareness	Propensity for reflection and thoughtfulness and ability to detect, trace, and label one's emotions.	Goleman, 1998; Langhorn, 2004
Self-management	Ability to regulate the rational and emotional operations of the mind in a balanced way and think before acting.	Goleman, 1998; Chung-Herrera et al., 2003
Cultural intelligence dimension		
Cognitive cultural intelligence	Knowledge about diverse cultures and cultural practices and intercultural interaction principles and ability to transfer experience from one kind of cultural encounter to another.	Ang et al., 2006
Motivational cultural intelligence	Intrinsic desire to successfully engage in cross-cultural encounters despite cultural unfamiliarity and ambiguity.	Earley and Ang, 2003
Behavioral cultural intelligence	Ability to exhibit the appropriate verbal and nonverbal behaviors while engaging with guests from diverse cultural backgrounds.	Ang et al., 2007; Mkono, 2010
Cultural sensitivity and mindfulness	Ability to draw on one's cultural knowledge to understand different cultural contexts and the needs of guests in an intercultural milieu.	Ang et al., 2007; Ng et al., 2009; Van Dyne et al., 2010

TABLE 7.2 *(Continued)*

Construct	Meaning	Author(s)
Hospitality experiential intelligence dimension		
Centricity of guest experience	Ability to personalize and enhance guest experience by making it central to the consumption activity.	Erdly and Kesterson-Townes, 2003; Berry and Carbone, 2007; Lashley, 2008
Creativity and innovation	Ability to interpret the needs of guests in unusual and exciting ways that create "lots of little surprises," leading to memorable experiences.	Morgan, 2004; Hemmington, 2007; Walls et al, 2011b
Generosity	Genuinely welcoming attitude and benevolence.	Lashley, 2000; Hemmington, 2007; Lashley, 2008
Professional behavior	Warm, courteous behavior, respect for guest privacy, and understanding of nuances of host-guest relationship.	Tas, 1988; Lashley, 2008; Walls et al, 2011b

A customer-facing employee can perform his task better if he/she has certain competencies that fall in the domain of EQ. Interpersonal intelligence as a component of EQ plays a key role in creating a memorable experience. Similarly, intrapersonal competencies such as emotional resilience, optimism, commitment, self-awareness, and self-management also play a crucial role in managing human interface in the hospitality industry. This can catapult the frontline employees from being merely a "service provider" to becoming an "experience provider."

Within the hospitality industry, another dimension which influences the ability of the frontline employees to deliver on the guest experience spectrum is the degree of cultural empathy and cultural proximity they share with their guests. When the frontline hospitality employees have similar cultural backgrounds and have had participatory exposure and enjoyed experiences similar to those which they are required to deliver to their guests, they can better "empathize and identify with the expectations and requirements of their customers, based on a shared cultural and experiential profile" (Baum, 2006, p. 133). Thus, they are able to place themselves culturally and emotionally in the shoes of their guests and thereby deliver on a superior guest experience.

In customer interactions, the employee and the customer may have very different cultures and orientations. Therefore, employees need to be sensitive to the values and expectations of global consumers. There might even be difference of values and perceptions and in such situations, organizational culture, which defines expectations on certain kind of behaviors, takes precedence.

In Western cultures, there is a shorter social distance between guests and hospitality employees owing to cultural and experientially proximity. On the other hand, in context of less developed countries like India the social distance between hospitality employees and guest is greater. The Western-centric nature of hospitality industry operations in countries like India which are more remote from the everyday lives of the local people, create a gap in the cultural and experiential exposure of the locally recruited frontline employees and that of their guests. To deliver superior guest experience, hospitality organizations have to recognize and bridge this gap by developing the HI of their customer contact employees through exposure training and skills and knowledge development which will enhance their CQ and EQ.

However, the framework proposed does not suggest that only individual aspects influence the nature of customer experience. There are organizational factors as well which have an overlap with other service mix elements such as processes, overall service design, policies, leadership, organizational culture, and employee satisfaction which impact service experience and in turn customer satisfaction. Further, customer satisfaction is not solely influenced by the service experience. Other organizational factors such as brand and physical evidence which is also referred to as "servicescape" (Bitner, 1992) do have an impact on customer satisfaction. However, with everything else in place, a poor interpersonal interface can actually ruin the customer experience. Hence, at the core of delivering a superior customer experience is a "people component." Thus, HI, which encompasses the competencies of frontline employees in terms of developing an emotional and cultural connect with a customer, which can have a huge impact on the nature of customer experience.

7.10 CONCLUSIONS

At the heart of each customer experience is a personal interface which is the front face of a brand or an organization. In face of increasing levels of competition and growing complexity in the global hospitality sector, the future survival and growth of hospitality organizations depends upon their ability to proactively and effectively elevate customer–employee interface from a simple interaction to a positive memorable experience. All other things being equal, the competencies of employees involved in customer interface become extremely important in ensuring effective customer engagement and cocreating memorable experiences. This paper puts forward a framework of competencies required by frontline hospitality employees who are involved in the guest/customer interface to transform them from being merely executors of service delivery mechanisms into facilitators of experience architecture.

This study proposes a new construct of "Hospitality Intelligence" (HI) and also a conceptual framework for the same. The conceptual framework and the HI construct proposed are largely based on secondary research done through a review of literature. Literature reviewed showed that there are number of factors such as physical environment, human interaction (of guests with employees as well as fellow guests), the personal characteristics of the guests themselves, and other trip-related factors which influence guest experience. With regards to guest–employee interaction, especially in the context of a frontline scenario, competencies of the frontline staff play an extremely important role. However, gaps exist in the current literature in terms of elaborating in greater detail which specific competencies are required to make frontline staff more effective in their job roles and could help in engendering a superior customer experience. This paper attempts to address this gap by proposing the construct of HI.

The paper clarifies the three main dimensions of HI–EQ (comprising interpersonal intelligence and intrapersonal intelligence), CQ, and hospitality experiential intelligence dimensions and elaborates on the sub-constructs which constitute these dimensions. The various sub-constructs which make up each of the HI dimensions have been drawn from existing competencies-related literature in the hospitality industry. The study suggests that the HI construct comprising EQ, CQ, and experiential intelligence when coupled with technical competence can lead to a more positive guest interaction by the frontline staff and hence contribute to a memorable guest experience. Though other factors do contribute to a larger guest experience, HI of the frontline staff would be a key enabler for a satisfying guest–employee interaction.

As with any exploratory study, the current study also has its limitations. The study is still at a very nascent stage and simply puts forward a preliminary conceptual framework and HI construct. The paper does not include empirical testing of the proposed conceptual framework. Future work could test the relationships put forward in the conceptual framework. The dimensions of intra- and interpersonal intelligence, CQ and hospitality experiential intelligence could be further explored for the relevance and priority in the context of hospitality industry. The inter-relationship and overlap, if any, between the various sub-constructs of HI could be examined. New evaluation tools could be developed or existing tools could be used to measure the HI of frontline employees and its impact on guest experience. However, while devising a new evaluation instrument, issues related to its validity and reliability as well complexity should be borne in mind.

7.11 IMPLICATIONS OF THE STUDY

The proposed framework of HI has certain implications for the practitioners. Intrapersonal and interpersonal intelligence which are components of EQ would be key factors contributing to personal effectiveness of an employee and a memorable engagement. The training initiated by the hospitality firms should ensure pedagogy that builds up interpersonal competencies. Also, the educational institutions should work toward building in elements such as team work, effective communication, and conflict management in the educational training. Jauhari (2006, p. 129) remarks that, "The role of academic institutions is inevitable in shaping competencies of future managers. The curriculum of the program determines the nature of the competence in industry." Experiential learning could also play an important role in developing these competencies.

The intrapersonal characteristics such as optimism and positive thinking, emotional resilience commitment, tolerance, self-awareness, and self-management would go a long way in building up self-confidence. In the initial years, they will help sustain the frontline staff through the harsh conditions in the hospitality industry, challenging situations and long work hours. Self-awareness and control would enable them to handle stressful situations effectively. Evaluation instruments which could assess the frontline recruits on these parameters could be developed to determine the level of preparedness of hospitality graduates.

Similarly, CQ would also play a vital role in delivering service offerings which match the consumer's exponentially rising expectation bar as would the hospitality-experience related competencies. Cross-cultural training could help build up cultural sensitivity toward the guests as well as at the peer level. The hotels could also initiate customer profiling. There could be sessions on values, rituals, and practices across various cultures across the globe. This would sensitize the work force on the food habits, interpersonal relationships, power distance, gender relationships, and other practices and service expectations across various cultures. This would help hospitality organizations to provide a better experience to guests who hail from different cultures.

Educational institutions should align themselves with the demands of the industry. Modules on cross-cultural communication could become an integral part of the curriculum. Internship exposure across various cultures would enable the future employees to have diverse cultural experiences which would sharpen their CQ.

The other implication is for hiring the right talent in the hospitality industry. Employers could test the potential employees for the various elements that make up HI. There could be recruitment tests which could be created which test a person's level of HI. This could be an effective tool which could serve as the basis of developing appropriate training interventions for the frontline hospitality staff.

Inculcating elements of HI would go a long way in having competent frontline staff who will become enablers of memorable guest experiences in the context of their interactions. Their superior ability to manage themselves and proactively understand the guest aspirations would be instrumental in building meaningful guest interactions and memorable experiences.

KEYWORDS

- **hospitality management**
- **competences**
- **employees' attitudes**
- **interpersonal skills**
- **hospitality intelligence**

- **frontline employees**
- **experience economy**
- **emotional intelligence**
- **cultural intelligence**

REFERENCES

Ang, S.; Van Dyne, L.; Koh, C.; Ng, Y.; Templer, K.; Tay, C.; Chandrasekar, N. A. Cultural Intelligence: Its Measurement and Effects on Cultural Judgment and Decision-Making Cultural Adaptation and Task Performance. *Manag. Organ. Rev.* **2007,** *3*(3), 335–371.

Aydin, M. D.; Leblebici, N. D.; Arslan, M.; Kilic, M.; Oktem, M. K. The Impact of IQ and EQ on Preeminent Achievement in Organizations: Implications for the Hiring Decisions of HRM Specialists. *Int. J. Hum. Resour. Manag.* **2005,** *16*(5), 701–719.

Baum, T. Reflections on the Nature of Skills in the Experience Economy: Challenging Traditional Skills Models in Hospitality. *J. Hosp. Tour. Manag.* **2005,** *13*(2), 124–135.

Berry, L. L.; Carbone, L. Build Loyalty through Experience Management. *Qual. Prog.* **2007,** *40*(9), 26–32.

Berry, L. L.; Carbone, L. P.; Haeckel, S. H. Managing the Total Customer Experience. *MIT Sloan Manag. Rev.* **2002,** *43*(3), 85–89.

Binkhorst, E.; Den Dekker, T. Agenda for CoCreation Tourism Experience Research. *J. Hosp. Mark. Manag.* **2009,** *18*(2/3), 311–327.

Bitner, M. Servicescapes: The Impact of Physical Surroundings on Customers and Employees. *J. Mark.* **1992,** *56*(2), 57–71.

Boyatzis, R. *The Competent Manager: A Model for Effective Performance;* John Wiley & Sons: New York, **1982**.

Boyatzis, R. E.; Stubbs, E. C.; Taylor, S. N. Learning Cognitive and Emotional Intelligence Competencies through Graduate Management Education. *Acad. Manag. J. on Learn. Educ.* **2002,** *1*(2), 150–162.

Brunner-Sperdin, A.; Peters, M. What Influences Guests' Emotions? The Case of High-Quality Hotels. *Int. J. Tour. Res.* **2009,** *11*, 171–183.

Carbone, L.; Haeckel, S. Engineering Customer Experience. *Mark. Manag.* **1994,** *3*(3), 8–19.

Chathoth, P.; Altinay, L.; Harrington, R.; Okumus, F.; Chan, E. Co-Production Versus Cocreation: A Process Based Continuum in the Hotel Service Context. *Int. J. Hosp. Manag.* **2013,** (32), 11–20.

Cherniss, C. *Emotional Intelligence: What It Is and Why It Matters?* Paper Presented at the Annual Meeting of the Society for Industrial and Organizational Psychology, New Orleans, LA, April 15, **2000**.

Chung, K. Y. Hotel Management Curriculum Reform Based on Required Competencies of Hotel Employees and Career Success in the Hotel Industry. *Tour. Manag.* **2000,** *21*(5), 473–487.

Chung-Herrera, B. G.; Enz, C. A.; Lankau, M. J. Grooming Future Hospitality Leaders: A Competencies Model. *Cornell Hotel Restaur. Adm. Q.* **2003,** *44*(3), 17–25.

Earley, P. C.; Ang, S. *Cultural Intelligence: Individual Interactions Across Cultures;* Stanford University Press: Palo Alto, CA, **2003**.

Earley, P. C.; Mosakowski, E. Cultural Intelligence. *Harv. Bus. Rev.* **2004,** *82*, 139–153.

Erdly, M.; Kesterson-Townes, L. Experience Rules: A Scenario for the Hospitality and Leisure Industry. *Strateg. Leadersh.* **2003,** *31*(3), 12–18.

Earley, P. C.; Ang, S.; Tan, J. S. *CQ: Developing Cultural Intelligence at Work;* Stanford University Press: Palo Alto, CA, **2006**.

Fitch, K. *Speaking Relationally: Culture, Communication and Interpersonal Connection;* Guilford Press: New York, **1998**.

Fitzgerald, H. *Cross-Cultural Communication for the Tourism and Hospitality Industry;* Hospitality Press: Melbourne, **1998**.

Flavell, J. H. Metacognition and Cognitive Monitoring: A New Area of Cognitive Inquiry. *Am. Psychol.* **1979,** *34*, 906–911.

Gardner, H. *Frames of Mind: The Theory of Multiple Intelligences;* Harper Collins: New York, **1982**.

Gardner, H. *Extraordinary Minds: Portraits of Exceptional Individuals and an Examination of our Extraordinariness;* Basic Books: New York, **1997**.

Goleman, D. P. *Emotional Intelligence: Why It Can Matter More Than IQ for Character, Health and Lifelong Achievement;* Bantam Books: New York, **1995**.

Goleman, D. What Makes a Leader? *Harv. Bus. Rev.* **1998,** *76*(6), 93–102.

Harris, R.; Harris, K.; Baron, S. Theatrical Service Experiences. *Int. J. Serv. Ind. Manag.* **2003,** *14*, 184–199.

Hemmington, N. From Service to Experience: Understanding and Defining the Hospitality Business. *Serv. Ind. J.*, **2007,** *27*(6), 747–755.

Hirschman, E. C.; Holbrook, M. B. Hedonic Consumption: Emerging Concepts, Methods and Propositions. *J. Mark.*, **1982,** *48*(3), 92–101.

Jauhari, V. Competencies for a Career in the Hospitality Industry: An Indian Perspective. *Int. J. Contemp. Hosp. Manag.* **2006,** *18*(2), 123–134.

Kandampully, J.; Suhartanto, D. Customer Loyalty in the Hotel Industry: The Role of the Customer Satisfaction and Image. *Int. J. Contemp. Hosp. Manag.* **2000,** *12*(6), 346–351.

Kanfer, R.; Heggestad, E. Motivational Traits and Skills: A Person-Centered Approach to Work Motivation. In *Research in Organizational Behavior;* Cummings, L.L., Staw, B.M., Eds.; Edward Elgar Publishing: Cheltenham, **1997**; pp 1–57.

Kay, C.; Russette, J. Hospitality-Management Competencies: Identifying Manager's Essential Skills. *Cornell Hotel Restaur. Adm. Q.* **2000,** *41*(2), 52–63.

Kihlstrom, J. F.; Cantor, N. Social Intelligence. In *Handbook of Intelligence;* Sternberg, R.J. Ed.; Cambridge University Press: Cambridge, **2000**; pp 59–379.

Knutson, B.; Beck, J.; Him, S.; Cha, J. Identifying the Dimensions of the Experience Construct. *J. Hosp. Leis. Mark.* **2006,** *15*(3), 31–47.

Kunnanatt, J. T. Emotional Intelligence: The New Science of Interpersonal Effectiveness. *Hum. Resour. Dev. Q.* **2004,** *5*(4), 489–495.

Kusluvan, S.; Kusluvan, Z.; Ilhan, I.; Buyruk, L. The Human Dimension: A Review of Human Resources Management Issues in the Tourism and Hospitality Industry. *Cornell Hosp. Q.*, **2010,** *51*(2), 171–214.

Langhorn, S. How Emotional Intelligence Can Improve Management Performance. *Int. J. Contemp. Hosp. Manag.* **2004,** *16*(4), 220–230.

Lashley, C. Marketing Hospitality and Tourism Experiences. In *Handbook of Hospitality Marketing Management;* Oh, H., Pizam, A. Eds.; Butterworth-Heinemann: Oxford, **2008**; pp 3–31.

Lenehan, T. A Study of Management Practices and Competences within Effective Organizations in the Irish Tourism Industry. *Serv. Ind. J.* **2000,** *20*(3), 19–42.

Lusch, R. F.; Vargo, S. L.; O'Brien, M. Competing Through Service: Insights from Service-Dominant Logic. *J. of Retail.* **2007,** *83*(1), 5–18.

Lynch, P. Sociological Impressionism in a Hospitality Context. *Ann. Tour. Res.* **2005,** *32*, 527–548.

McClelland, D. C. Testing for Competence Rather than for Intelligence. *Am. Psychol.* **1973,** *28*(1), 1–14.

Miao, L. Guilty Pleasure or Pleasurable Guilt? Affective Experience of Impulse Buying in Hedonic Driven Consumption. *J. Hosp. Tour. Res.* **2011,** *35*(1), 79–101.

Mkono, M. In Defense of Hospitality Careers: Perspectives of Zimbabwean Hotel Managers. *Int. J. Contemp. Hosp. Manag.* **2010,** *22*(6), 858–870.

Morand, D. The Emotional Intelligence of Managers: Assessing the Construct Validity of a Nonverbal Measure of "people skills". *J. Bus. Psychol.* **2001,** *16*(1), 21–33.

Morgan, M. From Production Line to Drama School: Higher Education for the Future of Tourism. *Int. J. Contemp. Hosp. Manag.* **2004,** *16*(2), 91–99.

Morgan, M. Making Space for Experiences. *J. Retail Leis. Prop.* **2006,** *5*(4), 305–313.

Morgan, M.; Elbe, J.; de Esteban Curiel, J. Has the Experience Economy Arrived? The Views of Destination Managers in Three Visitor-Dependent Areas. *Int. J. Tour. Res.* **2009,** *11*, 201–216.

Morgan, M.; Watson, P.; Hemmington, N. Drama in the Dining Rooms: Theatrical Perspectives on the Foodservice Encounter. *J. Foodserv.* **2008,** *19*(2), 111–118.

Ng, K.; Dyne, L.; Ang, S. From Experience to Experiential Learning: Cultural Intelligence as a Learning Capability for Global Leader Development. *Acad. Manag. Learn. Educ.* **2009,** *12*(4), 45–62.

Oh, H.; Fiore, A.; Jeoung, M. Measuring Experience Economy Concepts: Tourism Applications. *J. Travel Res.* **2007,** *46*, 119–132.

Otto, J. E.; Ritchie, B. The Service Experience in Tourism. *Tour. Manag.,* **1996,** *17*(3), 165–174.

Parasuraman, A.; Zeithaml, V. A.; Berry, L. SERVQUAL: A Multiple-Item Scale for Measuring Customer Perceptions of Service Quality *J. Retail.* **1988,** 12–40.

Pine, B.; Gilmore, J. Welcome to the Experience Economy. *Harvard Bus. Rev.*, July–August, **1998,** pp 97–105.

Pine, B.; Gilmore J. *The Experience Economy;* Harvard Business School Press: Boston, **1999**.

Prahalad, C. K.; Ramaswamy, V. *The Future of Competition: Cocreating Unique Value with Customers;* Harvard Business School Press: Boston, **2004**.

Pullman, M. E.; Gross, M.A. Ability of Experience Design Elements to Elicit Emotions and Loyalty Behaviors. *Decis. Sci.* **2004,** *35*, 551–578.

Raybould, M.; Wilkins, H. Generic Skills for Hospitality Management: A Comparative Study of Management Expectations and Student Perceptions. *J. Hosp. Tour. Manag.* **2006,** *3*(2), 177–188.

Reuland, R.; Coudrey, J.; Fagel, A. Research in the Field of Hospitality. *Int. J. Hosp. Manag.* **1985,** *4*(4), 141–146.

Salovey, P.; Mayer, J. Emotional Intelligence. *Imagin., Cogn. Personal.* **1990,** *9*(3), 185–211.

Schmitt, B. *Experiential Marketing: How to Get Customers to Sense, Feel, Think, Act, and Relate to your Company and Brands;* The Free Press: New York, **1999**.

Scott, N.; Laws, E.; Boksberger, P. The Marketing of Hospitality and Leisure Experiences. *J. Hosp. Mark. Manag.* **2009,** *18*(2–3), 99–110.

Scott-Halsell, S. A.; Blum, S. C.; Huffman, L. A Study of Emotional Intelligence Levels in Hospitality Industry Professionals. *J. Hum. Resour. Hosp. Tour.* **2008,** *7*(2), 135–152.

Shaw, G.; Bailey, A.; Williams, A. Aspects of Service-Dominant Logic and Its Implications for Tourism Management: Examples from the Hotel Industry. *Tour. Manag.* **2011,** *32*(2), 207–214.

Silberman, M. Developing Interpersonal Intelligence in the Workplace. *Ind. Commer. Train.* **2001,** *33*(7), 266–270.

Staton-Reynolds, J. A.; Ryan, B.; Scott-Halsell, S. A. A Comparison of Skills Considered Important for Success as an Entry Level Manager in the Hospitality Industry Vs the Skills Recent Graduates Possess **2009**, International CHRIE Conference-Refereed Track. http://scholarworks.umass.edu/refereed/Sessions/Wednesday/20 (accessed 17 July 2012).

Sternberg, R. J. A Framework for Understanding Conceptions of Intelligence. In *What is Intelligence? Contemporary Viewpoints on Its Nature and Definition;* Sternberg, R.J., Detterman, D.K. Eds.; Ablex: Norwood, **1986**; pp 3–15.

Sternberg, R. J. *Successful Intelligence;* Simon & Schuster: New York, **1996**.

Tas, R. F. Teaching Future Managers. *Cornell Hotel Restaur. Adm. Q.,* **1988,** *29*, 41–43.

Thorndike, E. L. Intelligence and Its Uses. *Harper's Mag.* **1920,** *140*, 227–235.

Van Boven, L.; Gilovich, T. To Do or to Have? That is the Question. *J. Personal. Soc. Psychol.* **2003,** *85*, 1193–1202.

Van Dyne, L.; Ang, S.; Livermore, D. Cultural Intelligence: A Pathway for Leading in a Rapidly Globalizing World. In *Leadership across Differences*; McFeeters, B., Booysen, L. Eds.; Pfeiffer: San Francisco, CA; pp 131–138.

Walls, A.; Okumus, F.; Wang, Y.; Joon-Wuk Kwun, D. An Epistemological View of Consumer Experiences. *Int. J. Hosp. Manag.* **2011a,** *30*, 10–21.

Walls, A.; Okumus, F.; Wang, Y.; Joon-Wuk Kwun, D. Understanding the Consumer Experience: An Exploratory Study of Luxury Hotels. *J. Hosp. Mark. Manag.* **2011b,** *20*(2), 166–197.

Wechsler, D. *The Measurement and Appraisal of Adult Intelligence* 4th edn; The Williams & Wilkins Company: Baltimore, MD, **1958**.

Williams, A. Tourism and Hospitality Marketing: Fantasy, Feeling, and Fun. *Int. J. Contemp. Hosp. Manag.* **2006,** *18*(6), 482–495.

Yoo, M.; Lee, S.; Bai, B. Hospitality Marketing Research from 2000 to 2009: Topics, Methods, and Trends. *Int. J. Contemp. Hosp. Manag.* **2011,** *23*(4), 517–532.

Further Reading

Ryu, K.; Han, H.; Jang, S. Relationships among Hedonic and Utilitarian Values, Satisfaction, and Behavioral Intentions in the Fast-Casual Restaurant Industry. *Int. J. Contemp. Hosp. Manag.* **2010,** *22*(3), 416–432.

PART IV
Quality Aspects

CHAPTER 8

EXPLORATION OF SERVICE QUALITY FACTORS IN THE RESTAURANT INDUSTRY: A STUDY OF SELECTED RESTAURANTS IN THE NEW DELHI REGION

GAURAV TRIPATHI[1*] and KARTIK DAVE[2]

[1]*BIMTECH, Greater Noida, India*

[2]*School of Business, Public Policy and Social Entrepreneurship, Ambedkar University Delhi, India*

[*]*Corresponding author. E-mail: tripathi_gaurav@hotmail.com*

CONTENTS

Originally published as Tripathi, G. and Dave, K. (2014) "Exploration of Service Quality Factors in Restaurant Industry: A Study of Selected Restaurants in New Delhi Region," in Journal of Services Research, 14:1, pp. 9-26. Published by the Institute for International Management and Technology. Reprinted with permission.

ABSTRACT

The purpose of this paper is to explore the underlying key dimensions of service quality in restaurants. Service quality items pertaining to the restaurants are extracted from extensive review of literature including the consideration of unique factors from Indian cultural orientation. The study was conducted in New Delhi and its adjoining cities wherein the restaurant customers were surveyed using a structured questionnaire. Factor analysis was used to bring out the underlying dimensions of service quality. The dimensions extracted are cultural orientation, aesthetics, ambient settings, empathy, privacy and entertainment, first Impression, reliability, and responsiveness. The Indian market is contextually different in contrast to various other countries where such research studies have been widely carried out. Hence, this study provides departure from previous studies and presents greater insight into the service quality factors as perceived by the consumers in India. This will help the restaurant managers to ponder on the factors, which are more pertinent for the Indian markets. Importantly, this study attempts to test the variables pertaining to cultural orientation from the Indian context as dimensions of the restaurant service quality and hence attempts to create a more suitable scale for the Indian market.

8.1 INTRODUCTION

The concept of service quality has emerged as the most important concept pertaining to the marketing of services in the last three decades. The original service quality model called SERVQUAL (Parasuraman et al., 1988) did not take into consideration the restaurant industry and hence DINESERV was conceptualized by Stevens et al. (1995). However, because of contextual and cultural issues various service quality models including SERVQUAL have been criticized on their universal applicability, as market conditions and the consumer perception change with the passage of time. Importantly, because the service quality is perceptual in nature, it is likely to vary due to the type of services and also due to cultural differences. Cultural differences hold importance, as they are likely to influence the dining orientations. Additionally, DINESERV has also been exposed to criticism due to its limited applicability in various contexts. DINESERV constitutes the same five dimensions as that of SERVQUAL to include restaurant services. Absence of restaurant services is one of its shortcomings of SERVQUAL, which although based on four service industries, does not include the restaurant services. Many studies have used DINESERV studies on restaurant service quality. These include the works of Kim et al. (2003, 2009), Markovic et al. (2010), Vanniarajan (2009), and many others. These studies have come up with new and different factors, as against the DINESERV factors, suggesting the limitation of the DINESERV model.

The present study attempts to refine the work of Vanniarajan (2009) which so far has been the only study in the Indian context focusing on service quality measurement in restaurants. There exists a dearth of scholarly literature in the Indian context focusing on service quality in restaurants. The present study provides a fresh insight into the service quality perceptions toward eating out in restaurants in Indian context.

India is one of the fastest growing economies in the world, which has shown growth in the services sector rather than manufacturing. The growth of restaurant industry in India is largely due to the presence of variety of cuisines. The liberalization policy of 1991 has opened India to the western cultures, which has resulted in increase of customers who look forward to eating out. People in India are craving for foreign delicacies, which is largely attributed to the growing tourism industry. An example of changing lifestyles can be seen among the youth who have made the fast-food restaurants popular. The modern Indians are giving higher priority to eating out. Service quality is what 24% of the customers look for; while making a decision for eating out. The other factors responsible for eating out include ambience, convenience, enjoyment, social gathering, and status (Anand, 2011).

The growth in the urban areas for the restaurant industry is also attributed to affluence, deskbound jobs, dual incomes, independence among youth, and paucity of time. The eating out culture in India has transformed to a more global style in the metro cities with consumers ready to pay more for ambience, convenience, and experience. In India, socializing with family and friends is strong way to stay connected with its culture. The quick service restaurants (QSRs) are popular among youth, which are understood as popular joint to spend time with friends while the full service restaurants (FSRs) are known for family gatherings. The changing demographics have strongly influenced the eating habits of the consumers especially in the metro cities and the lifestyle factors are responsible for this change, which are phenomenal (Anand, 2011). Moreover, the restaurants in metros are delivering services, which are comparable to the services delivered by restaurants at luxury hotels (Berry, 2008). New types of restaurants, theme-based or otherwise, display high quality of services, making them popular brands. This phenomenon though popular in metros, is gradually diffusing into relatively smaller cities with high levels of supply chain integration (Bhardwaj, 2011).

It is worth noting that India is ranked third globally in terms of growth forecast for next 5 years. This is even higher than most developed economies for both FSR and QSR. Moreover, for the last 5 years, India ranks third in terms of the growth rate, which is even higher than the developed economies for the combined segments of QSRs and FSRs. In addition, the Indian food service industry has shown a compound annual growth rate (CAGR) of 7.9% based on the value of food service for 5 years ending in 2010 (Euromonitor, 2011). Interestingly, the growth is highest in the leisure and retail segment, which reflects the consumers' readiness to pay more for high quality experiences involving comfort and leisure.

On the other side of growth story, the forecast from 2010 to 2015 in CAGR terms is 4% for the food service value (Euromonitor, 2011). It appears that the industry is maturing. However, it is a possibility that consumers might find some latent issues with the quality of service, etc., this provides a strong motivation to study these latent factors, which are significant determinants of service quality.

This research paper starts with the review of previous studies on service quality, which focuses on restaurant industry and then defines the existing gap in the literature. It is followed by exploring the service quality factors using data collected through a structured questionnaire. Further the latent factors pertaining to service quality in Indian restaurants are extracted which are tested for their reliability and validity. This is followed by discussion of the analysis and managerial implications.

8.2 REVIEW OF LITERATURE

Quality is defined as "fitness for use" (Stephens and Juran, 2005). Research on service quality has grown in the last three decades. Although there have been various researches based on service quality, and the SERVQUAL model is most referred in the literature, it is worth noting that most of the researches that cite SERVQUAL have criticized the model for its lack of applicability on all kinds of services. Many scholars have improved the

SERVQUAL model to fit to the needs of various service industries individually. Technically, most of these researches found the factor structure of their models different from that of SERVQUAL. The model was criticized by the original authors themselves. The model, which was developed by Parasuraman et al. (1988) collected data based on four types of service companies, and attempted to generalize the model for all the service industries, hence the name SERVQUAL. They attempted to retain the common scale items for most of the service industries. However, they might also have deleted the items, which were relevant to one or few firms thereby, ensuring the generalizability and applicability of the model to a wide range of service industries.

Various studies have attempted to measure service quality by using modified versions of SERVQUAL or DINESERV, or have attempted to pool the scale items from the literature to develop new scales. The divergence in the models proposed by various studies encourages an enquiry into the factors comprising service quality in restaurants in different cultural contexts.

Markovic et al. (2010) pointed out that evaluation of service quality in restaurant industry is difficult because both the process and delivery are at the focal point of customer's evaluation of service quality. Although many researchers have used SERVQUAL to assess the service quality in restaurants (Andaleeb and Conway 2006, Bojanic and Rosen 1994; Lee and Hing 1995; Yuksel and Yuksel 2002); yet, the development of DINESERV (Stevens et al., 1995) is a pivotal contribution. Because of the shortcomings of SERVQUAL Stevens et al. (1995) developed a 29-item scale and named it DINESERV. It was based on SERVQUAL's five factors but focused only on the restaurants.

Although the SERVQUAL studies have been extended to various industry settings, the work of Stevens et al. (1995) in shaping DINESERV is noteworthy. DINESERV is a service quality item-scale-based model focusing specifically on the restaurants. Post conceptualization of DINESERV in 1995, most of the authors have focused on either DINESERV or SERVQUAL as the base model for their study. Various studies which have used DINSERV includes the work of Kim et al. (2003, 2009), Markovic et al. (2010), and Vanniarajan (2009). The aforementioned models have been extended on the basis of literature review or focus group discussions to suit to specific cultural contexts. The models developed have been further utilized to test their effect on customer satisfaction and behavioral intentions. Various studies pertaining to this are discussed in the following paragraphs.

Becker et al. (1999) compared the restaurants of Hong Kong and USA by focusing on wait-staff behavior in which the scale-items were culled from focus groups. The authors derived the factors viz., professionalism, sanitation, cordiality, accommodation, knowledge, and entertainment. The most interesting feature of this research was that this research attempted to include the importance of cultural differences. Kivela et al. (2000) conducted a research on 15 theme restaurants in Hong Kong and came up with five factors viz., ambience excellence, first and last impressions, food excellence and feeling comfortable to eat there, reservations and parking, and service excellence. Kim and Kim (2004) discussed brand equity scale, which involved perceived quality as one of its factors. Lee et al. (2004) discussed competitive service quality improvement (CSQI), which was based on the SERVQUAL model. Hu (2005),while researching on senior citizens in USA came up with entertainment, front of the house(FOH) service and food, nutrition, and perceived value as the service quality factors. Ryu (2005) in the context of upscale restaurant came up with a new model called DINESCAPE, which composed of facility aesthetics, ambience, lightening, service product, layout, and social factors. Weiss (2005) while testing the intention to return for the theme restaurants used atmosphere, food, service, and experience and tested the model based on both importance and expectations. Andaleeb and Conway (2006) extracted responsiveness, food quality/reliability, physical design, and price as the factors of service quality. However, the authors suggested the results cannot be generalized. Kim et al. (2006) extracted factors similar to the service quality namely, relationship benefits, communication, price fairness, customer orientation, physical environment, food quality, as the factors which influenced relationship quality.

Qin and Prybutok (2009) discussed the same five factors of SERVQUAL with an exception of recovery while responsiveness and reliability loaded on the same factor. Markovic et al. (2010) discussed service quality in Croatian restaurants and came up with separate factors for perception and expectations. Assurance, basic demands, cleanliness and appearance of facilities and staff, individual attention, responsiveness, reliability and satisfaction, and loyalty constituted the expectation scale while the factors viz., overall dining experience and restaurant ambience formed the perception scale. More recently, Harrington et al. (2011) extracted six factors viz., promotion, price/value, quality expectations, settings, dietary, and variety/innovate.

The universal applicability of SERVQUAL has been under question (Gaur and Agrawal, 2006). DINESERV scale model (Stevens et al., 1995) is likely to have similar limitations as it is based on SERVQUAL. It comprises 29 scale-items constituting the five dimensions, which are similar to SERVQUAL's five dimensions. The individual scale items are however different. Interestingly, Stevens et al. (1995) themselves have discussed issues in the five dimensions of DINESERV model. Since these concepts are borrowed, a strong level of reliability and validity assessment for such scale models is advised (Oh and Parks, 1997). The aforementioned studies discussed in the previous paragraphs suggest the contextual limitations with differing dimensions.

In the Indian context, Vanniarajan (2009) came up with six dimensions viz., communication, empathy, food quality, price fairness, relationship benefits, and tangibles. However, Vanniarajan (2009) found problems with the generalizability of the results due to sampling issues, and since the six factors extracted differ from DINESERV, it was concluded that DINESERV also lacks universality. It was also felt that since the survey was carried out in non-metropolitan and non-cosmopolitan city of southern India its application cannot be justified for rest of the country. An earlier study by Jain and Gupta (2004) which used SERVPERF and SERVQUAL models on QSRs in Delhi did not test the dimensionality issue. Therefore, there exists a strong gap in the literature toward the factors structure of service quality of restaurants in the Indian context.

8.3 METHODS

8.3.1 SAMPLE DESIGN

Data was collected using questionnaire from various restaurant customers using the mall-intercept method in the major malls and market places of Delhi-NCR, as most of the popular restaurants in the New Delhi-NCR are located in various malls. 500 questionnaires were distributed out of which 369 were found usable in terms of completeness of the relevant data. Data was collected during 2 months from Feb 2013 to Mar 2013. In mall-intercept survey methods the respondents are contacted just after the service experience/encounter has taken place. Mall-intercept method is useful for collecting data in short duration and it helps in screening the potential respondents (O'Cass and Grace, 2008). The paucity of time and limitation of funds also supported the choice of mall-intercept method (Prasad and Aryasri, 2011).

8.3.2 INSTRUMENT AND SCALE ITEMS

The first section of the questionnaire comprised questions on the demographic profile of the respondents while the second part constituted the scale items. The questions on demographic profile included age, gender, income, occupation, religion, dietary orientation, core cultural food, etc. Respondents were from different ethnic food backgrounds including, Punjabi, Rajasthani, Mughlai, Gujarati, South Indian, Bengali, Bihar, Awadhi, Konkani, Kashmiri, etc. Although about half of the restaurants had their ethnic food background as Punjabi/North Indian their (respondents) favorite restaurants included cuisines from different cultural backgrounds. Moreover, the geographic region under study has numerous restaurants from different ethnic backgrounds. This strongly suggests that the population under study is cosmopolitan in terms of people, cultural aspects and ideas, a fact supported by the metropolitan status of the region and also due to the national capital which allows migration from various states making the region multi-ethnic.

Based on the aforementioned review of literature and unstructured interviews with ten restaurant consumers at different locations an initial pool of 54 items was generated. The scale items mainly consisted of scale items from the original DINESERV model created by Stevens et al. (1995). Other key sources of scale items include the works of Ryu (2005), Hu (2005), Harrington et al. (2011), and Weiss (2005). The remaining items, which were based on the interviews with the consumers, mainly related with culture including dietary and religious orientations. Since, this study is at an exploratory level wherein the focus is on developing a reliable and valid multiitem scale for measuring service quality in restaurants both the restaurant types viz. fast food restaurant and fine dining restaurants, are included for this study. In addition, no precise categorizing system exists in the Indian context, which is unlike the Michelin guide rating in Europe. Therefore, both quick service (fast food) and full service (fine dine) restaurants are used as broad categories. The scale items were scored on a 7-point Likert scale. A minimum response of 1 meant "Strongly disagree" and a maximum response of 7 meant "Strongly agree." The scale items were validated with the help of three academicians and three consultants in the field of hospitality research.

8.3.2.1 ANALYSIS AND DISCUSSION

The 54 scale-items were subjected to exploratory factor analysis. Principle component analysis with Varimax rotation was used. After six rounds of refinement, the number of remaining items was 22, which were grouped under seven factors. These seven factors are Cultural orientation, Tangibles 1 (Aesthetics), Ambient Settings, Empathy, Privacy and Entertainment, Tangibles 2 (First Impression), Reliability, and Responsiveness. A communality score of minimum 0.50 was used to retain any item. Apart from this a minimum score of 0.5 for factor loadings was used as the criteria for retention (Hair Jr. et al., 2006). Only those scale items which conformed to both these criteria were retained, and all items with significant cross-loading were excluded. After the final round of refinement total explained variance was 64% and The Kaiser-Meyer-Olkin (KMO) measure of sampling adequacy was 0.843. These values were higher than the benchmark values given by Hair Jr. et al. (2006). Cronbach α values were used to test the reliability of each factor which was above 0.6 and hence was acceptable (Hair Jr. et al., 2006). All the reliability scores for each factor with significant item loadings are listed in Table 8.1.

TABLE 8.1 Rotated Component Matrix with Reliability Scores.

Scale items	Factor loading	Factors	Reliability coefficient (α)
The restaurant premises and its facilities are maintained in a way which respects your religious values	0.795	Culture	0.788
This restaurant serves food that meets your religious dietary prohibitions (e.g., pure vegetarian, nonusage of onion and garlic, Jain food, Vaishnav food, Halal meat, etc.)	0.757		
This restaurant respects your culture while serving the food	0.753		
This restaurant respects your religious beliefs and values	0.720		

TABLE 8.1 *(Continued)*

Scale items	Factor loading	Factors	Reliability coefficient (α)
The restaurant interiors are visually attractive and makes you feel comfortable	0.790	Tangibles: aesthetics	0.677
The restaurant has comfortable seats in the dining room	0.673		
Table setting is proper and resembles high quality	0.634		
Lighting arrangement in the restaurant creates a comfortable atmosphere	0.813	Ambient settings	0.7
The temperature setting in the restaurant is appropriate	0.666		
The color settings in the restaurant makes you feel calm	0.628		
The restaurant anticipates your individual needs and wants	0.806	Empathy	0.722
The restaurant makes you feel as a special customer	0.709		
The restaurant has employees who are sensitive to your individual needs and wants, rather than always relying on policies and procedures	0.708		
The restaurant has appropriate noise levels to allow easy conversation	0.781	Privacy and entertainment	0.706
The restaurant maintains appropriate privacy levels	0.775		
The background music played in the restaurant is suitable to the dining atmosphere	0.610		
The restaurant has appropriate parking areas	0.798	Tangibles: first impression	0.691
The restaurant has visually attractive building exteriors	0.767		
The restaurant has visually attractive dining area	0.637		
The restaurant serves you within the time promised	0.788	Reliability and responsiveness	0.678
The restaurant serves your food exactly as you ordered it	0.685		
The restaurant provides prompt and quick service	0.643		

As exploratory factor analysis (EFA) has produced the latent constructs, the next step is to apply confirmatory approach of the factor analysis for validation. The confirmatory model is presented in Figure 8.1. It is essential to find out the unidimensionality of the model, which is the basis for construct validity. This is done by examining how well the individual items define a construct. A comparative fit index (CFI) value of more than 0.90 is adequate to represents unidimensionality (Byrne, 2010). A value of 0.901 indicated a fairly good fit. The other goodness of fit included (χ^2 = 420.688, df = 188, p < 0.001, χ^2/df = 2.238). In addition, the root mean square error of approximation (RMSEA) was 0.058 and GFI was 0.907. A value less than 0.08 for RMSEA is considered adequate for model fit (Hu and Bentler, 1999). In addition, all factor loadings were significant at p < 0.001 and the standardized regression weights were greater than 0.5 with all factor loadings in EFA greater than 0.5. According to Ford et al. (1986), these values should be above 0.4 for a good fit.

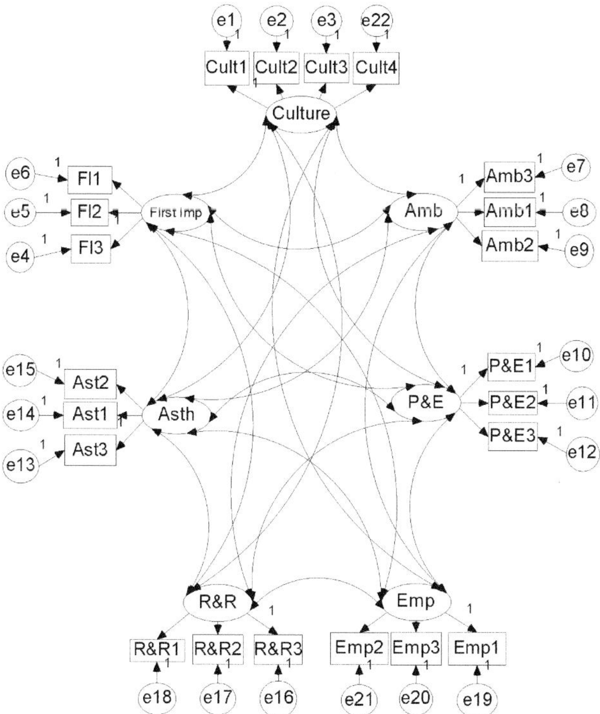

FIGURE 8.1 A confirmatory model of restaurant service quality factors in Indian context.

For achieving convergent validity, all factor loadings should be above 0.5 including the regression weights under CFA, variance extracted should be above 50% and reliability scores should be 0.70 (Hair Jr. et al., 2006). Looking at the validity of the model a convergent validity was established as all the factor loadings under EFA were above 0.6, variance extracted was above 64% and reliability scores were mostly above 0.7 and some are just below it and hence can be fairly accepted with slightest of exceptions. In addition, the standardized regression weights were all above 0.55.

Discriminant validity was achieved by comparing the square of the inter-construct correlation between the factors and AVE between them (see Table 8.2). For achieving discriminant validity average variance extracted (AVE) should be greater than the square of the inter-construct correlations else there could be issues with the validity of the model (Farrell and Rudd, 2009; Mechinda and Patterson, 2011, Patterson and Spreng, 1997).

TABLE 8.2 Discriminant Validity.

Correlation between factors		Interconstruct correlation	Square of interconstruct correlation	AVE (first factor)	AVE (second factor)
Culture	First Imp	0.305	0.093	0.483	0.439
Culture	Amb	0.412	0.170	0.483	0.459
Culture	P&E	0.392	0.154	0.483	0.455
Culture	Asth	0.281	0.079	0.483	0.426
Culture	R&R	0.456	0.208	0.483	0.415
Culture	Emp	0.430	0.185	0.483	0.475
First Imp	Amb	0.484	0.234	0.439	0.459
First Imp	P&E	0.541	0.293	0.439	0.455
First Imp	Asth	0.566	0.320	0.439	0.426
First Imp	R&R	0.581	0.338	0.439	0.415
First Imp	Emp	0.416	0.173	0.439	0.475
Amb	P&E	0.533	0.284	0.459	0.455
Amb	Asth	0.591	0.349	0.459	0.426
Amb	R&R	0.587	0.345	0.459	0.415
Amb	Emp	0.544	0.296	0.459	0.475
P&E	Asth	0.510	0.260	0.455	0.426

TABLE 8.2 Discriminant

Correlation between factors		Interconstruct correlation	Square of intercon-struct correlation	AVE (first factor)	AVE (second factor)
P&E	R&R	0.508	0.258	0.455	0.415
P&E	Emp	0.463	0.214	0.455	0.475
Asth	R&R	0.643	0.413	0.426	0.415
Asth	Emp	0.432	0.187	0.426	0.475
R&R	Emp	0.475	0.226	0.415	0.475

Abbreviations: First Imp – Tangibles: First Impression; Amb – Ambient Settings; P&E – Privacy and Entertainment; Asth – Tangibles: Aesthetics; R&R – Reliability and Responsiveness; Emp – Empathy.

8.4 IMPLICATIONS

This new service quality model pertaining to the restaurants will have strong implications due to its empirical nature. The implications for each of them are discussed in the following paragraphs.

8.4.1 CULTURAL ORIENTATION

A very important and notable finding of this research is the inclusion of the cultural orientation under service quality factors. Though this has not been previously discussed in the literature and it came from the unstructured interviews from the customers, the factor was highly significant. Some of the subcultures in India are sacrosanct toward their choice of food. Hence, they would only patronize a typical restaurant, which respects their cultural values. Common examples include the use of *Satvik* food by the Jains, only *Halal* meat by the Muslims, and prohibition toward eating *Beef* by the Hindus.

8.4.2 AMBIENT SETTINGS

The ambient settings are given a lot of importance in various studies. Clearly, they imply a lot of meaning for the restaurant managers as soothing color settings makes the customers feel comfortable. A good amount of lighting makes it comfortable for the customers to have a clear look at what they are served. Most importantly, the aroma inside the restaurant should make the customers feel happy. The outside environment is heavily polluted and customers would always prefer to breathe in a pleasant smelling environment. Bad ambient odors will never bring back a customer and hence proper cleaning and de-odorizing is essential for the modern day restaurants.

8.4.3 EMPATHY

The restaurant employees should understand the need to empathize with the customers. Every customer should be understood differently from others and hence the special individual needs should be addressed. A customer might want to sit at any place of his/her choice, for example, a couple would like to sit at their preferred location while the employees sometimes push them to sit at an uncomfortable location because the table for two is placed in an undesirable place. This might create a sense of distress in the minds of the consumers. The smarter employees understand that it is easy to retain an existing customer than acquiring a new one and hence minor adjustment in the policies and procedures can be done to satisfy the customers.

8.4.4 PRIVACY AND ENTERTAINMENT

Despite all good arrangements, the restaurants might not be able to make the customers feel good due to an unpleasant and noisy setup, which breaches the privacy and comfort levels of the customers. In a QSR, this cannot be avoided hence some good music should be regularly played. High-pitched conversations of the employees should also be very seriously accounted for, as it may send negative vibes to the customers. Some restaurants have televisions, etc. but with an uncomfortable view which should be addressed. In addition, soft musical orchestra arrangements like Ghazals, etc. have become popular in many restaurants. Many customers often revisit due to these special events. In other words, a customer intends to visit a restaurant for refreshment, which includes good food, entertainment, and a soothing experience.

8.4.5 TANGIBLES 1 (AESTHETICS)

Many customers are often pleased with the external setting of the restaurant. Magnificent buildings of the malls, with front location of the restaurant and clear glass walls to have a look inside always makes a genuine contribution in luring the customers. Difficulty in parking is another important issue, which has been well addressed by the mallculture in New Delhi region.

8.4.6 TANGIBLES 2 (FIRST IMPRESSION)

When a customer enters a restaurant, the first impression is very important. In places like New Delhi, the lifestyle changes are governed by the modern services businesses, which include restaurants. The interior design of the restaurant is considered important by the customers as it subscribes to their lifestyles. The dining area should have comfortable (soft/cushioned) seats so that customers should enjoy their meal in FSRs while for QSRs hard wooden chairs are used in order to manage the heavy footfall. The table setting is also important such that the customers are able to relax on the seats and enjoy their meals.

8.4.7 RELIABILITY AND RESPONSIVENESS

In an attempt to address the lifestyle needs through the intangibles, the restaurant should not forget that the customer has come to the restaurant to eat good food. The customers would like to have the food the way they had expected it. For this, any error in order taking can create a serious problem. In addition, the time taken to serve as per the promise should be strictly adhered to. The server should make a check of the availability of offerings before making any promise about the time to deliver and its availability. The customer may stay with a delayed service once or twice but not forever.

8.5 CONCLUSIONS

The present research work outlines seven key dimensions of service quality in restaurants. These are Cultural orientation, Tangibles 1 (Aesthetics),

Ambient Settings, Empathy, Privacy and Entertainment, Tangibles 2 (First Impression), Reliability and Responsiveness. The recommendations provided by (Gaur and Agrawal, 2006) are applied in the present work and have been found useful. It can be seen in the results that the review of literature has been useful in bringing out new factors pertaining to the service quality in Indian restaurants. These factors can be used in Indian restaurants for evaluating the service quality and hence it has strong practical implications. Strong reliability and validity measures also support this. It is worth noting that despite the criticism of service quality models existed since a long time along with very limited work in the Indian context a very significant gap remained in the literature. This study would provide departure from this gap in the literature.

From the academic point of view, it is widely discussed that service quality influences customer satisfaction, which subsequently influences behavioral (switching/loyalty) intentions. Future studies can focus on the same. Studies can be carried out for outlining any possible differences in the perceived service quality factors in various restaurant types along with their consequences.

From the practical point of view, the managerial implications would be useful in achieving customer satisfaction, which will result into positive behavioral intentions. The satisfied customers would make positive recommendations and would make revisits to the restaurant. This will result in increased profits.

8.6 LIMITATIONS

There are some limitations in the present research, which might affect the generalizability of the results. The study is conducted in New Delhi and its adjoining two cities, which might restrict the aspirations to use the same scale for national level studies or in other parts of India. However, it is noteworthy that New Delhi and its adjacent cities are cosmopolitan in the true sense because of its status of the national capital and metro city. The region under study has various embassies as well as restaurants of various cuisines of both Indian and foreign nature. Nevertheless, it is likely that the results might vary for smaller cities in the country. Further studies shall also look at measuring service quality and its consequences separately for fast food and fine dine restaurants.

KEYWORDS

- **DINESERV**
- **full service restaurants**
- **restaurant service quality**
- **quick service restaurants**

REFERENCES

Anand, R. A Study of Determinants Impacting Consumers Food Choice with Reference to the Fast Food Consumption in India. *Soc. Bus. Rev.* **2011,** *6*(2), 176–187.

Andaleeb, S. S.; Conway, C. Customer Satisfaction in the Restaurant Industry: An Examination of the Transaction-Specific Model. *J. Ser. Market.* **2006,** *20*(1), 3–11.

Becker, C.; Murrmann, S. K.; Murrmann, K. F.; Cheung, G. W. A Pan Cultural Study of Restaurant Service Expectations in the United States and Hong Kong. *J. Hosp. Tour. Res.* **1999,** *23*(3), 235–255.

Berry, P. Trends in the Indian Hospitality Industry. 2008. http://edissertations.nottingham.ac.uk/1892/1/08_MSc_lixpb9.pdf. (accessed 14 September 2011)

Bhardwaj, R. Perception about the Attributes of Selected Fast Food Retailers and their Impact on Consumer Satisfaction and Sales. *Manag. Converg.* **2011,** *1*(2), 83–102. URL: http://www. inflibnet.ac.in. (accessed 14 Sep 2011).

Bojanic, D. C.; Rosen, L. D. Measuring Service Quality in Restaurants: An Application of the SERVQUAL Instrument. *Hosp. Res. J.* **1994,** *18*(1), 3–14.

Byrne, B. M. *Structural Equation Modeling with AMOS: Basic Concepts, Applications, and Programming,* (2nd edn), Routledge, 2010.

Euromonitor. Consumer Foodservice by Location in India. 2011. http://www.euromonitor.com/. (accessed 15 August 2011).

Farrell, A. M.; John M. R. Factor Analysis and Discriminant Validity: A Brief Review of Some Practical Issues ANZMAC. 2009. http://www.duplication.net.au/ANZMAC09/papers/ANZMAC2009-389.pdf. (accessed 27 march 2013).

Ford, J. K.; MacCallum, R. C.; Tait, M. The Application of Exploratory Factor Analysis in Applied Psychology: A Critical Review and Analysis. *Pers. Psychol.* **1986,** *39*(2), 291–314.

Gaur, S. S.; Agrawal, R. Service Quality Measurement in Retail Store Context: A Review of Advances Made Using SERVQUAL and RSQS. *Market. Rev.* **2006,** *6*(4), 317–330.

Hair Jr., J. F.; Black, W. C.; Babin, B. J.; Anderson, R. E.; Tatham, R. L. *Multivariate Data Analysis,* (6th edn). Pearson Education: New Delhi, 2006.

Harrington, R. J.; Ottenbacher, M. C.; Kendall, K. W. Fine-Dining Restaurant Selection: Direct and Moderating Effects of Customer Attributes. *J. Foodserv. Bus. Res.* **2011,** *14*(3), 272–289.

Hu, S. M. A Structural Equation Model of the Senior Citizens' Purchasing Process in Foodservice: Considering the Quality of Food, Nutrition, Service and Entertainment', Doctoral dissertation, Oklahoma State University. 2005. http://digital.library.okstate.edu/etd/umi-okstate-1426.pdf. (accessed 14 September 2011).

Hu, L. T.; Bentler, P. M. Cut Off Criteria for Fit Indexes in Covariance Structure Analysis: Conventional Criteria Versus New Alternatives. *Struct. Equ. Model.: A Multidiscip. J.* **1999,** *6*(1), 1–55.

Jain, S. K.; Gupta, G. Measuring Service Quality: SERVQUAL vs. SERVPERF Scales. *Vikalpa.* **2004,** *29*(2), 25–37.

Kim, H. S.; Joung, H. W.; Yuan, Y. H. E.; Wu, C.; Chen, J. J. Examination of the Reliability and Validity of an Instrument for Measuring Service Quality of Restaurants. *J. Foodserv.* **2009,** *20*(6), 280–286.

Kim, H. J.; McCahon, C.; Miller, J. Assessing Service Quality in Korean Casual-Dining Restaurants Using DINESERV. *J. Foodserv. Bus. Res.* **2003,** *6*(1), 67–86.

Kim, W. G.; Lee, Y. K.; Yoo, Y. J. Predictors of Relationship Quality and Relationship Outcomes in Luxury Restaurants. *J. Hosp. Tour. Res.* **2006,** *30*(2), 143–169.

Kim, W. G.; Kim, H. B. Measuring Customer-Based Restaurant Brand Equity: Investigating the Relationship between Brand Equity and Firms' Performance. *Cornel. Hotel Restaur. Adm. Q.* **2004,** *45*(2), 115–131.

Kivela, J.; Inbakaran, R.; Reece, R. Consumer Research in the Restaurant Environment. Part 3: Analysis, Findings and Conclusions. *Int. J. Contemp. Hosp. Manag.* **2000,** *12*(1), 13–30.

Lee, Y. L.; Hing, N. Measuring Quality in Restaurant Operations: An Application of the SERVQUAL Instrument. *Int. J. Hosp. Manag.* **1995,** *14*(3–4), 293–310.

Lee, S. H.; Kim, Y. P.; Hemmington, N.; Yun, D. K. Competitive Service Quality Improvement (CSQI): A Case Study in the Fast-Food Industry. *Food Serv. Technol.* **2004,** *4*(2), 75–84.

Markovic, S.; Raspor, S.; Šegaric, K. Does Restaurant Performance Meet Customers' Expectations? An Assessment of Restaurant Service Quality Using a Modified DINESERV Approach. *Tour. Hosp. Manag.* **2010,** *16*(2), 181–195.

Mechinda, P.; Patterson, P. G. The Impact of Service Climate and Service Provider Personality on Employees' Customer-Oriented Behavior in a High-Contact Setting. *J. Serv. Mark.* **2011,** *25*(2), 101–113.

O'Cass, A.; Grace, D. Understanding the Role of Retail Store Service in Light of Self-Image–Store Image Congruence. *Psychol. Market.* **2008,** *25*(6), 521–537.

Oh, H.; Parks, S. C. Customer Satisfaction and Service Quality: A Critical Review of the Literature and Research Implications for the Hospitality Industry. *Hosp. Res. J.* **1997,** *20*(3), 35–64.

Parasuraman A.; Zeithaml, V. A.; Berry, L. L. SERVQUAL: A Multiple-Item Scale for Measuring Consumer Perceptions of Service Quality. *J. Retail.* **1988,** *64*(1), 12–40.

Patterson, P. G.; Spreng, R. A. Modelling the Relationship Between Perceived Value, Satisfaction and Repurchase Intentions in a Business-to-business, Services Context: An Empirical Examination. *Int. J. Serv. Indus. Manag.* **1997,** *8*(5), 414–434.

Prasad, C. J.; Aryasri, A. R. Effect of Shopper Attributes on Retail Format Choice Behaviour for Food and Grocery Retailing in India. *Int. J. Retail Distrib. Manag.* **2011,** *39*(1), 68–86.

Qin, H.; Prybutok, V. R. Service Quality, Customer Satisfaction, and Behavioural Intentions in Fast-food Restaurants. *Int J. Qual. Serv. Sci.* **2009,** *1*(1), 78–95.

Ryu, K. DINESCAPE, Emotions, and Behavioral Intentions in Upscale Restaurants. 2005.http://krex.k-state.edu/dspace/bitstream/handle/2097/71/KisangRyu2005.pdf?sequence=1. (accessed 14 September 2011).

Stephens, K. S.; Juran J. M. *Juran, Quality, and a Century of Improvement: The Best on Quality*. American Society for Quality, Quality Press: Milwaukee, 2004.

Stevens, P.; Knutson, B.; Patton, M. DINESERV: A Tool for Measuring Service Quality in Restaurants. *Cornel. Hotel Restaur. Adm. Q.* **1995,** 36(2), 56–60.

Vanniarajan, T. DINESERV: A Tool for Measuring Service Quality in Restaurants. *J. Market. Commun.* **2009,** *4*(3), 41–52.

Yuksel, A; Yuksel, F. Measurement of Tourist Satisfaction with Restaurant Services: A Segment-based Approach. *J. Vacat. Market.* **2002,** *9*(1), 52–68.

Weiss, R.; Feinstein, A. H.; Dalbor, M. Customer Satisfaction of Theme Restaurant Attributes and their Influence on Return Intent. *J. Foodserv. Bus. Res.* **2005,** *7*(1), 23–41.

PART V
Pricing

CHAPTER 9

CONSUMER BEHAVIOUR IN RESTAURANTS: ASSESSING THE IMPORTANCE OF RESTAURANT ATTRIBUTES IN CONSUMER PATRONAGE AND WILLINGNESS TO PAY

H.G. PARSA[1*], KIRTI DUTTA[2], and DAVID NJITE[3]

[1]*Daniels College of Business, University of Denver, 344 Joy Burns Center, 2044 East Evans Avenue, Denver, Colorado 80208, USA*

[2]*G.L. Bajaj Institute of Management & Research, Plot 2, Knowledge Park III, Greater Noida 201306, India*

[3]*University of New Orleans, Lester E. Kabacoff School of Hotel, Restaurant and Tourism Administration, 2000 Lakeshore Drive, New Orleans, LA 70148, USA*

[*]*Corresponding author. E-mail: hparsa@du.edu*

CONTENTS

Originally published as Parsa, H.G., Gregory, A., Self, J.T. and Dutta, K. (2012) "Consumer Behaviour in Restaurants: Assessing the Importance of Restaurant Attributes in Consumer Patronage and Willingness to Pay," in Journal of Services Research, 12:2, pp. 29-56. Published by the Institute for International Management and Technology. Reprinted with permission.

ABSTRACT

The purpose of the paper is to explore the relationship between restaurant attributes and consumers' willingness to patronize. Current research shows that the most common factors affecting restaurant guests while making this decision are: food quality, service quality, and overall restaurant environment. The present paper explores these three factors and their effect on consumers' willingness to pay and their willingness to patronize when these factors are modified from low to high and vice versa. A dynamic comparison method using scenario-based experimental primary research has been used for the current study. It is a 2 × 2 × 3 experiment with two types of restaurants (full-service and quick service), two levels of performance (high and low) and three major attributes (food quality, service, and ambience). Contrary to the commonly held notion in economic literature that the relationship between consumers' willingness to pay and the elasticity (intention to patronize) for restaurants' attributes is linear, the current results indicated that this relationship is not linear thus demanding further investigation. Additionally, questioning the earlier conclusions that all restaurant attributes are equally important in consumer decision-making, the current results indicated that consumers place differential importance on each attribute. And the level of importance placed on each attribute varies with the type of restaurant, upscale or quick service. This is one of the major contributions of the paper questioning the long-held belief and early empirical studies about restaurant attributes. The obtained results also indicated that food quality is more important than service and ambience for consumers in upscale restaurants while speed of service is more important than food quality and ambience in quick service restaurants. Customers in both upscale and quick service restaurants are willing to spend more if the restaurants' resources are focused on attributes that are appropriate for that segment. These findings are significantly important to the restaurant industry as they identify the critical attributes for each segment of the restaurant industry.

9.1 INTRODUCTION

Restaurants are one of the six major industries in the field of hospitality–tourism (Ottenbacher et al., 2009). According to the National Restaurant

Association (NRA, 2009), restaurant sales in 2009, were estimated to exceed $566 billion. The restaurant industry is estimated to be 4% of the gross domestic product of the USA and provides jobs for more than 13 million people. Restaurants are highly visible with nearly 945,000 locations throughout the USA. Industry sales represented an increase of approximately 2.5% in 2009 over 2008 sales. Despite the sluggish economy, unlike most other industries, the food service industry overall continued to maintain sales increases (NRA, 2009).

In order to continue the trend of increasing sales in the restaurant industry, overall guest satisfaction and repeat business must be a priority for organizations. Increasing guest satisfaction can lead to increased guest loyalty, which ultimately leads to increased revenues and profitability (Perutkova and Parsa, 2010). Because the restaurant industry consists of diverse segments with different types of guest service encounters, it is important for restaurants to determine the level of service expected from guests and deliver this level of service and quality effectively and consistently to achieve the desired level of guest satisfaction.

Current study investigates the important attributes in the two major segments of the restaurants industry, full-service restaurants and quick service restaurants, using a scenario approach. Earlier studies on this topic have used rank–order method in soliciting consumer preferences when patronizing a restaurant and their willingness to pay (WTP). In the rank–order method, consumers consider restaurant attributes in a sequential manner in order of their importance when making their restaurant decisions (Perutkova and Parsa, 2010). Unfortunately, the rank–order method compromises on realism in the sense that consumers do not necessarily follow a rank–order method in choosing a restaurant. In contrast, often consumers use a complex process evaluating all major restaurant attributes simultaneously in a dynamic manner. Thus, to better reflect the true consumer decision-making process, the current study substituted the traditional sequential process with a dynamic comparison of restaurant attributes: food quality, service, and ambience, and consumer's WTP, and intention to patronize (ITP) while choosing a restaurant. Understanding the functional structure of this relationship can help restaurant managers and owners make informed decisions in terms of reallocation of their funds for maximum return on investment.

9.2 LITERATURE REVIEW

9.2.1 *CUSTOMER SATISFACTION IN THE RESTAURANT INDUSTRY*

In reality, the success of restaurant managers/owners depends on the understanding of their customers' needs and expectations and meeting those needs better than their competition (Yang et al., 2009). While estimates may vary, a NRA report (2009) indicated that 60% of all new restaurants fail within the first three years in business, and roughly half of those fail in the first year (Parsa et al., 2005). This number shows the importance of ensuring customer satisfaction by providing excellent service, listening to customers' needs and complaints, and caring about the customer. Thus, customer satisfaction (CS) has become one of the most widely studied variables not only in hospitality literature but also in restaurant research due to the significant and direct impact on the financial performance of a restaurant.

Several researchers have tried to explore the relationship between customer satisfaction and restaurant performance, emphasizing the way that satisfaction affects customers' repeat purchase practices (Gupta et al., 2007; Sulek and Hensley, 2004; Soderlund and Ohman, 2005; Cheng, 2005). Some of these studies have identified various factors that influence customers' satisfaction with their dining experience including: wait time, quality of service, responsiveness of frontline employees, menu variety, food prices, food quality, food consistency, ambience of the facilities, and convenience (Sulek and Hensley, 2004; Iglesias and Yague, 2004; Andaleeb and Conway, 2006).

High customer satisfaction is an indication of consumers' willingness to revisit a restaurant. But the antecedents of consumer satisfaction (CS) are nonlinear as shown by the earlier research (Anderson and Mittal, 2000; Mittal et al., 1998; Oliver, 1995). Interestingly, Mittal et al. (1998) have found a S-shaped curve that is flat at the extremes and steep in the middle when measuring the effects of attributes on CS. There are only a few studies that have presented empirical evidence for nonlinear effects in the satisfaction–outcome link (with dependent variables such as customer loyalty and complaining behavior), and there has been no examination of the functional structure for specific relationships.

According to Okada and Hoch (2004), food service has received much attention in the restaurant industry. But ambience was also found to be working simultaneously with food and service. In a related study involving atmosphere in hotels, Heide and Gronhaug (2009) studied four components in atmosphere: distinctiveness, hospitality, relaxation, and refinement with hospitality found to be the most important.

In the hospitality industry, core, tangible, and intangible benefits (e.g., overall impression of restaurant, overall food quality, helpfulness of employees, friendliness of employees, and competence of employees, etc.) were found to have positive relationships with customer satisfaction and loyalty (Gupta et al., 2007; Heung et al., 2002; Matzler et al., 2006; Reich et al., 2005; Tepepci, 1999).

According to Kotler (1998), a product can be categorized into these three distinct benefit levels: the *core benefits* (core service/service product), the *tangible benefits* (servicescapes), and the *intangible benefits* (human element of service delivery). Fundamental benefits a customer receives are called core benefits. Benefits that are consumed and produced simultaneously during the service delivery process are called tangible benefits. Kim et al. (2006) pointed out that, in the restaurant business, tangible attributes include ambience with lighting, visual effects, layout, chairs/tables, carpet, art, lamp shades, and so forth. Ambience is primarily used as an indication of trustworthiness. It is considered as the tangible evidence of the strength of restaurant operations. For example, RainForest Café has unique and expensive ambience indicating that the customers' experience at these restaurants will be unique and special. On the contrary, some of the quick service restaurants such as McDonald's, Taco Bell, KFC offer simple and functional ambience indicating that their service will be functional and predominantly utilitarian.

Intangible benefits in the restaurant industry are conceptualized as quality service attributes where guests' needs are met with anticipation and courteousness. These are the "moments of truth." These include friendliness, knowledge, competence, and attitude of service staff (Kim et al., 2006; Reich et al., 2005). In a study by Sulek and Hensley (2004), only three restaurant attributes were found to be statistically significant: food quality, dining atmosphere, and seating order fairness; and several variables such as wait time, wait area comfort, and staff politeness were found to be statistically not significant.

9.2.2 LOYALTY

In addition to satisfaction, one key challenge to service marketers is to identify critical variables that determine customer loyalty. Oh (1999) stated there are only few studies that explored the relationship between critical variables and customer loyalty particularly in the restaurant industry setting. Earlier studies have primarily focused on the hotel industry (e.g., Bowen and Chen, 2001; Kandampully and Suhartanto, 2000; Mak et al., 2005; Mason et al., 2006) at the expense of the restaurant industry. Some variables that have been found to be related to customer loyalty included perceived value (Zeithaml, 1988), customer satisfaction (Fornell, 1992) and service benefits (Kotler, 1998; Zeithaml et al., 1996). But Skogland and Signuaw (2004) reported that there is no statistically significant relationship between satisfaction and loyalty. Studies by Sulek and Hensley (2004) and Clark and Wood (1998) showed that customer repeat purchase intentions are affected by service quality and food quality in full-service restaurants and speed of service was found to be the leading factor in quick service restaurants. Studies by Kivela et al. (2000) results showed that positive word of mouth is affected by the positive experience and consequential favorable attitude and greater value perceptions have resulted in higher likelihood of repeat patronage.

Contrary to the above literature, economic literature demonstrates that the relationship between consumers' willingness to patronize/pay and the demand elasticity of restaurant attributes is linear in direction. Consumers' patronage is directly related to the degree of change in restaurant attributes including food quality, service quality, and ambience (Gupta et al., 2007). Unfortunately, the commonly held above supposition has a limited empirical support from the restaurant industry. Thus, a greater understanding of the relationship between consumers' willingness to patronage and restaurant attributes is highly desired.

By using a more sophisticated statistical technique – conjoint analysis, Tse and Wilton (2001) have demonstrated that consumer trade-off between price and service while choosing a restaurant. These findings are consistent across various demographic variables such as gender and education. Studies by earlier researcher such as Taylor and Baker (1994) and Zeithaml et al. (1996) show customer satisfaction and overall service quality are directly related to core, tangible, and intangible benefits and overall service quality has significant effect on consumer satisfaction (Whittaker et al., 2007).

From the service literature, it is clear that perceived value perceptions have strong and direct relationship with consumer satisfaction (Huber et al., 2007; Lin et al., 2005; Whittaker et al., 2007). Lee et al. (2005) noted that, in the restaurant industry, perceived value is an important factor in affecting consumer patronage behavior, and greater customer satisfaction was to be a major impetus for customer loyalty (Oliver, 1980; Cronin and Taylor, 1992; Reichheld, 1996). In summary, perceived value is the primary factor that affects consumer loyalty and patronage (Bontis et al., 2007; Kwon et al., 2007; Lam et al., 2004; Woodruff, 1997).

9.2.3 RESTAURANT ATTRIBUTES: QUALITY, SERVICE, AND AMBIENCE

Typically, research in hospitality operations reveals three fundamental aspects that restaurant guests consider when determining where to dine: food quality, service quality, and the overall restaurant environment (Berry et al., 2002; Reuland et al., 1985; Sulek and Hensley, 2004). More specifically, Pettijohn et al. (1997) examined service quality in quick service restaurants to ascertain the characteristics that lead to guest satisfaction. Their research corroborates the notion that quality, cleanliness, and service are the most important attributes (Pettijohn et al., 1997).

Beyond academic research, the restaurant industry has operationalized measurements of customer satisfaction through inspection scores that assess a variety of attributes within the larger categories of quality, service, and ambience/environment in an effort to ensure operational consistency and ultimately improve customer satisfaction and repeat patronage. The concept of this type of score was originally pioneered by McDonald's Corporation and has since been mimicked throughout the industry (Love, 1987).

Typically, industry inspection scores measure three major attributes quality; service; and ambience (cleanliness/safety/environment) that are described here briefly.

Quality consists of, but is not limited to quality of raw and prepared products, following proper company procedures, food safety and sanitation standards as per local health departments, following effective inventory procedures, and so forth.

Service relates to the speed of service, level of convenience provided, drive-thru standards maintained, proper maintenance of service-related equipment (headsets, speakers, point of sales systems, etc.), accuracy of the orders, proper condiments, in "drive-thru" service, and so forth.

Ambience addresses the internal and external appearance/upkeep of a restaurant and how the standards of the company are maintained. This section includes two broad areas: external areas (parking lot, store front, enter/exit signage, windows, doors, recycling areas, "drive-thru" menus, etc.) and internal areas (dining room, public restrooms, condiment areas, service counters, inside menu boards, food service areas, production areas, storage areas, walk-in coolers, freezers, dry storage, etc.).

Inspection scores have three primary objectives in the restaurant industry. They have been used to evaluate operational efficiencies (Love, 1987; Kroc and Anderson, 1987; Aycock 2001); to qualify restaurant managers for financial incentives, such as quarterly bonus plans (Sasser and Pettway 1974; Raith, 2008); finally, inspection scores have been used to scrutinize management performance and ensure consistency among the various units; with poor scores often leading to corrective action, or perhaps termination of management employees (Sorenson and Sorenson, 2001; Raith, 2008; Tillotson, 2008; Coldwell et al., 2000; Costello et al., 1997).

The purpose of the current study is to identify the most important factors in the consumer decision-making process while choosing a restaurant. To more closely align the research with the true decision-making process, this study substitutes the typical rank–order response method with a dynamic comparison approach that considers the restaurant attributes (quality, service, and ambience) in addition to consumers' WTP and ITP while choosing a restaurant.

Current literature on the magnitude of restaurant food quality, service, and ambience on consumers' WTP and intentions to patronize (IIP) is not very clear. Moreover, research suggests that there is no established weighting of the various attributes: quality, service, and cleanliness (Love, 1985; Apte and Reynolds, 1995). As a result, the first hypothesis is stated in null form:

H1*: In the restaurant industry, there is no difference in importance of food quality, service, or ambience on consumer loyalty.*

The relationship of quality, service and ambience scores, and consumer loyalty is not well established. To investigate this relationship between quality, service and ambience attributes, and loyalty, the results of varying quality, service and ambience conditions were regressed over two measures (WTP and intention to re-patronize).

As previous literature has revealed, it is possible that consumers choose different types of restaurants for different reasons and that different attributes may be more important in determining loyalty toward different classifications of restaurants. Service and food quality were the critical attributes influencing repeat purchase intentions in full-service restaurants, while speed of service was the most important attribute in quick service restaurants (Sulek and Hensley, 2004; Clark and Wood, 1998). Toward clarification of this perspective, the research conditions were replicated for two scenarios: quick service restaurants and full-service restaurants. The following hypotheses address these conditions:

H2: *There is a positive relationship between food quality and service quality and loyalty indicators (willingness to pay (WTP) and willingness to return (WTR)) for full service restaurants.*

H3: *There is a positive relationship between speed of service and loyalty indicators (WTP and WTR) for Quick Service restaurants.*

And finally, based on economic literature previously mentioned, the following hypothesis addresses the presumed relationship between WTP and the elasticity of restaurant attributes.

H4: *There is a positive and linear relationship between the elasticity of restaurant attributes and consumers' willingness to pay.*

As mentioned previously, to better understand the consumer behavior process in choosing upscale, full-service, and quick service restaurants, the current study considers scenario-based survey research method as an appropriate choice. Scenario-based experiments are considered most effective in recreating the consumer experience in a chosen consumer behavior study.

9.3 METHODOLOGY

The proposed research hypotheses were tested with the help of a scenario-based experimental research method using two types of restaurants, high end (upscale, full-service) and low end (quick service restaurants). It is a

$2 \times 2 \times 3$ experiment with two types of restaurants (full-service and quick service), two levels of performance for each attribute (high and low), and three major attributes (food quality, service, and ambience). The first part of the instrument includes introduction in which the expectations are set for the use of four scenarios each containing a different restaurant experience (Appendix 1). The second section contains two full-service restaurant scenarios and two quick service restaurant scenarios. After reading a scenario, the participants were asked to provide their WTP on an absolute dollar scale and their IIP on a numerical scale of 1(lowest)–7 (highest) containing descriptive anchors (Appendix 1).

All scenarios were pretested with 64 subjects over a period of 3 months. The purpose of the pretesting process is to assure that the developed scenarios are relevant to the research subjects and to improve reliability of the instrument. Several alternative choices of descriptive terms were tested over a period of 3 months to arrive at the most reliable and relevant descriptive anchors for the attribute scales. Several modifications were made to the instrument based on the outcome of these pretests.

First, the participants were asked to read one written scenario at a time set in an upscale full-service restaurant context. Participants were then asked to evaluate their WTP and ITP for eight different possible combinations of restaurant attributes (food quality, service, and ambience) ranging from low (described as "good") to high (described as "excellent"). These descriptive anchors, "excellent" representing the high end and "good" representing the low end in full-service, upscale restaurants, were carefully chosen from a choice of several possible alternatives (Appendix 1). These two terms ("excellent" and "good") have received the highest preference scores during the pretesting process representing the high and low end of the full-service, upscale restaurants.

As a result, there were a total of eight possible combinations for two levels of restaurant attributes. For example, one of the attributes sets has all three attributes rated as being excellent at the high end (Condition 8) or all three attributes rated as being good at the low end (Condition 7) (Appendix 1) and some variations (six variations) in between such as excellent food, average service, and excellent ambience (Condition 6) and good food, good service, and excellent ambience (Condition 3), and so forth (Appendix 1). Respondents were required to consider all three attributes (quality, service, and ambience) in a dynamic fashion and present their WTP in absolute dollars, as well as express their IIP on a scale of 1 (lowest) to 7 (highest).

In case of the first two scenarios for full-service, upscale restaurants, based on the attribute preference, participants were expected to indicate their level of WTP on a range of $50–$150 and ITP on a scale of 1(least likely) to7 (most likely). The dollar range for WTP (guest check average of $50–$150) was determined based on the results of the pretesting process reflecting the local market conditions for menu pricing at full-service, upscale restaurants. The guest check average values below $50 and above $150 were not considered to be reflective of the local market as described by senior managers from the industry. This step was taken to enhance the realism of the experimental design as described by McGrath (1981; 1982) in his seminal "Dilemmatic" paper.

According to McGrath (1981; 1982), any research in social sciences has to satisfy at least two of the three criteria: generalizability, precision, and realism. McGrath refers this as "dilemmatic" as researcher can only maximize any two of the three criteria while compromising on the third one. For example, most survey research focuses on generalizability and precision (measured as reliability) but compromises on realism. Similarly most experimental research maximizes on realism and precision of an experiment but compromises on generalizability. Thus, research in social sciences, in essence, is a compromise trying to satisfy three criteria while able to maximize only two of those.

The current study, unlike the earlier researches using survey instruments focusing on generalizability, focuses on realism and precision using scenario-based experimental research methods. Thus, the authors strongly believe that the current results have greater precision and realism as the experimental scenarios have been tested repeatedly to capture the realistic nature of restaurant patronage. From this perspective, the current study is significantly different from the earlier studies.

In the third and fourth sets of the experimental studies, the participants were asked to evaluate the written scenarios that are set in quick service restaurant contexts. Participants were given the option to choose among food quality, speed of service, and attractiveness attributes ranging from high (described as "good" based on pretesting) to low (described as "average" based on pretesting). Based on the attribute preference participants were then asked to indicate how likely they were to visit the restaurant with a scale of the least likely (1) to most likely rated (7).

Respondents were also asked to indicate their WTP within a range of $5–$15 as predetermined from the data collected during the pretesting process. The values for WTP below $5 and above $15 for a meal at a quick service restaurant were found to be unrealistic for the local market during the pretesting process. In addition, the authors have also collected data from the local quick service restaurant menus to verify the accuracy and reliability of the obtained price range for quick service restaurant meals and it was found to be realistic. This range has provided the most reliable and realistic reflection of the quick service industry (McGrath, 1981; 1982) in the local market. The scenarios presented for quick service restaurants were also pretested for validity and reliability with the help of 64 subjects taken from the population pool. Demographic data from the participants were also collected.

In this experiment, there were total 380 cases with 190 cases representing high-end, upscale restaurants while 190 cases representing quick service restaurants. The total number of respondents are 95 from a major hospitality college located in the southeastern part of the USA. Hospitality students were chosen since they are more familiar with the high-end, full-service restaurants compared to the general population of undergraduate students from non-hospitality programs.

Subjects that are not familiar with the local upscale, full-service and quick service restaurants were excluded from the study by a self-declaration statement. Participation in the survey was voluntary and a small incentive was given to the participants that were consistent with the university (IRB) and human subject policies. On average the testing process took about 15 minutes and the respondents were debriefed at the end of the experiment. A manipulation check was conducted by asking the respondents four related questions. No problems were identified in the manipulation check.

9.4 RESULTS AND DISCUSSION

Consistent with the demographic composition of the chosen college, majority of the respondents were females (67%) which compares reasonable to the college composition of 64.5% of female students. Sample demographics include 27% of respondents between 19 and 20 years and 44% between 21 and 22 years of age. A majority of students are full-time students (91%) nearly half of them have a junior standing (third year of college). Good portion of the respondents were holding full-time employment (nearly 32 hours per week) and most of the respondents were residents of the state (Table 9.1).

TABLE 9.1 Demographic Information of the Sample.

Variable	Frequency (n)	Percent (%)	Variable	Frequency (n)	Percent (%)
Gender			*Degree*		
Male	31	32.6	Hospitality	45	47.4
Female	64	67.4	Restaurant	31	32.6
Age			Event	10	10.5
19–20	26	27.4	Other	9	9.5
21–22	42	44.2	*Status*		
23–24	18	18.9	Full-time	87	91.6
25 or more	9	9.5	Part-time	7	7.4
Education			*Employment*		
1st	3	3.2	Full-time	33	34.7
2nd	18	18.9	Part-time	60	63.2
3rd	46	48.4	Missing	2	2.2
4th	24	27.4	*Residency*		
Other	2	2.1	In state	89	93.7
			Out of state	6	6.3

9.4.1 FULL-SERVICE RESTAURANTS

In case of IIP the upscale, full-service restaurants, results from multiple regression indicated that all eight conditions were significantly different from each other (*F*-value 107.03). Current results indicated that Condition 8 (mean = 6.5) offering high-quality food, high service, and high ambience has the highest *R*-square value, followed Condition 4 (mean = 5.88) offering high-quality food and high service and low ambience and Condition 6 offering high-quality food, low service, and high ambience. The least amount of *R*-square value was explained by Conditions 5 (mean = 4.4) (low-quality food, high service, and low ambience) and Condition 3 (mean = 4.04) (low-quality food, low service, and high ambience).

For these comparisons, the Condition 7 (low quality, low service, and low ambience) was found to have lowest value in WTP and intentions to patronage, thus, it was chosen as the constant against which the other conditions were compared as shown in Table 9.2. This was found to be true in case of full-service and quick service restaurants.

TABLE 9.2 Results of Multiple Regression Analysis Comparing Food Quality, Service, Ambience at Upscale, Full-service Restaurants, and Quick Service Restaurants.

Independent variable	Model 1 Intention to patronize		Model 2 Willingness to pay	
	Upscale	Quick service		Upscale
Constant	3.53**	2.81**	Constant	3.53**
Condition 1	1.37**	0.28*	Condition 1	1.37**
Condition 2	1.52**	1.67**	Condition 2	1.52**
Condition 3	0.52**	0.33*	Condition 3	0.52**
Condition 4	2.12**	1.86**	Condition 4	2.12**
Condition 5	0.87**	1.12**	Condition 5	0.87**
Condition 6	1.73**	0.92**	Condition 6	1.73**
Condition 8	2.97**	3.39**	Condition 8	2.97**
Adj. R^2	0.33	0.37	Adj. R^2	0.33
F-value	107.03**	125.03**	F-value	107.03**

$^*p<0.05$, $^{**}p<0.001$

For upscale, full-service restaurants, among the eight different conditions, Condition 8, where a restaurant offers high levels of food, service, and ambience, as expected, had the highest WTP at $118.81; meanwhile, respondents indicated lowest WTP or least amount of money ($59.70) for a restaurant that provides low level of food quality, low service, and low ambience (Fig. 9.1, Table 9.2). Results with these two extreme conditions (highest and lowest) are fairly intuitive and there is no surprise. These results reflect the reality of consumers' WTP highest for highest offerings and vice versa.

The second highest value for WTP ($88.51) was obtained by Condition 4 (high food, high service, and low ambience, $88.51) followed by Condition 6 (high food, low service, and high ambience, $ 77.76), Condition 2 (low food, high service, and high ambience, $73.32), Condition 1 (high food, low service, and low ambience, $70.20), Condition 5 (low food, high service, and low ambience, $66.62), and Condition 3 (low food, low service, and high ambience, $61.40) in descending order (Fig. 9.1 and Table 9.2). These results provide partial support for H1 (there is no difference in importance of restaurant attributes on consumer loyalty).

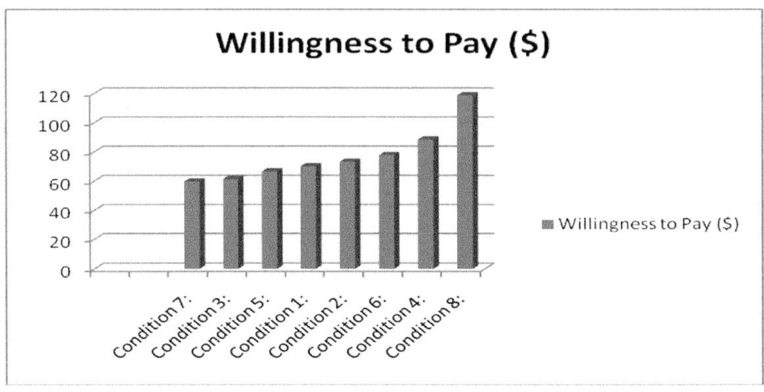

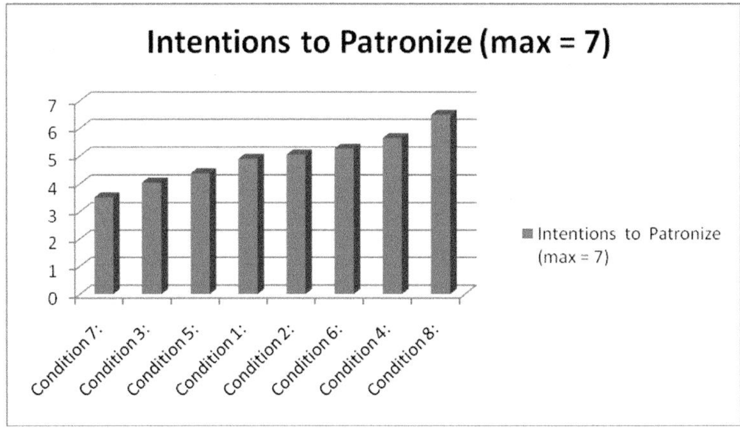

FIGURE 9.1 The mean values of willingness to pay and intentions to patronize at upscale, full-service restaurants by each scenario.

9.4.2 *QUICK SERVICE RESTAURANTS*

In the case of quick service restaurants, the highest WTP was reported as $12.65 for Condition 8 (high food, high service, high ambience) and the lowest WTP of $6.69 was reported for Condition 7 (low food, low service, low ambience) (Fig. 9.2, Table 9.2). Again, these results are fairly intuitive. Interestingly, in the quick service segment, the WTP for Condition 1 (high food, low service, low ambience) was $6.75 which is closer to Condition 3 (low food, low service, low ambience) of $6.80 and Condition 7 (low food, low service, low ambience) with $6.69 as indicated in Figure 9.2.

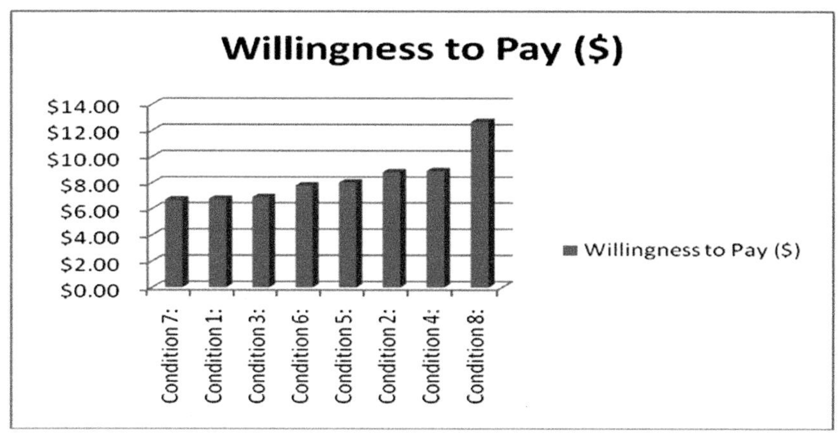

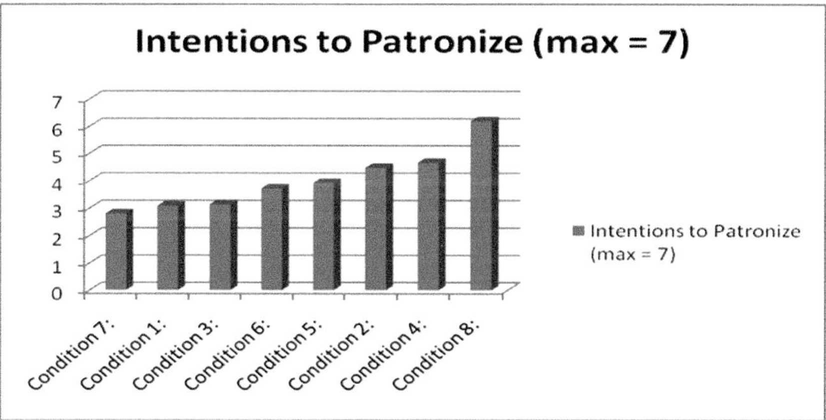

FIGURE 9.2 The mean values of willingness to pay and intentions to patronize at quick service restaurants for each scenario.

In the case of IIP quick service restaurants, Condition 8 explained the highest *R*-square value followed Condition 4 offering high food, high service, and low ambience and Condition 2 offering low food, high service, and high ambience. Unlike full-service restaurants, Condition 1 (high food, low service, low ambience) contributed the second lowest R-square value followed by Condition 3 (low food, low service, and high ambience). These results lend support to the previously stated hypotheses.

In order to achieve the objectives of the study, multiple regression analysis was conducted using dummy variables. Eight different conditions were coded as seven dummy variables and then entered as dependent variables in the model. Condition 7 having the lowest level for all three attributes was used as a base variable. According to the result of multiple regression analysis, the regression equations are presented here:

For Upscale Restaurants:

$$ITP = 3.53 + 1.37C_1 + 1.52C_2 + 0.52C_3 + 2.12C_4 + 0.87C_5 + 1.73C_6 + 2.97C_8$$

$$WTP = 59.70 + 10.50C_1 + 13.51C_2 + 1.69C_3 + 28.81C_4 + 6.92C_5 + 18.06C_6 + 59.10C_8$$

The expected ITP for a restaurant that provided low food, low service, and low ambience (Condition 7) was 3.53 out of 7-point scale and the expected WTP for this condition was $59.70. However, the ITP for a restaurant that offers high food, low service, and low ambience (Condition 1) increased by 1.327 from the expected intention of Condition 7 (3.53). Thus, the expected ITP this type of restaurant is 4.90. Also, based on the current results, consumers are likely to spend $10.50 more for a restaurant offering high food, low service, and high ambience (Condition 1) than a restaurant which provides low food, low service, and low ambience (Condition 7).

In upscale restaurants, consumers are most likely to patronize a restaurant (Condition 8, mean = 6.5) that provides high food, high service, and high ambience and WTP $118.80. Second place was occupied by Condition 4 offering high food, high service, and low ambience consistent with H2, with IIP of 2.12 as well as WTP of $28.81. Thus, consumers are willing to pay $28.81 more for the Condition 4 (high food, high service, and low ambience) and intend to patronize more by 2.12 compared to the base of Condition 7 (low food, low service, and low ambience). Table 9.2 summarizes the result of regression analysis.

For Quick Service Restaurants:

$$ITP = 2.81+0.28C_1+1.67C_2+0.33C_3+1.86C_4+1.12C_5+0.92C_6+3.39C_8$$

$$WTP = 6.69+0.05C_1+2.14C_2+0.19C_3+2.23C_4+1.10C_5+1.33C_6+5.97C_8$$

The expected ITP for a restaurant that offers average food, slow service, and low ambience (Condition 7) was 2.81 on a 7-point scale, and the expected WTP for this restaurant was \$6.69. On the other hand, it was expected that consumers intend to patronize Condition 8 (high food, high service, high ambience) more (6.20) and they are WTP (\$5.97) more than a restaurant with least desirable attributes as in Condition 7 (low food, low service, low ambience).

To elaborate further, consumers IIP (0.28) and WTP (0.05) change minimally from the base Condition 7 (low food, low service, and low ambience) to Condition 1 (high food, low service, low ambience) but increase dramatically with Condition 2 (low food, high service, and high ambience) with values for IIP 1.67 and WTP 2.14, as anticipated in H3.

The next step is to determine the most influential factor among three variable, food, service, and ambience (H1). Toward this goal, an additional multiple regression analysis was conducted. The regression model included three restaurant attributes and two levels of performance.

In case of upscale, full-service restaurants, food was found to be the most influential factor affecting the ITP as well as the WTP. In the condition of "Excellent" food quality, the consumer ITP has increased by 1.32 and WTP has improved by \$23.59. Meanwhile, in case of service quality, WTP has increased by \$19.52 when service is high and IIP have improved by 0.97. In case of ambience, WTP changed by only \$11.53 and ITP has changed by 0.59 (Table 9.3). These results clearly indicate that in case of full-service, upscale restaurants, food quality is the most important attribute in choosing a restaurant followed by service and ambience.

In case of quick service restaurants, service attribute showed to be a most important factor for both ITP and WTP. In the condition of fast service, consumers' ITP has increased by 1.63 and WTP also increased by \$2.47 (Table 9.3). In the condition of highest quality food, consumers' IIP have increased by 0.83 and WTP has increased by \$1.53. When ambience was introduced in the model, consumers' ITP has improved by 0.76 WTP has increased by \$1.56 with high ambience; but it is significantly lower than when service attribute is high (faster).

TABLE 9.3 Results of Multiple Regression Analysis of Consumers' Intentions to Patronize and Willingness to Pay for Restaurant Attributes at Upscale, Full-service, and Quick Service Restaurants.

Independent variable	Model 1 Intentions to patronize		Model 2 Willingness to pay	
	Upscale	Quick service		Upscale
Constant	0.58**	−0.84**	Constant	0.58**
Food	**1.32****	0.83**	Food	1.32**
Service	0.97**	1.63*	Service	0.97**
Ambience	0.59**	0.76**	Ambience	0.59**
Adj. R^2	0.33	0.34	Adj. R^2	0.33
F-value	246.31**	254.91**	F-value	246.31**

*$p<0.05$, **$p<0.001$

Thus, H1 is not supported as the results from the current study indicated that food quality is more important in selecting upscale, full-service restaurants; and speed of service is more important in selecting quick service restaurants. Contrary to the common belief that all restaurants should emphasize food quality as the primary target (Sorenson and Sorenson, 2001; Raith, 2008; Tillotson, 2008; Coldwell et al., 2000; Costello et al., 1997), the current results indicated that though food quality may be important in upscale, full-service restaurants, it is not the case with quick service restaurants. In case of quick service restaurants, consumers prefer faster service over any improvements in food quality and ambience after minimum acceptable standards of food quality, food safety, and sanitation are met.

These results also demonstrate that consumer patronage patterns and WTP practices are significantly different when selecting upscale, full-service restaurants, and quick service restaurants (H4). Current results also indicated that the relationship between change in level of restaurants attributes and consumers' WTP and ITP is not necessarily linear as commonly believed. Further research is needed to better understand the nature of change in restaurant attributes and consumers WTP and IIP.

To further confirm the current results, data were analyzed using analysis of variance (ANOVA). The ANOVA statistical method was chosen as the choice method of data analysis since there were three treatments (food, service, and ambience) and two levels for each treatment with the same dependent variables (WTP and ITP).

Results from the ANOVA indicated that, in case of full-service restaurants, all eight conditions are significantly different (Levene statistic = 23.883; p>0.001). Regarding the dependent variable, ITP, results from the ANOVA analysis have indicated that the presented eight sets can be organized into five distinct groups (Table 9.4). The first group consisted of Condition 8 (high food, high service, and high ambience) with a mean value of 6.50. It was followed by Condition 4 (high food, high service, and low ambience) with a mean value of 5.88; Conditions 1, 2, and 6 with a mean value of 5.07 formed the third subset; Conditions 3 and 5 with a mean value of 4.22 formed the second subset; the last choice was Condition 7 offering low food, low service, and low ambience with a mean value of 3.53, as expected. In subsets 3, 4, and 5 representing five conditions (8, 6, 4, 2, and 1), the dominant attribute was found to be food quality, thus, confirming the results from multiple regression. Similar results were obtained for WTP with five subsets from eight conditions.

TABLE 9.4 Results of ANOVA for Intentions to Patronize Full-service Restaurants.

n	Full-service restaurant scenarios (max = 7)				
	Subset 1	**Subset 2**	**Subset 3**	**Subset 4**	**Subset 5**
189	Condition 7 Low food Low service Low ambience (mean = 3.53)				
189		Condition 3 Low food Low service High ambience (mean = 4.04)			
189		Condition 5 Low food High service Low ambience (mean = 4.40)			

TABLE 9.4 *(Continued)*

n	Full-service restaurant scenarios (max = 7)				
	Subset 1	**Subset 2**	**Subset 3**	**Subset 4**	**Subset 5**
189			Condition 1 High food Low service Low ambience (mean = 4.90)		
189			Condition 2 Low food High service High ambience (mean = 5.05)		
189			Condition 6 High food Low service High ambience (mean = 5.26)		
189				Condition 4 High food High service Low ambience (mean = 5.88)	
189					Condition 8 High food High service High ambience (mean = 6.50)

In the case of quick service restaurants, unlike the case of full-service restaurants, there were only four subsets for the dependent measure ITP. The highest (Condition 8, mean = 6.20) and lowest (Condition 7, mean = 2.81) subsets have remained constant across both the restaurant segments as expected (Table 9.5). But in case of quick service restaurants, in addition to Condition 7 (low food, low service, low ambience), the subset 1 (mean = 3.01) also had Conditions 1 (high food, low service, low ambience) and Condition 3(low food, low service, high ambience). The subset 2 (mean = 3.83) was represented by Condition 6 (high food, low service, and high ambience) and Condition 5 (low food, high service, low ambience). The subset 3 (mean = 4.58) consisted of Condition 2 (low food, high service, high ambience) and Condition 4 (high food, high service, and low ambience). The highest ITP (subset 3 and 4) has occurred when service is high (faster service) than food and ambience. Thus, these results clearly indicated that the attribute "faster service" is the dominant factor contributing to the high incidence of ITP compared to food quality and ambience. These findings affirm the results obtained for multiple regression.

TABLE 9.5 Results of ANOVA for Intentions to Patronize Quick Service Restaurants.

n	Quick service restaurant scenarios (max = 7)			
	Subset 1	**n**	**Subset 1**	**n**
187	Condition 7 Low food Low service Low ambience (mean = 2.81)	187	Condition 7 Low food Low service Low ambience (mean = 2.81)	187
187	Condition 1 High food Low service Low ambience (mean = 3.09)			
187	Condition 3 Low Food Low Service High Ambience (mean = 3.13)			
187		Condition 6 High food Low service High ambience (mean = 3.73)		

TABLE 9.5 *(Continued)*

n	Quick service restaurant scenarios (max = 7)			
	Subset 1	**Subset 2**	**Subset 3**	**Subset 4**
187		Condition 5 Low food High service Low ambience (mean = 3.92)		
187			Condition 2 Low food High service High ambience (mean = 4.49)	
187			Condition 4 High food High service Low ambience (mean = 4.67)	
187				Condition 8 High food High service High ambience (mean = 6.20)

9.5 CONCLUSIONS

Based on the results of this study, it can be concluded that customers in both upscale and quick service restaurants are willing to spend more if the restaurant's attention and resources are focused on the proper attribute, that is, equally of food in upscale restaurants and fast service in quick service restaurants. In the case of upscale restaurants, the ITP increased by 1.32 and consumers were willing to pay on average $23.59 more if the quality of food is high. In the case of quick service restaurants, the ITP increased by 1.63 and consumers were willing to pay on average $2.47 more if the service is faster.

These results can help managers in high-end restaurants develop strategies that place emphasis and resources on achieving higher food quality rather than spending their limited resources on other factors that have less real value to its customers. Similarly, managers at quick service restaurants could focus on improving speed of service since customers place greater value on faster service and are willing to pay more for it than food or ambience. Quick service restaurant managers may want to invest in improving their staffing, systems, and training in order to yield faster speed of service rather than quality of food or ambience.

9.6 MANAGERIAL IMPLICATIONS

While restaurant managers/owners may not fully appreciate the importance of the relationship between their restaurant concept and their customers' priorities, they do recognize that customer satisfaction is linked to repeat business. The typical drivers of restaurant customer satisfaction, however, namely food, decor, and service, are not created equally; at least when related to the type of restaurant. For the restaurant manager/owner, knowing the core attribute for their type of restaurant allows them to make strategic decisions regarding their resources, to focus on the most important attribute of their particular concept; for example, high-end restaurants should focus on food quality, while quick service restaurants should focus on speed of service. This emphasis on their core attribute allows for spending dollars that immediately address their customer expectations rather than spending on other attributes that would not be fully appreciated by their particular customer.

This information can have significant impact on the ability of both high-end and quick service restaurants to better differentiate themselves between their competition for a clear competitive advantage with a resulting increase in sales and greater return on investment in the long term.

9.7 LIMITATIONS AND FUTURE SUGGESTIONS

Since it is an experimental research, emphasis is placed on precision and realism as suggested by McGrath thus generalizability may be compromised. Such a compromise is expected in experimental research. To overcome this limitation, it is highly desirable to replicate the study with a different research design that involves a survey of restaurant customers.

There is a possibility of respondents' stress factors as subjects were asked to review four scenarios. Thus, future studies may address this aspect by having larger samples with fewer scenarios for each study. Interestingly, replication of the study from different part of the country or different parts of the world from another nation would be desirable.

KEYWORDS

- **customer satisfaction**
- **consumer behavior**
- **restaurant attributes**
- **upscale restaurant**
- **quick service restaurant**
- **consumer patronage**
- **willingness to pay**

REFERENCES

Andaleeb, S. S.; Conway, C. Customer Satisfaction in the Restaurant Industry: An Examination of the Transaction-Specific Model. *J. Serv. Mark.* **2006,** *20*(1), 3–11.

Anderson, E. W.; Mittal, V. Strengthening the Satisfaction-Profit Chain. *J. Serv. Res.* **2000,** *3*(2), 107.

Apte, U. M.; Reynolds, C. C. Quality Management in Kentucky Fried Chicken. *Interfaces.* **1995,** *25*(3), 6–21.

Aycock, A. Training for QSC: How McDonald's Makes Library Managers. *Community Jr. Coll. Libr.* **2001,** *10*(4), 29–37.

Berry, L. L.; Carbone, L. P.; Haeckel, S. H. Managing the Total Customer Experience. *Sloan Manag. Rev.* **2002,** *43*(3), 85–89.

Bontis, N.; Booker, L. D.; Serenko, A. The Mediating Effect of Organizational Reputation on Customer Loyalty and Service Recommendation in the Banking Industry. *Manag. Decis.* **2007,** *45*(9), 1426–1449.

Bowen, J. T.; Chen, S. L. The Relationship Between Customer Loyalty and Customer Satisfaction. *Int. J. Contemp. Hosp. Manag.* **2001,** *13*(5), 213–217.

Cheng, K. A Research on the Determinants of Consumers' Repurchase Toward Different Classes of Restaurants in Taiwan. *Bus. Rev.* **2005,** *4*(2), 99–105.

Clark, M. A.; Wood, R. Consumer Loyalty in the Restaurant Industry-a Preliminary Exploration of the Issues. *Int. J. Contemp. Hosp. Manag.* **1998,** *10*(4), 139–44.

Coldwell, D. S.; Blakeway, J.R.; Husted, C. B.; Goldean, P. Franchise Law. *South. Methodist Univ. Law Rev.* **2000,** *53,* 1056–1080.

Costello, K. R.; Levin, B. A.; Wieczorek, D. E. Encroachment and Duty of Good Faith: Camp Creek Resurrects Scheck. *Franch. Law J.* **1997,** *17,* 140.

Cronin, J. J.; Taylor, S. A. Measuring Service Quality: A Reexamination and Extension. *J. Mark.* **1992,** *56,* 55–68.

Fornell, C. A National Customer Satisfaction Barometer: The Swedish Experience. *J. Mark.* **1992,** *56,* 6–21.

Gupta, S.; McLaughlin, E.; Gomez. M. Guest Satisfaction and Restaurant Performance. *Cornell Hotel Restaur. Adm. Q.* **2007,** *48*(3), 284–298.

Heide, M.; Gronhaug, K. Key factors in Guests' Perception of Hotel atmosphere. *Cornell Hosp. Q.* **2009,** *50*(1), 29–43.

Heung, V. C. S.; Wong, M. Y.; Qu, H. A Study of Tourists' Perceptions, Satisfactions and Post Experience Behavioural Intentions in Relation to Airport Restaurant Services in Hong Kong SAR. *J. Travel Tour. Mark.* **2002,** *12*(2/3), 111–135.

Huber, F.; Herman, A.; Henneberg H. C. Measuring Customer Value and Satisfaction in Services Transactions, Scale Development, Validation and Cross-Cultural Comparison. *Int. J. Consum. Stud.* **2007,** *31,* 554–564.

Iglesias, M. P.; Yague, M. Perceived Quality and Price: Their Impact on the Satisfaction of Restaurant Customers. *Int. J. Contemp. Hosp. Manag.* **2004,** *16*(6), 373–379.

Kandampully, J.; Suhartanto, D. Customer Loyalty in the Hotel Industry: The Role of Customer Satisfaction and Image. *Int. J. Contemp. Hosp. Manag.* **2000,** *12*(6), 346–351.

Kim, W. G.; Lee, Y. K.; Yoo, Y. J. Predictors of Relationship Quality and Relationship Outcomes in Luxury Restaurants. *J. Hosp. Tour. Res.* **2006,** *30*(2), 143–169.

Kivela, J.; Inbakaran, R.; Reece, J. Consumer Research in the Restaurant Environment; Part 3: Analysis, findings, and conclusions. *Int. J. Contemp. Hosp. Manag.* **2000,** *12*(1), 13–30.

Kotler, P. *Marketing Management: Analysis, Planning, Implementation, and Control;* Prentice-Hall, Inc: Englewood Cliffs, NJ, 1998.

Kroc, R.; R., Anderson. *Grinding it Out: Making of McDonald's;* Contemporary Book: Chicago, IL, 1987.

Kwon, H. H.; Trail, G.; James, J. D. The Mediating Role of Perceived Value: Team Identification and Purchase Intention of Team-Licensed Apparel. *J. Sport Manag.* **2007,** *21,* 540–554.

Lam, S. Y.; Shankar, V.; Murthy, M. Customer Value, Satisfaction, Loyalty and Switching Costs: An Illustration from Business to Business Context. *J. Acad. Mark. Sci.* **2004,** *32*(3), 293–311.

Lee, Y. K.; Park, K. H.; Park, D.W.; Lee, K. A.; Kwon, Y. J. The Relative Impact of Service Quality on Service Value, Customer Satisfaction and Customer Loyalty in Korean Family Restaurant Context. *Int. J. Hosp. Tour. Adm.* **2005,** *6*(1), 27–51.

Lin, C. H.; Sher, P. J.; Shih, H. U. Past Progress and Future Directions in Conceptualizing Customer Perceived Value. *Int. J. Serv. Ind. Manag.* **2005,** *16*(4), 318–336.

Love, J. F. *McDonald's: Behind the Golden Arches;* Bantom Publications: New York, NY, 1985.

Love, J. F. *McDonalds: Behind the Golden Arches*; Bantam Books: New York, NY, 1987.

Mak, B.; Sim, J.; Jones, D. Model of Service Quality: Customer Loyalty for Hotels. *FIU Hosp. Rev.* **2005,** *23*(1), 96–104.

Mason, D.; Tideswell, C.; Roberts, E. Guest Perceptions of Hotel Loyalty. *J. Hosp. Tour. Res.* **2006,** *30*(2), 191–206.

Matzler, K.; Renzl, B.; Rothenberger, S. Measuring the Relative Importance of Service Dimensions in the Formation of Price Satisfaction and Service Satisfaction: A Case Study in the Hotel Industry. *Scand. J. Hosp. Tour.* **2006,** *6*(3), 179–196.

McGrath, J. E. Dilemmatics: A Study of Research Choices and Dilemma. *Am. Behav. Sci.* **1981,** *25*(2), 179–210.

McGrath, J. E. Dilemmatics: Judgment Calls in Research. In *Judgment Calls in Research;* McGrath, J. E., Ed.; Sage Publications: Beverly Hills, CA, 1982; pp. 69–102.

Mittal, V.; Ross, W.; Baldasare, P. The Asymmetric Impact of Negative and Positive Attribute-Level Performance on Overall Satisfaction and Repurchase Intentions. *J. Mark.* **1998,** *62(*January), 33–47.

National Restaurant Association. 2009. http://www.restaurant.org/pdfs/research/index/200912.pdf. (accessed 22 May 2011).

Oh, H. Service Quality, Customer Satisfaction, and Customer Value: A Holistic Perceptive. *Int. J. Hosp. Manag.* **1999,** *18*(1), 67–82.

Okada, E.; Hoch, S. Spending Time Versus Spending Money. *J. Consum. Res.* **2004,** *31*(2), 313–314.

Oliver, R. A Cognitive Model of the Antecedents and Consequences of Satisfaction Decisions. *J. Mark. Res.* **1980,** *8*(4), 460–69.

Oliver, R. Attribute Need Fulfillment in Product Usage Satisfaction. *Psychol. Mark.* **1995,** *12*(January), 1–17.

Ottenbacher, M.; Harrington, R. J.; Parsa, H. G. Defining Hospitality: A Classificational Analysis of the Term and Discussion of Pedagogical and Research Implications. *J. Hosp. Tour. Res.* **2009,** *38*(3), 1–19.

Parsa, H. G.; Self, J.; King, T.; Njite, D. Why Do Restaurants Fail? *Cornell HRA Q.* **2005,** *46*(3), 304–322.

Perutkova, J.; Parsa, H. G. Consumers' Willingness to Pay and to Patronize According to Major Restaurant Attributes. *Undergrad. Res. J.,* **2010,** *4*(2), 1–11.

Pettijohn, L. S.; Pettijohn, C. E.; Luke, R. H. An Evaluation of Fast Food Restaurant Satisfaction: Determinants, Competitive Comparisons and Impact on Future Patronage. *J. Restaur. Foodserv. Mark.* **1997,** *2*(3), 3–20.

Raith, M. Specific Knowledge and Performance Measurement. *RAND J. Econ.* **2008,** *39*(4), 1059–1079.

Reich, A.; McCleary, K.; Tepanon, Y.; Weaver, P. The Impact of Product and Service Quality on Brand Loyalty: An Exploratory Investigation of Quick-Service Restaurants. *J. Foodserv. Bus. Res.* **2005,** *8*(3), 35–53.

Reichheld, F. *The Loyalty Effect;* Harvard Business School Press: Boston, MA, 1996.

Reuland, R.; Coudrey, J.; Fagel, A. Research in the Field of Hospitality. *Int. J. Hosp. Manag.* **1985,** *4*(4), 141–146.

Sasser, W. E.; Pettway, S. H. 1974 Case of Big Mac's Pay Plans, *Harvard Bus. Rev.*, July, 30–46.

Skogland, I.; Siguaw, R. Are Your Satisfied Customers Loyal? *Cornell Hotel Restaur. Adm. Q.* **2004,** *45*(3), 221–234.

Söderlund, M.; Öhman, N. Assessing Behavior before it Becomes Behavior: An Examination of the Role of Intentions as a Link between Satisfaction and Re-Patronizing Behavior. *Int. J. Serv. Ind. Manag.* **2005,** *16*(2), 169–85.

Sorenson, O.; Sorensen, J. B. Finding the Right Mix: Franchising, Organizational Learning, and Chain Performance. *Strategic Manag. J.* **2001,** *22*, 713–724.

Sulek, J.; Hensley, R. The Relative Importance of Food, Atmosphere, and Fairness of Wait. *Cornell Hotel Restaur. Adm. Q.* **2004,** *45*(3), 235–247.

Taylor, S.; Baker, T. An Assessment of the Relationship between Service Quality and Customer Satisfaction in the Formation of Consumers' Purchase Intentions. *J. Retail.* **1994,** *70*(2), 163–179.

Tepeci, M. Increasing Brand Loyalty in the Hospitality Industry. *Int. J. Contemp. Hosp. Manag.* **1999,** *11*(5), 223–229.

Tillotson, J. E. Fast Food-Ray Kroc and the Dawning of the Age of McDonald's. *Nutr. Today.* **2008,** *43*(3), 107–113.

Tse, D. K.; Wilton, P. C. Models of Consumer Satisfaction Formation: An Extension. *J. Mark. Res.* **2001,** *8*(4), 460–469.

Whittaker, G.; Ledden, L.; Kalafatis, S. A Re-Examination of the Relationship between Value, Satisfaction and Intentions in Business Services. *J. Serv. Mark.* **2007,** *21*(5), 345–357.

Woodruff, R. B. Customer Value: The Next Source for Competitive Advantage. *J. Acad. Mark. Sci.* **1997,** *25*(2), 139–153.

Yang, C.; Cheng, L.; Sung, D.; Withiam, G. Strategic Pricing Policy Based on Analysis of Service Attributes. *Cornell Hosp. Q.* **2009,** *50*(4), 498–509.

Zeithaml, V. Consumer Perceptions of Price, Quality, and Value: A Means End Model and Synthesis of Evidence. *J. Mark.* **1988,** *52*(July), 2–22.

Zeithaml, V.; Berry, L; Parasuraman, A. The Behavioral Consequences of Service Quality. *J Mark.* **1996,** *60*, 31–46.

CHAPTER 10

DRIVING VALUE THROUGH PRICING: STRATEGIES ADOPTED BY MANAGERS IN PRICE-SENSITIVE AND FIERCE COMPETITIVE MARKETS

ANJANA SINGH[1] and KAMAL MANAKTOLA[2*]

[1]*Institute for International Management and Technology, Gurgaon, India*

[2]*School of Hospitality, Auro University, Surat, India*

[*]*Corresponding author. E-mail: kamal.manaktola@aurouniversity.edu.in*

CONTENTS

ABSTRACT

Hotel managers have always faced the challenge of use of pricing strategies to achieve both revenue and customer satisfaction. The objective of this paper is to identify existing practices of price setting in hotels of National capital region and strategies adopted by managers in price sensitive and fierce competitive market. This information will enable us to analyze the thoughts and price pressures hotel managers go though in driving value for customers through pricing strategies and to make recommendations accordingly.

The chapter uses qualitative primary research through structured open ended interview to discuss in detail pricing strategies. The interviews will be conducted with senior management responsible for pricing decisions like revenue managers or General Managers from a spectrum of hotels in National Capital Region of India. It is imperative for the hotels to understand the perceived customer value of the product or service in a global context and respond appropriately to change in the market conditions. This research will provide the understanding of the intentions of the hotels towards pricing strategies and the overall aim to be achieved through pricing. This makes this research quite valuable for academic researchers and practitioners to understand the factors that could be important for sustainable pricing strategy.

10.1 INTRODUCTION

Buffett told the Financial Crisis Inquiry Commission in an interview that "If you've got the power to raise prices without losing business to a competitor, you've got a very good business. And if you have to have a prayer session before raising the price by 10%, then you've got a terrible business." Yet, pricing has been neglected area in many hospitality organizations. Mc Kinsey and Company has estimated that fewer than 15% of the organizations have a dedicated function in pricing and fewer than 10% of the colleges teach pricing (Hinterhuber, 2004). Quite a few academicians have confirmed that pricing has been of the neglected components as compared to other components of marketing mix (Avlonities and Indounas, 2006; Hoffman et al., 2002). Hotel room prices face challenges of intangibility, perishability, fixed supply, administrative costs, brand image, customer relationship, and so forth, making it more difficult, challenging, and complex for revenue managers. In the focus of balancing all potentially differing objectives, room pricing may not get due attention but the financial impact may be enormous and destroying for the organization.

Hotel managers have always faced the challenge of use of pricing strategies to achieve both revenue and customer satisfaction. The objective of this paper is to identify existing practices of price setting in hotels of National Capital Region and strategies adopted by managers in price-sensitive and fierce competitive market. This information will enable us to analyze the thoughts and price pressures hotel managers go through in driving value for customers through pricing strategies and to make recommendations accordingly.

The chapter uses qualitative primary research through structured open-ended interview to discuss in detail pricing strategies. The interviews were conducted with senior management responsible for pricing decisions like revenue managers or general managers from renowned international and Indian chains of National Capital Region of India. The similar views were taken from India's leading travel brand to understand in-depth pricing practices followed by hotels in general. It is imperative for the hotels to understand the perceived customer value of the product or service in a global context and respond appropriately to change in the market conditions.

10.2 PRICING AND PRICING STRATEGY

Pricing has been very demanding and tricky especially when prices of raw materials are changing frequently due to market and economic conditions. Researchers have retreated the importance of role of price in marketing mix as it can directly affect the customers, profit, market share, and sales (Monroe, 2003; Nagle and Hogan, 2006;). Engaging with costs would result in sales but engaging with price would result in profits. The rise of Internet and information technology (IT) has helped in strategic implementation of pricing. Singh and Munjal (2013) confirmed that role of IT is quite strategic and helps in providing real-time information when dealing with sensitive customers and fierce competitive market.

"Strategy is concerned with planning how an organization will achieve its goals" (Grant, 2005), whereas a price strategy would signify by how organizations can achieve its pricing objectives. Establishing effective pricing strategies is crucial for marketing managers; therefore, pricing strategy has to be present and prepared quite well in advance. Pricing strategy is quite a conscious decision and needs to be reviewed and modified due to anticipated changes in the business environment. Hence, apart from kinds of transactions, pricing strategy should include kinds of services, customer perception, market segment behavior and competition.

Pricing strategies usually refers to the attention given to pricing based on cost, competitors, or customer perception (Ingenbleek et al., 2003). Noble and Gruca (1999) has provided a framework to support rationale on 10 different pricing strategies supported under majorly three pricing conditions, which are new product, competitive, and product line. The strategies are beyond these three approaches like penetration, skimming, bundling, and so forth.

Pricing objectives give directions for future price strategies (Shipley and Jobber, 2001).Pricing objectives can be combined and intertwined to achieve long-term business objective. Many researchers have mentioned the profitability as main pricing objective as compare to others like market share, sales, and so forth (Meidan and Chin, 1995; Morris and Fuller, 1989). Indounas and Avlonitis (2009) mentioned broadly eight pricing objectives combining qualitative versus quantitative, short terms versus long term, customer satisfaction versus profit objectives. These are:

"Stability in the market; customer-related pricing objectives; service quality-related pricing objectives; financial objectives; achieving satisfactory profits and sales; market share and capacity-related pricing objectives; competition-related pricing objectives; and maximization of profits and sales." Pricing decisions are affected by a variety of external and internal factors. Internal factors are related to organization like cost of service, business objective, and so forth, whereas external factors include customer price sensitivity, competition, and so forth (Shipley and Jobber, 2001).

The price setting process involves positioning of the price indicated by different pricing strategies like skimming, leadership, bundling, and so forth (Table 10.1), to practice; and organizations would require different kinds of data and information to process the same. The price setting concerns with the methods the organizations would use to establish final selling price. Hospitality organizations might differ in their approaches but broadly keen on three major category which are cost-based pricing, competition-based pricing, and values-based pricing and are commonly used by majority of literature (Avlonitis and Indounas, 2005; Nagle and Hogan, 2006; Hinterhuber and Liozu, 2012).

Cost-based pricing is an approach where an organization calculates the cost and return on the investment or certain markup of the cost. Sometimes also known as break even pricing or markup pricing, this approach is easy to implement due to availability of data. This approach ignores the customer perception on value of the services and competition or market price levels.

Competition-based pricing: A market- or competitors-driven approach where prices are influenced with competitors are charging to their customers. This approached monitors both existing and prospective competition to determine the price levels. The pricing overlooks the cost but reduces the risk of price war. Competition-based pricing has been in practice, justified as price has been one of the prime factors for the consumers.

Customer value-based pricing: The customer value-based pricing identifies and uses data on perceived value that the customer has determined for your product or service. This approach is influenced with the reference price or value that has been assigned by the customer. It is driven by the knowledge of customer needs, elasticity, and willingness to pay can be increased despite increasing competition. This approach has given prime importance to customer's value rather that cost and competitor pricing.

10.3 REVENUE MANAGEMENT PRICING

Revenue management (RM) is defined as "an integrated, continuous and organized approach to maximize room revenue through the manipulation of room rates in response to forecasted patterns of demand" (Chiang et al., 2007). RM is a pricing strategy with disciplined tactics and effective forecasting with a focus of price optimization and selling it to micro-segmented markets. It would be important to first understand the concept of RM and then discuss the strategic role of price in hospitality industry. RM strategy has been one of the profitable sources of hospitality sector. There has been little research that has witnessed its application and success in varied areas like restaurants, health clubs, spas, theme parks, and even hospitals. Cross (1998) has witnessed and argue that "Revenue Management systems and strategies have the capability to increase your Return on Investment by 200%." The application and discipline of Yield management initiated with the airline industry and was adopted by hotels in the late 1980s by famous chain Marriott. The strategy managed to increase their incremental revenue by $150–200 million (Marriott and Cross, 2000). RM is successful with certain specific characteristics which are the fixed capacity, ability to segment in markets, perishable inventory, variable demand, high fixed cost, and advance bookings (Kimes and Wirtz, 2003). As against airlines, hotels look for additional revenues from other profit center departments like restaurants, health clubs, conference centers, and spas.

10.3.1 REVENUE MANAGEMENT PRICING APPROACHES AND CHALLENGES

According to Kimes (2010a), RM pricing is based on two dimensions, that is, price discrimination and demand-based pricing. RM pricing is special and unique due to unconstrained demand and the choice is left to hotel to choose customers who are paying most or fulfilling the conditions. This condition gives you the perfect opportunity to increase occupancy as well as average room rate. Price discrimination allows hotels to charge multiple prices to different market segments which ultimately lead to improved revenue as compared to one single rate to all customers. This discrimination could be presented with conditions or fences in terms close to arrival or length of stay controls. Marriott hotels have implemented multiple rates for each day of guest stay and customers have started accepting these multiple rates than traditional single pricing (Kimes, 2010b). The hotels demarcate these multiple prices in forms of physical fences like room view, floor, and so forth, controlled availability where lower rates are possible only through few channels like website, customer characteristics like age, gender, and so forth, transaction characteristics like advance bookings, distribution channel, and so forth, and product line where levels of services are differentiated.

Though effective pricing decisions can increase revenue, hotel should also think about impact of RM pricing on customer satisfaction. The satisfaction is usually affected with the notion of perceived fairness of these prices. Many researchers have confirmed that customers are unlikely to patronize those hotels who are implementing unfair pricing practices (Wirtz and Kimes, 2007; Choi and Matilla, 2005; Kahneman et al., 1986).

Ingenbleek and Lans (2010) have drawn and discussed the framework of pricing strategies developed by Noble and Gruca (1999). This model has talked about three pricing conditions that are competition pricing, new product pricing, and product line pricing. The framework also suggests different strategies under these subheads.

With respect to hospitality, this study has added RM pricing which revolves around the dynamic and differential pricing validated with benefits and restrictions. As previously discussed, the RM pricing includes price discrimination and demand-based pricing. The price discrimination is then justified with different fences and conditions on different customers. These two strategies covers broadly every aspect related to RM pricing (see Table 10.1).

TABLE 10.1 Different Pricing Strategies Under Different Situations.

Situation	Strategy	Description
New product pricing situation	Price skimming	Opening prices are set high and then decrease with time
	Penetration pricing	Opening prices are set low to gain and increase product acceptance
	Experience curve	Set price low to build economies of scales and it benefits to experience players
Competitive pricing situation	Leader pricing	Begin the price change and others pursue it
	Parity pricing	Match the price with overall market
	Low-price supplier	Set lowest price in the market
	Premium pricing	Set highest price in the market
Product line pricing situation	Complementary product pricing	The price of main product is low and charge higher for other miscellaneous services
	Price bundling	Set one price for combination of products or services
	Customer value price	Set prices based on perceived customer value
RM pricing (inventory is fixed and perishable)	Price discrimination	Multiple prices or variable pricing to different market segments
	Demand-based pricing	Customer who are willing to pay the most in unconstrained demand

Source: Adapted from Noble and Gruca (1999), cited in Ingenbleek and Lans (2010).

10.4 PRICE SENSITIVE

Price transparency and high competition make target market quite price sensitive and it becomes key component for revenue manager while making strategies for prices.

Price-sensitivity measurement indicates the value the customer perceives through pricing and quality of product or service. Gabor and Granger (1966) introduced this concept through their research where they identified the price limit of the consumers. They concluded that within the identified limit, price indicates level of quality and outside the limit it acts as a buying barrier. Therefore, price sensitivity of demand or elasticity of demand is the percentage of change in demand due to percentage in price. If a price is too low, it will attract huge demand but will dilute revenue. If the price is too high, it might not generate enough demand to generate potential revenue (Mehrotra, Ideas, No date).

Lewis and Shoemaker (1997) differentiated reference price and price sensitivity and stressed on studying the range of acceptable price by specific market segments. Hoteliers can remove the resistance to purchase by influencing the factors affecting the perception value of customers. Kimes (2003) has also highlighted the need to have in-depth understanding of price sensitivity of customers and rates applied in different distribution channels. The author also highlighted the gap in price optimization methods as hotels possess less knowledge in understanding the relationship between hotel demand and room rates. Guha (2013) in his conversation with global CEO of Alcatel-Lucent, Michel Combes mentioned that India is a very competitive and price-sensitive market signifying that price sensitivity can have a significant impact on revenue and eventually profits.

10.5 PRICE OPTIMIZATION

Pricing has become more multifaceted with loads of information and unique features of hotels like perishable inventory, seasonal demands, and varied market segments. The data have given the opportunity to the hotels to improve the probability of decision-making especially related to price optimization. Hoteliers or managers are becoming revenue managers to understand the demand and price elasticity. Hotel's revenue manager is in charge of price optimization by implementing the key RM strategies like demand management, overbooking and forecasting, and differential pricing with restrictions (Koushik et al., 2012). Hence, the goal of using all these effective strategies is not to receive more business but superior and healthy business. We have all witnessed the evolution of RM from yield and inventory management. In future, revenue optimization is evolved and meaningful description of what hotels have been engaging in rather than RM. Revenue or price optimization is a system that calculates buyer behavior with respect to price and product and generates more profit. (Hayes and Miller, 2011, P. 121). Price optimization model has helped IHG (International Hotels Group) in enhancing the present systems and becoming the forecasting center of excellence and demand intelligence (Koushik et al., 2012). Price optimization techniques or systems help in aligning all strategic decisions related to marketing, budgeting, and inventory of the hotel.

10.6 ANALYSIS AND DISCUSSION

The primary aim achieved through pricing seems to be increasing the operational performance of the hotel by analyzing the revenue per available room and overall profit. Travel portal Yatra.com specified that the hotels are also interested in increasing the market share and dominate the competition. IHG also emphasized the aim of optimum mix of different segments through demand management. While segmentation, hotels should have information on price perceptions and willingness to pay or price value that the customer has attached with your services (Rondan-Cataluna and Rosa-Diaz, 2014). Both these variables cannot operate in isolation and hotels would have to consider the competition and positioning of the hotel in the market. Hinterhuber and Lizou (2012) pointed out that customer value-based pricing is effective in highly competitive industries and this sometimes prevents hotels and managers to be innovative. The possibility of differentiation gives hotel a need to superior pricing through creation of value in the product or services. The hotels have considerable opportunities to differentiate form competitors by create and communicate the same value-based pricing strategies to customers. Becerra et al. (2013) have also confirmed in their study that differentiation strategies give opportunity to hotels to escape from the competitor's pressure of reducing prices.

Pricing at hotels has changed dramatically and with the advent of Internet and the explosion of online travel agents has led to price transparency, and online detailed reviews and feedback (Mcguire and Noone, 2014).

10.6.1 PRICING STRATEGIES AND PRACTICES BY HOTELS

Oberoi Group of Hotels, India

The Oberoi group was founded in 1934 by Late Rai Bahadur Mohan Singh Oberoi. It owns and controls more than 30 properties across India and other various countries. It has received many awards from World Travel awards, Conde Nast Traveler, Forbes and Galileo (Oberoi Hotels, 2014).

Views of Revenue Manager on Pricing Strategies

The overall aim that hotel seeks to achieve through pricing is to create a *right balance between positioning by having a threshold price and achieving optimum Revenue per available room.*

Hotels adopt a pricing strategy of a combination of *competitive and product line pricing.* We are the leaders in the market and the prices are dictated/influenced by us to the rest of the market. We bundle our product or services to a very limited extent and the pricing most of the times are directly proportional to demand.

In price setting process and to implement pricing strategy, the information hotel would be interested is a *combination of costs (which decides the threshold pricing), demand competition pricing, and guest value.*

Segmentation of guests based on their price elasticity is also employed wherever possible specific ***price strategies*** need to be adopted by hotel keeping in view of price-sensitive and fierce competitive market.

Most of the hotels are built with a long-term vision as building hotels is capital intensive and has a long gestation period in India. *Hence, sustainable pricing strategy would be customer value pricing and will precede over revenue management.*

InterContinental Hotels Group, India

InterContinental Hotels Group with nine hotel brands and largest rooms inventory of more than 6 million rooms spread over in 100 countries over the world. IHG owns prestigious brands like InterContinental hotels and resorts, Holiday Inn, Crowne Plaza, Candlewood suites, Hotel Indigo, and so forth.

Views of Revenue Head on Pricing strategies

The aim for most hotel chains is to appropriately price in order to capture an *optimum mix of demand available across segments in order to drive maximum top-line performance of the hotel* (perishable product).

Pricing is critical whether it be rooms/F&B or hotel health clubs and spas. Most hotels try to establish positioning and *retain customers through service, value proposition, competition differentiation, and recognition.* Hotels follow a pricing strategy of combination of pricing methods depending upon demand, lead time, segment, and product type. When setting prices *apart from costs and competition, key elements that hotels always take into account is unconstrained and constrained demand, lead time, price elasticity, and on-the-books performance.*

Revenue Management will be sustainable pricing strategy and would encompass value proposition and price sensitivity etc.

Yatra.com, Travel Organization, India

Yatra.com is a renowned travel portal formed in 2006. In 2012, it was declared as second largest online website in India. It offers ranges of services for both business and leisure traveler. Its reservation facility is extended to more than 12,000 hotels in India and 4 million hotels around the world. It has won many accolades by institutions like Matrixlab, Brand Equity, and CNBC Awaaz.

Views of VP Marketing on Pricing Strategies of Hotels

The overall aim that the hotel seeks to achieve through pricing primarily is *combination of achieving satisfactory profits and sales, market share and capacity-related pricing objectives, and competition-related pricing objectives.*

Hotels pricing strategy is a combination of costs, competition, value and revenue management pricing. *Value-based pricing and competitive pricing are the pricing strategies* adopted by hotel keeping in view of price-sensitive and fierce competitive market.

In future, *Revenue management is the key*. Indiscriminate discounting does not work and needs to be carefully thought out.

Hotels and hospitality organizations are utilizing the competitive information related to rate, revenue, and performance of players in the market. The overloading of the competitive information might lead to "follow the leader" or follow the market which does not indicate a healthy sign of pricing practices. The competitive rate information coupled with demand patterns will help the hotel organizations to analyze the hotel pricing and its influence on the demand in the market.

Price sensitivity has become an important term in RM pricing due to increase in competition and price transparency. RM pricing has always indicated the higher price for higher demand but do really customers want to pay that higher or different price with every time change in demand. According to CHRS (2012), the three pillars to price optimization are demand, competition, and price sensitivity. As discussed above, price optimization manages the complexity by addressing competition and value-based pricing in combination with demand and price sensitivity. Price sensitivity helps in structured representation of how demand would react to change in price positioning in the market and price optimization builds further recommendations.

We can infer from above discussion that pricing has a prominent role in driving value for consumers. Hotels organizations are practicing various modules like price optimization, segmentation, differentiation, demand management, and so forth, to engage with customers especially in sensitive and competitive markets. Information on competition and customer value has always helped hotels to strategize and retain customers in fierce competitive and sensitive markets.

10.6.2 ENGAGING CUSTOMERS WITH REVENUE MANAGEMENT PRICING

Best practice pricing is the combining all the pricing practices and implement in different situations. RM pricing has been voted as sustainable pricing strategy for coming years which would encompass technology for real-time application, customer value, and demand patterns to implement strategically for all target markets with customized services. A winning pricing strategy will be clear, rational, fair, and simple to communicate to stakeholders (Steed and Gu, 2004). Information, familiarity, and communication play a key role in building up customer agreement with the pricing strategies (Choi and Matilla, 2005; Wirtz and Kimes, 2007; Xia et al., 2004). RM pricing is getting popular and getting accepted by the consumer due to its visibility in the allied industries. The information over the Internet is quite accessible leading to price transparency, which makes it easy for customers to weigh the alternatives. Price should not be the only reason left for customers to negotiate. To attain sustainable profits, hotels must use price as a strategic weapon and should concentrate more on superior and exceptional service.

There is need to inform the customers regarding the practice and communicate the fact that it is "Fair." For RM pricing to make inroads, it needs to become customer centric, as stated earlier, the customer needs to be on the same page as the business, and should identify the practice as favorable and fair. Hotels have the opportunity to understand the most profitable and valuable customer and derive *responsible revenue strategies* where customers also have the options of selecting the optimum deal offered to them. Authors describe "Responsible Revenue Management" as strategies which give equal opportunities to both hotels and customers to make their own share of profits. To earn incremental revenues, hotels attract different segments of customers by devising the right yield strategy and to get value, customers will choose the optimum deal from various plans offered to them. Responsible RM offers win-win situations for both involved stakeholders.

10.7 CONCLUSIONS AND RECOMMENDATIONS

RM pricing has been the relevant tool for generating incremental revenue and adding value to the bottom line. The age of tactical RM toward rooms is fading away, hence it needs to be viewed as strategic and should be interfaced with marketing and operating strategies. It is in the interest of the hotel to build a revenue optimization culture that looks beyond rooms alone as drivers of optimization. It should increase its scope toward group RM and other revenue centers like restaurants, banquets, and spas. Application of RM holds relevance beyond demand and supply patterns. It is the response which matters even in high demand and low demand. It is important that the hotels do not panic and be proactive in devising strategies that helps them to sail through the economic crisis in future. RM pricing strategies need to be more responsible and customer centric. The level of communication with the customers will remain crucial to avoid any loss of loyal and valued customers. Pricing and packaging have always played an important role in attracting and retaining customers, hence need to be substantiated with customers information on their buying behaviors. Hotels need to start interacting with its customers and understand their needs and pricing behavior rather making strategies in one room with few managers and competing with few competitors.

10.8 MANAGERIAL IMPLICATIONS

While RM in the Indian hospitality sector has evolved from a mere room inventory management tool, there is a tremendous potential on the one hand and multiple challenges on the other for its further growth.

Consumers have a need, interest, and above all intelligence to negotiate for the services but are willing to pay extra if given genuine value and benefits. We should not aim to confuse customers with hollow and false innovations because that may lead to loss of faith from the brand itself. It is imperative to create, classify, and communicate the price positioning of the product or service and continue to reflect a distinct character of the offerings in the market.

ACKNOWLEDGMENT

Authors acknowledge and thank all the participants for their kind support and the cooperation provided during the interview and conduct of the research.

KEYWORDS

- **price-sensitive markets**
- **fierce competitive markets**
- **pricing strategy**
- **revenue management**
- **information technology**

REFERENCES

Avlonities, G.; Indounas, K.. Pricing Practices of Service Organizations. *J. Serv. Mark.* **2006,** *20*(5), 346–356.

Becerra, M.; Santalo, J.; Silva, C. Being Better vs. Being Different: Differentiation, Competition, and Pricing Strategies in the Spanish Hotel Industry. *Tour. Manag.* **2013,** *34*, 71–79.

Chiang, W. C.; Chen J. C. H.; Xu, X. An Overview of Research on Revenue Management: Current Issues and Future Research. *Int. J. Revenue Manag.* **2007,** *1*(1), 97–128.

Choi, S.; Mattila, A. C. Impact of Information on Customer Fairness Perceptions of Hotel Revenue Management. *Cornell Hotel Restaur. Adm. Q.* **2005,** *46*(4), 444–452.

CHRS Pricing as a Competitive Weapon: How IHG's Price Optimization Capability Revolutionized Pricing for Hospitality [Online] 2012. https://www.hotelschool.cornell.edu/industry/events/chrs/documents/programweb.pdf (accessed Sept 1, 2014).

Cross, R. *Revenue Management: Hard Core Tactics for Market Domination*; Broadway Books: New York, 1998; pp. 50–65.

Frye, A.; Campbell, D. (2011) *Buffet Says Pricing Power More Important than Good Management.* http.bloomberg.com.

Gabor, A.; Granger, C. W. J. Prices as an Indicator of Quality: Report on an Enquiry. *Economica.* **1966,** *33*(129), 43–70.

Grant, Robert M. *Contemporary Strategy Analysis*. Blackwell: Cornwall, UK, 2005; pp. 10–23.

Guha, R. Alcatel-*Lucent: India is a very Competitive and Price Sensitive Market, Times of India.* [Online] 2013. http://timesofindia.indiatimes.com/tech/it-services/Alcatel-Lucent-India-is-a-very-competitive-and-price-sensitive-market/movie-review/22626860.cms (accessed Aug 27, 2014).

Hayes, D. K.; Miller.A. A. *Revenue Management for the Hospitality Industry*. John Wiley & Sons: Hoboken, N.J., 2011; pp. 110–120.

Hinterhuber, A. Towards Value Based Pricing: An Integrative Framework for Decision Making. *Ind. Mark. Manag.* **2004,** *33*(8), 765–778.

Hinterhuber; Lizou. (Is it Time to Rethink your Pricing Strategy? *MIT sloan Manag. Rev.* **2012,** *53*(4), 69–77.

Hoffman, K. D.; Turley, L. W.; Kelley, S. W. Pricing Retail Services. *J. Bus. Res.* **2002,** *55*(12), 1015–1023.

Indounas, K.; Avlonitis, G. J. Pricing Objectives and their Antecedents in the Services Sector. *J. Serv. Manag.* **2009,** *20*(3), 342–374.

Ingenbleek, P.; Debruyne, M.; Frambach, R.T.; Verhallen, T. M. M. Successful New Product Pricing Practices: A Contingency Approach. *Market. Lett.*. **2003**, *14*(4), 289–305.

Ingenbleek, P. T. M.; Van der Lams, I.A. Relating Price Strategies and Price Setting Practices, *Eur. J. Mark.* **2010,** *77* (1/2), 27–48.

Kahneman, D.; Knetsch, J. L.; Thaler, R. H. Fairness as a Constraint on Profit Seeking: Entitlements in the Market. *Am. Econ. Rev.* **1986,** *76*, 728–741.

Kimes, S. *A Strategic Approach to Yield Management.* In A. Ingold; U. McMahon-Beattie; I. Yeoman Eds. *Yield Management: Strategies for the Service Industries.* (2nd ed.): Continuum Press: London, 2003, pp 3–14.

Kimes, S. E.; Wirtz, J. Has Revenue Management Become Acceptable?: Findings from an International Study on the Perceived Fairness of rate fences. *J. Serv. Res.* **2003,** *6*, 125–135.

Kimes, S. The Future of Revenue Management. *Cornell Hosp. Rep.* **2010a,** *10*(14), 4–15.

Kimes, S. *Strategic Pricing through Revenue Management.* In C. Enz Ed.; *The cornell School of Hotel Administration Handbook of Applied Hospitality Strategy.* 2010b;pp 502–513. [Online]. http://scholarship.sha.cornell.edu/cgi/viewcontent.cgi?article=1348&context=articles/ (accessed on July 26, 2014.

Koushik, D.; Higbie, J.; Eister, C. (2012) *Retail Price Optimization at IHG. Interfaces, 42*(1), 45–57 [Online]. http://revenueanalytics.com/wp-content/uploads/2014/03/Retail-PO-at-IHG1.pdf (accessed Aug 28, 2014).

Lewis, R.; Shoemaker, S. Price-sensitivity Measurement: A Tool for the Hospitality Industry. *Cornell Hotel Restaurant Admin. Quarterly.* **1997,** *38*(2), 44–54.

Marriott, J.; Wiard, Jr.; Cross, R. G. *Room at the Revenue Inn. In the Book of Management Wisdom: Classic Writings by Legendery Managers*;:Peter Krass, Ed.;. Wiley: New York, 2000, pp 199–208.

Mcguire, K. A.; Noone, B. M. (2014) Price Ratings and Reviews: Value Transparency in Hotel Pricing, Hospitality Upgrade. [Online]. http://mag.hospitalityupgrade.com/publication/frame.php?i=201234&p=38&pn=&ver=flex (accessed Sept 1, 2014).

Mehrotra, R. *Rate Optimization: Enhancing Your Hotel's Pricing Strategy, IdeaS, White Paper* [Online]. http://revenuemanagement.cc/analysis-rate-optimization-enhancing-your-hotels-pricing-strategy/ (accessed on July 26, 2014.

Meidan, A.; Chin, A. C., Mortgage-pricing Determinants a Comparative Investigation of National, Regional and Local Building Societies. *Int. J. Bank Mark.* **1995,** *13*(3), 3–11.

Monroe, Kent B. (2003), *Pricing: Making Profitable Decisions*, 3d ed. Burr Ridge, IL: McGraw-Hill/Irwin.

Morris, M. H.; Fuller, D. A. (1989), Pricing an Industrial Service. *Ind. Mark. Manag.* **1989,** *18*(2), 139–46.

Nagle, T. T. and Hogan, R. K. *The Strategy and Tactics of Pricing: A Guide to Profitable Decision Making*; Prentice Hall: Englewood Cliffs, NJ, 2006; pp. 130–140.

Noble, P. M.; Gruca, T. S. Industrial Pricing: Theory and Managerial Practice. *Mark. Sci.* **1999a,** *18*(3), 435–54.

Rondan-Cataluña, F. J.; Rosa-Diaz, I. Segmenting hotel clients by pricing variables and value for money, Current Issues in Tourism, [Online]. http://www.turisme.gva.es/turisme/es/files/pdf/Biblio_revistas/2014/Current_Issues_Tourism/Current%20Is.Tour%202014-17-1_60-71.pdf (accessed Aug 28, 2014).

Singh,Anjana and Munjal, Sandeep (2013) "Emerging revenue management practices and its challenges: Indian luxury hotelier's perspective proceedings of the International conference on Global Competitiveness and Corporate Governance Imperatives in Emerging Economies which is being organized by Ansal University (School of Management studies) on February 15-16, 2013

Shipley, D. D.; Jobber, D. Integrative Pricing via the Pricing Wheel. *Ind. Mark. Manag.* **2001,** *30*(3), 301–14.

Steed, E.; Gu, Z. An Examination of Hotel Room Pricing Methods: Practised and Proposed. *J. Revenue Pricing Manag.* **2004,** *3*(4), 369–379.

Wirtz, J.; Kimes, S. E. The Moderating Role of Familiarity in Fairness Perceptions of Revenue Management Pricing. *J. Serv. Res.* **2007,** *9*(3), 229–240.

Xia, L.; Monroe, K. B.; Cox, J. L. The Price is Unfair! A Conceptual Framework of Price Fairness Perceptions. *J. Mark.* **2004,** *68*, 1–15.

PART VI
Technology

CHAPTER 11

MANAGING TECHNOLOGIES FOR CONSUMER ENGAGEMENT

PARUL WASAN*

Associate Professor, Manav Rachna International University, Faridabad, Haryana, India

**E-mail: Parul.wasan@yahoo.co.in*

CONTENTS

ABSTRACT

"The passive consumer of analog media has rapidly evolved into an active creator of content moving across multiple digital media channels." (Baker, 2010)

The emerging technologies epitomize the consumer lifestyles. Additionally, it also points towards increased internet activity and social media usage through integrated media apps through mobile devices.

The consumer is usually at the epicenter of the convergence trend, and more often than not, consumer leads the technology adoption curve, while a hotel enterprise is forced to play catch up in order to pursue customers in the domain of consumer engagement. According to Adam Cahill, EVP co-media director, responsible for digital strategy and media across all Hill Holliday clients, "*it boils down to three key consumer behavior changes... (they are) more mobile, (do) more simultaneous consumption, and (they are) more social.*"

According to a white paper from Mindtree titled *Mindtreedigital: Insights into consumer engagement in hospitality*, there are two major forces that have influenced the growth of digital technology in the hospitality industry today. (A) Increasing importance of the social media as a way of life, (B) use of social media as a platform for interaction with each other and with brands, products, and services, and (C) growing adoption of technology devices for interaction with an enterprise viz. the hotels.

Additionally, "adoption of technology" has altered both the operational and the philosophical aspect of how any hotel enterprise looks at customer engagement.

Therefore, a new class of technology is evolving termed as *customer engagement technologies* (CETs). According to *Customer engagement technology study: 2013*, "**CETs can be defined as technologies and/or applications which are utilized to create deeper, more meaningful connections between a company and its customers to enhance the overall quality of their experiences, drive customer loyalty, and ultimately lead to increased sales and profitability**."

Emerging insights are now pointing toward trends that fuel merger of consumer technologies, mobile and convergence technology and the social media – for creating opportunities and expectations for enhancing guest services and guest expectations in hospitality industry. Then they are brands that are scaling up the social competencies of their websites, in order to bond with their customer. Additionally they synchronize their strategies to achieve deeper customer engagements.

The industry has started to use new technologies (also known as "funware") and the power of social networking.

An example of a new strategy is the new buzz word "**Gamification,**" it is the new concept on the block. It offers a powerful marketing strategy to hospitality companies for little or no cost. Gamification techniques challenge and motivate customers through competition, recognition, and rewards. Further, because the dynamics of gamification are highly transferable, they can be applied to achieve many different goals: to create viral PR and buzz, increase loyalty or compliance, crowd source new products or solutions, gain feedback, recruit talent, and so forth.

11.1 INTRODUCTION

Technology has become the central theme of the hospitality industry. Customers are increasingly flocking around new applications, purchasing new devices, and visiting new hospitality sites. This has guided the industry towards innovative ways of approaching and bringing together the new age but fragmented customers.

The role of technology in nurturing the growth of the hospitality industry and increasing its effectiveness has been widely recognized through its widespread influence over the industry. Hence technology is viewed as a viable weapon and a strategic resource. This calls for effective technology management at all levels of the hospitality industry. Gaynor in 1989, defined technology management as:

> "A method of operation that leverages human resources, technologies and other assets by *optimising* the relationship between the business enterprise and technological functions. It is a process of integrating managing, science and engineering with research, development and manufacturing in order to meet the operational goals of the business unit efficiently, effectively and economically. It includes managing the totality of the technological operations from concept through commercialization."

Technology management therefore includes many interconnected issues viz. – technology policy; technology strategy; technological forecasting and assessment; technology transfer; technology-induced as well as market-oriented Research and Development (R&D); human resource management in terms of innovative capabilities, process technology and product technology and their continuing improvement; flexibility and contribution; and technology project management.

11.1.1 MANAGING TECHNOLOGIES FOR CUSTOMER ENGAGEMENT

Technology management (as listed above) embraces several interrelated issues ranging from policy planning at the group level to strategic planning at the property level, it calls for decisions and effective macro–micro relationships, and result-oriented actions both at the macro as well as micro levels.

Macro technology management at the corporate or group level primarily concerns about planning for:

- Improving technological competency at the corporate level
- Identifying strategic sector specific technology and related fields that needs to be developed
- Ascertaining in-house development competency or considering "buy" decisions
- Instituting formal mechanisms for directing and coordinating the development of technological capabilities
- Proposing policy measures for controls

Micro technological management on the other hand is primarily concerned about technology management at the hotel level. It includes:

- Taking counter measures to block any fallout that may ensue because of technology use by the competitor
- Integrating technology strategy into the overall corporate strategy
- Identifying and assessing technological options and improvements along with the factors relating to their success and failure
- Guiding research and development, including determination and definition of project feasibility at the corporate level
- Reviewing and planning technological obsolescence and replacement

Together, thcy cnable the industry to better plan, link, control, evaluate, and manage technological processes so that they are mutually synergistic.

This also implies linking various levels of management and departments, infrastructure and business strategy, bringing various stakeholders into the fold, and keeping pace with the technological processes, customer requirements. In all this entails a three-step mechanism of technology management, namely integration of technology identification, implementation, and potential technology commercialization processes at the frontline. This brings us to the management of technologies that operate within a hotel ecosystem. Central to these are the backbone technologies that form the customer engagement ecosystem of the hotel viz. Property Management Systems (PMS), Central Reservations Systems (CRS), Global Distribution Systems (GDS), point of Sales (POS), Loyalty Programs, and so forth.

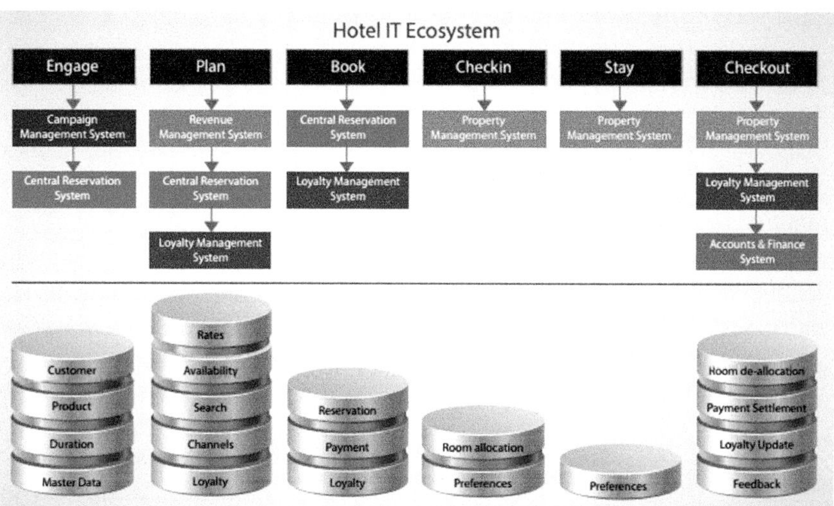

Source: Infosys (2013) White paper – Integrated property and Guest Management System (online).

A large number of hotel properties worldwide have integrated technologies in their day-to-day operations, to provide their customers with the top of the line hospitality products and services at the optimum value. So when it comes to ensuring success in the hospitality industry, it's all about integrating technology solutions to deliver optimal connectivity, better business management, and data quality; along with goal of increasing productivity, better customer service, and optimizing revenue and maximizing margins.

The remaining are seriously considering new solutions to gather better guest intelligence, compete in the market, and gain control of distribution on a global scale. Most importantly, they have begun to inquire about IT solutions that would help them to increase revenue and profitability. Not only are they dealing with decreasing commission cuts and low profits, they also have to keep up with emerging competitors. This has forced the technological laggards in the hospitality to drastically retool their business models, in order to effectively compete and offer their customers the best hospitality and value for money. They therefore are now scouting for providers of seamless integration, at the most cost effective price.

11.2 THE BACKBONE TECHNOLOGIES

11.2.1 PROPERTY MANAGEMENT SYSTEMS (PMS)

Standard definitions define it is a comprehensive software application used to cover some basic objectives such as coordinating the operational functions of front office like guest bookings, guest details, online reservations, point of sale, and so forth. and functions of sales and planning, banquets, food, and beverage costing, besides materials management, HR and payroll, maintenance management, quality management, and other amenities in the hospitality industry. Additionally, hotel property management systems may interface with yield management systems, payment card authorization, back office, pay-TV, door-locking, house-keeping optimization, energy management, and channel management systems.

Since actions and activities such as above take place simultaneously, it falls upon PMS to automate the entire range of functions. This leads to optimized hotel operations, besides gathering business intelligence.

Business Intelligence: An Effective Offshoot of PMS

A good business intelligence and the associated software can always benefit a hotel/hospitality entity because it helps them to access:

- Industry benchmarks which are focused around profitability, and not just revenue

- Market-linked cost optimization connected with the distribution strategy
- Behavioral economics rooted into pricing and marketing decisions
- Forecast to control availability and product management

Not only do these software's and solutions help hoteliers to answer why, where, what and how of sales, they also facilitate marketing and revenue management and strategic decision making.

An effective BI tool would therefore enable the hoteliers to continually optimize their profit margins by (a) efficiently sifting through the enormous customer data that is generated every day and (b) analyzing the customer behaviors, buying patterns, and references. This in turn can guide the hotel in identifying profitable guests/customers; leading to designing effective service offerings.

Adapted from: Technology for Better Business Intelligence (online) (10th July 2014) http://hospitalitytechnology.wordpress.com/2012/03/26/technology-for-better-business-intelligence/

PMS is an important part of the strategic management of a hotel since it pervades through various functionalities of the organizations and is also involved in exploring innovative ways to make the system more customer centric.

Property management strategies, technologies, and capabilities address various demands of the hotel.

11.2.2 PROPERTY MANAGEMENT STRATEGIES

1. Numerous studies carried out by experts revolve around (a) data and IT integration of business function silos and across customers, (b) developing loyalty initiative and customer insights. The foremost strategic action, therefore being carried out at the hotel level is the aligning the business and customer requirements with IT for business optimization. This lowers the ownership costs of

the applications, helps in expansion of customer touch points, increases the customer service efficiency and positively impacts the revenue margins. These strategies eliminate the gap that exists between the business, the IT infrastructure, and the customer requirements – which centers around the extended in-room and other value added services the enable the hotel to become more profitable and efficient.

2. Another strategic action that many experts have pointed out is to develop standards that can help to integrate the back-office data with the front-office data. Integrating these standards is therefore the new action being taken by both old school and the new school hotels and the hospitality segments. Not only does it help in obtaining a unified view of the property but also of the guest. This results in – (a) efficient performance and service allocation, (b) enhanced forecasting and revenue capabilities, (c) improved customer service capabilities, and (d) increased revenue accountability.
   Another advantage of such a strategic action is that employees can have an over view of the facility. This helps them to optimize reservations, room allocation, and staffing among other things. These in turn would help the service personnel to access customer data viz. spending habits, on-premise expenditure, preferences, and so forth, long before the arrival of the customer. The industry is as of now in a critical phase of expanding in a contracting economic scenario. The standards for data integration for – (a) internal procurement, (b) room inventory, (c) finance, (d) marketing, and (e) customer information have therefore become essential to its survival.
3. Reward based strategic action on the other hand focuses on data collaboration techniques. In other words an increase in customer/business data allows a hotel property to use enhanced analytic techniques to create more precise offers and loyalty programs. It is an industry observation that the best in their class hotels/chains focus on retaining the current customers by utilizing reward based loyalty incentive. These properties often use multi-tiered reward strategies; additionally they also share this data across all their properties thus arming their employees with actionable customer data, thereby enhancing customer retention at a staggering rate.

11.2.3 PROPERTY MANAGEMENT CAPABILITIES

1. Leading Hotel properties invest in regular upgrades of their IT systems to retain competitive edge over their rivals. These more often than not are in the area of real-time reporting capabilities for optimizing property management. The trigger for these actions is usually both external (customers or environment) and external (employee). Broadly speaking these upgrades are in the areas like – (a) Customer centric network enhancement, (b) application performance for employees, (c) new application integration competency, (d) requirements for regulatory compliance. Consequentially, employees are armed with competent operations and customer related technology and functionality. This results in reduced manual labor costs and better overall guest experience.
2. Real-time or near-real-time reporting often result in evaluation of the organizational performance resulting in changes in the stand point of – inventory, workforce, marketing or pricing. An interesting fall out of such actions is the creation of a mentality of a "unified version of the reality" for the employees. All departments have a clear knowledge of the overall performance of the property thereby improving interdepartmental collaboration, increase in customer touch points and service availability.
3. Managing property connectivity applications is an important part of the property management exercise. These help in optimizing activities like inventory management, revenue management, central reservation programs, customer loyalty, and CRM programs along with business intelligence. Additionally, connectivity between various functionalities ensures that there are no gaps in the performance and in keeping each other in the communication loop. This allows seamless flow of information and the availability of the property management data in real time.
4. One of the key functions of a property management system is being able to predict the customer flow and forecast the availability of amenities. This also ensures proper staffing levels across the property. Also based on this information, the front desk utilizes incoming guest records to upgrade different packages and offerings.

5. An offshoot of the property management capabilities is the "planned property management capability" of a hotel. This enables the hotel to retain high performing employees and ensure constant upgrade of skills. Incentive systems based on application integration and business performance and automated training cycles for both customer and operation processes; ensures that the employees remain vested in their jobs. Increasing use of the automated training portals has enabled the organizations to do away with costly off-site training. Hotels have integrated training systems into the property management capabilities and thus allowing "on the move" training for the new employees. These systems use pop-up web based tutorials programed within the system. This ensures streamlined training exercises and reduction in costs and time.

11.3 TECHNOLOGY AS AN ENABLER IN PROPERTY MANAGEMENT

Given the ever evolving technological and customer scenario, most hotels often quickly step into systems upgrade. Technological management at the crucial touch points therefore becomes important and is often the focus of constant review. In order to facilitate efficiency a hotel therefore often integrates property management applications into the PMS. Managing this very critical aspect is crucial for operational success of customer touch points and operations related areas. Yet misalignment exists between the existing systems and the newer applications. Alert organization overcomes this critical issue by utilizing service-oriented architecture (SOA) for integrating systems and applications. A service-oriented architecture is essentially a collection of services. Simply put these services communicate with each other. This can involve either simple data passing or it could involve two or more services coordinating some activity.

"A SOA has been defined as the underlying structure supporting communications between services. SOA explains how two computing entities, such as programs and applications, interact with each other to enable one entity to perform a unit of work on behalf of another entity. Service interactions use a description language. Each interaction is self-contained and loosely coupled, and is independent of any other interaction." (Margaret Rouse)

Although, the current economic situation around the world necessitates that a hotel property give more importance to guest services, yet there has been a concerted effort to integrate various applications like inventory management, revenue management, and central reservation system. This is in addition to integration of various CRM applications into the PMS. Thus, signalling the importance of PMS in hotel operations.

According to Hospital Technology (2013) about 19% of the total IT budget of a hotel is spent on PMS. According to Barb Bowden (2012), general manager of "The Peabody Orlando," "Today the critical point (that) we are focusing on with our PMS is overall improvements to the guest experience. The whole concept of understanding your guest and understanding their preferences and behaviors to enhance the experience goes along with a hotel's ability to market to the guest in a better way."

11.4 FUTURE DIRECTIONS IN PMS

11.4.1 SOCIAL MEDIA PRESENCE

Increasing social media presence has forced the hospitality industry to integrate its systems with the capabilities of the social media. Many experts and hoteliers have therefore come to the conclusion that the PMS can be further developed to respond to guest chatter on various social media sites. It is gradually being felt that as a part of social branding, designated employees armed with appropriate tools could manage, monitor, and analyze social media chatter while interacting with the guests online. Future could see new applications that could help integrate social media profiling with PMS.

11.4.2 DATA INTEGRATION, CLOUD, AND CUSTOMIZATION

The future of data PMS systems lies in applications that recognize guest preferences in order to create a unique offering complete with a comprehensive tailor made rate charts, service packages, and options for avenues for guest to spend upon or make purchases. As the thin line between data entry by guests on the internet and the hotel entry of the guest information at check-in diminishes, PMS systems would have to evolve to anticipate guest preferences and requirements while simultaneously track guest behavior. In future the PMS systems would be expected to pick up nuances of the guest behavior and become more specific by accommodating tidbits of the customer's personality. Such systemic modifications can allow the guest to fill in data about their specific requirements, like allergies, preferences of pillows, sheets, room temperature, coffee/tea/food requirements, wake-up call, and so forth long before they set foot on the hotel premises. In addition to incorporating "do it yourself facility" into the hotel processes for the guests, future of PMS systems would include the mobile distribution of data for increasing the efficiency of the staff and hotel associates. This would enhance their ability to provide assistance to the guest anywhere and anytime.

As hotel chains move into uncharted territories and expanded international markets, because of regional languages, government rules and regulations, and localization, it will become imperative to implement globalized common enterprise solutions across all the properties both in operational and financial areas. Additionally, a globalized PMS system could also act as a tool to map the currency and time conversions, the location of goods, assets, inventories, and supply chain networks both at the local and global level.

Cloud based technologies have become instrumental in cost reduction and increasing interoperability in the hotel departments. Not only have they expanded the functionality of the property they have also reduced the operating costs and depending on the size of the property it is also the way of the future. Hoteliers are seriously considering unifying the pricing across similar properties and therefore need to understand the components and how much each one costs. It would be an interesting development if all the PMS vendors could get together and leverage the cloud and PCI component to provide a solution that can be run on the least common denominator of technology.

Customization is always a desired by-product of the hotel industry. It is this aspect which distinguishes one hotel property from another. It is therefore not surprising that hotels also look for unique customizations of their PMS systems. There is a call from all small and medium sized properties that– the PMS developers create a unique ability or an interface perspective, within the system that would allow each guest to customize it according to their needs, yet at the same time the system could remain within the purview of the property– in other words hoteliers are now demanding that the guests may be allowed to "*have their cake and eat it too.*" They argue that one size of the PMS cannot fit all the customer requirements because the needs are different from an interface perspective.

11.5 CONSUMER ENGAGEMENT – THE DIGITAL ENABLER

Customers of today operate round the clock through social networks, mobile devices. They want instant gratification and control over their situations. Not only are they sophisticated, they are demanding and informed, as a result they are in a position to enforce their desires and demands. It thus becomes important that an organization recognizes that guests appreciate and understand effective technology. Therefore, it is essential to integrate customer contact with the technological connect in order to achieve strategic goals. Hoteliers have thus recognized that customers of today have immense desire to engage and control. A desire that is fuelled by new channels, emerging technology platforms, the dominance of social media platforms, and mobile devices. Hoteliers therefore not only need to manage (a) Customer Engagement Technology (CET) and (b) think about ways and means where systems, practices, and individuals can collaborate and share optimum results in other words move toward convergence.

Customer engagement can be defined as influencing the customer to act in accordance with the strategic objectives of a hospitality organization through a unique aspect that is (or could be) important to the customer. Accordingly when a brand identifies with a customer and promises satisfaction by offering bundle of attributes, it assumes that a transaction will take place because the consumer perceives a value addition to self when relating to the brand.

In line with this thought distribution practices and constantly evolving digital marketing exercises have begun to defy traditional marketing and sales structures. Not only do they challenge traditional way of doing things, they also force hoteliers to take a comprehensive and holistic approach to digital distribution, revenue optimization, and demand generation. Thus gently nudging them to see how the technologies are converging together under one umbrella. This requires a whole new mindset and fresh strategies that demand collaboration and connectivity.

In other words, the hospitality industry needs to reconfigure its resources and expertise to stay ahead of consumer behavior change with dynamic technology adoption. Additionally, the key to delivering the new reality is through relevant content and services. This can be achieved through people and technology engagement, and optimizing processes across rapidly evolving set of customer touch points. Given the fact that the consumer is at the eye of the raging technology storm, it becomes a thought point to investigate the customer preferences from through multiple vantage points.

11.5.1 CUSTOMER ENGAGEMENT TECHNOLOGIES

These technologies have been defined by Gartner (2013), as "set of technologies and business applications that provide customer service and support, regardless of the interaction (or engagement) channel, including social media and community forums, while retaining the customers' context, but also to deliver the appropriate business rule to determine the next best action, information or process with which to engage the customers." Falling under this umbrella are the efforts of hotels to engage customers through digital technologies be it smartphones, tablets, and various other near field communication technology (NFC) devices.

According to a white paper from Mindtree, titled *Mindtreedigital: Insights into Consumer Engagement in Hospitality*, there are two major forces that have influenced the growth of digital technology in the hospitality industry today. (a) Increasing importance of the social media as a way of life, (b) use of social media as a platform for interaction with each other and with brands, products, and services, and (c) growing adoption of technology devices for interaction with an enterprise viz. the hotels. Additionally another 2013 Customer engagement technology study point towards four technology trends that drive the progression of consumer engagement technologies in the hospitality and restaurant industry namely (a) consumerization of IT, (b) social media, and (c) mobile technologies and convergence.

Consumerization of IT: Prevalence of "bring your own device" (BYODs) and "Buy-your-own-content"(BYOC) among the customers creates challenges within the IT infrastructure within hotel premises. Because this calls for increase in bandwidth and the need for number of power outlets in the hotel, if the hotel wishes to enhance the customer experience during the stay and contribute to the guest expectations.

Social Media: Role of social media has evolved as that of a coordinator of different aspects of guest life cycle. A transparent organization attracts an informed customer and creates greater expectations. Both digital and social media marketing are now emerging as the future battle ground as more and more hotels and restaurants involve interactive technologies in the hope of capturing that elusive market share, drive revenue, and generate customer loyalty. The approach is to encourage participation of the customers in contests, video blogging activities, and take pictures to compete for various prizes. A 2013 study by Hospitality technology suggests that by 2015, nearly all hotels and restaurants would achieve 97% market penetration through social media. Additionally, it is hoped that these organizations will integrate their loyalty programs with their social media initiatives. Through these initiatives they hope to overcome cost complexities created to achieve technological integration and the need to take incremental steps. Facebook and Twitter are the social media sites of choice not because they are the most popular (1.11 billion Facebook users, 5.5 million Twitter users), but also because they are relatively easy to use. Another eye opener has been that hoteliers and restaurateurs consider these services a goldmine for mining data to gain customer feedback and insights, which then are incorporated into their continuous improvement process.

As the industry improves its exposure to novel social media platforms it has started to experiment with various social media tools that match its customer base in order to justify time spent, attract critical user mass, drive customer visitation and purchase behavior, customer value, and engage the target customer over long periods of time. This may appear as a daunting challenge for many hotels, yet for today's hyper-connected customers, the ability to engage through social media is no longer a novelty but an expected piece of the customer experience. An example of such an event was an initiative taken by Hyatt Hotels in 2011 to directly engage its customers on Facebook. It invited suggestions from its customers on how to improve its FB page. Hyatt harnessed this information to further increase its promotions and games for residents. In this way it elicited proactive response and was able to transfer conversation into action.

Convergence

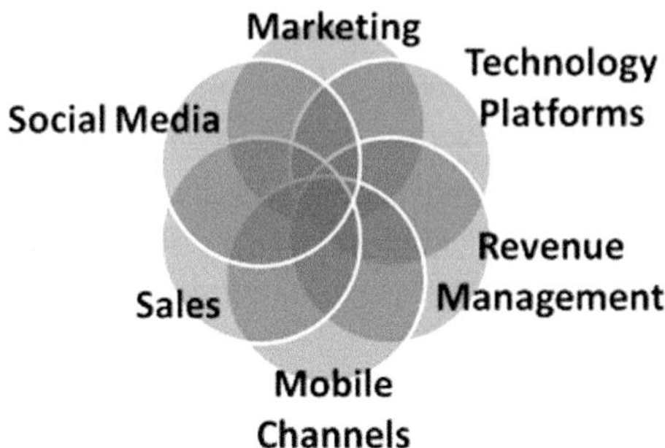

Source: Schnieder, Taryn (2012) Converging on Success: Best Practices for Managing Convergence in Hospitality Sales, Marketing and Revenue Optimization, Hospitality Sales and Marketing Association International *in* partnership with Sabre Hospitality Solutions.

Hospitality sales and marketing today is driven by the new travel consumer who wishes to be engaged and be in control at all times. He is ably assisted in this endeavour by emerging technology platforms, new channels, endless touch points, along with ever present mobile devices. Evolving digital marketing practices and distribution landscape is defying the traditional thinking and sales and marketing structure, forcing hoteliers to take a holistic approach to digital distribution, demand generation, and revenue optimization. Additionally, it also requires a new mindset that seeks to combine strategies of collaboration and connectivity.

Convergence looks at ways that individuals practices and systems work together for optimum results in the travel scape the world over. The reason for this technology convergence is the shift in the consumer behavior. For example behavioral marketing customer relationships management solutions are converging with the hotel reservation technology. CRM on the other hand is converging with e-commerce in order to support a multi touch-point customer experience. Another example of this convergence would be demand generation information with advanced analytics in the hotel. The flip side of this system would be chaos that could be generated at crucial areas, overlap and redundancy between jobs, in the absence of a systematic plan, which could result in empty rooms, facilities, and restaurants. Convergence therefore requires systematic preparation and professional guidance if disorder in the system is to be avoided. It would be safe to say that organizations need to sort out their resources and identify their abilities to be at par with consumer technology adoption and consumer behavior change. Convergence therefore creates quality in the customer interactions, which is fashioned by different technologies, platforms, disciplines, and channels to generate solutions that are greater than individual parts.

As a hotelier moves toward enhancing the customer engagement he/she requires the right technology framework to enable this transition. Convergence includes everything from content distribution, online presence, social engagement, and how a product offering by a hotel is assessed, booked, and reviewed by the customer. For example the convergence of PMS (PMS), customer relationship management systems (CRM) and central reservation systems (CRS) enhances revenue management, pricing, and inventory control. Additionally it also gives a holistic view of individual customer which in turn can be applied to each initiative like CRM, distribution management, rate and inventory control, and guest management.

Convergence: Personalizing Customer Interaction: Integrating systems for optimizing customer interactions may entail identifying right technology framework. A hotelier may therefore look at a converged enterprise platform with a single data model and point management to support distribution, marketing, rate and inventory control, guest management, and property operations.

Content and relevancy become very important when the customer becomes the center of the operation. It becomes all the more important to deliver personalized and dynamic content that is uniform across all channels, in order to convert queries into confirmed bookings. In this context the role of the content management system (CMS) would be to simultaneously place information on the hotel website as well as on the social media channels, email lists, and on the mobile web. Ideally a hotel CMS should push the content beyond marketing channels and into call center, front desk, open travel alliances (OTAs), and in-room TV.

Mobiles have become a powerful tool to create a meaningful experience. Together social, local, and mobile platforms can be used to deliver more personalized and relevant content to engage the existing and potential customer. A hotelier's mindset therefore has to go beyond being a provider to being an enabler of distribution channels, social networking, customer relationship, and marketing services. Additionally, the hotelier needs to dominate the complete travel experience of the customer on the social media, by anticipating customer desires at every step of the travel experience. The new data points can therefore affect the bottom line of the hotel and influence both the marketing messages and distribution channels of the property.

Revenue management is no longer about juggling numbers; it has transitioned to being customer centric and is being driven by competitive pricing strategies and distribution insights. It has therefore become imperative that a hotelier fine tunes its pricing and marketing strategies to gain a fair share of the market. Additionally a well thought of distribution strategy in conjunction with pricing and branding across all channels and search engines would affect the bottom line.

It is interesting to note that social media has become the preferred channel for reward programs, a hotelier can converge this insight into the business intelligence and create better promotions, incorporate customer preferences, and pricing decisions to generate buzz and short-term revenue.

Convergence is essentially all about a multichannel approach. Following the customer across various channels would ensure that as a hotelier you are able to create personalized transactions and guest experience at every touch point. A contextually relevant insight about what guests want, what they use, how they use, and when they use becomes a crucial nugget of information for tailoring the next generation of services.

As more and more areas become dependent upon each other, it is essential to gain insight into how roles and responsibilities have evolved in order to create a comprehensive and collaborative environment. Convergence ensures this relationship between (a) revenue management, (b) distribution, (c) marketing and sales. Additionally, this ensures accountability, communication, and cooperation. This is necessary to understand each other's roles, identify areas in which to collaborate, talk in the same language, and use same set of metrics for revenue enhancement and customer satisfaction.

A moot question at this point would be "Does the customer prefer the automated digital engagement in all contexts?," or "do they look forward to the tablet apps for room service and mobile check-ins'?," especially when (a) there is an increasing comfort level and presence of digital consumer devices among the customers and (b) we have so far been advocating digitalization at all levels in the hotel industry.

11.6 NEED FOR ENHANCING CONSUMER ENGAGEMENT

11.6.1 ENGAGING THE CUSTOMER WITHIN THE PROPERTY OR ON-PREMISE ENGAGEMENT

Technology is profoundly impacting every facet of the hospitality industry, through "disruptive innovation." It is a term coined by Clayton Christensen, who describes it "as a process by which a service or a product enters at the bottom of the market in the form of simple application and rapidly moves up the market chain, in the process it displaces existing competitors," *for example, cell phones have disrupted the technology of land lines, while tablets and PCs have replaced the mini and mainframe computers.* These technological advances have mandated that changes take place in operating procedures, hotel design, and the architecture of service delivery processes. Technologies like these have significantly altered the competitiveness of the hospitality industry, especially in the way a hotel interacts with the guests. For the hospitality industry this represents an opportunity to be different (Exhibit-1).

The Future of On-premise Engagement in Managed Technology: iBeacons

The latest innovation currently being tested in the hotel industry is the use of iBeacons' for on premise engagement of the customer. As a technology for guest engagement ibeacon is making inroads across the industry. Additionally, it offers enhanced customer experience and increased revenue opportunities.

Not so long ago, capabilities of iBeacons' were limited to the public spaces like parks, museums, and stadiums. This technology has however opened up new possibilities for resorts and hotels that use geo-fencing. Additionally this technology (app) acts as personal concierge to the guest. These iBeacon's use a Bluetooth Low Energy profile for locating small objects or for "micro-location" to assist hotel guests in many aspects such as interacting with staff, room service or for in-room entertainment. Simply put these are "low-powered-transmitters" that are used by the hotels and others to deliver context and proximity based information like opening. This technology is currently at an early stage and few hotels like Marriott International which has launched Local Perks, a new feature within its Rewards program that uses iBeacons to follow and reach hotel patrons with push notifications.

Leading hospitality organizations are increasingly maximizing opportunities at on premises facilities such as restaurants, spas, and function spaces by taking advantage of sophisticated technology to increase revenue generation within the four walls of the property. They engage with on premises guests by sending them "location-aware" recommendations and offers, thereby increasing the likelihood of guest spending additional money on hotel services. This results in greater use of the hotel facilities, besides additional revenue generation. Additionally hoteliers have recognized that hotel rooms must be equipped with the technologies to which guests have become accustomed in their work places and at homes. Not surprisingly it puts immense pressure on budgets and the technology infrastructure, especially on the internet bandwidth. A hotel also has to invest in employee training, so that they can assist guests with connecting and using their devices during their stays. Additionally, hotels are working round the clock with technology companies to keep up with their gadget obsessed guests and retain their market edge. No sooner does the guest checks in, their mobiles are automatically synchronized with the dedicated hotel network. The connection is customized to the type of device the guest is using. The hotel also ensures personalized content and network bandwidth in relation to the guest's loyalty level, and/ or as a service available at an additional cost. There is a twofold advantage of such a provision (a) the hotel anonymously tracks these signals and provides hoteliers with an insight and analytics on guest flow and behavior, that is, how the guests move around the hotel property and (b) understand the customer "dwell time" in public spaces and/or in amenity areas. Such connectivity helps the customer to find their way around the hotel. These provisions display "turn-by-turn" directions, indoor mapping information of the property, and other contextual information. These deliver more personalized and relevant services to the guests, as and when they need it. The hotel also uses real-time personalized location-based messaging to entice the guests with contextual offers based on guests' interests and his current location in the hotel. Such applications also ensure that the guests can shop from anywhere and anytime within the hotel, change their itinerary or order room service. These transactions can be posted back to the guest folio in the hotel PMS and be used to increase operational efficiencies and guest experience.

Hotels therefore establish long term business relationship with technology companies in order to keep up with new products and trends. Conversely, this also means that they establish a symbiotic relationship, wherein the technology company can show case its latest innovations to the customer within the premises of the hotel without any additional cost. According to Sandra Andrews, hospitality industry solutions director for Microsoft, "The guests that walk through the hotel lobby are the same consumers that Microsoft targets." Under the current economic situation, experts caution that hotels need to focus on essential technologies and on increasing bandwidth that can justify additional room rent or attract bring in more guests.

- Hotels like the Sheraton have joined hands with Microsoft to create Link@Sheraton Lounges to create space in lobbies. Guests can use these spaces to check their e-mail, print boarding passes, and skype greetings to their family and friends.
- Westin hotel on the other hand has made arrangements with Nintendo to provide its fitness centers with Wii consoles and games like Wii fit. Clients at the fitness center can use these games to exercise and do yoga.
- Smaller hotels have also taken a cue from this emerging trend and have turned to technology leaders like Sony to equip their guest rooms and public spaces with the latest electronics. A few of them have revamped their public spaces to suit the needs of both the leisure and business travelers'.

11.6.2 ENGAGING THE CUSTOMER OUTSIDE THE PROPERTY OR OFF-PREMISE ENGAGEMENT:

Gamification: Customer loyalty is important for the hotel industry. However, more competitors and better informed customers have made this difficult. It is therefore important that hotels forge bonds with their customers by using new strategies. Gamification is one such strategy, which has been around for some time now but off lately it has reinvented itself. It uses powerful elements of game to connect and engage with customers. It uses "Funware" and social networking to challenge customers through rewards, competition, and recognition. Gamification can also be applied to (a) increase loyalty/compliance, (b) create buzz and viral PR, (c) gain feedback, (d) recruit talent, and (e) crowd source new products or solutions.

Travelers using frequent flier programs are used to planning their itinerary in such a manner so as to optimize their points. They would be familiar with the way strategizing works and result in upgrades, free flights or free hotel stays which are tangible in nature. However, unlike these programs, gamification motivates people with virtual rewards very much like a virtual game that have little or no monetary value. Gamification is similar to the frequent flier programs in as much as it offers rewards and incentives to drive consumer behavior. It deepens the engagement of the customer with the brand by exposing them to something that has an intangible value. This opens up limitless possibilities for the hotel property at no extra cost. An example of one such "Gamified loyalty" program is "*Win it in a Minute*" program of the InterContinental Hotel Group. It's a daily online trivia game which rewards customers with free miles in lieu of correct answers. This program was created for young customers who are not known for their brand loyalty.

Marriot hotel, on the other hand, has extended its HR functionality by launching a Facebook game " My Marriott Hotel" to introduce future employees to the hospitality industry. The aim of this game is to identify and fill over 50,000 positions globally. This game allows future employees to play the role of a hotel manager in the kitchen, buy supplies and cook dishes before taking them to the virtual counter. Visitors to this site who may be interested to take up hospitality as a career can do so by going to the "Do it for Real" button, which then helps the visitor to navigate to the career sit of the Marriott.

Sites like TripAdvisor, publish traveler reviews on its site to help viewers make better judgments about credibility of the reviews and also of the place or location. It also gives a Star badge and assigns the status of "Senior Reviewer" to the person who posts more than 6–10 reviews. By awarding status to traditional loyalty program, the gamification adds a "community" dimension. Such programs celebrate individual achievements and add a powerful social "halo" to these online games. The key aspect of "Status" is a strong motivator that engages people. Additionally, the fact that this status can be on the world wide web makes people work very hard to maintain it through loyalty tasks.

Gamification combines technology to turn loyalty programs into enjoyable online social experiences. It employs motivational psychology by leveraging people's need to compete for reward, self-expression, achievement, and status.

A lot of hotel brands have gamified their loyalty programss by using game mechanics such as leaderboards, ranks, avtars, and also by awarding badges and virtual points, for doing program–related activities and then displaying these screen shots on the customer's profile on the game website. This in turn has promoted competition and increased customer engagement. This gamification approach drives the viewer traffic and also boosts the bottom line of the company.

Another loyalty program of such nature is the Starwood Preferred Guest program (Starwood has partnered with Foursquare), wherein the guest earns additional loyalty points and badges for checking in participating hotels. Frequent guests to these properties are appointed as SPG Mayor, whose duties would include sharing a favorite insider tip and destination hotspot with other frequent travelers, around the world.

The intention of gamification exercise is to motivate and engage participants through fun and games in order to enhance the appeal of the hotel property and make a difference in the profit margins.

11.6.2.1 MOBILE TECHNOLOGIES FOR OFF-PREMISE CUSTOMER ENGAGEMENT

Increasing number of mobile platforms empower consumers to easily look for a hotel property, additionally such platforms also make automated recommendations through applied customer intelligence. As more and more customers turn to their mobile devices to read reviews, compare costs and amenities or redeem loyalty offers on the frequent fliers programes, they expect that the hospitality/travel company should deliver efficient mobile experience. Mobile therefore offers a unique opportunity to the hospitality industry to enhance its brand awareness and customer engagement resulting in improved bottom line at the end of the process. Besides drawing in new customers, mobile has become critical after the initial point of purchase, because companies can then immediately reach the customer through mobile messaging. This exercise serves a twofold purpose (a) to deliver timely and relevant information, and (b) to build lasting relationships. The hospitality industry can leverage the flexibility of mobile to reach their targets and create a brand awareness, and achieve better customer service in the bargain. Additionally they have now started to install mobile applications on the mobile devices of the customers, which could be both interactive or passive. Such a value driven communication keeps the brand on the top of the customer recall, ensuring positive customer reviews and long term loyalty. Together these drive customer spend and repeat business.

It would thus be extremely prudent of the hospitality industry, if a mobile strategy that takes into the account promotion, customer experience, and loyalty and rewards, could be the order of the day. Mobile is an important aspect of the customer engagement strategy in the hospitality industry. It is also an efficient channel with which to deliver timely and personalized experience throughout the guest life cycle.

1. This strategy would enable the industry to deliver in-time information on hotel deals, price discounts and of parking discounts, besides offering promotional information for free upgrades or on property discounts in restaurants, spas or gyms.
2. This strategy would enable to restructure its information systems and gear them towards keeping guest informed about new destinations, facilities, and properties. Additionally, this would ensure real-time information sharing with the guests prior to their arrival and also during their stay at the property. This information could be about weather, local events or the availability of some seasonal speciality.
3. Mobiles could also be used for personalizing reward points, mileage balance, reservation numbers, and confirmation codes. They can also be used to send advance information about discount codes, solicit post-travel feedback or invitation of a future stay.

An integrated approach using variety of channels such as MMS, SMS, Push services, Push e-mails, and Voice can be used to maintain multi-channel communication with guests at a number of touch points during their travel experience. This would also create more opportunities for business and deepen the understanding of customer behavior resulting in profit maximization. In all a multi-channel approach can help the industry to directly connect with their customers and thereby deliver an exceptional customer experience.

It is thus imperative to develop a balanced customer engagement strategy in order to operate competitively in the current economic scenario, especially when it comes to attracting and retaining customers. The industry can thus use mobiles to differentiate itself from its competitors and ensure a long-term customer loyalty.

11.6.2.2 ONLINE MARKETING TOOLS FOR OFF-PREMISE CUSTOMER ENGAGEMENT

Customer engagement is the heart of the hospitality industry and online marketing has become the new soul. Whether a property is introducing a new facility, announcing a loyalty system or offering a season's discount, it's all about putting the right message in front of the right user at just the right time. This needs precise customer targeting, and that's a formidable task.

Hospitality industry leaders now have access to many online marketing tools. These use advanced text analytics. These in turn carry out intensive analysis of what the consumers think. Hoteliers can then use these insights to drive key business decisions, deliver proactive service, and formulate competitive business strategies. These tools unlock the wealth of information that lies within the customer chatter, and accurately pull out sentiment and key issues. These tools also have the ability to express such insights in an easy-to-use business-oriented applications. Hoteliers have started to use numerous online marketing tools to supplement their marketing strategy. These tools help to (a) fill the operational gap that may or may not be achieved either strategically or manually and (b) augment the prevailing ROI initiative that may require engineering of resources efficiently. For example a tool that helps hotels deliver the right message to the customer just at the very time when he/she browses the web and then targets the user with a focused message. These tools could also direct the client additional content or an offer, which could result in higher conversion or engagement rate. Hoteliers are aware that customers value efficiency and thoroughness and they also want their problems resolved the first time without too much explaining or by transferring the call to other agents or by being kept on hold for a long period of time. These tools pull out the precise gist of customer conversations about a particular service. This can be very useful in terms of the detail customers give about themselves, especially– the reasons for what they buy, who they buy from/ for, and more. This demographic and behavioral data is very revealing; and therefore it can be used to deliver a degree of granularity, for better customer segmentation. The marketing team can thus make their systems more customer centric, and maintain an individualized view of their customer's on-site experience and understand the areas of concern and improvement. Their capability to take initiative based on these insights can establish business processes which are critical in today's competitive hospitality market. Such systems also help the marketing team at the hotel to eliminate tunnel vision, visualize and comprehend the customer's user experience across platforms and thereby boost customer engagement by highlighting issues that may not be otherwise evident.

Financial constraints may at times be a limiting factor, hoteliers therefore need to choose solutions that enable scalability of customer engagement tools to meet different marketing needs of hotel without changing its core business intelligence and CRM platforms. At the same time they should also fit into the existing technology infrastructure.

11.7 CUSTOMIZING CUSTOMER INTERACTIONS

Certain interactions do not take kindly to digitization, because they are unstructured in nature they do not lend themselves easily to automation. Customer experience has to be designed for specific contexts if digitization has to be optimized. So far the industry has taken the path of "one size fits all," this has created many areas of discontent in customer engagement. Although transactional interactions like reservations, placing orders, and cab bookings lend themselves more easily to automation via tablet apps and touchscreens (Mindtree 2013), customers wish for face to face interactions especially for casual, on the spot conversations viz. asking for local information, events, directions, and other routine information.

It is not surprising that customers of all age groups prefer face to face interactions. Such interactions fulfil various needs of the customer and also provide an opportunity to the hotel to influence the last minute purchase decisions at the transit point. Digital technology can be leveraged at such points to introduce cost effective human interaction in such contexts leading to increase in topline and increased customer satisfaction. An example of such exercise would be integrating contexts into the mobile apps. For any application to be effective, location is the most effective trigger of action and therefore apps that can efficiently leverage accuracy and granularity for optimum customer satisfaction, need to be identified and used for maximum impact.

11.8 CONCLUSION

There has been an increase in the use of customer engagement technologies in the hospitality industry. Hotels have creatively used social media for enhancing brand awareness and to assist guests at every stage of their travel journey. Additionally, they also have a potential to offer guests a whole range of new services and tools besides helping them in hotel bookings. Travelers have come to expect that the hotels that they stay in will always assist them in staying connected.

Customer engagement technologies are being newly deployed in various functional areas of the hotel. Hoteliers are in turn also looking for an integration of these technologies in the overall operations of the hotel primarily in the PMS. Although still new, these technologies have begun to prove their efficacy in creating transformative and exciting ways to serve guests and win them over for life. Mobile and social tools have additionally ushered in new service paradigms.

An all pervasive impact of these technologies have encouraged hoteliers to develop "interaction maps" for each of their customer so that they remain at the forefront of ever growing customer expectations. A hotel not only determines what information or services guests need, they also identify what a guest expects at each phase of his/her stay.

Additionally these technologies help hotels to enhance service through technology capabilities that create potential customer centric delivery tools for websites and mobile apps. These would help the customer to prioritize features according to his requirements.

Lastly, technologies for consumer engagement also give an in-depth insight into various customer issues. However, since the detail about these issues is usually hidden in textual feedback, identifying them and understanding their magnitude can be challenging for any hotel. By analyzing online customer chatter a hotel can come to know about issues at an early stage and track them over a period of time to improve customer service, and hotel's offerings that could result in significant savings.

KEYWORDS

- **PMS**
- **social media**
- **convergence**
- **on-premise**
- **off-premise**

REFERENCES

Baker, M. President & CEO, DataXu (online), 10th July 2014. https://www.dataxu.com/blog/the-future-of-advertising-how-technology-is-transforming-consumer-engagement/

CISCO *Connected Mobile Experiences for Hospitality* [Online] 2014. URL: <http://www.cisco.com/c/dam/en/us/products/collateral/wireless/mobility-services-engine/at_a_glance_c45-726723.pdf> (accessed Aug 1, 2014).

Creamer, D. *6 Property Management Predictions That May Impact your Next Buy* [Online] 2012. URL: <http://hospitalitytechnology.edgl.com/news/6-Property-Management-Predictions-that-May-Impact-Your-Next-Buy81481> (accessed Jul 10, 2014).

Cunnane, C. *Property Management Integration: Redefining the Role of PMS in Hospitality* [Online] 2010. URL:<http://www.tblat.com/facebook/pdf/aberdeenpms.pdf> (accessed Jul 10, 2014).

Customer Engagement Technology Study [Online] 2014. URL: <http://hospitalitytechnology.edgl.com/reports/2014-Customer-Engagement-Technology-Study94392> (accessed Aug 1, 2014).

Findings on Your Competitors Are Engaging guests: 2013 Customer Engagement Tech Study [Online] 2013. URL:<http://hospitalitytechnology.edgl.com/reports/143-Findings-on-How-Your-Competitors-are-Engaging-Guests--2013-Customer-Engagement-Tech-Study87653> (accessed Aug 14, 2014).

Gartner, Customer Engagement Centre (CEC) [Online] 2013. URL: <http://www.gartner.com/it-glossary/customer-engagement-center-cec/> (accessed Aug 10, 2014).

Gaynor, G. H. Managing Technology - Managers don't Grow on Trees, Proceedings of the Second International Conference on Engineering Management, Ontario, Canada, 1989.

Infosys *White Paper - Integrated Property and Guest Management System* [Online] 2013. URL: <http://www.infosys.com/industries/hospitality-leisure/white-papers/Documents/guest-management-system.pdf> (accessed Jul 10, 2014).

Marinkovic, S. *Management of Technology and development* [Online] 2014. URL: <http://mtr.fon.bg.ac.rs/attachments/article/218/Technology%20management.pdf (accessed Jul 10, 2014).

Prakash, Sai L. *Technology Management* [Online] 2014. URL: <http://nptel.ac.in/courses/IIT-MADRAS/Management_Science_II/Pdf/5_1.pdf> (accessed Jul 10, 2014).

Rouse, Margaret. *Service-Oriented Architecture* [Online] 2014. URL:<http://searchsoa.techtarget.com/definition/service-oriented-architecture> (accessed Jul 10, 2014).

Schnieder, T. Converging on Success: Best Practices for Managing Convergence in Hospitality Sales, Marketing and Revenue Optimization, Hospitality Sales & Marketing Association International in Partnership with Sabre Hospitality Solutions, 2012

Technology for Better Business Intelligence [Online] 2014. http://hospitalitytechnology.wordpress.com/2012/03/26/technology-for-better-business-intelligence/ (accessed Jul 10, 2014).

PART VII
Social Media

CHAPTER 12

SOCIAL MEDIA AND ENGAGING WITH CONSUMERS IN THE HOSPITALITY SECTOR

NAVDEEP KAUR KULAR*

Visiting Faculty, Vedatya Institute (formerly IIMT), Gurgaon, India

E-mail: novikular@rediffmail.com; novikular@gmail.com

CONTENTS

ABSTRACT

Social media is a valuable tool to engage with the customers. The emerging media landscape has provided new opportunities for the consumer connect. It has altered the manner in which consumers search for information and make their decision choices. The academic literature along with the technology literature available from vendors in public domain has been synthesized to present the opportunities and challenges for hospitality sector.This chapter ponders over the importance ofsocial media and how businesses can interact, engage and participate with the online users. It suggests the ways and means to enhance customer acquisition, customer development and retention.Customer opinions and evaluation of services can be used for collaboration and co-creation of products and services. It also highlights the challenges in quantifying social media's influence on the customers. The case studies illustrate the social media measures adopted by various hospitality organizations for consumer engagement. These can provide insights to others to emulate the best practicesand develop a sustainable social media strategy.

12.1 INTRODUCTION

Social media is an important tool to connect and engage with the customers. It is more so in the hospitality sector where the essence of service is at the core of the product. This is an ever changing field with exponential growth and there is a paucity of academic research on current initiatives of hospitality organizations. The evolving dynamics of social media and its impact on the travel, tourism, and hospitality industry have been studied in this chapter.

There has been an unprecedented growth in the human interactions with the advent of social media. Radio reached the audience of 50 million in 38 years, the internet in 7 years whereas Facebook in its third year of operations achieved the same (Ernst and Young, 2011). Facebook launched in 2004 had 1.28 bn monthly active users in March 2014 (Facebook, 2014). Twitter boasts of 255 monthly active users in the year 2013 (Twitter, 2014). The videos are constantly being uploaded on video sharing platform Youtube and images on Flickr. Ever since the advent of internet when there was a rush to create a website for the organization the time has come when the focus is on achieving competitive advantage through user generated content. According to the estimates of eMarketer the number of social network users is going to increase by 12.5% this year reaching 1.79 billion worldwide which is 63.4% of the internet users and one-fourth of the global population (eMarketer, 2014). Social media platforms have easy to use tools and applications that allow the users to build profile, develop relationships, and maintain the same. With the advent of social media the networking capacity of individual user has multiplied manifolds and at the same time the cost is low (Hvass and Munar, 2012). Social media provides a platform to interact with family and friends, acquaintances and strangers, and definitely brands. More and more people are using it to record and broadcast their experiences, post feedback and complaints, research, and to make bookings.The consumers in today's world have more control over how information is created, presented, and shared. The social media enables customers to take a more active role as it can reach and can be reached by almost everyone anywhere and anytime (Hennig-Thurau et al., 2010).

12.2 EMERGENCE OF SOCIAL MEDIA

There is multiplicity of terms in social media with *online social networks, social networking sites, social technology, social web, consumer generated media, user generated content, WEB 2.0, and Travel 2.0* being interchangeably used. It is rapidly replacing e-mail as the primary form of communication on the internet. It allows the internet users to create, edit, modify, share, and discuss online information adding more value to the experience.The social software provides a base to collaborate and share information and form communities online (Weinberg and Pehlivan, 2011). The social media has placed an unprecedented power in the hands of the consumers. The consumers today can help an organization build its reputation or harm it through active use of social media. This trend can significantly impact the company's reputation, sales and even survival (Keitzmann et al., 2011). Businesses need to learn how to use the social media to their advantage. Amersdorffer et al. (2012) have used the term social innovation for the emergence of the social web which has transformed the way in which companies and people interact and communicate. It is going to change the media landscape, media consumption and the development of tourism imaginations.

The consumers can disseminate through social media with unknown users their consumption preferences and experiences which influences their behavior. Organizations need to respond to the brand-related discussions and utilize the social capital (Canhota and Clark, 2013). The social media has enabled businesses to communicate with large number of consumers. The visibility of the organization is magnified through the actions of the consumers on the social media platforms. This has led to the increased reach of organizations and reduced the cost of communication and transaction. There is no direct control of the company on the content, timing and frequency of interactions happening between consumers (Mangold, and Faulds, 2009).

Gironda and Korgaonkar (2014) examined the motivations that drive the consumers to join the business's social networking site page or click on the advertisement on social networking page. The study showed that attitude, relative advantage, compatibility, complexity, normative influences, and self-efficacy impact the use of social media.

As the social media is a community so pushing sales is not enough. The companies have to take out the time to engage on a personal level to draw the consumers into meaningful conversation. It is important to know what the travelers are talking about, researching for and recommending to others on the social media in order to engage with them. The emphasis has now shifted on what the consumers of the hospitality sector expect and how they behave on social media platforms.

12.3 TYPES OF SOCIAL MEDIA

Social media sites can be of pure review type, social networking, social sharing, social bookmarking, and purchase review type. The common characteristic of these sites is that they invite feedback, comments, polls, sharing, and discussion from all users.

12.3.1 FACEBOOK

Facebook is one of the foremost social media sites that has become part and parcel of millions of people's lives around the world. In 10 years of existence the monthly active users of Facebook have increased from

1 million to 1.28 bn in 2014 which comprise one-sixth of the world's population (Facebook, 2014). Had Facebook been a country then it would have been the third most populous country in the world. There are 146.6 mn users from USA followed by 84.9 mn from India, 61.2 mn from Brazil, and 60.5 mn from Indonesia on Facebook. Facebook allows users to create, present, and maintain their profiles. The organizations can connect with the users through their wall posts, contests, events, and discussions. Facebook has a huge repository of information on consumer interests and their online web browsing behavior which it can use to build consumer profiles and target ads. The sheer size of the Facebook membership makes it imperative for the hospitality organistions to have a strong presence on this platform. According to the research by Social Bakers, photographs accounted for 75% of the content posted worldwide on Facebook followed by links that accounted for 10%. The Edge-rank algorithm used by Facebook to spread posts gives higher rank to those that have been commented on or shared than those that have been liked (Leposa, 2013). Using Facebook Graph Search consumers can combine the places with preferences. It allows users to have structured queries based on their travel interests.

12.3.2 TWITTER

Twitter is a micro-blogging site that permits the posts upto 140 characters and allows users to organize in the follower–followee pattern. Twitter has overtaken Facebook in new registrations. The growth of Twitter in emerging markets is phenomenal. The Asia-Pacific region has more users of this social platform than those in the North America or Western Europe. The real-time capability of Twitter can be leveraged by organizations to give the travelers frequent updates. One study found that one-third of the tweets were for tourism professionals. This platform is used in all stages of the travel cycle starting from information search for travel, deals, hotel bookings, mid-trip engagement, and posttravel reviews and sharing of the experience.

Airports on Twitter can update the flight take off and landing information to interested travelers enhancing their experience. The Leeds Bradford Airport is already sharing its flight arrival and departure information on its Twitter account of @LBIA with interested members (Beese, 2014).

The South African Tourism has an official Twitter account at @GoTo-SouthAfrica. In 2013, it invited four bloggers to travel on separate routes covering its nine provinces and then share the personalized experience with the online community in an attempt to market the country as a tourist destination.

Twitter can be an effective tool for publicity as many journalists are active on this platform. In Social Reservations guests can book the hotels directly from the Twitter account.

12.3.3 GOOGLE+

Google+ is growing fast and is expected to surpass Facebook in registered users by 2016. It has more than 1.5 billion registered users and monthly active user base of 359 million which is more than that of Twitter. The hotel's Google+ page can enhance the organic search of the hotel on Google as it will be indexed more quickly (Hospitality net, 2014). Google purchased Youtube in 2006 and comments posted on Youtube videos get displayed in all G+ circles. The owned, paid, and earned content can be integrated to engage the customer in any stage of the travel for information, localization, and socially relevant content. Google Hangout distinguishes Google+ from other social networking sites. The sales team can have a video chat with potential corporate clients or an executive can help the guest plan a vacation using it.

12.3.4 PINTEREST

Pinterest is a visual social platform which the businesses can leverage for achieving competitive advantage. Launched in 2012, it already has over 70 mn monthly users out of which 40 mn are active users. It is an image-focused site where interesting visuals and videos can garner the attention of the users. Users can upload, save, sort, and mange the images which are known as pins and also videos and also browse, like and comment through the pins of other users. Users can create a board on the upcoming trip and the experts pin their recommendations. The social technology can be leveraged to create a personal experience for the consumer. This is an excellent place for promotion of destination weddings as there is heavy wedding presence on this platform (Hospitality Net, 2014).

12.3.5 YOUTUBE

The results from comScore's research show that more than 85% of the online audience in the USA viewed the online video content in June 2013 (comScore2013). Google sites, Youtube being the primary one among them had 158.3 mn unique viewers and had the highest average engagement. In this context, the Youtube which is a video-driven social media site and is also the second largest search engine becomes an important channel in the social media space (The Times of India, 2011). The video content online is more engaging and helps the organization to stand out in the clutter. Videos related to the property or general documentaries can be used. The videos posted on Youtube can give the virtual tour of the hotel, testimonials from guests or have other engaging content. Visitors can get an inside view of the hospitality destinations around the world through videos uploaded on Youtube. High-quality video is the tool to attract visitors.

12.3.6 INSTAGRAM

Instagram with 200 mn users currently and 60 mn photos being uploaded each day is a good visual platform to promote hotels (Instagram, 2014). Its integration with the hotel's Facebook account and the mobile interface facilitatesthe online visibility, engaging with customers and augmenting the marketing initiatives. It is a great medium to connect with the influencers through eye-catching photos.

12.3.7 FOURSQUARE

Foursquare is a location-based mobile service which allows users to find the nearest places of interest. More than 50 mn people are using Foursquare to find the great places to go to. Also 1.7 mn businesses are using the Merchant platform of Foursquare.

Stay Connected With Hilton

The Hilton hotels and resorts with more than 550 locations in 80 countries around the world has presence on multiple social media platforms. It's Facebook site with 1.2 mn likes and 7.2 mn visits showcases the amazing destinations, provides information about offers around the world, and is host to a vibrant community. It's Twitter account with 150.3 k followers tracks happenings in destinations located in 80 countries and gives latest information about offers there. The queries and comments from visitors are solicited to encourage engagement with the brand. The brand's Pinterest has 24 boards and 448 pins and is the place to discuss about any topic related to the Hilton brand from destinations to cuisine to pools to spas to weddings. Hilton hotels and resorts, Youtube videos provide an inside look of the hotels at various destinations and also the performance arts events held at various Hilton hotels. The brand's presence on the Foursquare platform ensures that guest can check for Hilton hotel in the vicinity of their location and make the most of the offers and tips provided. The Hilton Global Media Center has all the facts and news items related to the brand. Customers can download this application on their mobiles and can get access to all the information anytime anywhere in the world. With guests from emerging economies playing a vital role in the hospitality industry, the Hilton Hotels and Resorts has taken note of it and has extended its social media range. The hotel's social media initiatives are not limited to the above mentioned channel but also incorporate the Chinese video site and social network Tuduo and Sina Weibo, respectively.

(Hilton Hotels and Resorts, 2014)

12.4 INCREASED USE OF SMART PHONES

The smartphones have changed the way people search for information and make purchase decisions. The people using smartphones in 2014 will be just under a quarter of the global population and this will rise to one-third by the year 2017 (eMarketer, 2014). The travelers have access to online information all the time and are connected the world. The US mobile travel sales are expected to increase from $16.36 billion in 2013 to $64.69 billion in 2018 (eMarketer, 2014). The comScore research found that nearly half of the smartphone or tablet owning travelers in United Kingdom who had booked their travel in the past 6 months had planned their trip using these devices (eMarketer, 2014). The influence of the social media is there throughout the duration of the trip as the network is always with the travelers through their mobiles. Out of the monthly active members on Facebook, 1.01 bn have access to the site on their phones (Facebook, 2014). The travelers today are increasingly social and mobile (Jayawardena et al., 2013). The location-based services such as Facebook Places, Google Latitude, and Foursquare let the tourists share and recommend their destination to their friends and the small and medium scale operators to promote their businesses (Ruzic et al., 2012).

The MMGY Global's Portrait of American Travelers reveals a six-fold increase in the "digital elite" in 2 years from 2011 to 2013 (MMGYGlobal, 2013). These are the people who use at least two digital devices (a smartphone and a tablet) to plan and book their vacation. They travel more and spend more than other travelers. Eight out of 10 are active on Facebook, one-third on Twitter and nearly a quarter on Youtube and Google+. A total of 90% of them made their travel reservations online the previous year and expect sophisticated web content from the hospitality organizations. The demand of the customers would make the organizations optimize the websites for mobiles, adopt easy to use booking technology, provide virtual tours of the hotels and preview of rooms.

12.5 CHANGING CONSUMER PROFILE

The use of social media is not limited to the Gen Y but is increasingly being adopted by Gen X and the baby boomers (Kaplan and Haenlein, 2010). By 2016, the Gen Y and Gen X will have greater influence over the purchase decisions of others (Ernst and Young, 2011). Google+ is being visited by 23% of Gen X, 28% of Gen Y, 29% of Gen Z, 19% of younger Boomers, 16% of older Boomers, and 15% of the Golden Generation every month. (Forrester Research cited Hospitality Net, 2014).

The Gen Y is heavy user of technology with higher information search capability and higher expectations from the products. Generation Y has a different standard for measuring brands as compared to the generations before. This generation has grown up on the social media and the traditional advertising methods are outdated for reaching them. For the digital savvy consumers going through the user-generated content is an important step before purchasing. The millenials make product evaluations on the basis of online reviews (Mangold and Smith, 2012). A total of 39% of millenials read through other people's opinions before renting a room (Steinbirk, 2013).

Bilgihan et al. (2014) have also noticed that Gen Y is a heavy user of social networking sites and consumer opinion leadership and consumer susceptibility to interpersonal influence affect GenY's dining information seeking and sharing behavior on social networking sites. The influence of the social media is going to grow with each passing year and the hospitality organizations cannot afford to ignore it. Frequent engagement with the consumers on the various social media sites is required to create a positive brand perception.The social media should be leveraged to reach the important audience of young consumers (Hanna et al., 2011). The hospitality organizations need to be part of the worldwide social media community in order to keep up with the Gen Y's expectations and majority of the customers who own smartphones.

12.6 OPPORTUNITIES FOR CONSUMER ENGAGEMENT IN HOSPITALITY SECTOR

The hospitality industry is diverse, complex, and constantly evolving (Bagley and Lanz, 2014). The social media is not only a technological innovation but a lifestyle revolution which has changed the way people interact, look for information and purchase products and services. Hospitality marketers need to take note of the consumer advocacy revolution which is taking place making the user reviews more important than the travel agents advice (Ong, 2012). Tham et al. (2013) have identified little known source–receiver relationship, channel variety, content retention capabilities, opportunities for solicitation, and motive for disclosure as the distinctive features of electronic word-of-mouth. It is important to know about the role of the social media in travel information search for devising better tourism marketing practices (Xiang and Gretzel, 2010). In the hospitality sector, the social media provides opportunities for building brand awareness, increasing bookings, and engaging with customers.

Customer engagement behaviours are those which customers exhibit beyond the purchase and which may have various motivational drivers. These include recommendations, writing reviews, blogging, word-of-mouth, solving others problems, and even legal action (van Doorn et al., 2010). Verhoef et al. (2010) emphasize the fact that the increasingly networked society with the use of social media and other new media provides an opportunity for consumer engagement which is a behavioural manifestation of the consumer toward the brand and goes beyond transactions. There is an opportunity for the organizations to engage the existing and potential customers through the consumer-initiated content on the internet (Vivek et al.,2012).

The social media provides the opportunity to the organizations to understand their customers better, interact with them, and measure their activities and outcomes (Hvass and Munar, 2012). Taking user-generated data has the advantage that it is collected in the natural setting and can provide valuable insights (Horster and Gottschalk, 2012). Brejla and Gilbert (2014) have demonstrated how data mining approach can lead to knowledge discovery and co-creation of value on board cruise ships. The interactions among guests and those with the staff can be analyzed for providing better service. Knowledgeable consumers through discussion and sharing of their restaurant experiences alter the nature of experience for other consumers giving shared values and identity (Watson et al., 2008).

Consumers can engage and create value for the firm in number of manners. Kumar et al. (2012) propose that the total customer engagement value comprises customer lifetime value, customer referral value, customer influencer value, and customer knowledge value.

Customer lifetime value – this depends on the consumer purchase behavior.

Customer referral value – referrals of new customers.

Customer influencer value – the ability to influence current and potential customers (to increase customer acquisition, retention and spend on products and services through word-of-mouth). Tham et al. (2013) propose that destination managers should have greater engagement with the social media in order to create opportunities to visitors to narrate their memorable visits to others as well as work with the industry partners to build relevant destination images.

Customer knowledge value – the value gained by the company through feedback provided by the customer. The social media provides an arena for collecting ideas from large number of consumers and which can be brought back to the market in adapted, transformed, and enriched form (Mladenow et al., 2014). Martini et al. (2014) studied how the social media was utilized in the customer co-creation from the initial stage of idea exploitation to a more complex stage of exploitation and exploration being carried out simultaneously. Online customer interactions trigger the emotions and cognition which lead to further refined ideas for new services. Companies should nurture, develop, and moderate the customer interactions to enhance the new service development processes (Sigala, 2012).

12.6.1 INCREASE PRODUCT AWARENESS/ADVERTISING

The internet has taken over the role of information provider for travel search in addition to the travel journalism and traditional media. The online travel search is increasing used by customers all around the world to look for the most suitable property that matches their need. With millions of consumers having internet access, the social media and new technology will play an important role in the next 5 years in the hospitality industry (Deloitte,2010). It is an economic and effective way to make the potential customers aware of the hotel's presence. Consumers are increasingly sharing their opinions online and it impacts how the hotel is perceived by potential guests. It is imperative for hotels to be present where their customers are. McCarthy et al. (2010) found that recommendations from friends and family were the chief source of information for leisure travelers while making hotel choice decisions.

12.6.2 CUSTOMER ACQUISITION

Hospitality and tourism organizations have adopted the internet as one of the main channels to acquire and retain customers (Pan et al., 2011). Now hospitality organizations are adopting technology that makes it possible for the consumer to make bookings through social media platforms.

The recommendations of consumers can encourage others to choose a specific property over competitors which boost the revenue. Consumers trust other consumer more than advertizing, so user-generated content and images, social endorsements such as likes, pluses, and shares influence the consumer's decision to book a particular property. About 92%

of the consumers go through the online reviews of a hotel before making a booking (Bagley and Lanz, 2014). The consumers can post compliments and complaints on the multiple social media channels available. The speed and the response to these determine how other consumers are influenced. Litvin and Hoffman (2012) in their empirical study have found that both rebuttal and response by the hotel management to negative postings on travel review boards have positive influence on consumer attitudes towards the property.

12.6.3 CUSTOMER SERVICE

When consumers are encouraged to give their comments, it provides insight to the management on service aspects that are appreciated and enhanced the experience of the consumers. The customer service time and cost has reduced through the use of social media. Real-time connectivity between businesses and customers is there. The candid and genuine feedback of consumers on the social media can be a valuable source for service recovery mechanisms (Litvin et al., 2008). The researchers emphasize the fact that comments on travel review sites too should be taken note of and appropriate response should be given. Sites such as TripAdvisor give the management an opportunity to post response but as seen by Chan and Guillet (2011) in their study on Hong Kong hotels only a quarter of the hotels posted their response to customer reviews on TripAdvisor.

12.6.4 CUSTOMER LOYALTY/RETENTION

The customers expect the hotels to entertain them and provide an experience rather than providing a standard service so that they can make a return trip and/or have ongoing positive relations through Tweets (Jayawardena et al., 2013). It is of utmost importance to take note of any negative comments and reply, rebut, or rebuff at the earliest so as to counter any negative influence on prospects views regarding the hotel or restaurant. Positive experiences at hospitality destinations lead to customer loyalty and generate word of mouth advertising. The long-term engagement of consumers leads to brand loyalty and brings in repeat customers who themselves advocate the brand to others. There is a strong correlation between the customer retention rate and sustainable profits. The focus should be on making an emotional connect with the brand.

12.6.5 PERSONALIZATION/CUSTOMIZATION

Products and services that are customized to the customer's need and location provide them a unique and memorable experience. Through the social media, the social profiling of the customer can be done and then the right offer to the right prospect can be communicated. The social media is playing an important role in the search engine results. The social media is getting linked with the search results offering each prospective consumer a personalized search result based upon his social graph. The intent of businesses to find the most valuable customer can be met with new media. There are many digital media companies that enable organizations to accomplish this objective. The Glow Digital Media helps clients build, manage, optimize, and evaluate their Facebook campaigns (Broughton, 2014). The professional expertise is deployed to target, optimize, and track the most valuable customers through social media. The search results will become more meaningful and personal for the consumers.

12.6.6 CUSTOMER RELATIONSHIP MANAGEMENT

The traditional customer relationship management is carried out using databases to send e-mails, mails, or phone calls to the customers. The advent of social media has opened up opportunities to connect with the customers on one to one basis and build trust.The customer relationship management and marketing have reached a new level through the usage of social media. The marketers now can engage, inform, interest, and entertain the consumers through social media and provide them a medium to transact (Woodcock et al., 2011). Over time as knowledge about the customer builds, the services can be personalized leading to increased revenues and decreased costs.

12.6.7 CUSTOMER COLLABORATION AND CO-CREATION

The new uses and the future consumption trends can be discovered using the interactive platform of the online communities and the social media.

There is opportunity to observe, test and develop new value propositions with consumers (Prahalad and Ramaswamy, 2004; Fuller, 2010). There is opportunity for both upstream and downstream co-creation with the consumers (Vernette and Hamdi-Kidar, 2013). The downstream co-creation happens when value is created by the user while consuming the product or service. The upstream co-creation with consumers can take place from idea generation to test phase to creating advertising messages and videos for promotion. Consumers create media products and images which are uploaded for consumption for other tourists. They are influenced and in turn create a new product. Thus, tourists are active participants in the ongoing consumption and production process related to travel destinations in social media (Mansson, 2011).The latent, hidden, and evolving needs of the customers can be integrated through co-development and crowdsourcing into the offerings which are important value co-creation mechanisms to achieve sustained competitive advantage for the firm (Mattson, 2010; Sarijaarvi, 2012). Starbucks uses social media to transform its passive customers of beverages to contributors in the innovation process (Chua and Banerjee, 2013). The company can collaborate and co-create by engaging with the lead users possessing creative abilities and the emergent nature users with visionary capabilities for product creation, adaptation, and modification process.

The involvement and participation of the existing or potential customers is the prerequisite for consumer engagement which leads to value, trust, loyalty, word-of-mouth, affective commitment, and brand community involvement (Vivek et al., 2012).

Taj's Presence on the Social Media

The Indian Hotels Company Limited, branded as Taj Hotels Resorts and Palaces owns and operates 93 hotels spread over 55 locations in India. It also has 16 international hotels at destinations ranging from Maldives to South Africa. The company is present in luxury, premium, midmarket and economy segments with its offerings namely Taj, Taj Exotica, Taj Safaries, Vivanta by Taj Hotels and Resorts, The Gateway Hotel and the Ginger brand. The finest luxury and resort hotels span from exotic beach resorts to modern business hotels to authentic royal palaces. The former royal palaces converted into luxury hotels such as Umaid Bhawan at Jodhpur, Taj Lake Palace at Udaipur, Falaknuma Palace in Hyderabad, and Rambagh Palace in Jaipur offer a unique product coupled with perfect hospitality difficult to replicate anywhere else in the world. Taj Hotels are present on multiple social media channels propagating the Taj experience and services. The Taj Hotels and Resorts, Vivanta by Taj, and The Gateway hotel are present on Facebook, Twitter, and YouTube. The Gateway hotel also has its presence on the Foursquare platform. The Facebook page of the group with more than 74 k likes posts pictures with short descriptions and links of its hotels and testimonials by guests of the perfect hospitality offered by the Taj. It also promotes the brand by posting the recent certifications and awards achieved by the group and performance arts events held at its properties. The offers at Taj are available on the If a customer likes the Facebook page of a particular hotel, the website takes him there. The group's Twitter page @Taj Hotels with over 9 k tweets and 8 k followers retweets the photographs sent by guests which engage others to share their experience at the Taj hotel. The customer recommendations are acknowledged and complaints listened to. Standard wording is used for responses. The response time is 1 day with the customer being encouraged to discuss further and resolution arrived at. The links, blogs, and pins sent by customers are shared too. The customers are assisted in making their trip plans. There is consistency in the content posted on the Facebook, Twitter, and Pinterest account of Taj Hotels.

(Taj Hotels Resorts and Palaces, 2014)

12.7 CHALLENGES IN CONSUMER ENGAGEMENT

12.7.1 FINANCIAL

The hospitality organizations need to set aside financial resources for being present on the social media and to continuously monitor and engage customers. In difficult times like the present where there is competition in every sphere of the hospitality industry this is an additional requirement to be fulfilled. Hede and Kellett (2012) in their study of building online brand communities on social media platforms for events in Australia and found that the capability to resource this particular sphere of marketing is one of the key challenges. Measuring the success of social media strategies and its return on investment is a difficult task.

12.7.2 TECHNOLOGY

The technical platforms to collect, analyze, and process vast information needs to be in place for the social media initiatives. The cost of research and development is high and the life span of new technological products is low. The frequent technology upgrades require additional financial resources and training of manpower for efficient use. The innovative technology is only useful if it is used in the right manner through appropriate business model (Chesbrough, 2010).

12.7.3 HUMAN RESOURCES

The options for responding to consumers available for organizations are posting tailored messages by media personnel or prescripted approved messages by employees or impromptu reply by the employee. The freedom can only be given to employees to judge the context, situation, and profile of consumer and review previous messages and then respond if they are adequately trained. Global brands have an additional challenge of managing the cultural and language differences to effectively route the query to the employee who can handle it. Feedback and coaching is important to project consistency in policy. The employees interactions on the social media should be guided and managed to enhance the public image of the organization otherwise it would be time bomb waiting to explode having a devastating impact on the organization's reputation (Miles and Mangold, 2014). Qualified in-house trainers or consultants are required to accomplish this task. Also demand is placed on the time of the employees. The effectiveness of the training is also an issue in an industry which has high attrition rate. Inversini and Masiero (2014) have pointed out the need for employing personnel with specific skills who can respond and react to the opportunities that emerge in the online media.

12.7.4 INCONSISTENT BRAND IDENTITY

Social media has changed the brand building exercise from a one-way process to a two-way communication with the consumers participating in development of destination brand identity and image. Lim et al. (2012) provide insights into the destination branding strategies. They found that consumer-generated destination videos on the social media do not carry the same brand as the organization's marketing videos. There is a risk of emergence of counter- and alter-brand communities when the organization's measures to build brands are not effective on the social media (Hede and Kellett, 2012).

12.7.5 COMPETITIVE MEASURES

Hospitality organizations are continuously making efforts to not only to match their competitors in the social media measures taken up by them but also trying to keep one step ahead. Already scarce resources need to be deployed on the monitoring the organizations's social media analytics and analysis of competitive moves in this sphere. This is an ongoing process in this dynamic field which is evolving every second.

12.7.6 ORGANIZATION STRUCTURE AND CULTURE

Chathoth et al. (2014) in their study of three upscale Hongkong hotels have found that firm's strategy, organizational structure, and culture are the most important barriers to implementing the consumer engagement in hotels. The present hierarchies and departments may undergo changes in order to assimilate a new channel for customer engagement. This would mean changes in the organizational structure which may not go down well with individuals who see their power diminished. The strong culture of being responsive to what the customer says needs to be ingrained in employees at all levels to make any consumer engagement initiative a success. The top leadership needs to demonstrate their strong support toward consumer engagement measures taken up by the organization.

12.7.7 POLICIES AND STANDARDS

The hospitality organizations have to build their social media platforms and manage them within the governance frameworks. The technology policies and standards of the countries in which the operations take place must be adhered to. The operations in this new area of social technologies should be carried out with utmost care within the permissible boundaries set by the state. Any social media initiative of the organization should not be impinge upon the law of the land so as to avoid any unnecessary litigation.

12.7.8 CONSUMER ADOPTION/USE

Inspite of the proliferation of the social media not all consumers are on it. The traditional channels of consumer engagement need to be used along with new media for effective results.

Gartner Inc's research indicates that the expectations from social networking tools may exceed the perceived benefits derived from them. Inks et al. (2012) found that the use as well as improvements to productivity by these social networking tools by the sales people is limited. The perception is that at some point these tools may become critical to success.

Bijmolt et al. (2010) have studied the analytics for customer engagement and discuss the barriers for introducing analytics for customer engagement.

12.8 SOCIAL MEDIA ANALYTICAL TOOLS

Marketing spend on social media expected to grow 300% by 2016 from 2011 levels (Ernst and Young, 2011). Hospitality organizations need to know what search terms customers use to find them. In addition, they should be aware of topics of current interest in the travel and tourism industry on which people are posting comments in order to devise their social media strategy. The relevant customer interactions from millions of posts need to be identified for action. These objectives can be accomplished by using analytics tools. Most of the hospitality organizations have adopted the social media but the results from their social campaigns vary. Measuring the impact of the organization's social media initiatives is of paramount importance for future investments in this channel. The strategy to guide the social media campaign should be composed of the following steps:

1. State clearly the business goals;
2. Formulate social media goals;
3. Identify key performance indicators for social media goals and monitor the same.

The crowd sourcing in the innovation processes requires analytic support (Mladenow et al., 2014). The crowd sourcing in the innovation processes requires analytic support (Mladenow et al., 2014). Different social media analytical tools are available such as Circos, GuestCentric Systems, Milestone Internet Marketing, Radian6, Omniture and Overtone. The online reputation management companies such as Revinate, ReviewPro, and Digital Alchemy helps hotels to engage with the customers by monitoring reviews and utilizing them to enhance services (Bagley and Lanz, 2014).

Ranking of Restaurant Brands on Social and Digital Performance

The Digital CoCo is a digital agency focused on return on investment for social media for the restaurants and hospitality. It does comprehensive analysis through analytics to build the restaurant social media index. It is tracking thousands of restaurants and hospitality brands and millions of consumers engaged in producing user-generated data in over 208,000 locations. It is not merely a count of the likes but digs deeper into the data of multiple social platforms such as Facebook, Foursquare, Google+, and Youtube to arrive at results. The quality of the brand content, consumer interactions, influence, engagement and the reach of the brand are analyzed to measure the social footprint and do predictive analysis of the brand. The social and digital performance of restaurants in the USA is measured on the basis of three parameters, namely influence, sentiment, and engagement. The following are the top 10 restaurant brands according to the restaurant social media index for the first quarter performance in the year 2014.

Rank	Restaurant	RSMI Score (2014 Q1)
1.	Subway	403.17
2.	McDonald's	402.19
3.	Panera Bread	400.68
4.	Buffalo Wild Wings	397.88
5.	Starbucks	394.00
6.	Taco Bell	392.72
7.	Wendy's	388.24
8.	Chipotle	384.66
9.	Sonic Drive-in	382.77
10.	Hard Rock Café	374.28

(Restaurant Social Media Index, 2014)

12.9 SOCIAL MEDIA STRATEGY

The strategy of the organizations should be to manage customer relationships through customer engagement by the means of social media so as to build trust and brand loyalty (Woodcock et al., 2011). Organizations need to comprehend the manner in which the consumers expect them to interact, behave, and engage in the social media. It is not a question of whether to be on the social media or not, it is about where to be present and what measures to take up.

The foremost reason for businesses to be on social media is to build communities followed by building brand, for customer service, use it for research and to generate leads (Ernst and Young, 2013). When a brand is able to build a community then it provides a platform to reach numerous customers at one go for marketing initiatives. Customers can bond, share experiences and generate stronger word of mouth leading to increased brand loyalty, quicker resolution of queries reducing the service costs and generating innovative ideas.

The social media strategy needs to engage the consumer at each stage of the travel continuum. It needs to support the entire customer lifecycle in order to increase sales and decrease costs. The services need to be targeted to the right consumers. The ease of purchase and use should be ensured so as to provide memorable experience through personalization of the products and services according to the needs of the consumer.

Companies need to evaluate what to post, when to post, where to post and how often. Companies should develop and post content that the consumers find interesting, enjoyable and valuable interesting (Kaplan and Heinlein, 2010). By becoming friends with consumers on the social networking sites, companies have access to the personal information which is otherwise difficult to obtain. This can be used to create the content for future uploads. The links to industry news and trends of interest to the consumers can be posted. Posting customer testimonials on the social media sites is a quick and easy way to reach huge audience. Engage with bloggers and other online influencers in order to make them loyal towards the organization.

12.9.1 PARTICIPATION AND TRANSPERENCY

Whether the company is listening or not customer feedback is all over the social media. The users should be allowed to initiate discussions on the social media channels. The company should relinquish control and allow the customers to freely express their views. This would engage the users to create content. The business should notadminister tight control over what is being said about it but should focus on ways to take corrective actions in the areas found deficient in service. There is no longer a private conversation between and the company and the customer about the things gone wrong. Brands have become fragile and vulnerable to millions of empowered customers coming online every day. The brand does not own the channel. It is part of the online community although a powerful and influential member but should not censor the comments of other members. Placate online followers so that they refrain from posting negative comments. Once the company acknowledges receipt the customer anticipatesthat solution would soon be offered. Complaints can be put on the public platform and quick response and redressal is required to show empathy in real time on social media so that it is visible to all that the company cares. Timely response, apology or compensation saves the company from bad word of mouth. Deleting or censoring the negative feedback only shows the organization's inability to rectify the situation. Listen to what customers are saying in reviews and social media. Share it with the staff and build a culture of paying attention to what the customers are saying and make necessary changes. The positive comments should also be graciously acknowledged. The user generated content is more authentic and trustworthy in the eyes of other consumers. The brands that re-tweeted comments of the users have 264% more followers as compared to the one that did not.

12.9.2 PROACTIVE ENGAGEMENT

Engaging with customers on a daily basis would lead to growth in the consumer base. The quality of content matters more than the quantity. The business should listen and interact with the past guests and brand enthusiasts (TripAdvisor, 2014). The business intelligence can be collected and analyzed to determine what should be posted to keep the consumers engaged. The company can analyze what travelers are asking for on sites like TripAdvisor. The competitor analysis through their customer feedback, marketing channels, tactics, and best practices can be done in order to optimize your marketing and public relations. Simple short sentences should be used to gain visitors attention as they may be on the page for few seconds only. Eye catching pictures can tell the whole story and can be engaging and sell the product. The language should be kept positive . Negative language can harm reputation. Content can be curated or original. The ratio of curated to original content is recommended by experts is four or five is to one. Links to news stories and blog posts already available on the internet can be posted.

Organizations should surprise and delight the customers with offers and contests at regular intervals. Deals and exclusive promotions only for online fans keep the interest in the site. Thereviews, images or videos can be solicited from the users as a prerequisite to participate in contests. This would boost the organization's user content database for further uploads and keep the customers engaged. This is an easy and economic way to generate new content. The own, user and paid content can be integrated to keep the consumers engaged. The organization should try to engage the individual members as well as the community at large. The success in this sphere can be gauged by the size and strength of likes, followers, uploads and shares. Likes indicate that there is traffic on the site but how much of it is getting converted in business terms is difficult to estimate. Shares on the other hand can determine whether the posts are valuable or not. The retweets, repins, and shares happen only when a visitor takes some action on the original post and tries to influence others. The social sharing of content is more likely to happen on weekends when the visitors have more time on hand to read the posts. Frequency of interaction should be more on Twitter as guest expectations are to be connected with the brands in real time on this platform. Cost of creating new content on Youtube more as high-quality videos need to be made. As 75% of Twitter content is generated by 5% of the users, it is important to manage the key influencers. Time of post and the duration after which the company takes a remedial action also matters. In most cases there should be speedy solution to the query or resolution of the complaint.

12.9.3 FACILITATE DEEPER SHARED MEANINGS

The customers should derive added value from the knowledgeable contributions to discussion on online forums about their travel and hospitality experiences. They should be able to relive their experience through narration to others and induce a desire to repeat the experience for themselves and initiate it in others. They should emotionally connect with the brand and should have a deeper, shared meaning of the experience. The customers articulation of opinions on subjects of importance to the company should delight them and enhance the brand image of the company. Their position as brand advocates is cemented by demonstration of excitement and content at the experiences provided by the brand during and after the travel. They become brand ambassadors in the community and spread electronic word-of-mouth which reaches thousands of customers at the press of few key strokes. Their social endorsements should influence potential customers and bring in revenues for the company. The social capital of the organization should be leveraged to provide a competitive advantage in the marketplace.

Customer Engagement through Social Media

Sources of origin – Visitor

Interaction Format	*What to do?*
Queries	Respond; provide information; facilitate bookings
Positive Comments	Acknowledge, increase visibility through retweets and shares; more valuable than own content
Negative comments/ Complaints/Greviances	Respond, redress, apologise, and compensate

Sources of origin – Organization

Interaction Format	*Purpose*
Industry news/trends	Generate interest; get traffic to the site
Values of the brand	Brand awareness; social endorsement through shares, likes, retweets, and pluses
Offers	Get traffic to the site; Keep the customers interested; novelty of the site
Quizzes/Games	Get user information; data generation; enhance customer's knowledge about the brand
Story/experience sharing contest	Get authentic content for electronic-word-of-mouth
Picture/video contest	Get access to high-quality pictures and videos depicting customer delight
Ideas solicitation	Crowd sourcing of ideas; improvement/refinement of service; development of new service
Product/service reviews	Improvement/refinement of service; development of new service

12.9.4 CONSISTENT ENGAGEMENT

There is emergence of hybrid online channel because of the presence of businesses on multiple social media channels. The customer should have the option to effortlessly move across channels and social media sites. It should be the customer's choice regarding where he wants to engage. The brand message and brand identity communicated should be consistent across platforms. It is important to integrate the owned content and the earned content and post it in byte sized pieces that engage customers across social media channels to amplify visibility and reach. The social networks can be searched so tag the images with description and brand name and use consistent hashtags across platforms. The online engagement measures should be in tune with the offline endeavours so as to project a consistent policy. There should be integration of all consumer engagement channels.

12.9.5 COLLABORATE AND CO-CREATE

The consumer reviews can provide deep insights into the features of the products and services that have touched a chord with the consumers and where there is scope for improvement. The companies can garner free development resources for ideas for potential products and services. The crowd sourcing helps in refining the new services and can point to areas where there might have been oversight from the managers. Scarce resources can be allocated to those products in which there is greatest interest and are likely to be successful. The sales potential of different geographical territories can be studied on the basis of traffic coming on the social media sites indicating consumer interest shown in potential products and services. The social innovation process can be devised by having appropriate mechanisms to integrate the learned insights of the consumers with the efforts of the company personnel to have strategic advantage.

12.9.6 IDENTIFY AND SHARE BEST PRACTICES

The company should identify and share the best practices across properties for improved performance of the entire portfolio (Tripadvisor, 2014 The content for the article provided by Revinate). The learnings from success of various initiatives at one hotel should be communicated to other hotels for emulation. The challenges encountered while in progression and the measures taken to overcome those should also be shared so that the knowledge about this new field is codified, replicated, improvised, and enhanced.

The organizations need to monitor, understand, and respond to the activities on the social media in a timely and comprehensive manner. Managers need to learn to steer the discussion on the social media which is congruent with the mission and business goals of the organization (Mangold and Faulds, 2009). The social platforms such as Youtube, Facebook, and Twitter should not be seen as standalone components but should be built into an ecosystem of related elements and should fit into the company's marketing communications strategy (Hanna et al., 2011). In the dynamic and interconnected international world, the companies need to engage customers, embrace technology, and invest in its employees to harness the power of the social media (Berthon et al., 2012).

The product needs to be prepared on the customer and market requirements. The social media campaign needs to be devised, launched, managed, and evaluated in the right manner. The success of the social media campaign needs to be measured and businesses need to follow the social media best practices. The content and engagement strategy should be relevant for the current times. As the technology is evolving, the organizations need to make a cultural and behavioral change in engaging with the customers to make the process more transparent and be prepared to adopt the platforms that the consumers are moving on to.

12.10 CONCLUSION

Inversini and Masiero (2014) have recommended that the presence of hospitality organizations on the social media and online travel agent sites is imperative to create a platform for social booking technologies to increase the visibility and sales. The social media outreach is going to impact all operations in the hospitality industry and add value to the experience of the customer. Leadership intervention and inclusion of consumer feedback at all stages can lead to creation of value (Chathoth et al., 2014).The full potential of the social media is not being exploited at present by the hotels and it is sometimes used incorrectly (Rosman and Stuhara, 2014). Integrative and comprehensive approach is required to manage consumer engagement behavior so that its evolution and consequences over time can be taken into account ((van Doorn et al., 2010). Thus customer-generated product reviews and advertisements, contributions to new product development and discussions on various forums should provide the company with a competitive advantage in the marketplace.There is a need to build one-to-one, direct, stronger, relevant, and meaningful relationships with consumers. These efforts of the organizations would provide them with insights from the interactions and which can be leveraged to gain commercial success.

KEYWORDS

- **analytics**
- **consumer engagement**
- **hospitality sector**
- **personalization**
- **social media**
- **social networking**
- **user-generated content**

REFERENCES

Amersdorffer, D.; Bauhuber, F.; Oellrich, J. The Economic and Cultural Aspects of the Social Web: Implications for the Tourism Industry. *J. Vacat. Mark.* **2012,** *18*(3), 175–184.

Bagley, E.; Lanz. L. The Evolution of Digital Marketing and the Significance of Earned Content' The Digital Direction: Content Management and the Marketing Communication of Today HVS (February), pp. 2–5. 2014. Downloads/HVS%20-%20The%20Digital%20Direction...Two-Part%20Series.pdf. (accessed 2 July 2014).

Beese, J. Learn How 3 Innovative Travel Brands Found Success on Twitter. 2014. http://sproutsocial.com/insights/find-3-innovative-travel-brands-succeeding-twitter/. (accessed 2 May 2014).

Berthon, P. R.; Pitt, L. F.; Plangger, K.; Shapiro, D. Marketing meets Web 2.0, social media, and creative consumers: Implications for international marketing strategy. *Bus. Horiz.* **2012,** *55*(3), 261–271.

Bijmolt, T. H. A.; Leeflang, P. S. H.; Block, F.; Eisenbeiss, M.; Hardie, B. G. S.; Lemmens, A.; Saffert, P. Analytics for Customer Engagement. *J Ser. Res.* **2010,** *13*(3), 341–356.

Bilgihan, A.; Peng, C.; Kandampully, J. Generation Y's Dining Information Seeking and Sharing Behaviour on Social Networking Sites: An Exploratory Study. *Int. J. Contemp. Hosp. Manag.* 2014, *26*(3), 349–366.

Brejla, P.; Gilbert, D. An Exploratory Use of Web Content Analysis to Understand Cruise Tourism Services. *Int. J. Tour. Res.* **2014,** *16*(2), 157–168.

Broughton, M. All that glitters is GLOW' Casino International, February, pp.64–66. 2014. http://www.casinointernational-online.com/all-that-glitters-is-glow.aspx. (Accessed 15 April 2014).

Canhota, A. I.; Clark, M. Customer Service 140 Characters at a Time: The Users' Perspective. *J. Market. Manag.* **2013,** *29*(5/6), 522–544.

Chan, N. L.; Guillet, B. D. Investigation of Social Media Marketing: How Does the Hotel Industry in Hong Kong Perform in Marketing on Social Media Websites? *J. Travel Tour. Market.* **2011,** *28*(4), 345–368.

Chathoth, P. K.; Ungson, G. R.; Altinay, L.; Chan, E. S. W.; Harrington, R.; Okumus, F. Barriers Effecting Organizational Adoption of Higher Order Customer Engagement in Tourism Service Interactions. *Tour. Manag.* **2014,** *42,* 181–193.

Chua, A. Y. K.; Banerjee, S. Customer Knowledge Management via Social Media: The Case of Starbucks. *J. Knowl. Manag.* **2013,** *17*(2), 237–249.

Chesbrough, H. Business Model Innovation: Opportunities and Barriers. *Long Range Plan.* **2010,** *43,* 354–363.

comScore. comScore Releases June 2013 U.S. Online Video Rankings. 2013. http://www.comscore.com/Insights/Press-Releases/2013/7/comScore-Releases-June-2013-US-Online-Video-Rankings. (accessed 14July2014).

Deloitte. Hospitality 2015 Game Changers or spectators. 2010. http://www.deloitte.com/assets/Dcom-Malta/Local%20Assets/Documents/Industries/dt_Hospitality_2015.pdf. (accessed 10 July 2014).

eMarketer. US Mobile Travel Sales to Increase 60% in 2014. 2014. http://www.emarketer.com/Article/US-Mobile-Travel-Sales-Increase-60-2014/1010828. (accessed 26 June 2014).

eMarketer. Mobile Devices Trending for UK Travel Researchers. 2014. http://www.emarketer.com/Article/Mobile-Devices-Trending-UK-Travel-Researchers/1010939. (accessed 26 June 2014).

eMarketer. Company Mentions on Social Channels Peak on Thursdays. 2014. http://www.emarketer.com/Article/Company-Mentions-on-Social-Channels-Peak-on-Thursdays/1010926. (accessed 26 June 2014).

eMarketer. World Smartphone Usage to Grow 25% in 2014. 2014. http://www.emarketer.com/Article/Worldwide-Smartphone-Usage-Grow-25-2014/1010920. (accessed 26 June 2014).

Ernst & Young. Social media: New game, new rules, new winner. 2011. http://www.ey.com/Publication/vwLUAssets/Social_media_-_New_game_new_rules_new_winners/$FILE/EY_Social_media.pdf. (accessed 2 May 2014).

Ernst &Young. Social Media Marketing – India Trends Study 2013. 2013. http://www.ey.com/IN/en/services/advisory/social-media-marketing-india-trends-study-2013. (accessed 2 May 2014).

Facebook. Company Info. 2014. http://newsroom.fb.com/company-info/. (accessed 14 July 2014).

Foursquare. About Foursquare. 2014. https://foursquare.com/about. (accessed 14 July 2014)

Fuller, J. Refining Virtual Co-creation from a Consumer Perspective. *Calif. Manag. Rev.* **2010,** *52*(2), 92–122.

Gironda, J. T.; Korgaonkar, P. K. Understanding Consumers Social Networking Site Usage. *J Market Manag* 2014, *30*(5/6), 571–605.

Gretzel, U.; Kang, M.; Lee, W. Differences in Consumer-Generated Media Adoption and Use: A Cross National Perspective. *J. Hosp. Leis. Market.* **2008,** *17*(2), 99–120.

Hanna, R.; Rohm, A.; Crittenden, V. L. We're All Connected: The Power of the Social Media Ecosystem. *Bus. Horiz.* **2011,** 54(3), 265–273.

Hede, A.; Kellett, P. Building Online Brand Communities: Exploring the Benefits, Challenges and Risks in the Australian Event Sector. *J. Vacat. Market.* **2012,** *18*(3), 239–250.

Hennig-Thurau, T.; Malthouse, E. C.; Friege, C.; Gensler, S.; Lobschat, L; Rangaswamy, A.; Skiera, B. The Impact of New Media on Customer Relationships. *J. Ser. Res.* **2010,** *13*(3), 311–330.

Hilton Hotels and Resorts. 2014. http://www3.hilton.com/en/about/stayconnected.html?WT.mc_id=zEWWATB0US1HH2REP4Social7GW841484. (accessed 15 June 2014).

Horster, E.; Gottschalk, C. Computer-Assisted Webnography: A New Approach to Online Reputation Management in Tourism. *J. Vacat. Market.* 2012, *18*(3), 229–238.

Hopitality Net. Why Pinterest is a Must Have For Hoteliers. 2014. http://www.hospitalitynet.org/news/154000320/4064371.html. (accessed 2 May 2014).

Hopitality Net. Why Google+ is so Important to Organic SEO. 2014. http://www.hospitalitynet.org/news/global/147000382/4064905.html. (accessed 2 May 2014).

Hvass, K. A.; Munar, A. M. The Takeoff of Social Media in Tourism. *J. Vacat. Market.* **2012,** *18*(2), 93–103.

Inks, S. A.; Schetzsle, S.; Avila, R. A. Exploring the Use of Business Networking Tools in Sales: Current Perceptions and Furure Expectations. *Market. Manag. J.* **2012,** *22*(1), 1–16.

Instagram. Stats. 2014. http://instagram.com/press/. (accessed 14July 2014).

Inversini, A.; Masiero, L. Selling Rooms Online: The Use of Social Media and Online Travel Agents. *Int. J. Contemp. Hosp. Manag.* **2014,** *26*(2), 272–292.

Jayawardena, C.; McMIllan, D.; Pantin, D.; Taller, M.; Willie, P. Trends in the International Hotel Industry. *Worldw. Hosp. Tour. Themes* **2013,** *5*(2), 151–163.

Jeong, M.; Jeon, M. M. Customer Reviews of Hotel Experiences through Consumer Generated Media (CGM). *J. Hosp. Leis. Mark.* **2008,** *17,* 121–138.

Kaplan, A. M.; Haenlein, M. Users of the World Unite! The Challenges and Opportunities of Social Media. *Bus. Horiz.* **2010,** *53,* 59–68.

Keitzmann, J. H.; Hermkens, K.; McCarthy, I. P.; Silvestre, B. Social Media? Get Serious! Understanding the Functional Building Blocks of Social Media. *Bus. Horiz.* **2011,** *54*(3), 241–251.

Kumar, V.; Aksoy, L.; Donkers, B.; Venkatesan, R.; Wiesel, T.; Tillmanns, S. Undervalued or Overvalued Customers: Capturing Total Customer Engagement Value. *J. Serv. Res.* **2010,** *13*(3), 297–310.

Lee, S. To Tweet or Not To Tweet: An Exploratory Study of Meeting Professionals' Attitude Toward Applying Social Media for Meeting Sessions. *J. Conv. Event Tour.* **2011,** *12,* 271–289.

Leposa, A. Social Media Tips from the Experts. *Travel Agent* **2013,** *22,* 30–35.

Lim, Y.; Chung, Y.; Weaver, P. A. The Impact of Social Media on Destination Branding: Consumer-generated Videos Versus Destination Marketer-generated Videos. *J. Vacat. Market.* **2012,** *18*(3), 197–206.

Litvin, S. W.; Hoffman, L. M. Responses to Consumer-generated Media in the Hospitality Marketplace: An Empirical Study. *J. Vacat. Market.* **2012,** *18*(2), 135–145.

McCarthy, L.; Stock, D.; Verma, R. How Travelers Use Online and Social Media Channels to Make Hotel-choice Decisions. *Cornel. Hosp. Rep.* **2010,** *10*(18), 4–18.

Mangold, W.G.; Faulds, D. J. Social Media: The New Hybrid Element of the Promotion Mix. *Bus. Horiz.* **2009,** *52*(4), 357–365.

Mangold, W. G.; Smith, K. T. Selling to Millennials with Online Reviews. *Bus. Horiz.* **2012,** *55*(2), 141–153.

Mansson, M. Mediatized Tourism. *Anna. Tour. Res.* 2011, *38*(4), 1634–1652.

Martini, A.; Massa, S.; Testa, S. Customer Co-creation Projects and Social Media: The Case of Barilla of Italy. *Bus. Horiz.* 2014, *57*(3), 425–434.

Miles, S. J.; Mangold, W. G. Employee Voice: Untapped Resource or Social Media Time Bomb? *Bus. Horiz.* 2014, *57*(3), 401–411.

Mladenow, A.; Bauer, C.; Strauss, C. Social Crowd Integration in New Product Development: Crowdsourcing Communities Nourish the Open Innovation Paradigm. *Glob. J. Flex. Syst. Manag.* **2014,** 15(1), 77–86.

MMGY Global. Survey Reveals New Class of Travelers: The Digital Elite. 2013. http://www.mmgyglobal.com/news/survey-reveals-new-class-of-travelers-the-digital-elite/. (accessed 14July, 2014).

O'Conner, P. Managing a Hotel's image on TripAdvisor. *J. Hosp. Market. Manag.* **2010,** *19*(7), 754–772.

Ong, B. S. The Perceived Influence of User Reviews in the Hospitality Industry. *J. Hosp. Market. Manag.* **2012,** *21*(5), 463–485.

Pan, B.; Xiang, Z.; Law, R.; Fesenmaier, D. R. The Dynamics of Search Engine Marketing for Tourist Destinations. *J. Travel Res.* **2011,** *50,* 365–377.

Prahalad, C. K.; Ramaswamy, V. Co-creation Experiences: The Next Practice in Value Creation. *J. Interact. Market.* **2004,** *8*(3), 25–14.

Restaurant Social Media Index. Overall top 250 RSM Index. 2014. http://rsmindex.com/2014-top-250-index-q1/. (accessed 14 July, 2014).

Rosman, R.; Stuhura, K. The Implications of Social Media on Customer Relationship Management and the Hospitality Industry. *J. Manag. Pol. Pract.* **2013,** *14*(3), 18–26.

Ruzic, D.; Bilos, A.; Kelic, I. Development of Mobile Marketing in Croatian Tourism Using Location-Based Services. *Tour. Hosp. Indus.* **2012,** *21*, 151–159.

Saarijarvi, H. The Mechanisms of Value Co-creation. *J. Strat. Market.* **2012,** *20*(5), 381–391.

Sigala, M. Social Networks and Customers Involvement in New Service Development (NSD) The Case of www.mystarbucksidea.com. Int. *J. Contemp. Hosp. Manag.* **2012,** *24*(7), 966–990.

Sigala, M. Web 2.0 and Customer Involvement in New Service Development: A Framework, Cases and Implications in Tourism. In *Social media in travel, tourism and hospitality: Theory, practice and cases;* Sigala, M., Christou, E., Gretzel, U., Eds.; Ashgate Publishing Limited: Surrey, 2012; pp. 25–38.

Steinbirk, S. *Digital Technologies in Travel: Light at the End of the Funnel*? PhoCusWright Inc, 2013.

Stringham, B. B.; Gerdes Jr. J. An Analysis of Word-of-Mouth Ratings and Guest Comments of Online Hotel Distribution Sites. *J. Hosp. Market. Manag.* **2010,** *19*(7), 773–796.

Taj Hotels Resorts and Palaces. Company Information. 2014. http://www.tajhotels.com/About-Taj/Company-Information/default.html. (accessed 27 June 2014).

Tham, A.; Croy, G.; Mair, J. Social Media in Destination Choice: Distinctive Electronic Word-of-Mouth Dimensions. *J. Travel Tour. Market.* **2013,** *30*(1/2), 144–155.

The Times of India. Google owns worlds' second-largest engine too! 2011. http://timesofindia.indiatimes.com/tech/tech-news/Google-owns-worlds-second-largest-search-engine-too/articleshow/7804930.cms. (accessed 14 July 2014).

TripAdvisor. Creating Your Hotel Social Media Action Plan. 2014. http://www.tripadvisor.in/TripAdvisorInsights/n2147/creating-your-hotel-social-media-action-plan. (accessed12 June 2014).

Valluari, D. J. Sharing Compelling Stories on Social Mediais Boosting Bookings, Driving Loyalty. 2014. http://www.hospitalitynet.org/news/154000320/4064611.html. (accessed 2 May 2014).

van Doorn, J.; Lemon, K. N.; Mittal, V.; Nass, S.; Pic, D.; Pirner, P.; Verhoef, P. C. Customer Engagement Behavior: Theoretical Foundations and Research Directions. *J. Serv. Res.* 2010, *13*(3), 253–266.

Vernette, E.; Hamsi-Kidar, L. Co-creation with Consumers: Who has the Competence and Wants to Cooperate? *Int. J. Market Res.* **2013,** *55*(4), 2–20.

Verhoef, P. C., Reinartz, W. J.; Krafft, M. Customer Engagement as a New Perspective in Customer Management. *J. Serv. Res.* 2010, *13*(3), 247–252.

Vivek, S. D.; Beatty, S. E.; Morgan, R. M. Customer Engagement: Exploring Customer Relationships Beyond Purchase. *J. Market. Theory Pract.* **2012,** *20*(2), 127–145.

Watson, P.; Morgan, M.; Hemmington, N. Online Communities and the Sharing of Extraordinary Restaurant Experiences. *J. Foodserv.* **2008,** *19,* 289–302.

Weinberg, B.; Pehlivan, E. Social Spending: Managing the Social Media Mix. *Bus. Horiz.* **2011,** *54*(3), 275–282.

Woodcock, N.; Green A.; Starkey, M. Social CRM as a Business Strategy. *J. Database Market. Cust. Strat. Manag.* **2011,** *18,* 50–64.

Xiang, Z.; Gretzel, U. Role of Social Media in Online Travel Information Search. *Tour. Manag.* **2010,** *31,* 179–188.

CHAPTER 13

HERITAGE HOTELS IN INDIA: OFFERING UNIQUE EXPERIENCES TO CUSTOMERS WITH SUSTAINABLE PRACTICES AS A DIFFERENTIATOR

PARUL G MUNJAL[1*] and SANDEEP MUNJAL[2]

[1]*Sushant School of Art and Architecture, Ansal University, Gurgaon, India*

[2]*Vedatya Institute, Gurgaon, India*

[*]*Corresponding author. E-mail: parul.g.munjal@gmail.com*

CONTENTS

ABSTRACT

Objective

Adaptive reuse of heritage structures in the form of hotels has shown impressive growth in India in recent years. While this conversion poses challenges, it also presents opportunities as end users are showing interest in staying at heritage hotels to experience our rich cultural heritage.As sustainable practices, conservation of heritage and social responsibility take center stage, heritage hotel owners/ management are increasingly marketing the overall experience with its intended societal benefits to its consumers. It is important to establish if the existing heritage hotels have been sensitive to concerns of the local communities while setting up and managing their business. In the current paradigm of development, where the process of any project conception and implementation is professed to be based on stakeholder participation, the best practices represented by existing heritage hotels can chart the way forward for responsible development and management of heritage resources as hotels to ensure superior consumer experiences in a sustainable manner.

The objective of the research is to explore the success of heritage hotels in India in offering a value-added product to the customers, and also probe the sociocultural and economic impact of heritage hotels from a perspective of sustainability. The study focuses especially on heritage hotels, because these have emerged as a high growth segment, typically located in areas with historical contexts. They offer an inimitable experience due to the physical features and heritage value on one hand and are also receiving patronage due to the sustainable practices they are adopting.

Methodology/Approach

An update of the heritage hotel scenario in India has been presented, as extracted from the Ministry of Tourism database and other heritage hotel associations. Secondary research in the form of existing literature and data has been used to build the understanding of various factors that contribute to the social, cultural and economic impact and sustainability. The analysis and inferences of the study are based on information collected on sample cases of heritage hotels. The approach is to document qualitative inputs based on a questionnaire instrument to draw inferences on respective experiences of heritage hotel developers. The sustainability indicators prescribed by the Ministry of Tourism have been used to assess the impact of selected heritage hotels taken up for study.

The Major Findings

The research effort highlights the success or challenges that the case study hotels have achieved in offering a unique experience to its expanding customer base, with the practice of principles of sustainability as a distinguishing feature. These findings can be helpful directives for more reutilization of heritage structures as potential heritage hotels.

Conclusions

Heritage hotels represent opportunities for putting heritage assets to commercial use and simultaneously ensuring their conservation. Many such structures are unlikely to find resources required to sustain these without reuse options that open revenue streams. Integration of such reuse with the local socioeconomic context will render feasibility to any projects conceived by developers, private or government linked.

Implications

The inferences can help establish heritage hotels as drivers of social development, especially in regions that are suffering from poverty, unemployment and lack of education. If appropriate processes are followed, a mutually interdependent and beneficial relationship can be forged and promoted that can sustain the cultural component at the local, regional and as a result, national level.

Target Audience

The target audience includes all stakeholders in the realm of heritage and hospitality such as hoteliers, governmental and nongovernmental organizations, students of hospitality and heritage studies schools, heritage property owners and heritage consultants.

13.1 INTRODUCTION

India has for long been recognized as a heritage tourism destination. In keeping with that credential, more recently, the hotel industry has seen a strong growth in number of heritage hotels that have come up all over the country. This growth has been driven by a demand that is both domestic as well as international. The consumer interest in patronizing heritage hotels is based on the unique experience that these offer both in terms of their structural and situational context, and also the sustainable practices that they tend to represent. The sociocultural and economic impacts that these businesses bring forth are a differentiation point that feeds into their commercial success as well as their acceptance with today's guests.

13.2 DEFINING HERITAGE HOTELS

Heritage hotels, also termed as "historic hotels" (Historic Hotels of America, 2013), are considered a subset of boutique hotels (Henderson, 2011; Lim & Endean, 2009) in most parts of the world. These range from monumental grand hotels to urban vernacular "shophouses" of Singapore (Chang & Teo, 2009). Chang and Teo (2009, p. 347) give Malaysian examples of the Cheong FattTze Mansion in Penang and Puri Hotel in historic Malacca that demonstrate successful adaptive reuse of urban–vernacular architecture into heritage hotels by the private sector. In the Indian context, while researchers may include the historic properties built for the purpose of being run as hotels such as the Oberoi Maidens in Delhi and the Taj Mahal Palace and Tower in Mumbai (Kapoor, 2012), these are not included in the list of heritage hotels approved by the Government of India (GOI) and are not under consideration for the current study.

The Ministry of Tourism, GOI has developed guidelines for various categories of hotels and defines criteria for classification under each. The definition of "heritage hotels" as per the Ministry guidelines is (Ministry of Tourism, n.d. a):

> ...running hotels in palaces/castles/forts/*havelies*/hunting lodges/ residence of any size built prior to 1950. The facade, architectural features and general construction should have the distinctive qualities and ambience in keeping with the traditional way of life of the area. The architecture of the property to be considered for this category should not normally be interfered with. Any extension, improvement, renovation, change in the existing structures should be in keeping with the traditional architectural styles and constructional techniques harmonising the new with the old. After expansion/renovation, the newly built up area added should not exceed 50% of the total built up (plinth) area including the old and new structures. For this purpose, facilities such as swimming pools, lawns etc. will be excluded.

Hence, the classification as "heritage hotels" are based on the following conditions:

- Original function–not being a hotel
- Historicity–built prior to 1950
- Architectural characteristics–distinctive ambience and qualities
- Sensitivity in renovation–using traditional styles and techniques
- Extent of addition–new built up area not more than 50% of total area

Along with these, a number of general conditions have also been outlined that ensure professional management of the premises and maintenance of good standards in terms of infrastructure and services, including appropriate water and waste management mechanisms and authentic entertainment of guests (Ministry of Tourism, 2013). The "heritage" category hotels are organized into three subcategories: basic, classic and grand according to the Ministry. The classification is revisited and approved periodically, every five years. The factors on which the classification is dependent are as follows.

TABLE 13.1 Factors Defining Subclassification of Heritage Hotels (Ministry of Tourism, n.d. a)

Factor	Heritage basic	Heritage classic	Heritage grand
Historicity	Built prior to 1950	Built prior to 1935	Built prior to 1935
Min. no. of rooms	5 (10 beds)	15 (30 beds)	15 (30 beds)
Ambience, comfort and imaginative readaptation	Concept of heritage and architectural distinctiveness	Concept of heritage and architectural distinctiveness	Concept of heritage and architectural distinctiveness Public and private areas including rooms with superior appearance and decor Atleast 50% rooms air conditioned and/or heated
Sporting facilities	none	Atleast one of listed[1] sporting facility	Atleast two of listed[2] sporting facilities
Cuisine offered	Traditional cuisine of the area	Traditional cuisine and four to five items from continental cuisine	Traditional and continental cuisine
Bar (if permitted by law)	Desirable	Required	Required
Quality of service and years of experience of owner/staff	Subject to evaluation		

Hence, the Ministry of Tourism guidelines for "heritage hotels" are sensitive to the issues and opportunities that heritage properties of India provide, rather than positioning them in competition with the star categorization. This encourages heritage owners to approach the required standards in terms of number of room requirements and other considerations, for a heritage classification, though there are perceived limitations due to the classification, as well due to which a number of heritage hotel properties, especially, the smaller ones are reluctant to apply for the classification.

[1]Swimming pool, health club, lawn tennis, squash, riding, golf course, provided the ownership vests with the concerned hotel. Apart from these facilities, credit would also be given for supplementary sporting facilities such as golf, boating, sailing, fishing or other adventure sports such as ballooning, parasailing, wind-surfing, safari excursions, trekking,etc. and indoor games (Ministry of Tourism, 2013).

[2]Same as above.

The Indian Heritage Hotels Association (IHHA), a nongovernmental affiliating body for heritage hotels, qualifies for membership: "palaces & castles or stately homes and residences that have been lovingly restored to meet the comforts expected by the modern traveler, and yet retain the character and flavor of traditional homes", serving as "a continuation of the past tradition of hospitality" (India Heritage Hotels Association, 2013).

13.3 UNIQUENESS OF HERITAGE HOTELS

Heritage hotels may be close to "boutique hotels" in terms of their uniqueness, hence qualifying as a subset of these in most parts of the world, but the historicity and associational values of heritage hotels present challenges and opportunities that are incomparable with a nonheritage hotel. The concept of heritage hotels has gained popularity due to the need for a unique experience they offer, as compared with a typical luxury hotel room (Kapoor, 2012, p. 5). Culturally oriented tourists are not usually price-sensitive (Murzyn-Kupisz, 2013) and the rich experience offered by heritage hotels is the main attraction for such tourists.

The location and setting of current or potential heritage hotels such as historic palaces, forts, hunting lodges and residences have strategic locations for defense, leisure or symbolic purposes. Hence, the setting of such properties is unique, be it in the form of medieval hill forts, palaces along the lake, hunting lodges in the middle of forest or palaces at the centers of cities or towns as political centers. This is an inherent advantage that heritage hotels have over other properties that can be capitalized very well to provide the guest a unique experience.

In a number of cases of heritage hotels in India, the association of royal or noble families with the properties lend a unique "continuity value" to these properties. The heritage hotel properties of HRH group are owned and managed by the Sisodia royal family; WelcomHeritage is a joint venture of ITC Ltd. and Jodhana Heritage Resorts of H.H. Maharaja Gaj Singh II of Jodhpur (WelcomHeritage, 2013; Jodhana Heritage Resorts, 2013), lending a spirit of custodianship to these. Stand-alone heritage hotels such as the Jehan Numa Palace, Bhopal exemplify properties that continue to be owned and run by the royal families who earlier used these as forts, palaces, residences, hunting lodges or guest houses.

According to Abakerli (2012, p. 10), "...heritage properties are valuable socioeconomic endowments". Infrastructure associated with cultural tourism development also provides services to the local communities, especially, in remote areas (Roe & Urquhart cited by Abarkeli 2012, p. 8). Heritage hotel establishment and management is also a form of cultural tourism development that impacts the surrounding communities.

Maskey (2008, p. 80) emphasizes "historic buildings are unique resources that hold various use and nonuse values for society. In order to protect these values, preservation and maintenance of these buildings is required. Neglecting these resources may lead to inefficiencies due to loss of historic value". The adaptive reuse of historic buildings as heritage hotels allows the maintenance and management of these structures that would have otherwise fallen to disuse and neglect. Abakerli (2012, p. 10) points out the reduced environmental impact of retrofitting existing dwellings, as less waste material is produced in the form of demolition debris.

13.4 CHARTING THE COURSE: SOCIAL AND ECONOMIC FACTORS

The history of establishment of heritage hotels in India goes back to 1957, when the Rambagh Palace in Jaipur was converted to a palace hotel by Maharaja Man Singh of Jaipur, the head of the royal family of Jaipur, in order to provide the state capital with a hotel. While the numerous princely states of India were absorbed in to the Indian union in 1947, the withdrawal of the privy purses of the royal families who owned the numerous forts, palaces, hunting lodges *etc.* in 1971, was one of the major reasons for their inability to maintain heritage properties (Kapoor, 2012). As a result, custodians of some of the properties resorted to adaptive reuse in the form of museums or hotels in order to sustain these, instead of letting them fall to disuse and neglect.

Some were bought and converted to heritage hotels by individuals such as Aman Nath and Francis Wacziarg, who bought the fort at Neemrana from the royal family in 1986 (Indian Heritage Hotels Association, 2013) and started the Neemrana Group of Hotels with its conversion to a heritage hotel. Relatively new regional entrants into the business are groups such as Chevron Hotels & Resorts established in 1995 that runs four heritage hotel properties in Kumaon, Uttarakhand and INDeco Leisure Hotels established in 1996 managing three heritage hotels in Tamil Nadu (Borgia, 2012). The story of INDeco Leisure Hotels is similar to Neemrana Group. Both cases reflect the keen interest of these individuals in restoring and reusing the properties that lay in poor state of repair and contributing to the development of the local rural communities around the properties through generation of livelihoods and the capacity building toward the restoration and management of the heritage buildings. Their commitment toward social, cultural, and economic development of the heritage imbedded in the properties and the local communities functions as a social responsibility of these business entities.

As of now there are 53 basic, 1 classic and 5 grand heritage hotels approved by the Ministry of Tourism (2013), while some are under evaluation. Besides the approved heritage hotels, India has many more heritage properties adapted to reuse as hotels, though not approved by the GOI. The IHHA (2013) has over 140 members across the country. Some of these are attached to groups that specialize in managing hotels in heritage properties, the prominent ones being WelcomHeritage with 40 hotels across 13 states, Historic Resort Hotels (HRH) with 10 hotels in the state of Rajasthan and Neemrana Group of Hotels with 27 "non-hotel" hotels across the country, with the earliest property dating to the 14th century.

The HRH Groups of hotels is an example of a heritage hotel group owned by the House of Mewar, "the world's oldest serving dynasty" that diverts contributions toward initiatives of the Maharana of Mewar Charitable Foundation (MMCF). Hence, the House of Mewar continues to be a custodian of the heritage resources of Mewar till date, under the umbrella of Eternal Mewar, "a unique heritage brand exemplifying hospitality, cultural preservation, philanthropy, education, sports & spirituality for global audiences" (Eternal Mewar, 2013).

The private sector and local communities are important active participants in the process of sustainable tourism development, while the government plays the role of an enabler through the creation of a favorable policy environment (Ministry of Tourism, n.d. b). One of the challenges is that the benefits of setting up heritage related hospitality establishments may reach the local community to some extent in terms of providing job opportunities, but the maximum benefit may go to external owners (Murzyn-Kupisz, 2013, p. 157).

Governments at both central and state level have, over the last few decades, made efforts to offer incentives in the form of capital subsidies and interest subsidies to encourage investments in heritage hotels and organize the buyer–seller meets to bring the heritage property owners and the hospitality industry face-to-face. The objective is guided by economic policy that identifies tourism as a potential high growth sector plagued by a shortfall in hotel rooms across all categories. From 1973 when the initial capital subsidy was declared, to 1993 when state capital subsidy scheme offered subsidy to a tune of 15% of eligible investments, specifically for heritage hotels,[3] many initiatives have been taken. Ministry of Tourism,GOI introduced a scheme of "Capital Investment Subsidy" in the year 2002 that was available during the 10th plan period till 2007, for setting up hotels in one to three star category and heritage hotels with an objective to increase the supply of hotel rooms in the budget category in the country (Tourism Finance Corporation of India Limited, 2007). The response from heritage hotels has been lukewarm due to the fact that being a part of the star classification subjects them to higher taxes, and even being branded as a heritage hotel comes with a tax tag. Being in the unaffiliated category is more profitable from a taxation perspective. This is food for thought for the policy makers.

13.5 ECONOMIC POSITIONING IN THE CURRENT CONTEXT

The economic impact of heritage structures being converted or utilized as hotels can be visited from multiple stakeholder perspectives. The key aspect here, however, remains the fiscal success of the business model that envisages the deployment of heritage buildings as commercial hotels. The HVS (2012) report identifies "heritage" as a category separate from the typical star-rating-based hotel classification and comments on the performance of this segment. While the hotel sector at large charts a decline of 1.9% in occupancy levels, heritage segment grew by 4%. An interesting facet impacting the decline in overall occupancy levels is the fact that a supply growth at 15% was not adequately compensated by demand growth that charted 13% growth. In the heritage segment the supply grew at 10% but demand was stronger, resulting earlier stated occupancy growth. From a cost-management perspective the impact of 8.8% inflation is quite pronounced on the hotel sector in general, with top line receding by 3–1% across board. Here again the heritage segment was relatively insulated, given the dependence on local (in some cases self-produced) raw materials and lower payroll costs (again due to employment of cheaper local talent). Also, an average room inventory of 46 rooms enabled the hotels in the

[3]Subject to a cap of INR 15 lacs.

heritage segment to sell inventory at good price, given the demand growth. An average room rate of INR 4,261 in 2011–2012 saw heritage hotels stand head-to-head with four-star category hotels. A healthy net profit margin of 22.6% validates the business model from a fiscal perspective (HVS, 2012).

There are other indicators that can be interpreted to argue the "business risk" aspect of converting heritage buildings to commercial hotels. The hotels drew more than 50% of their customer base from the domestic market, indicating a healthy domestic demand and hence limited dependence on the fickle international traveler. The average length of stay of 4.4 for domestic customers is the highest across all hotel segments and is indicative of revenue potential per customer (*ibid.)*. As stated by Munjal and Munjal (2011), the international visitors travelling to India have been impacted by external macroeconomic factors impacting their respective economies and the result has been a demand shift to less expensive months and overall stagnation in international tourist visitor growth rates. The heritage hotel segment has reacted to this trend by focusing attention to the domestic market that has shown a healthy growth. This focus has not been restricted to the "leisure" segment alone, but has included the lucrative "meetings, incentives, conferences and exhibitions" segment (Srivastava, 2013). In fact, Shriji Arvind Singh Mewar, Chairman of HRH Group mentions that investments in infrastructure elements that would support the needs of this segment have been wellreceivedby the domestic corporate market (*ibid.)*.In essence, the revenue generating potential of heritage hotels, today, is relatively insulated from fickle international demand and this expansion in the width of customer base bodes well for the segment, fiscally speaking.

13.6 SELECTION OF CASE STUDIES

In order to revalidate the unique positioning, inherent sustainability mechanisms and impact of the heritage hotels, five heritage hotels, representing diverse perspectives have been taken up for analysis, namely:

- Hill Fort Kesroli, Village Kesroli, Alwar, Rajasthan, Neemrana Hotels
- Shiv Niwas Palace, Udaipur, Rajasthan, HRH Group of Hotels
- Noor-Us-Sabah Palace, Bhopal, Madhya Pradesh, ITC Welcom Heritage

TABLE 13.2 Diversity Represented in the Case Studies.

	Hill Fort Kesroli	Shiv Niwas Palace, Udaipur	Noor-Us-Sabah Palace, Bhopal	JehanNuma Palace, Bhopal	INDeco Hotel, Swamimalai
Period of origin	14th century AD	Early 20th century AD	1920s	1890	1896
Original use	Hill Fort of Yaduvanshi Rajputs who converted to Islam to be called Khanzadas	Royal guest house of Maharana Fateh Singh of Mewar (period of reign: 1884-1930)	Palace of Abida Sultan, eldest daughter of the 15th ruler of the erstwhile princely state of Bhopal, Hamid Ullah Khan	Palace of General Obaidullah Khan, second son of 14th ruler of the erstwhile princely state of Bhopal, Nawab Sultan Jehan Begum	Villa of Sri Srinivas Iyer
Location	Village Kesroli, Alwar, Rajasthan	City of Udaipur, Rajasthan	City of Bhopal, Madhya Pradesh	City of Bhopal, Madhya Pradesh	Village Thimmakudi, Kumbakonam, Tamil Nadu
Setting	On a hill top, surrounded by agri-cultural fields	Along Lake Pichola, in the heart of the city	On slope of Shamla Hill,	On hill, at edge northern eastern edge of Upper Lake of Bhopal	Rural setting
Year of conver-sion to heritage hotel	1998	1982	1997	1983	1996
Use just prior to conversion	Not in use	Royal guest house	Not in use, in poor condition	In use by the royal family	State of disuse and neglect
Motivation for conversion	Heritage conservation and rural development	Owners motivated to maintain the property well	Heritage conservation and revenue generation	Owners motivated to maintain the property well and fulfil require-ment of hotel in Bhopal	Heritage conser-vation and rural development

TABLE 13.2 *(Continued)*

	Hill Fort Kesroli	Shiv Niwas Palace, Udaipur	Noor-Us-Sabah Palace, Bhopal	JehanNuma Palace, Bhopal	INDeco Hotel, Swamimalai
No. of rooms	21 rooms (including 11 suites)	36 rooms (including 17 suites)	57 (expansion plans – addition of 100 more rooms)	100	30
Heritage classification (Govt.) and memberships	None as per Govt. of India. Member of IHHA	Heritage Granc. Member of IHHA	Under review. Heritage Classic (2008-2013). Member of IHHA	Heritage Basic. Heritage Grand Hotel (2008-2013). Member of IHHA	None as per Govt. of India. Member of IHHA
Architectural style	Medieval Rajput, defensive architecture	Blend of European and Rajput	Nawabi / Indo-Saracenic	Medley of British Colonial, Italian Renaissance & Classical Greek	Rural vernacular of the region
Ownership	Wing Commander Mangal Singh of Thakur family	Maharana Shriji Arvind Singh Mewar	Reliable Ventures India Ltd	Royal Family	INDeco Leisure Hotels
Management	Neemrana Hotels (40 yr lease)	HRH Group of Hotels (owned by the Maharana)	ITC WelcomHeritage	Self-managed by the family	INDeco Leisure Hotels

- JehanNuma Palace, Bhopal, Madhya Pradesh
- INDeco Hotel Swamimalai, Village Thimmakudi, Kumbakonam, Tamil Nadu, INDecoLeisure Hotels

13.6.1 LOCATION, SETTING, CHARACTER AND ORIGINAL PURPOSE

Each of the five properties is unique in its setting, location, architectural style and form and associational values attached. Three of these are in an urban setting while two are in a rural area, across the states of Rajasthan, Madhya Pradesh and Tamil Nadu. The properties reflect a close relationship with the topography and environment,and authentically represent the architectural character of the times that these were constructed in, along with providing appropriate services for the guests. None of the properties was conceived as a hotel originally; hence demonstrated the case of an adaptive reuse into a heritage hotel. One was originally a fort, two were royal palaces, one was a royal guest house and one was a villa.

FIGURE 13.1 View of agricultural landscape surrounding the 14th century Hill Fort at Kesroli, near the city of Alwar in Rajasthan, from a bastion of the fort, converted to a heritage hotel by the Neemrana Group.

13.6.2 OWNERSHIP AND MANAGEMENT

While the three major heritage hotel groups, ITC WelcomHeritage, Neemrana and HRH have been represented through the cases, Swamimalai Hotel characterizes a smaller group spearheaded by an individual committed to rural development setting. The Shiv Niwas Palace, Udaipur and JehanNuma Palace, Bhopal are examples of properties that are owned and managed by the royal families who were the original custodians and reflect a continuity in associational value. This in turn resulted in the properties being maintained by the royal families through their existence and the decision to convert them to heritage hotels, in order to continue the spirit of custodianship and royal legacy. The attitude and commitment of the owners and the management are reflected in the uniqueness of the services and experience offered to the guests. Hill Fort Kesroli and Noor-Us-Sabah Palace follow the model of owner leasing out the properties to a heritage hotel group, namely Neemrana and ITC WelcomHeritage groups respectively.

13.7 ANALYSING THE IMPACT

13.7.1 WHAT IS ON OFFER FOR THE CUSTOMERS?

A guest visiting/patronizing a heritage hotel property is essentially looking for a unique experience setting. This includes the "built form" which is the building structure, in addition,what differentiates these properties is the sociocultural impact or value that they create and the economic benefits that they have to offer to a range of stakeholders. In fact while the level of services that are typical of a star rated hotel may not be available at some of the heritage hotels, the sustainable practices that define their functioning are the reasons for customers to choose them.

Information about the five heritage hotels taken up for study was gathered on the basis of primary visit to and interviews with the general managers of the hotels and in the case of INDeco Hotel Swamimalai, on the basis of a published case study (Borgia, 2012). The impact of the respective hotels, as divulged through the primary and secondary data collection, is categorized into sociocultural and economic impacts and presented as follows:

13.7.1.1 HILL FORT KESROLI

- Sociocultural impact:
  - The fort was a local landmark in state of disrepair that was conserved resulting in continuity of built heritage.
  - Sets an example of a sustainable adaptive reuse of historic structure for guests, investors, local community, professionals, and so forth.
  - Guests offered a unique experience of residing in a 14th century hill fort in a picturesque rural setting.
  - Regional art and craft promoted through platform provided for performing arts and craft products as souvenirs.
  - Local cuisine offered to guests along with other options, promoting the same.
  - Choice of local agricultural produce impacted by demand generated by the hotel. Eg. Exotic vegetables like broccoli, zucchini *etc.*
  - Capacity building of the local people employed, enhancement of their skill sets, enabling them to get groomed as trained hospitality professionals and in traditional building crafts.
  - Promotion of natural and cultural heritage tourism, as a base to visit the Sariska Tiger Reserve, Kankwari fort, Neelkanth temples, Pandupol, monuments of Tijara, Siliserh and Jaisamand lakes, hot springs of Talavriksh and Koeladeo Ghana bird sanctuary in Bharatpur.

- Economic impact:
  - All line employees belong to the village or nearby areas, providing them an alternate source of income.
  - Indirect economic gains for local agriculturists as produce such as milk, vegetables, flour etc. is purchased locally for hotel consumption.
  - Engagement of local artisans in restoration and maintenance of the property.
  - Revenue realization from room sales, as well as food and beverage sale has ensured financial sustainability.
  - Career growth paths within the chain/other hospitality employers is enabled through in-house training and experiential learning for employees bringing economic growth for families with multiple social impacts including better education for children and so forth.

13.7.1.2 SHIV NIWAS PALACE, UDAIPUR

- Sociocultural impact:
    - Carries forward the spirit of custodianship of the House of Mewar
    - The guests are offered an extension of the Mewari cultural heritage and engagement with the royal legacy.
    - Experience of unique location along the lake offered to guests. City Palace Museum managed by MMCF finds financial support in the form of funding for organizing festivals and cultural events that enable continuity of traditions.
    - Many families in employment of the royal family have found continued employment support due to commercial use of the erstwhile royal palace.
    - Promotes cultural heritage tourism by hosting domestic as well as international tourists and strongly positioning Udaipur as a cultural heritage tourism destination.

FIGURE 13.2 Shiv Niwas Palace, an early 20th century palace along the Lake Pichola.

- Economic impact:
  - Revenue generation from room and food and beverage sales, meetings, incentives, conferences and exhibitions.
  - Except for few managerial positions, the entire staffing of nearly 220 people is from the city of Udaipur.
  - Almost 40% of raw product used for food production purposes is drawn from local vendors.
  - Maintenance contracts for electrical, plumbing, landscaping and other related interventions find local representation.
  - At a macro-level, Udaipur has emerged as tourist destination due to presence of heritage; the rooms' demand for top tier visitors is largely supported by conversion of palaces into hotels, bringing macroeconomic gains for the city in general.

13.7.1.3 NOOR-US-SABAH PALACE, BHOPAL

FIGURE 13.3 Entrance porch of Noor-Us-Sabah Palace, Bhopal, showcasing a historic carriage. The hotel is located on lakeside, enabling picturesque views of the lake from the various terraces.

- Sociocultural impact:
  - Restoration of a rundown heritage property in state of disuse, disrepair and neglect.
  - 80% of the staff employed that amounts to about 150 persons are local, who are trained periodically, resulting in their capacity building.
  - Spearheads sustainable measures of waste, waste and electricity management for the hospitality industry of the city with use of 40% solar energy, plantation of trees, sewage treatment, recycling of water and composting.
- Economic impact:
  - With 92% occupancy through the year, the property demonstrates an economically sustainable model.
  - 90% of business is from corporate clients, 8% leisure tourists and 2% international guests, hence, supporting macroeconomics of the city and the region.
  - Souvenir shop sells products from the city of Bhopal, indirectly feeding the local economy.

13.7.1.4 JEHAN NUMA PALACE, BHOPAL

- Sociocultural impact:
  - Carries forward the spirit of custodianship of the royal Nawabi family.
  - The guests are offered an extension of the Nawabi cultural heritage of Bhopal and engagement with the royal legacy.
  - Authenticity of built fabric maintained during conversion to hotel with sizes of rooms unaltered.
  - Later additions in the form of anew block follow similar architectural vocabulary as the original block in terms of planning, building heights, color scheme, materials used such as lime mortar and bricks for walls, Agra sandstone for flooring, metal girders and stone slabs for roofing *etc.*

FIGURE 13.4 Block added later at Jehan Numa Palace, Bhopal, following the same architectural vocabulary as the original block.

FIGURE 13.5 New block added at Jehan Numa Palace, Bhopal, recently, maintaining the essence of the original structure in terms of scale, proportion, color scheme, etc.

  - Capacity building of staff through in-house training programs and sending key employees for 3- to 6-month training programs to other hotels at company expense as a part of "train the trainers" initiative.
  - Good retention of staff for 15–20 years, hence a deeper social impact.
  - Sponsoring of joint ventures promoting literature, art and culture, continuing the spirit of cultural patronage.
  - Traditional Nawabi cuisine is promoted, being offered at one of the restaurants in the hotel.
  - Some guests have continued patronage of the hotel for the last 15 years, reflecting the quality of hospitality and overall experience offered.
  - Spearheads sustainable practices such as having an in-house sewage treatment plant, recharging of rain water that is recycled and reused and plans for installation of composter for waste management.

- Economic impact:

  - Expansion of the hotel from 15 room capacity at the start to 100 room capacity is indicative of its fiscal sustainability supported by demand as well as investment ability.
  - Directly employs 300 local people for upkeep, repair, maintenance and services
  - Indirectly about 450 people provided livelihoods in the form of vendors, suppliers etc.
  - Raw materials to manufacture designer products and artefacts sold in the gift shop are procured from the local market. Local tailors employed in garments reflecting the Mughal era sold at the shop.
  - 60% of the business is generated from banquets, conferences, product launches, seminars etc.,for companies such as IBM and Oracle from across the country, bringing economic impact due to incremental revenue for the city such as transport services and food retail.
  - 40% leisure tourists, promoting the cultural economy.
  - The bakery sustains not only in-house demand but also citywide demand for upmarket bakery products.

13.7.1.5 INDECO HOTEL, SWAMIMALAI

- Sociocultural impact:
    - Heritage conservation (tangible and intangible) and rural development at the heart of the project.
    - Use of vernacular architecture during restoration and conversion, using local skills.
    - Skill development, training and employment
    - Promotion of locally produced traditional cloth as uniforms, music of the region
    - Local tile makers trained by potters from other regions in production of almost extinct country tiles
    - Involvement of local elders in training the chefs in preparing authentic local recipes
    - Revival of traditional utensils and their use in recipes offered at the hotel
    - Museum integrated with hotel
    - Participation of local people in promotion of the hotel, reflecting their engagement and sense of ownership in the initiative
    - Excess milk from in-house dairy distributed to pregnant women in the village.
    - Employment information disseminated to the unemployed youth
    - Skill development, training and employment to the local people within the hotel and in the hotel construction process.
- Economic impact:
    - 60% of project budget spent on local labor and wages.
    - 70% of operational budget spent in the vicinity, directly beneficial to the local communities.
    - Use of locally produced towels, mirror frames, produce and so forth.
    - Employment opportunities for all, including the specially abled and senior citizens.
    - Employment for local craftspeople and engagement of musicians originally from the region, for performances at the hotel with an allocated budget for the same

The analyses of the five cases bring forth some observations regarding the uniqueness and impact of the heritage hotels in sociocultural and economic terms. In each of the cases, a commitment toward cultural heritage conservation and socioeconomic development of the local communities was seen as paramount.

- At Noor-Us-Sabah Palace, Bhopal, the systems are in place, as it is managed by the largest hospitality groups of India that focuses specifically on management of heritage hotels. Hence, there isavailability of support for any technical issues, structured training programs for staff and standard operating procedures that ensure sustainable maintenance and management of the business.
- The other cases demonstrate the commitment of the royal families who are directly involved or individuals who are driven toward the cause of heritage conservation and social development in the rural areas.
- The spirit of custodianship and association with a royal legacy is strongly inbuilt in the properties owned and managed by the royal families.
- A clear impact is visible in the rural projects that have been able to reposition the villages on the tourist circuit, promising further development in a direct or indirect manner.
- In the urban settings as well, the heritage hotels have contributed toward promotion of natural and cultural heritage tourism.
- Livelihood generation for local population and capacity building through training programs are common to all cases.
- The high retention rates of staff and continued guest patronage reflect a long term approach.
- The inclusive approach is most evident in case of INDeco Hotel Swamimalai, where all the resources that the rural setting has to offer have been optimally incorporated in the visitor experience and promoted through the various activities; while, in the case of Hill Fort Kesroli, any negative cultural impact due to influx of tourists has been kept to a minimum.

The "Sustainable Tourism Criteria for India" applicable to the accommodation sector (Ministry of Tourism, n.d. b) outline five main principles, namely:

A. Demonstrate effective sustainable management
B. Design and construction of buildings and infrastructure
C. Maximize social and economic benefits to the local community and minimize negative impacts
D. Maximize benefits to cultural and historical heritage and minimize negative impacts
E. Maximize benefits to the environment and minimize negative impacts

The analyses of the five case studies of heritage hotels reflect the following response to each of the sustainability principles:

TABLE 13.3 Response of Heritage Hotels to Sustainability Principles.

Sustainability principle	Response of heritage hotels
A	The management of heritage hotels is as per long-term sustainable management system, as objective is to ensure the continuity of the heritage resources in the long-term.
	There is no issue of noncompliance with legislative and regulatory frameworks
	Customer satisfaction is a prime concern, hence any issues in that respect are acted upon
	Periodic training of staff is carried out in all the properties, whether stand alone or part of a chain.
	Promotional materials are accurate as personally observed in four of the cases[4]
B	The case studies reflect a very strong emphasis of heritage hotels toward the use of traditional materials and technology, sensitivity toward the context in addition of new parts and interpretation about natural and cultural heritage sites or environment, as these are the unique selling points of heritage hotels, with a strong link to natural and cultural heritage tourism.
	The addition of lifts becomes a challenge, in ensuring an inclusive approach allowing access for all as observed in most cases, due to incompatibility with the existing built fabric.
C	The case studies represent a strong inclusive approach with a mutually beneficial relationship with the local communities in the sociocultural and economic terms. The impact is prominently visible in the rural examples of INDeco Hotel Swamimalai and Hill Fort Kesroli, while the spirit of custodianship by the royal families has ensured the same for Jehan Numa Palace, Bhopal and Shiv Niwas Palace, Udaipur.

[4]The author was unable to visit INDeco Hotel Swamimalai to confirm the same.

TABLE 13.3 *(Continued)*

Sustainability principle	Response of heritage hotels
D	The heritage hotels exemplify commitment toward cultural and historical heritage by ensuring the continuity of the built fabric through sensitive adaptive reuse and promotion of the tangible as well as intangible heritage resources of the area. The commitment is clear in case of the properties owned and run by royal families, as well as those managed by the groups, namely Neemrana, ITC WelcomHeritage and INDeco Leisure Hotels.
E	The heritage hotels covered as case studies reflect a commitment toward environmental conservation through use of alternate source of electricity, maintaining the green cover, sustainable waste and water management practices.

Hence, the case studies fare well in terms of following the sustainability principles. This strengthens the unique position of heritage hotels as sustainable initiatives that ensure the protection and continuity of the cultural heritage resources along with causing responsible social and economic development of the local region through both direct and indirect channels.

13.8 CONCLUSION

In the Indian context, the following statement from the Neemrana Group defines how heritage hotels have an inseparable relationship with sustainable heritage tourism: "The word "Neemranification" has now come to symbolize a viable and sustainable heritage tourism involving the local communities, so that their rural pride resurges to win the battle to counter migration to urban slums" (Neemrana Hotels, 2011).

The development of heritage hotels has very high potential of minimizing negative and maximizing positive impact of tourism on the environment, local communities, heritage, and inclusive economic growth that are requirements defined for sustainable tourism by the Ministry of Tourism (n.d. b).The unique position of heritage hotels, in their location, setting, inclusive approach and commitment toward heritage conservation and socioeconomic development of the local communities promises a long-term sustainable approach toward heritage and hospitality management.

The success of the case studies in terms of financial viability and providing the visitors a unique experience has inspired others to follow suit. The challenge lies in a true commitment from the ownership and management, to ensure that a long-term sustainable model for heritage conservation and social development be established, without looking at short-term gains.

The stage is set for further focus and growth of this hospitality segment, closely linked with promotion of cultural heritage tourism. The government at all levels local, state and central is demonstrating a positive orientation that is being expressed through policy initiatives, incentives and developing frameworks for sustainability in the accommodation sector. On the other hand, the demand for the "heritage room" has grown from strength to strength, drawing patrons from both domestic and international markets. The setting up of such businesses is a challenge that can be driven by heritage property owners, hospitality professionals or entrepreneurs who are keen on inclusive, sustainable development and management of the numerous heritage resources that the country possesses, irrespective of the size of the property being converted. The above discussed success stories make a case in point that states: protecting our heritage makes as much business sense as social sense.The heritage "room product" has taken off, it is clear from the discussed case studies that the sustainability focus is a differentiated that has worked for this segment and will continue to drive its growth.

KEYWORDS

- **heritage**
- **hotels**
- **tourism**
- **management**
- **sustainability**
- **ownership**
- **cultural tourism**
- **communities**

REFERENCES

Abakerli, S. Crafting India's Economic Growth and Development. *Context: Built, Living and Natural, a Special Issue on Cultural Economics and Livelihoods.* **2012,** *9*(2), 4–11.

Borgia, S. Responsible Development through Tourism Initiatives: Villages of Tamil Nadu. *Context: Built, Livingand Natural, a Special Issue on Cultural Economics and Livelihoods.* **2012,** *9*(2), 69–76.

Chang, T. C.; Tep, P. The Shophouse Hotel: Vernacular Heritage in a Creative City. *Urban Studies*. **2009,** *46*(2), 341–367.

Chevron Hotels (2013) (online) (cited 13 March 2013). Available from <http://www.chevronhotels.com/>.

Eternal Mewar (2013) (online) (cited 5 March 2013). Available from <http://www.eternalmewar.in/about/index.aspx>.

Henderson, J. C. Hip Heritage: The Boutique Hotel Business in Singapore, *Tourism and Hospitality Research.* **2011,** *11*(3), 217–223.

Hergnyan, M. *Tufenkian Heritage Hotels: Enhanced Employment Opportunities in Distressed Rural Areas,* Growing Inclusive Markets, UNDP. 2010

Historic Hotels of America (online)(cited 19 March 2013). Available from <http://www.historichotels.org/>.

HRH Group of Hotels (2013) (online) (cited 2 February 2013). Available from <http://www.hrhhotels.com/>.

HVS. *Indian Hotel Industry Survey 2011-2012*, Federation of Hotel & Restaurant Associations of India, New Delhi. 2012

IHHA (2013) (online) (cited 4 March 2013). Available from <http://indianheritagehotels.com>.

Jalfon, J. Operating in a Green and Energy Friendly Environment, *Hospitality*. **2008,** 13–17.

JchanNuma Palace (2010) (online) (cited 4 March 2013). Available from <http://www.hoteljehanumapalace.com/>.

Jodhana Heritage Resorts (2013) (online) (cited 2 April 2013). Available from <http://www.jodhanaheritage.com/>.

Kapoor, A. *Indian Heritage Hotels: Legacy of Splendour*; Roli Books: New Delhi, 2012

Lewis, R. A.; Mottier, E. M. A "Hotel Within a Hotel" in Bangkok, *Emerald Emerging Markets Case Studies*. 2012

Lim, W. M.; Endean, M. Elucidating the Aesthetic and Operational Characteristics of UK Boutique Hotels. *Int. J. Contemp. Hosp. M.* **2009,** *21*(1), 38–51.

Market Research Division. *India Tourism Statistics at a Glance*, Ministry of Tourism, Government of India, New Delhi. 2012

Maskey, V. *Economic Analyses Explaining Historic Preservation: The Impact of Social and Economic Values,* ProQuest Information and Learning Company, Michigan, USA. 2008

Ministry of Tourism, Govt. Of India (2013) (online) (cited 4 March 2013). Available from <http://tourism.gov.in/TourismDivision/AboutDivision.aspx?Name=Hotels%20and%20Restaurants>.

Ministry of Tourism, Govt. of India (n.d. a) *Guidelines for Classification of Heritage Hotels*(online) (cited 12 January 2013). Available from <http://tourism.nic.in/writereaddata/Uploaded/Guideline/051820120222241.pdf>.

Ministry of Tourism, Govt. of India(n.d. b) *Sustainable Tourism for India: Criteria and Indicators Applicable to Accommodation Sector and Tour Operators* (online) (cited 2 March 2013). Available from <http://tourism.gov.in/writereaddata/CMSPagePicture/file/marketresearch/Survay&Study/sustainable%20tourism/Sustainable%20Tourism%20Criteria%20For%20India.pdf>.

Munjal, S.; Munjal, P. G. City Palace Udaipur: A Case Study for Sustainable Heritage Tourism through Services Enhancement, *Proceedings of the 5th International Conference on Services Management,* 23–30, 2011.

Murzyn-Kupisz, M. The Socio-economic Impact of Built Heritage Projects Conducted by Private Investors, *J. Cult. Herit.* **2013,** *14*, 156–162.

Neemrana Hotels (2011) (online) (cited 19 April 2013). Available from <http://neemrana-hotels.com>.

Singh, A. V. *The Golden Rs of Heritage Hotels in India,* HVS, 2013, Available from <http://www.hvs.com/article/4057/the-golden-rs-of-heritage-hotels-in-india/>. 2009.

Srivastava, M. (2012*) Heritage hotels shift focus to corporates* (online) (cited 4 January 2013). Available from <http://www.livemint.com/Consumer/XQHSd262BGY4Mkx-W0L7EUL/Heritage-hotels-shift-focus-from-foreign-tourists-to-corpora.html>.

Tourism Finance Corporation of India Limited (2007) *Final Report on Evaluation of the Scheme "Incentives to Accommodation Infrastructure in India",* Ministry of Tourism, Govt. of India, New Delhi.

WelcomHeritage (2013) (online) (cited 1 February 2013). Available from <http://www.welcomheritagehotels.in/>.

INDEX